School-Based Mental Health

School-Based Mental Health

A Practitioner's Guide to Comparative Practices

Edited by

Ray W. Christner
Rosemary B. Mennuti

Routledge
Taylor & Francis Group
New York   London

Routledge
Taylor & Francis Group
270 Madison Avenue
New York, NY 10016

Routledge
Taylor & Francis Group
2 Park Square
Milton Park, Abingdon
Oxon OX14 4RN

© 2009 by Taylor & Francis Group, LLC
Routledge is an imprint of Taylor & Francis Group, an Informa business

Printed in the United States of America on acid-free paper
10 9 8 7 6 5 4 3 2

International Standard Book Number-13: 978-0-415-95558-4 (Hardcover)

Library of Congress Cataloging-in-Publication Data

School-based mental health : a practitioner's guide to comparative practices / [edited by] Ray W. Christner and Rosemary B. Mennuti.
        p. ; cm.
    Includes bibliographic references and index.
    ISBN 978-0-415-95558-4 (hardbound : alk. paper)
    1. School children--Mental health services. 2. School psychology. I. Christner, Ray W., 1972- II. Mennuti, Rosemary B., 1947-
    [DNLM: 1. Mental Health Services--United States. 2. School Health Services--United States. 3. Adolescent--United States. 4. Behavior Therapy--methods--United States. 5. Child--United States. 6. Mental Disorders--therapy--United States. WA 352 S368 2009]

    LB3430.S383 2009
    371.7'13--dc22
                                                                        2008024922

Visit the Taylor & Francis Web site at
http://www.taylorandfrancis.com

and the Routledge Web site at
http://www.routledge.com

I must express my sincere gratitude to my wife, Andrea, and my daughters, Alyssa and Sydney, who provided me with unending support and patience during the countless months of work on this project that can never be repaid. No matter how frustrated and tired I became during this process, I always knew I could count on you to keep me going.

RWC

My love and appreciation to Jean and Alex for all the joy you bring me. Your gentle holding and support always move me forward with excitement and pleasure.

RBM

Contents

SECTION I Introduction

SECTION II Foundation of Universal Interventions

SECTION III Targeted and Intensive Interventions

SECTION IV   Nontraditional Interventions

SECTION V   Summary

Figures and Tables

Acknowledgments

As is the case with most books, this work is the product of the efforts of many people. Whether directly or indirectly, many practitioners, students, workshop participants, and colleagues contributed to the ideas and thoughts comprising this volume. Most of all, this book would not have been possible without the countless children, adolescents, and families whom we have encountered and who have allowed us to enter into rewarding experiences with them. We are continually amazed by the strength and conviction of many of the students and families we work with, who take chances and believe in our work with them. We are indebted to them for these experiences, the relationships forged, and their dedication in treatment.

This book would never have been possible without the innovation and commitment of the chapter authors. Through their willingness to share their experiences and expertise, we were able to compile a volume consisting of innovative ideas. Thank you to all of you who dedicated your time and effort to this project. Also, we are grateful to Dr. Arthur Freeman for his ongoing mentorship and inspiration, which started us on the path of publishing.

Finally, we wish to thank Routledge/Taylor & Francis Group for their recognition and appreciation of the growing interest in school-based mental health and the potential this book has to offer clinicians and graduate students. A special thanks to Dana Bliss, Chris Tominich, and George Zimmar, who were exceptionally helpful and patient in making this project come to life.

Ray W. Christner

Rosemary B. Mennuti

About the Contributors

Howard Adelman, PhD, is professor of psychology and codirector of the School Mental Health Project and its federally supported national Center for Mental Health in Schools at the University of California, Los Angeles.

Heather K. Alvarez, PhD, is assistant professor of psychology at The Ohio University in Athens, Ohio.

Barry Barbarasch, PhD, is a school psychologist with Hamilton Township Schools in Princeton Junction, New Jersey.

Jennifer Block-Lerner, PhD, is assistant professor in the Department of Psychology at La Salle University, Philadelphia, Pennsylvania.

Katherine Brehm, PhD, is associate professor of school psychology in the Department of Educational Psychology and Special Services at the University of Texas at El Paso.

Linda Caterino, PhD, ABPP, is training director of the School Psychology Program at Arizona State University in Tempe, Arizona, and she is currently the vice president for professional affairs for Division 16 of the American Psychological Association.

Ray W. Christner, PsyD, NCSP, is school psychologist with the South Middleton School District, Boiling Springs, Pennsylvania, and clinical assistant professor at the Philadelphia College of Osteopathic Medicine.

Beth Doll, PhD, is professor and director of the School Psychology Program at the University of Nebraska–Lincoln.

Athena Drewes, PsyD, is director of clinical training and APA internship for the Astor Home for Children in Poughkeepsie, New York.

Dianne Dulicai, PhD, ADTR, founded and directed graduate dance–movement therapy programs in Philadelphia and London, and she taught in numerous countries.

Maurice Elias, PhD, is professor of clinical psychology and intradisciplinary health and director of the Social-Emotional Learning Lab at Rutgers University, New Brunswick, New Jersey.

Anne F. Farrell, PhD, is assistant professor in the Department of Human Development and Family Studies at the University of Connecticut, Storrs.

William C. Freeman, PhD, ADTR, has directed and facilitated professional development, parent education, and direct service programs in movement therapy and the expressive arts for over 30 years. He maintains a practice and provides consultative services and teaching for educational, mental health, and arts agencies.

Michael A. Holston, MA, is currently a third-year student in the doctoral program in clinical psychology at LaSalle University, Philadelphia, Pennsylvania.

Kirk John, EdD, NCSP, is professor and coordinator of the school psychology program at the California University of Pennsylvania in California, Pennsylvania.

Marjory J. Levitt, PhD, maintains a private practice in Philadelphia, and she supervises practicum and internship students at Temple University, Philadelphia.

Rosemary B. Mennuti, EdD, NCSP, is professor and director of the School Psychology Program at the Philadelphia College of Osteopathic Medicine.

Maggee Messing, MA, is a third-year doctoral student at LaSalle University, Philadelphia, and she is a New Jersey–certified school psychologist.

Loren Person, MS, is a doctoral student in the School Psychology Program at the Philadelphia College of Osteopathic Medicine, and she is a Pennsylvania-certified school psychologist.

Amanda Sullivan is a doctoral student in school psychology at Arizona State University in Tempe, Arizona.

Linda Taylor, PhD, is codirector of the School Mental Health Project and its federally supported National Center for Mental Health in Schools at the University of California, Los Angeles.

Elise Billock Tropea, MA, ADTR, is a faculty member in the Creative Arts in Therapy Program at Drexel University, Philadelphia, and she is in private practice and provides body-centered clinical services to children and adults.

Ann Vernon, PhD, is professor and coordinator of counseling at the University of Northern Iowa in Cedar Falls, Iowa; the vice president of the Albert Ellis Board of Trustees; and the director of the Midwest Center for RET in Janesville, Iowa.

Elana Weinstein, MS, is a student in the Educational Specialist Program in School Psychology at the Philadelphia College of Osteopathic Medicine.

James S. Whitaker, MS, is a doctoral student in the School Psychology Program at the Philadelphia College of Osteopathic Medicine, and he is a Pennsylvania-certified school psychologist.

Robert E. Wubbolding, EdD, is director of the Center for Reality Therapy in Cincinnati, Ohio.

Section I

Introduction

1

An Overview of School-Based Mental Health Practice
From Systems Service to Crisis Intervention

Ray W. Christner

Rosemary B. Mennuti

James S. Whitaker

Why Write This Book?

A number of children and adolescents enter schools each day struggling with emotional, behavioral, and family problems that affect their learning as well as the learning of others. This has a reciprocal effect, in that these students internalize their academic difficulties, which further exacerbates some of the emotional and behavioral problems they face. This idea of supporting the social and emotional growth of youth to enhance their success at school is not a new one, yet there remain questions regarding how to overcome the barriers, how to deliver these services in a multileveled framework, and which orientation to interventions should be used.

When we set out to compile this book, we did so with the intention of offering a resource for frontline providers, as well as those at an entry level, that would provide an overview of a service delivery framework, as well as a guide to offering interventions at multiple levels. These would range from a system-wide climate issue to direct one-on-one service to students. Numerous of excellent resources exist that discuss school-based services from a single orientation (see Bush, 1997 [for art therapy]; Drewes, Carey, & Schaefer, 2001 [play therapy]; Mennuti, Freeman, & Christner, 2006 [cognitive-behavioral therapy]; Sklare, 1997 [solution-focused therapy]; Walsh & Williams, 1997 [family systems]; etc.), that review models of how to deliver services (Doll & Cummings, 2007; Nastasi, Bernstein Moore, & Varjas, 2003), and that provide interventions for specific disorders (Atkinson, 2002). However, we designed this book to be a single volume that addresses three main goals: (a) to provide practitioners a broad overview of school-based mental health services, (b) to review different theoretical orientations for clinicians to use in their practice, and (c) to offer a discussion and integration of the commonalities and differences in approaches.

An Understanding of the Need for School-Based Mental Health

School plays a significant role in the lives of youth, as nearly 50 million children and adolescents attend public schools in the United States, with an average daily attendance of over 44 million students (National Center for Education Statistics, 2005), not including the additional number of students attending private educational programs. However, children and adolescents come to school each day with a number of life factors and barriers that affect their learning, behavior, and development, including family stress, academic difficulties, peer conflicts, health issues, cultural differences, as well as community concerns.

Approximately 10% of children and adolescents in the United States will meet criteria for a mental health disorder during their school years (National Institute of Mental Health, 2004), and many will have the first onset of symptoms that may lead to mental health concerns later in life (Kessler, Berglund, Demler, Jin, & Walters, 2005). Moreover, regardless of a formal diagnosis, between 12% and 22% of youth under the age of 18 have a need for mental health intervention to address emotional or behavioral difficulties (Center for Mental Health in Schools, 2006). In large urban schools, some researchers have noted a greater concern, in that it has been estimated that over 50% of children attending these schools demonstrate significant emotional, behavioral, and learning difficulties (Center for Mental Health in Schools, 2003).

Evidence has shown that youth with emotional or behavioral difficulties in school often have less academic success and a greater number of negative social interactions (Coleman & Vaughn, 2000). In addition, these students are prone to higher frequencies of truancy, suspensions, tardiness, expulsions, attention-seeking behaviors, and poor peer relationships (Epstein & Cullinan, 1994). Adelman and Taylor (1998, 2000) noted that mental health concerns and stressors are major barriers to learning. Not only is this the case for individual students with difficulties, but in some cases these concerns may affect their classmates as well.

Although the primary mission of schools is academic education, we cannot ignore that schools comprise one of the primary socialization agents in a child's life, charged with the task of shaping the "whole child." As such, early attention to mental health factors can prevent greater difficulties for students that may result in school failure or dropout. This is an issue that schools and educators must not ignore, and instead, they must find ways to enhance the mental health of all students. The *Final Report* of the President's New Freedom Commission on Mental Health (2003) provided support for these efforts, as it concluded that "strong school mental health programs can attend to the health and behavioral concerns of students, reduce unnecessary pain and suffering, and help ensure academic achievement" (p. 58). In addition, this report recommended that any attempts to alter the manner in which mental health treatment is delivered must take into consideration the opportunities and needs of schools (Center for Mental Health in Schools, 2006).

Given this information, as well as considering the dominant role education plays in the lives of youth, we see schools as an essential entry point for mental health services for children, adolescents, and, in some cases, families. When we think of school-based mental health, however, we need to focus our efforts not only on the treatment of mental health disorders, but also on the prevention of difficulties by teaching students the necessary coping skills to deal with life's challenges. Moreover, and perhaps most relevant, offering mental health services in schools has the potential to eliminate barriers to learning and to help schools achieve their mission of educating children.

School-Based Service Delivery

In the context of schools, *mental health services* refer to the broad array of services designed to prevent and treat behavioral and emotional difficulties that may or may not be symptoms of specific mental disorders. In some cases, interventions may be universal and applied to entire schools or school districts, whereas other cases may require targeted or intensive interventions geared toward specific students who are at risk for certain problems. Regardless of the level at which the interventions are provided, it is best to offer them within the context of a supportive learning environment. This includes schools that promote positive emotional development, increased resiliency, and enhanced protective factors and that facilitate smooth transition into different life stages.

Unlike traditional conceptions of mental health services, where there is one client and one therapist, the clients in school-based mental health services include students, teachers, administrators, families, and entire systems. Although in most cases pupil services professionals (e.g., special education staff, school counselors, social workers, and school psychologists) take a primary role in the delivery of school-based mental health programs (Center for Mental Health in Schools, 2006), within the unique environment of schools, other educators such as teachers, administrators, and paraprofessionals can also have an important and prominent role in the implementation and maintenance of these services.

The method of mental health service delivery in schools can be varied depending upon the resources and organizational structure of the school system. Some schools have established their own school-based mental health programs that are delivered using professionals within their system. However, other schools have had to rely on and join with outside mental health agencies (Center for Mental Health in Schools, 2006). Either of these approaches can be acceptable, as long as the services are delivered in a manner that is structured and includes sound methods to identify students in need, to conceptualize the cases of students and groups, to offer interventions at multiple levels, and to monitor the progress of students as well as the system as a whole.

Conceptual Design for School-Based Mental Health Delivery

Schools can address social and emotional factors of students most appropriately and effectively if these services are offered within a multilevel design that embraces intervention and prevention (Christner, Forrest, Morley, & Weinstein, 2007; Smallwood, Christner, & Brill, 2007). These services must move from a level of working with all students within a specific school or school district to working with an individual child who presents the highest level of need. To accomplish this, schools must seek to offer help across four main levels of intervention—*universal, targeted, intensive,* and *crisis.* However, it must be noted that in some cases, the needs of students may go beyond the resources of a given school system and require collaboration and possible referral to outside professionals and agencies. Figure 1.1 illustrates the interactive dynamic of this design. Within and across each of these levels are the inherent components that

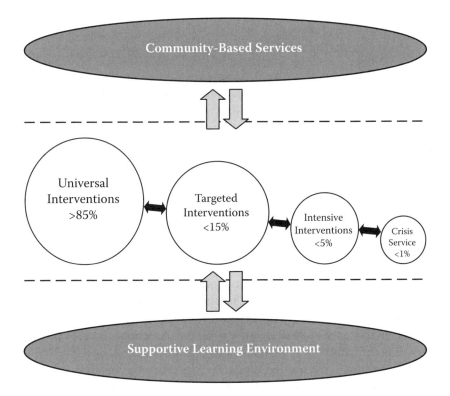

Figure 1.1   Multileveled Design of School-Based Mental Health Services

make up a systematic approach to understanding, conceptualizing, assessing, intervening in, and monitoring problems of students and systems. This systematic approach allows for a fluidness that offers providers a way to determine if interventions are working and, if not, to reconceptualize the case and modify the interventions as needed. The following sections will provide a brief overview, a review of assessment and case conceptualization, and quick tips to interventions at each level.

Universal Interventions

Interventions offered at the *universal* level are designed for implementation to all students within a particular school or, in some cases, a particular school district. The goals of *universal interventions* are threefold: (a) to build protective factors in order to reduce vulnerability for future problems or maladaptive ways of coping, (b) to prevent problems for students before they occur, and (c) to offer global resources to students who are at risk or those who have existing vulnerabilities. In essence, these services have an impact on all members of the school community. With universal mental health interventions, there is the goal of increasing social and emotional competence and decreasing risk for emotional, behavioral, and learning difficulties. Examples of interventions at this level may include preventing bullying, building resiliency, and promoting adaptive coping skills (e.g., social problem solving). Although universal interventions are provided to all students, we must realize that not all students will respond to this level of service. Our goal is for universal services to meet the needs of at least 85% of the school population, and others may require specific intervention offered at the lower levels.

To select the focus and to monitor the effect of universal interventions, it is necessary to use an assessment process that is global enough to capture schoolwide and systemic issues. Baseline assessment may yield information regarding the frequency and intensity of identified issues, as well as the contexts in which these occur. Assessment to monitor the effectiveness of universal interventions may yield information regarding the need to change or adapt the approach or the goals for the school, whereas postintervention assessment will produce outcome data that may be useful in justifying program costs and continuation. Specific assessment practices at the universal level will obviously vary based on factors such as the nature of the issue being addressed, the availability of resources, and the institutional-specific practices and methods of data collection. Nonetheless, a number of general assessment strategies may be useful when attempting to gather baseline data, to monitor intervention progress, and to determine intervention effectiveness.

Table 1.1 provides a review of data collection and assessment practices for intervention at this level. In general, it is recommended that use of a combination of these or other assessment methods is the best way to ensure a thorough appraisal necessary for intervention development and monitoring at this level. Readers are encouraged to see the work of Simonsen and Sugai (2007), who have offered an excellent discussion of using schoolwide assessment data.

Programs designed for universal use provide all students with exposure opportunities for the same interventions. The first section of this book contains chapters dedicated to a detailed explanation of interventions at this level, including building resiliency, fostering social competence, and providing schoolwide positive behavioral support programs. We are unable to provide a comprehensive list of all possible programs

TABLE 1.1   Assessment at Each Level

Assessment for Universal Interventions

Focus Group Data	Focus groups can be conducted with students, faculty, administrators, and/or parents to determine issues that are present within the schools. This can be accomplished by using a random selection of members from each group and using a semistructured interview format. For information on conducting focus groups, see Krueger and Casey (2000).
Survey Data	Surveys can be developed and used with students, faculty, administrators, and/or parents to identify specific needs within the school community. These can be designed in an open-ended format, allowing those completing the survey to offer qualitative data (e.g., *Tell me about concerns you have experienced in the cafeteria*). Surveys can also be used to gather quantitative data about specific areas of need using "yes/no" questions or ratings on a Likert scale (e.g., *Using the following scale, how much of a concern is bullying to you?*).
Preexisting School Data	Schools maintain many sources of data that can be used to identify areas of need as well as monitor changes following an intervention. These data typically exist and do not require additional work, other than analyzing the information that has been previously collected. This information could include the number of discipline referrals for specific problem behaviors, the number of out-of-school placements, the dropout rate, the truancy rate, student grades, and the school's performance on statewide testing.
Preexisting Community Data	Local government and community agencies often gather and maintain data on various community issues that also have relevance to school-based intervention. Issues of teen drug use, suicide rates, and so on can provide information on needs that can be addressed in school. This information not only offers insight into local issues but also yields information on more global trends facing youth.

Assessment for Targeted Interventions

Preexisting School Data	The preexisting school data described above can be used to identify students who may require more intensive services. These data typically exist and do not require additional work, but if the data are stored in an efficient manner, they can be used effectively to identify students. This information could include discipline referrals by specific student, specific students demonstrating risk factors of dropping out, students who are frequently tardy or truant, and the like.

TABLE 1.1   Assessment at Each Level (Continued)

Prereferral Data	Many schools collect data as part of their prereferral process. This will include student response to schoolwide interventions. Through monitoring the progress that students make on schoolwide goals, students who may require more intensive and direct interventions can be identified. Using a response-to-intervention (RTI) model, these would be students who do not progress on Tier I or universal interventions.
Screening Programs	Schools have the opportunity to conduct screening programs for a variety of different areas. For instance, there are a number of commercially available screening programs for anxiety, depression, eating disorders, and so on. The results of these programs can be used to develop intervention programs targeting specific behaviors.
Student Referral	Although there are a number of school-initiated screening tools, it is essential that schools have a safe and accessible method for students to self-refer or to refer other students. For these means to be usable, it is necessary that they be done in a confidential manner for those referring themselves and in an anonymous way for those referring peers.

Assessment for Intensive Interventions

Response to Intervention	Students who are part of a prereferral process or who receive Tier II interventions should be monitored to determine their response to interventions at that level. Those students who do not progress from interventions provided at that level should be considered for interventions that are more intensive to better meet the students' needs.
Rating Scales	School personnel should have broad-band and narrow-band rating scales accessible to them in order to collect information from observers, such as parents or teachers. It is important that broad-band instruments be utilized first in order to assess a variety of behaviors or areas to rule out other causes of difficulties, as well as to look for comorbid factors. When general areas are identified, narrow-band instruments can then be used to pinpoint specific symptoms or behaviors that can serve as goals for the interventions.
Observations	Observations are a means of viewing the students' behaviors within the context of their environment. This may include classroom interventions, but for mental health concerns, observations in less structured settings (e.g., the playground and cafeteria) are often most beneficial. Looking at social skills (e.g., students' interaction styles) or academic-related behaviors (e.g., time on task) may also be most beneficial.

TABLE 1.1   Assessment at Each Level (Continued)

	Assessment for Crisis Interventions
Psychological Evaluation and Risk Assessment	Despite our efforts on the aforementioned levels, some students continue to need a higher level of care. This may be for threats of harm to self or others, or because of frequent and chronic behavioral outbursts. For these students, it is important that a comprehensive psychological evaluation or risk assessment be conducted. This evaluation may be conducted by the school psychologist or by an individual who is trained in this type of assessment. Many schools contract with outside agencies to offer these assessments or may utilize local crisis response units.

that can be implemented at this level; however, we do offer several key points to consider when identifying universal interventions or programs (see Table 1.2).

Targeted Interventions

Targeted interventions are designed for children who are "at risk" for developing an emotional or behavioral disorder or who have not responded to universal interventions. Targeted interventions are more specialized and intensive than universal interventions and are sometimes referred to as *early-intervention activities*. These interventions are appropriate for students who demonstrate ongoing need but whose level of need is not significant enough to require more intensive and individualized treatment. For example, a targeted intervention may be appropriate for a small number of students who continue to demonstrate minor anger or aggressive behavior, despite exposure to the school's universal bullying prevention and reduction program.

In addition to those children demonstrating emotional or behavioral difficulties that may be indicative of emerging psychological problems, children having specific risk factors or vulnerabilities to life stressors may also receive services at this level (Christner et al., 2007). Coie and colleagues (1993) focused on identifying these risk factors, which are thought to increase the risk that children will be unable to develop into healthy functioning adults. Coie et al. identified seven domains of risk factors (see Table 1.3), and within each of the domains exists a number of generic risk factors that may be found individually or in combination. Risk factors such as poverty, minimal parent education, marital discord or

TABLE 1.2   Intervention Implementation Considerations

Universal Interventions

Key Points	Examples of Programs
Focus on prevention and building competencies for all students Use schoolwide data to identify need and to monitor progress Emphasize skill development and generalization Provide schoolwide opportunity and supports for practice of specific skills Offer direct instruction as well as adult and peer modeling of all skills taught	*I Can Problem Solve* (Shure, 2001) *Positive Alternative for Thinking Strategies* (PATHS; Kusche & Greenberg, 1994) *School-Wide Positive Behavior Support* (Sugai & Horn, 1999) *Resilient Classrooms* (Doll, Zucker, & Brehm, 2004) *PREPARE* (Goldstein, Glick, & Gibbs, 1998) *Social Decision Making* (Elias & Butler, 2005)

Targeted Interventions

Key Points	Examples of Manual Approaches
Focus on minimizing risk for students with specific needs Use group and individual data to identify specific needs and to monitor progress Emphasize skill development and generalization around a specific need area Provide opportunities and supports for the practice of specific skills aimed at goals to reduce risk Offer small-group or individual instruction and modeling of all skills taught	Anxiety: *Coping Cat* (Kendall, 1993) Anger: *Coping Power Program* (Larson & Lochman, 2002) Aggression: *Aggression Replacement Training* (ART; Goldstein et al., 1998) Depression: *Coping With Stress* (Clarke & Lewinsohn, 1995)

Intensive Interventions

Key Points	Examples of Treatment Orientations
Focus on direct and ongoing interventions on the individualized needs of specific students Use data on each individual to conceptualize his or her needs, to identify detailed goals, and to monitor progress Utilize individual, group, and/or family treatments designed to address individual goals and needs Provide opportunities and supports for the practice of skills aimed at stabilizing and treating a student with a specific disorder Offer individual and/or group therapy to foster growth and enhance functioning	Cognitive-behavioral therapy (CBT) Rational emotive behavior therapy (REBT) Behavior therapy or modification Reality therapy Client-centered therapy Family systems therapy Adlerian therapy Psychodynamic therapy

TABLE 1.2   Intervention Implementation Considerations (Continued)

Crisis Interventions

Key Points	Examples of Crisis Intervention Models
Focus on stabilizing a student or group of students following a crisis or traumatic event Provide interventions based on a school's existing brief crisis intervention model Utilize group and individual crisis approaches to reduce the severity and incidences of stress reactions and maladaptive coping responses Offer screening for stress-related disorders (e.g., posttraumatic stress disorder [PTSD]) Provide a system of referral to outside agencies	PREPARE (Brock, Nickerson, Reeves, & Jimerson, 2008) Critical incidence stress management (CISM; Mitchell & Everly, 1996) National Organization for Victim Assistance (NOVA) model (Young, 2002) BASIC Ph (Lahad, 1997)

family dysfunction, ineffective parenting, child maltreatment, poor physical health of the child or parents, parent mental illness or inadequacy, and large family size are of particular concern (Doll & Lyons, 1998). Even though schools are unable to control for many of these specific factors, the information they provide serves as a basis for professionals to identify at-risk students and to design protective interventions (Mennuti, Freeman, & Christner, 2006).

The identification process is essential for this level of service to be effective. When assessing students who have preexisting vulnerabilities to stress and life circumstances, it is common to determine the level of impact of specific risk factors and how well protective factors may be serving the child. Other students who are symptomatic can benefit from early

TABLE 1.3   Categories of Risk Factors

Constitutional handicaps
Skill development delays
Emotional difficulties
Family circumstances
Interpersonal problems
School problems
Ecological risks

Source: Modified from Coie et al. (1993).

attention in order to prevent the development of severe symptoms and the need for intensive treatment. An example of an acute symptom may be a sudden uprise in suspensions and detentions for aggressive behaviors. In either case, these students are in need of service at the targeted level, and therefore, they should be part of the instructional support program or another building-based problem-solving team process (Smallwood et al., 2007).

Assessment practices to identify children in need of targeted interventions may overlap some of the assessment tools utilized at the universal level. At the targeted level, however, the goal is not to develop a schoolwide intervention but, instead, to focus on specific areas that affect a smaller group of students. For instance, data on students who have frequent contact with teachers and administrators due to discipline referrals (e.g., verbal or physical altercations) can be used to identify students for inclusion in a group intervention (e.g., an anger and aggression management group). The challenge for school-based practitioners will be identifying those students who demonstrate risk factors for or emerging symptoms of more internalizing disorders, such as anxiety disorders. In these cases, assessment techniques may have to go beyond review of disciplinary records to include consultation with school staff who, because of direct contact, are in a better position to identify students in need of intervention. For instance, teachers in a particular school may identify a number of academically competent students who are not demonstrating their academic skills due to a high level of anxiety during testing situations. The data provided by these teachers can be used to develop a group intervention focusing on stress reduction.

In addition to the aforementioned techniques, the use of formal and informal screening instruments or programs can be an effective way to identify students at risk. For instance, the Columbia University TeenScreen® Program (Coleman & Vaughn, 2000) is a national screening program used to help identify students who are at risk for mental health issues and suicide. This voluntary program offers youth the opportunity for mental health checkups. Schools may also develop their own informal screening process by using various standardized and/or informal rating scales and questionnaires.

Assessment before, during, and after implementation of targeted interventions is necessary to obtain knowledge about response to the intervention, as well as to measure an individual student's progress. Given that targeted interventions may be designed to address particular skill deficits or eliminate some specific undesired behavior, the assessment methods need to be more specific, and for monitoring purposes, they should be used to assess progress toward a specific goal. In these cases, practitioners may choose to use an already established rating scale addressing a set of symptoms (e.g., the Beck Youth Depression Scales; Beck, Beck, Jolly, & Steer, 2005). Table 1.1 also offers examples of assessment data that can be used at the targeted intervention level.

Programs at the targeted level of intervention can be applied with individual students; however, we recommend utilizing group interventions at this level whenever possible. The type of targeted intervention utilized will depend on the developmental level of the students, the nature of the target behaviors, and the organizational climate of the school, which may support or impede the application of different strategies. Throughout this book, there are examples of programs and interventions that can be used at this level. In addition, a variety of programs is available commercially. Although we do not offer a review of all available programs, Table 1.2 provides several key points to consider when identifying targeted interventions or programs.

Intensive Interventions

Although many students will respond to interventions offered at the *universal* and *targeted* levels, a small group of students will continue to be in need of more intensive supports and individualized interventions. In some cases, these services may go beyond what can be provided as part of a comprehensive school-based mental health program, as depicted in Figure 1.1. However, for many of these students, services could be provided within the school system alone or in conjunction with those services provided through community-based programs. Intensive interventions are designed to decrease the level of impairment associated with an existing emotional or behavioral disorder and to enhance a student's level of functioning and ability to learn. The interventions at this level can be provided in a group intervention format; however, in most cases, students in need of services at this level will require individualized intervention or treatment plans (Smallwood et al., 2007).

Interventions at this level must be highly individualized based on the student's areas of need, and intervention selection should be guided by assessment and case conceptualization (Mennuti et al., 2006). Assessment can include obtaining new data (e.g., rating scales, observations, and functional behavior assessment) as well as previously conducted evaluations. It is important that the frequency and severity of the student's symptoms and/or target behaviors be assessed so that operational intervention goals can be developed and monitored. To assist with case conceptualization, Murphy and Christner (2006) developed a framework and worksheet to assist practitioners. Although this framework was designed from a cognitive-behavioral orientation, it can be extended and modified for use with any theoretical model. For detailed information, the reader is referred to Murphy and Christner's chapter in *Cognitive-Behavioral Interventions in Educational Settings: A Handbook for Practice* (Mennuti et al.).

The individual delivering intensive interventions typically has some formal training and experience in the assessment and treatment of emotional and behavioral disorders. In the school setting, intensive interventions may be delivered by school psychologists, school counselors, social workers, or other mental health specialists. In other cases, school districts contract with community-based providers who come into the school to provide mental health treatment. In contrast to universal and targeted interventions, intensive interventions are typically presented in a more traditional psychotherapy format. The focus is not exclusively on skill building via psychoeducational activities, as the goals further include symptom reduction, increasing coping skills, and the like. The specific goals and strategies employed in intensive interventions will depend on the clinician's theoretical orientation. Part 2 of this book contains descriptions of various intensive interventions based on several different theoretical orientations. As readers view each chapter, they should keep in mind the key points for intensive interventions noted in Table 1.2.

Crisis Interventions

Although not often distinguished as a separate component of school-based mental health services, crisis intervention is essential in any comprehensive attempt to meet the emotional needs of children. Crisis intervention services can be conceptualized as involving three primary activities— namely, those activities involved in planning for crises and those involved in preventing and intervening with crises when they occur. Thus, crisis prevention and intervention services can be implemented at the universal, targeted, and intensive levels of service.

However, in the school-based mental health framework offered in Figure 1.1, *crisis services* refer to brief counseling for students who are suicidal or are experiencing some other personal crisis, such as abuse or the death of a parent. As compared to intensive interventions designed to produce lasting behavioral changes, the focus of crisis services is stabilization via an emphasis on student strengths and preexisting coping resources. In addition, Brock and Jimerson (2004) identified the need for interventions to reduce the severity and incidence of stress reactions and maladaptive coping responses. They also recommended the development of procedures to identify students who are at risk for developing a stress-related mental health problem (i.e., posttraumatic stress disorder) and make referrals to mental health providers for ongoing care.

Within the school setting, crisis services are typically provided by pupil services personnel such as school counselors, school psychologists, and social workers. However, in some instances, school districts may utilize the services of outside mental health agencies that are called in to assist during crises. Like other intensive interventions, crisis intervention is typically provided on an individual basis. However, some group crisis intervention models have been developed (Brock, 2002). Table 1.2 offers a review of key points of crisis services and examples of various models.

How to Use This Book

As we have introduced in this chapter, school-based mental health providers must have a conceptualization not only of individual students but also of service delivery within the unique setting of schools. Following the service delivery model described above, part 1 of this book offers a review of system-level issues as well as interventions that can be applied school-wide or at the universal level. However, universal interventions alone will not address the needs of all children, and thus, part 2 of this book reviews school-based mental health from varying theoretical orientations, which can be applied in work with students at the targeted or intensive level of service delivery.

Designing this book was done with a purpose in mind—that is, to expose readers to different theoretical orientations in order to facilitate their developing a solid theoretical style consistent with their personal characteristics as well as the culture of their particular school environment. Having a theoretical orientation is grounded in a set of beliefs, which become the lenses through which practitioners view the individuals or groups with whom they work. Although we believe that understanding a number of theoretical perspectives and orientations is essential to good therapy, we discourage readers and practitioners from becoming theoretically eclectic—that is, attempting to conceptualize cases from multiple views. By doing this, there is greater chance of having contra-dictory hypotheses about those we work with, which has the potential to decrease our effectiveness. However, although we are discouraging practi-tioners from conceptualizing cases from an eclectic viewpoint, we encour-age them to be technically eclectic in their selection of interventions. For instance, a practitioner may conceptualize a student's behaviors using a cognitive-behavioral perspective, but through this conceptual framework the practitioner may identify that interventions often used in family ther-apy may be particularly useful for this student. Although the practitioner does not change his or her orientation, he or she may incorporate family system intervention to enhance treatment outcomes.

Therefore, this book provides the basic knowledge needed to provide mental health services in the school; however, to take this information and implement it in a cookbook manner may lead to service delivery with minimal effectiveness. One size does not fit all practitioners. Best practice in school-based mental health is more than theoretical knowledge, prin-ciples, techniques, and strategies. Rather, we must come to know ourselves as individuals—our way of being in the world in an authentic way. How this self-awareness interfaces with our knowledge of theory develops into our personal therapeutic philosophy. In so doing, we integrate our theo-retical orientation with a sense of self that leads to a personal style that is real, thus transforming theory into effective relational practice.

To help this book come alive, we asked the chapter authors from Parts 2 and 3 of this book to each address the same case from their particular framework. The appendix to this chapter provides a copy of the case pro-vided to the authors, which you can follow through each chapter in order to help identify the similarities and disparities between various approaches. As you read each chapter, keep the following question in mind: "How would you use this knowledge to promote Todd's development?"

Appendix: The Case of Todd

Todd is a 10-year-old African American boy who is in the fourth grade. He lives with his biological mother and maternal grandmother, and he has no siblings. The family resides in a lower- to middle-class com-munity. His mother and classroom teacher referred him to the school-based intervention team. A difference in his behaviors began in the third grade, and they have worsened over the past 3 months.

Todd's mother noted that he is an organized child who has always liked structure. His mother and previous teachers indicated that he is a hardworking and motivated student who is well mannered. Notes from his preschool teacher stated, "Todd is a perfect little gentleman." His mother reported that she initially viewed his organization and work ethic as being positive attributes, but within the past few months, she noticed that it seems to have begun to affect him greatly.

Starting in the third grade, Todd began reporting being "stressed out" and frustrated with schoolwork. His mother thought this was due to the curricular changes in the third grade and demands, as his homework seemed to increase at that time. Todd's mother also began receiving notes that Todd was not turning in his homework, although she knew he was completing it the night before. When asked about homework, Todd's mother indicated that he starts his homework as soon as he gets home from school (3:30 p.m.) and works for about 2 hours. He then stops to eat dinner with his family and works until bedtime (9:00 p.m.). She also noted that he works for several hours over the weekend. His classroom teacher reported that homework should be about 45 to 60 minutes per night Monday through Thursday. The teacher has informed Todd's mother that if he is not finished after 60 minutes, she should note it in his homework book, and the teacher will work with Todd at school. When this was presented to Todd, he became very "worked up" and insisted that he do his work at home.

Despite Todd's long hours of work and continued effort, his grades this year have been all C's, and on occasion lower. This is a notable change from his straight A's in past years. The school had Todd evaluated by the school psychologist to rule out any learning problems, and the testing showed that he had above-average cognitive abilities, and his academic achievement scores were all within the average to high-average ranges. Behavioral rating scales completed by Todd, his mother, and his teacher revealed generally appropriate externalizing behaviors across settings. His mother's responses showed some tantrum behaviors that have become apparent this year. All of the ratings, however, suggested that Todd had clinically significant signs of anxiety and worry. Much of his anxiety was performance based, especially with regard to school performance and the perception of others.

The recommendation for Todd is for mental health services provided at school, to include individual weekly counseling as well as parent and teacher consultation. Upon your interview with Todd, you find him to be a charming and friendly youngster. He reported a desire to please others and to do well in school.

References

Adelman, H. S., & Taylor, L. (1998). Reframing mental health in schools and expanding school reform. *Educational Psychologist, 33,* 135–152.

Adelman, H. S., & Taylor, L. (2000). Looking at school health and school reform policy through the lenses of addressing barriers to learning. *Children Services: Social Policy, Research, and Practice, 3,* 117–132.

Anderson, J. A., Kutash, K., & Duchnowski, A. J. (2001). A comparison of the academic progress of students with EBD and students with LD. *Journal of emotional and Behavioral Disorders, 9,* 106–115.

Atkinson, M. (2002). *Mental health handbook for schools.* London: RoutledgeFalmer.

Beck, J. S., Beck, A. T., Jolly, J., & Steer, R. (2005). *Beck youth inventories, second edition for children and adolescents.* San Antonio, TX: Harcourt.

Brock, S. E. (2002). Group crisis intervention. In S. E. Brock, P. J. Lazarus, & S. R. Jimerson (Eds.), *Best practices in school crisis prevention and intervention* (pp. 367–384). Bethesda, MD: National Association of School Psychologists.

Brock, S. E., & Jimerson, S. R. (2004). School crisis interventions: Strategies for addressing the consequences of crisis events. In E. R. Gerler (Ed.), *The handbook of school violence* (pp. 285–332). Binghamton, NY: Haworth.

Brock, S. E., Nickerson, A. B., Reeves, M. A., & Jimerson, S. R. (2008). Best practices for school psychologists as members of crisis teams: The PREPaRE Model. In A. Thomas & J. Grimes (Eds.), *Best practices in school psychology* (Vol. 4; pp. 1487–1504). Bethesda, MD: National Association of School Psychologists.

Bush, J. (1997). *The handbook of school art therapy: Introducing art therapy into a school system.* Springfield, IL: Charles C. Thomas Publisher.

Center for Mental Health in Schools, University of California, Los Angeles. (2003). *Youngster's mental health and psychosocial problems: What are the data?* Los Angeles: Author. Retrieved June 20, 2008, from http://smhp.psych.ucla.edu/pdfdocs/prevalence/youthMH.pdf

Center for Mental Health in Schools, University of California, Los Angeles. (2006). *The current status of mental health in schools: A policy and practice analysis.* Los Angeles: Author.

Christner, R. W., Forrest, E., Morley, J., & Weinstein, E. (2007). Taking cognitive-behavior therapy to school: A school-based mental health approach. *Journal of Contemporary Psychotherapy, 37*(3), 175–183.

Clarke, G., & Lewinsohn, P. M. (1995). *The adolescent coping with stress in class: Leader's guide.* Portland, OR: Kaiser Permanente Center for Health Research.

Coie, J. D., Watt, J. F., West, S. G., Hawkins, J. D., Asarnow, J. R., Markman, H. J., et al. (1993). The science of prevention: A conceptual framework and some direction for a national research program. *American Psychologist, 48,* 1013–1022.

Coleman, M., & Vaughn, S. (2000). Reading interventions for students with emotional/behavioral disorders. *Behavioral Disorders, 25,* 93–105. New York: Columbia University TeenScreen® Program.

Doll, B., & Lyons, M. A. (1998). Risk and resilience: Implications for the delivery of educational and mental health services in the schools. *School Psychology Review, 27,* 348–363.

Doll, B., Zucker, S., & Brehm, K. (2004). *Resilient classroom: Creating healthy environments for learning.* New York: Guilford.

Doll, B., & Cummings, J. A. (2007). *Transforming school mental health services: Population-based approaches to promoting the competency and wellness of children.* Thousand Oaks, CA: Corwin Press.

Drewes, A., Carey, L. J., & Schaefer, C. E. (2001). *School-based play therapy.* New York: Wiley.

Elias, M. J., & Butler, L. B. (2005). *Social decision making/social problem solving: A curriculum for academic, social, and emotional learning.* Champaign, IL: Research Press.

Epstein, M. H., & Cullinan, D. (1994). Characteristics of children with emotional and behavioral disorders in community-based programs designed to prevent placement in residential facilities. *Journal of Emotional and Behavioral Disorders, 2*(1), 51–58.

Evans, S. W., Weist, M., & Serpell, Z. (Eds.) (2007). *Advances in School-Based Mental Health Interventions: Best Practices and Program Models (Vol. 2).* New York: Civic Research Institute.

Goldstein, A. P., Glick, B., & Gibbs, J. (1998). *Aggression replacement training: A comprehensive intervention for aggressive youth* (2nd ed.). Champaign, IL: Research Press.

Kendall, P. C. (1993). *A coping cat workbook.* Ardmore, PA: Workbook Publishing.

Kessler, R. C., Berglund, P., Demler, O., Jin, R., & Walters, E. E. (2005). Lifetime prevalence and age-of-onset distributions of DSM-IV disorders in the national comorbidity survey replication. *Archive of General Psychiatry, 62,* 593–602.

Krueger, R. A., & Casey, M. A. (2000). Focus groups. A practical guide for applied research (3rd ed.). Thousand Oaks, CA: Sage Publications.

Kusche, C. A., & Greenberg, M. T. (1994). *The PATHS (promoting alternative thinking strategies) curriculum.* Seattle, WA: Developmental Research and Programs.

Lahad, M. (1997). BASIC Ph: The story of coping resources. In M. Lahad & A. Cohen (Eds.), *Community stress prevention* (Vols. 1–2, pp. 117–143). Kiryat Shmona, Israel: Community Stress Prevention Centre.

Larson, J., & Lochman, J. E. (2002). *Helping schoolchildren cope with anger: A cognitive-behavioral intervention.* New York: Guilford.

Mennuti, R. B., Freeman, A., & Christner, R. W. (Eds.). (2006). *Cognitive-behavioral interventions in educational settings: A handbook for practice.* New York: Routledge.

Mitchell, J. T., & Everly, G. S. (1996). *Critical incident stress debriefing: An opera-tions manual for the prevention of traumatic stress among emergency services and disaster workers* (2nd ed., Rev. ed.). Ellicott City, MD: Chevron.

Murphy, V. B., & Christner, R. W. (2006). A cognitive-behavioral case conceptual-ization approach for working with children and adolescents. In R. B. Mennuti, A. Freeman, & R. W. Christner (Eds.), *Cognitive-behavioral interventions in educational settings: A handbook for practice.* New York: Routledge.

Nastasi, B. K., Bernstein Moore, R., & Varjas, K. M. (2003). *School-based men-tal health services: Creating comprehensive and culturally specific programs.* Washington, DC: American Psychological Association.

National Center for Education Statistics. (2005). *Digest of education statistics, 2004.* NCES Publication No. 2006005. Retrieved May 16, 2006, from http://nces.ed.gov./programs/digest/d04

National Institute of Mental Health. (2004). *Treatment of children with mental dis-orders* (NIH Publication No. 04-4702). Bethesda, MD: Author.

President's New Freedom Commission on Mental Health. (2003). *Final report to the president: Full version.* Washington, DC: Author.

Shure, M. B. (2001). I can problem solve (ICPS): An interpersonal cognitive problem solving program for children. In L. A. Reddy & S. Pfeiffer (Eds.), *Innovative mental health programs for children: Programs that work* (pp. 2–14). Binghamton, NY: Haworth.

Simonsen, B., & Sugai, G. (2007). Using school-wide data systems to make deci-sions efficiently and effectively. *School Psychology Forum: Research in Practice, 1*(2), 46–58.

Sklare, G. B. (1997). *Brief counseling that works: A solution-focused approach for school counselors.* Thousand Oaks, CA: Corwin Press.

Smallwood, D. L., Christner, R. W., & Brill, L. (2007). Applying cognitive-behav-ior therapy groups in school settings. In R. W. Christner, J. L. Stewart, & A. Freeman (Eds.), *Handbook of cognitive-behavior group therapy: Specific set-tings and presenting problems* (pp. 89–105). New York: Routledge.

Sugai, G., & Horner, R. H. (1999). Discipline and behavioral support: Practices, pitfalls, and promises. *Effective School Practices, 17*(4), 10–22.

Walsh, W. H., & Williams. G.R. (1997). *Schools and family therapy: Using systems theory and family therapy in the resolution of school problems.* Springfield, IL: Charles C. Thomas Publisher.

Young, M. (2002). The community crisis response team: The National Organization for Victim Assistance protocol. In S. E. Brock, P. J. Lazarus, & S. R. Jimerson (Eds.), *Best practices in school crisis prevention and intervention* (pp. 333–354). Bethesda, MD: National Association of School Psychologists.

Section II

Foundation of Universal Interventions

2

Ending the Marginalization of Mental Health in Schools
A Comprehensive Approach

Howard Adelman

Linda Taylor

What is the current context for efforts to advance mental health in schools? To begin with, there is long-standing acknowledgment that a variety of psychosocial and health problems affect learning and performance in profound ways (Center for Mental Health in Schools, 2006; Marx & Wooley, 1998). Moreover, it is clear that such problems are exacerbated as youngsters internalize the debilitating effects of performing poorly at school and are punished for the misbehavior that is a common correlate of school failure. Because of all this, school policy makers have a lengthy history of trying to assist teachers in dealing with problems that interfere with schooling, including a wide range of psychosocial and mental health concerns.

Over the past 20 years, an enhanced movement to increase linkages between schools and community service agencies has added impetus to advocacy for mental health in schools. Recently, some advocates for school-linked services have coalesced their efforts with those engaged in initiatives for youth development and community schools. These coalitions have expanded interest in social-emotional learning and protective factors as ways to increase students' assets and resiliency and reduce risk factors. All this activity has been bolstered by local, state, federal, and private foundation initiatives.

A prominent example of federal efforts to advance the field is the U.S. Department of Health and Human Services' Mental Health in Schools Program, established in the mid-1990s (Anglin, 2003). The emphasis of this program is on increasing the capacity of policy makers, administrators, school personnel, primary care health providers, mental health specialists, agency staff, consumers, and other stakeholders so that they can enhance how schools and communities address psychosocial and mental health concerns. Particular attention is given to prevention and responding early after the onset of problems as critical facets of reducing the prevalence of problems. Other examples of noteworthy current federal initiatives that have potential to advance the field of mental health in schools include the multiagency Safe Schools/Healthy Students grant program and the Integration of Schools and Mental Health Systems grant program from the U.S. Department of Education's Office of Safe and Drug-Free Schools.

Despite all this, addressing psychosocial and mental health concerns is not assigned a high priority on a regular basis in schools. Such concerns gain temporary stature whenever a high-visibility problem arises—such as a shooting on campus, a student suicide, and an increase in bullying. However, student supports in general and mental health in particular commonly have low status in current policy and practice (Center for Mental Health in Schools, 2005a). As a result, interventions are developed in an ad hoc, piecemeal, and highly marginalized way. In addition, the marginalization not only produces fragmented approaches, but also contributes to wasteful redundancy, counterproductive competition, and inadequate results. The marginalization spills over and negatively affects how schools pursue special education and connect with systems of care and wraparound services. Moreover, it hampers efforts to incorporate evidence-based practices.

Because of the marginalization, the current context for efforts to advance mental health in schools can be summarized as follows:

- Too many students continue to perform poorly in too many schools across the country.
- To change this, schools should be, but are not, playing a major role in addressing mental health and psychosocial concerns and other barriers to learning and teaching.
- As a result, support programs and services as they currently operate cannot meet the needs of the majority of students experiencing behavior, learning, and emotional problems.
- Linking a few more community health and social services to a few schools does not enable schools to meet the demand.
- What schools need to develop is a comprehensive support system that can ensure that all students have an equal opportunity to succeed at school.
- However, the development of such a system is unlikely as long as school policy and practice continue to marginalize student supports.

This chapter highlights four fundamental matters that our work suggests must be pursued if the marginalization is to end. One involves enhancing the *policy* framework for school improvement in ways that incorporate mental health and psychosocial concerns under a broad and unifying umbrella concept that is established as a primary and essential component of a school's mission. The second matter is that of reframing *interventions* in ways that are consistent with such a broad, unifying concept. The third matter calls for rethinking the organizational and operational *infrastructure* at a school, for the feeder pattern of schools, and at the district level. In addition, finally, there is the problem of facilitating major *systemic change* in organizations such as schools that have well-established institutional cultures.

Reworking Policy

It is essential to constantly remember that schools are not in the mental health business. They are in the education business. Educators will continue to marginalize mental health in schools as long as the work is formulated narrowly in terms of meeting the needs of students with mental health problems.

Given that schools are not in the mental health business, it is strategic to move beyond simply stressing that good health is a prerequisite to good learning. That is, the health and mental health agenda must be embedded into the broader need for schools to play a major role in addressing barriers to learning and teaching. From a policy perspective, ending the marginalization requires adopting the type of unifying concept for this role that elevates its importance with school policy makers and fully integrates the work into school improvement and reform efforts.

Current Policy Making Is Piecemeal and Ad Hoc

At the school level, analyses consistently find that programs, services, and special projects for addressing student problems are the product of piecemeal and ad hoc policy making (Adelman & Taylor, 1997a, 2006a; Dryfoos, 1994; Gardner, 2005). The result is a tendency for student support staff to function in relative isolation of each other and other stakeholders, with a great deal of the work focusing on discrete problems and overrelying on specialized services for individuals and small groups. In some schools, a student identified as at risk for dropout, substance abuse, and grade retention may be assigned to three counseling programs operating independently of each other. Furthermore, in every facet of school operation, an unproductive separation often is manifested between those focused on instruction and those concerned with student problems. Such fragmentation not only is costly in terms of redundancy and counterproductive competition, but also works against developing comprehensive, multifaceted, and cohesive systems to address barriers to learning and teaching (Adelman, 1996; Adelman & Taylor, 1997a, 1999).

Widespread recognition of the fragmentation has produced some efforts to enhance coordination. Better coordination is a good idea. Nevertheless, it does not address the fundamental systemic problem of *marginalization.* Given the marginalization, it is not surprising that student support personnel almost never are a prominent part of a school's planning processes and organizational structure. Even worse, such staff usually are among those deemed dispensable as budgets tighten.

Moving From a Two- to a Three-Component Policy Framework

Analyses by our research group indicate that school improvement policy is currently dominated by a two-component model (Adelman, 1995, 1996; Adelman & Taylor, 1994, 1997a, 1998). That is, the primary thrust is on improving instruction and school management. Although these two facets obviously are essential, ending the marginalization of efforts to effectively address student problems requires establishing a third component as primary, essential, complementary, and overlapping (see Figure 2.1).

As illustrated in Figure 2.1, we designate the third component as an *enabling component*; others who have adopted it use terms such as a *learning supports component* (e.g., Iowa Department of Education, 2004). The concept of an enabling or learning supports component is formulated around the proposition that a comprehensive, multifaceted, integrated continuum of enabling activity is essential in addressing the needs of youngsters who encounter barriers that interfere with their benefiting satisfactorily from instruction. The concept embraces healthy development, prevention, and interventions to correct problems.

Various states and localities have adopted this third component as a policy basis for developing the type of comprehensive intervention framework that is described in the next section. (See information about these

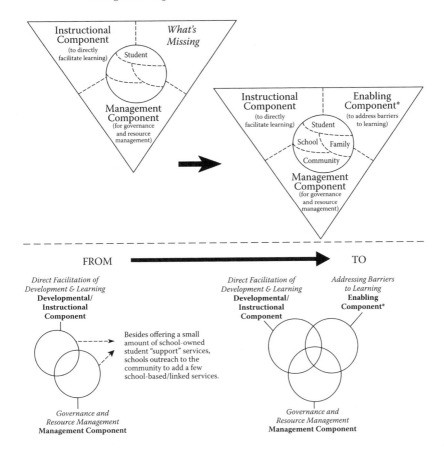

Figure 2.1 Moving From a Two- to a Three-Component Model for School Improvement

trailblazing initiatives online at Center for Mental Health in Schools, n.d., http://smhp.psych.ucla.edu/summit2002/wheresithappening.htm.)

Reframing Intervention

There are about 90,000 public schools in about 15,000 districts in the United States. Over the years, most (but obviously not all) schools have instituted programs designed to address a range of mental health and psychosocial concerns, such as school adjustment and attendance problems, dropouts, physical and sexual abuse, substance abuse, relationship difficulties, emotional upset, delinquency, and violence. Some programs are mandated for every school; others are carried out at or linked to targeted schools. The interventions may be offered to all students in a school, to those in specified grades, or to those identified as "at risk." The activities may be implemented in regular or special education classrooms or as "pull-out" programs, and may be designed for an entire class, groups, or individuals. Moreover, besides those that are owned and operated by schools, community agencies also are bringing services, programs, and personnel to school sites.

Despite the range of activity, it is common knowledge that few schools come close to having enough resources to deal with a large number of students with behavior, learning, and emotional problems. In addition, many schools report that large numbers of students are affected (Foster et al., 2005; Kutash, Duchnowski, & Lynn, 2006; U.S. Department of Education, 1996).

Who's the Client? A Few Students, or the School and All Its Students?

If schools are to achieve their mission, they must effectively address the problems of the many students who are not benefiting from instructional reforms. This will require fundamental, systemic changes. Yet, most school improvement plans pay little attention to substantially enhancing the ways in which schools provide student and learning supports. Instead, there has been an emphasis on initiatives to link a few community resources to a few schools and enhance coordination of services (e.g., through establishing "Family Resource Centers," "Full-Service Schools," and multidisciplinary teams that focus on specific students).

Connecting school and community resources ultimately is a good idea (Dryfoos, 1994). The reality, however, is that the number of schools and the number of students in need of support far outstrip what publicly supported community agencies can make available. Even when one adds together community and school assets, the total set of services in impoverished locales is woefully inadequate. Moreover, it must be recognized that poorly conceived and designed strategies for community involvement at schools can exacerbate marginalization and compound fragmentation and counterproductive competition. Part of the reason this happens is because too often the primary focus is only on coordinating *community* services and colocating them at schools, rather than braiding resources and integrating interventions with the ongoing efforts of school staff (Adelman & Taylor, 2006a).

As inadequate as school-owned student support services are at most schools, the resources invested in student support staff (e.g., school psychologists, counselors, social workers, and nurses) usually exceed to a considerable degree what local public agencies can afford to link to a school. Moreover, schools have other resources they can use to meet the challenge of ensuring all students have an equal opportunity to succeed at school. Besides traditional "pupil service personnel," student support is provided by compensatory education personnel (e.g., Title I staff), resource teachers who focus on concepts such as *response to intervention* and *prereferral interventions*, and staff associated with a variety of schoolwide programs (e.g., after-school, safe, and drug-free school programs).

Regardless of who offers the support, the current tendency is to overemphasize *services*. This inevitably means there is too little focus on making fundamental changes in how a school addresses the needs of the many students who are experiencing problems. It seems evident that persons working in and with schools need to be more concerned about improving schools for all students and not just providing services to a few student clients. Indeed, if the complex problems experienced by large numbers of students are to be dealt with effectively, all support staff must appreciate that the school and all its students are their "clients."

Complex Problems Require a Comprehensive, Multifaceted, Cohesive Systemic Approach

The complexity of factors interfering with learning and teaching underscores the need for a comprehensive enabling or learning supports component. The question then arises as to how to operationalize such a component. To this end, we offer a framework that encompasses (a) an integrated continuum of interventions and (b) a multifaceted and cohesive set of content arenas (Adelman, 1995, 1996; Adelman & Taylor, 1994, 2006a, 2006b).

A Continuum of Integrated School–Community Intervention Systems
In effect, the intent, over time, is for schools to play a major role in establishing a full range of interventions, including:

- Systems for promoting healthy development and preventing problems
- Systems for intervening early to address problems as soon after onset as is feasible
- Systems for assisting those with chronic and severe problems

As illustrated in Figure 2.2, the desired interventions can be conceived along a continuum. In keeping with public health and public education perspectives, such a continuum encompasses efforts to enable academic, social, emotional, and physical development and address behavior, learning, and emotional problems at every school. Most schools have some programs and services that fit along the entire continuum. However, the tendency to focus on the most severe problems has skewed the process so that too little is done to prevent and intervene early after the onset of a problem. As a result, public education has been characterized as a system that "waits for failure."

Properly pursued, the continuum spans the concepts of primary, secondary, and tertiary prevention and incorporates a holistic and developmental emphasis that envelops individuals, families, and the contexts in which they live, work, and play. The continuum also provides a framework for adhering to the principle of using the least restrictive and most nonintrusive forms of intervention required to appropriately respond to problems and accommodate diversity.

Moreover, given the likelihood that many problems are not discrete, the continuum can be designed to address root causes, thereby minimizing tendencies to develop separate programs for each observed problem. In turn, this enables increased coordination and integration of resources, which can increase impact and cost-effectiveness.

Operationalizing the Continuum to Fit School Improvement Efforts
In our work, we operationalize the continuum in terms of the concept of an enabling or learning supports component. This helps to coalesce and enhance programs to ensure all students have an equal opportunity to succeed at school. A critical matter is defining what the entire school must do to enable *all* students to learn and *all* teachers to teach effectively. Schoolwide approaches are especially important where large numbers of

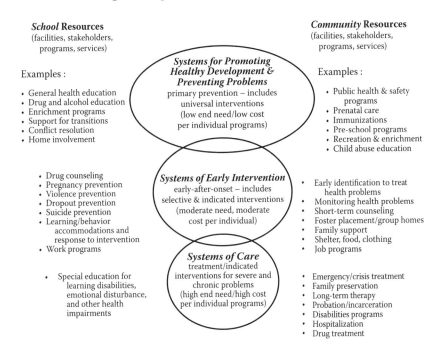

School Resources
(facilities, stakeholders,
programs, services)

Examples :

- General health education
- Drug and alcohol education
- Enrichment programs
- Support for transitions
- Conflict resolution
- Home involvement

- Drug counseling
- Pregnancy prevention
- Violence prevention
- Dropout prevention
- Suicide prevention
- Learning/behavior
  accommodations and
  response to intervention
- Work programs

- Special education for
  learning disabilities,
  emotional disturbance,
  and other health
  impairments

Community Resources
(facilities, stakeholders,
programs, services)

Examples :

- Public health & safety
  programs
- Prenatal care
- Immunizations
- Pre-school programs
- Recreation & enrichment
- Child abuse education

- Early identification to treat
  health problems
- Monitoring health problems
- Short-term counseling
- Foster placement/group homes
- Family support
- Shelter, food, clothing
- Job programs

- Emergency/crisis treatment
- Family preservation
- Long-term therapy
- Probation/incarceration
- Disabilities programs
- Hospitalization
- Drug treatment

Systems for Promoting Healthy Development & Preventing Problems
primary prevention – includes
universal interventions
(low end need/low cost
per individual programs)

Systems of Early Intervention
early-after-onset – includes
selective & indicated interventions
(moderate need, moderate
cost per individual)

Systems of Care
treatment/indicated
interventions for severe and
chronic problems
(high end need/high cost
per individual programs)

Systemic collaboration* is essential to establish interprogram connections on a daily basis and over time to ensure seamless intervention with each system and among *systems* of *prevention, systems of early intervention, and systems of care.*

*Such collaboration involves horizontal and vertical restructuring of programs and services
(a) within jurisdictions, school districts, and community agencies (e.g., among departments, divisions, units, schools, clusters of schools)
(b) between jurisdictions, school and community agencies, public and private sectors; among schools; among community agencies

Adapted from various public domain documents written by Adelman and Taylor.

Figure 2.2   Interconnected Systems for Meeting the Needs of All Students

students are affected and at any school that is not yet paying adequate attention to equity and diversity concerns.

Pioneering efforts have operationalized such a component into six programmatic arenas. Exhibit 2.1 outlines the prototype for the six arenas.

EXHIBIT 2.1   "Content" Areas for a Component to Address Barriers to Learning

1. Classroom-Based Approaches Encompass the Following:
   - Opening the classroom door to bring in available supports (e.g., peer tutors, volunteers, and aides trained to work with students in need; resource teachers and student support staff work in the classroom as part of the teaching team).
   - Redesigning classroom approaches to enhance teacher capability to prevent and handle problems and reduce the need for out-of-class referrals (e.g., personalized instruction, special assistance as necessary, developing small-group and independent learning options, reducing negative interactions and overreliance on social control, expanding the range of curricular and instructional options and choices, and the systematic use of prereferral interventions).
   - Enhancing and personalizing professional development (e.g., creating a learning community for teachers; ensuring opportunities to learn through coteaching, team teaching, and mentoring; and teaching intrinsic motivation concepts and their application to schooling).
   - Curricular enrichment and adjunct programs (e.g., varied enrichment activities that are not tied to reinforcement schedules, and visiting scholars from the community).
   - Classroom and schoolwide approaches used to create and maintain a caring and supportive climate.
   - Emphasis at all times is on enhancing feelings of competence, self-determination, and relatedness to others at school, and on reducing threats to such feelings.
2. Crisis Assistance and Prevention Encompass the Following:
   - Ensuring immediate assistance in emergencies so students can resume learning.
   - Providing follow-up care as necessary (e.g., brief and longer term monitoring).
   - Forming a school-focused crisis team to formulate a response plan and take leadership for developing prevention programs.
   - Mobilizing staff, students, and families to anticipate response plans and recovery efforts.
   - Creating a caring and safe learning environment (e.g., developing systems to promote healthy development and prevent problems, and creating bullying and harassment abatement programs).
   - Working with neighborhood schools and the community to integrate planning for response and prevention.
   - Capacity building to enhance crisis response and prevention (e.g., staff and stakeholder development, and enhancing a caring and safe learning environment).
3. Support for Transitions Encompasses the Following:
   - Welcoming and social support programs for newcomers (e.g., welcoming signs, materials, and initial receptions; and peer buddy programs for students, families, staff, and volunteers).

- Daily transition programs (e.g., before school, during breaks and lunch, and after school).
- Articulation programs (e.g., from grade to grade, for new classrooms and new teachers, from elementary to middle school, from middle to high school, and in and out of special education programs).
- Summer or intersession programs (e.g., catch-up, recreation, and enrichment programs).
- School-to-career and higher education (e.g., counseling, pathway, and mentor programs; broad involvement of stakeholders in planning for transitions; and students, staff, home, police, faith groups, recreation, business, and higher education).
- Broad involvement of stakeholders in planning for transitions (e.g., students, staff, home, police, faith groups, recreation, business, and higher education).
- Capacity building to enhance transition programs and activities.

4. Home Involvement in Schooling Encompasses the Following:
   - Addressing specific support and learning needs of family (e.g., support services for those in the home to assist in addressing basic survival needs and obligations to the children; and adult education classes to enhance literacy, job skills, English as a second language, and citizenship preparation).
   - Improving mechanisms for communication and connecting school and home (e.g., opportunities at school for family networking and mutual support, learning, recreation, and enrichment, and for family members to receive special assistance and to volunteer to help; phone calls and/or e-mails from teachers and other staff with good news; frequent and balanced conferences—student led, when feasible; and outreach to attract hard-to-reach families—including student dropouts).
   - Involving homes in student decision making (e.g., families prepared for involvement in program planning and problem solving).
   - Enhancing home support for learning and development (e.g., family literacy, family homework projects, and family field trips).
   - Recruiting families to strengthen school and community (e.g., volunteers to welcome and support new families and help in various capacities; and families prepared for involvement in school governance).
   - Capacity building to enhance home involvement.

5. Community Outreach for Involvement and Support Encompasses the Following:
   - Planning and implementing outreach to recruit a wide range of community resources (e.g., public and private agencies; colleges and universities; local residents; artists and cultural institutions; businesses and professional organizations; service, volunteer, and faith-based organizations; and community policy and decision makers).
   - Systems to recruit, screen, prepare, and maintain community resource involvement (e.g., mechanisms to orient and welcome, enhance the volunteer pool, maintain current involvements, and enhance a sense of community).

- Reaching out to students and families who don't come to school regularly—including truants and dropouts.
- Connecting school and community efforts to promote child and youth development and a sense of community.
- Capacity building to enhance community involvement and support (e.g., policies and mechanisms to enhance and sustain school–community involvement, staff and stakeholder development on the value of community involvement, and "social marketing").

6. Student and Family Assistance Encompasses the Following:
   - Providing extra support as soon as a need is recognized and doing so in the least disruptive ways (e.g., prereferral interventions in classrooms; problem-solving conferences with parents; and open access to school, district, and community support programs).
   - Timely referral interventions for students and families with problems based on response to extra support (e.g., identification and screening processes, assessment, referrals, and follow-up—school based, school linked).
   - Enhancing access to direct interventions for health, mental health, and economic assistance (e.g., school-based, school-linked, and community-based programs and services).
   - Care monitoring, management, information sharing, and follow-up assessment to coordinate individual interventions and check whether referrals and services are adequate and effective.
   - Mechanisms for *resource* coordination and integration to avoid duplication, fill gaps, garner economies of scale, and enhance effectiveness (e.g., braiding resources from school-based and linked interveners, feeder pattern and family of schools, and community-based programs; and linking with community providers to fill gaps).
   - Enhancing stakeholder awareness of programs and services.
   - Capacity building to enhance student and family assistance systems, programs, and services.

Source: Adapted from various public domain documents written by Adelman and Taylor.

In essence, this constitutes the "curriculum" or content of an enabling or learning support component (Adelman, 1996; Adelman & Taylor, 1998, 2006b; Center for Mental Health in Schools, 2004). Encompassed are programs to

- *enhance regular classroom strategies to enable learning* (i.e., improving instruction for students who have become disengaged from learning at school and for those with mild–moderate learning and behavior problems).
- *support transitions* (i.e., assisting students and families as they negotiate school and grade changes and many other transitions).

- increase home and school connections.
- respond to and, where feasible, prevent crises.
- increase community involvement and support (outreach to develop greater community involvement and support, including an enhanced use of volunteers).
- facilitate student and family access to effective services and special assistance as needed.

Combining the six content arenas with the continuum of interventions illustrated in Figure 2.2 provides an umbrella intervention framework to guide and unify school improvement planning to develop a system of learning supports (Adelman & Taylor, 2006a, 2006b; Center for Mental Health in Schools, 2005b). The resulting matrix is shown in Figure 2.3. This framework facilitates mapping and analyzing the current scope and content of how a school, a family of schools (e.g., a feeder pattern of schools), a district, and the community at each level address barriers to learning and teaching. Encompassed throughout is a full range of mental health and psychosocial concerns.

Beginning in the classroom with differentiated classroom practices, such a comprehensive, multifaceted, cohesive systemic approach

- addresses barriers through a broader view of "basics" and through effective accommodation of individual differences and disabilities.
- enhances the focus on motivational considerations with a special emphasis on intrinsic motivation as it relates to individual readiness and ongoing involvement and with the intent of fostering intrinsic motivation as a basic outcome.
- adds remediation, treatment, and rehabilitation as necessary, but only as necessary.

For individual youngsters, the intent is to prevent and minimize as many problems as feasible and to do so in ways that maximize engagement in productive learning. For the school and community as a whole, the intent is to produce a safe, healthy, nurturing environment or culture characterized by respect for differences, trust, caring, support, and high expectations. In accomplishing all this, the focus is on reframing support programs and melding school, community, and home resources.

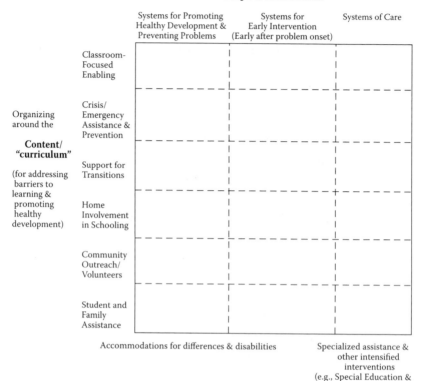

*Note that specific school-wide and classroom-based activities related to positive behavior support, "prereferral" interventions, and the eight components of Center for Prevention and Disease Control's Coordinated School Health Program are embedded into the six content ("curriculum") areas.

Adapted from various public domain documents written by Adelman and Taylor.

Figure 2.3 Matrix for Reviewing the Scope and Content of a Component to Address Barriers to Learning

Rethinking Infrastructure

Any discussion of ending the marginalization of mental health in schools must address the modification of existing infrastructure mechanisms in ways that guarantee that new policy directions are translated into appropriate daily practices. A well-designed and supported infrastructure establishes, maintains, and evolves the type of comprehensive approach to addressing barriers to student learning outlined above. It ensures local ownership, a critical mass of committed stakeholders and processes that overcome barriers to stakeholders working together effectively. It generates strategies that mobilize and maintain proactive effort so that changes are implemented and there is renewal over time. Such an infrastructure includes mechanisms for coordinating among enabling activity; for enhancing resources by developing direct linkages between school and community programs; for moving toward increased integration of school and community resources; and for integrating the instructional, enabling, and management components (Adelman & Taylor, 2006a; Center for Mental Health in Schools, 2005c, 2007).

In developing an organizational and operational infrastructure, the fundamental principle is that *structure follows function*. Based on clear functions, a differentiated infrastructure must be established to enable the accomplishment of functions and related tasks. Minimally, the need is for mechanisms to steer and do work on a regular basis. Moreover, because the work usually overlaps with that of others, there is a need to establish connections among various mechanisms. Properly redesigned infrastructure changes are needed to ensure, for example, integration, quality improvement, accountability, and self-renewal. Examples of major functions and tasks needed to develop a comprehensive approach to addressing barriers to learning and teaching are highlighted in the following discussion of key infrastructure mechanisms.

Key Mechanisms

From our perspective, the infrastructure for an enabling or learning supports component is designed from the school outward. That is, the emphasis is first on *designing* an integrated infrastructure at the school level. Then, the focus expands to include the mechanisms needed to connect a feeder pattern or complex of schools and establish collaborations with surrounding community resources. Ultimately, central district and community agency offices need to be rethought in ways that best support the work at the school and school complex levels.

Institutionalizing a comprehensive, multifaceted intervention component necessitates restructuring the mechanisms associated with at least six infrastructure concerns. These encompass processes for daily (a) governance, (b) leadership, (c) planning and implementation of specific organizational and program objectives, (d) coordination and integration for cohesion, (e) management of communication and information, and (f) capacity building. In redesigning mechanisms to address these matters, new collaborative arrangements must be established, and authority (power) redistributed. Those who do the restructuring must have appropriate incentives and safeguards for making major systemic changes, and those who operate essential mechanisms must have adequate resources and support. All this is easy to say, but extremely hard to accomplish.

Focusing on Resources
Obviously, administrative leadership is key to ending the marginalization of efforts to address behavior, learning, and emotional problems. Another key is the establishment of a team that focuses specifically on how learning support resources are used.

Every school is expending resources on student support to enable learning. In some schools, as much as 25% of the budget may be going to problem prevention and correction. Few schools have mechanisms to ensure the appropriate use of existing resources and enhance current efforts. Resource-oriented mechanisms contribute to the cost efficacy of student support activity by ensuring all such activity is planned, implemented, and evaluated in a coordinated and increasingly integrated manner. Creation of such mechanisms is essential for braiding together existing school and community resources and encouraging services and programs to function in an increasingly cohesive way.

Although resource-oriented mechanisms might be created solely around psychosocial programs, they are meant to focus on resources related to all major student support programs and services. In addition, when the mechanisms include a "team" (see next section), a new means is created for enhancing working relationships and solving turf and operational problems.

One of the primary and essential tasks that resource-oriented mechanisms undertake is that of delineating school and community resources (e.g., programs, services, personnel, and facilities) that are in place to support students, families, and staff. A comprehensive "gap" assessment is generated as resource mapping is aligned with unmet needs and desired outcomes. Analyses of what is available, effective, and needed provide a sound basis for formulating priorities, redeploying resources, and developing strategies to link with additional resources at other schools, at district sites, and in the community. Such analyses guide efforts to improve cost-effectiveness and enhance resources.

Resource-Oriented Teams

Resource-oriented teams do not focus on specific individuals, but on how resources are used. Such a team has been designated by a variety of names, including *resource coordinating team, resource management team,* and *learning supports resource team.* For the purposes of this discussion, we will use the last of these. We initially demonstrated the feasibility of such teams in the Los Angeles Unified School District, and now they are being introduced in many schools across the country (Center for Mental Health in Schools, 2005d; Lim & Adelman, 1997; Rosenblum, DiCecco, Taylor, & Adelman, 1995). Properly constituted at the school level, such a team provides on-site leadership for efforts to address barriers comprehensively and ensures the development, maintenance, and improvement of a multi-faceted and integrated approach (Adelman & Taylor, 2006a, in press-a).

A resource-oriented team exemplifies the type of mechanism needed to pursue overall cohesion and ongoing development of school support programs and systems. Minimally, it can reduce fragmentation and enhance cost efficacy by guiding programs to function in a coordinated and increasingly integrated way. More generally, the group can provide leadership in guiding school personnel and clientele in evolving the school's vision, priorities, and practices for student and learning support.

In pursuing its functions, the team provides what often is a missing link for managing and enhancing programs and systems in ways that integrate, strengthen, and stimulate new and improved interventions. For example, such a mechanism can be used to (a) map and analyze activity and resources to improve their use in preventing and ameliorating problems; (b) build effective referral, case management, and quality assurance systems; (c) enhance procedures for the management of programs and information and for communication among school staff and with the home; and (d) explore ways to redeploy and enhance resources—such as clarifying which activities are nonproductive, suggesting better uses for resources, establishing priorities for developing new interventions, as well as reaching out to connect with additional resources in the school district and community.

To these ends, efforts are made to bring together representatives of all relevant programs and services. This might include, for example, school counselors, psychologists, nurses, social workers, attendance and dropout counselors, health educators, special education staff, after-school program staff, bilingual and Title I program coordinators, safe and drug-free school staff, and union representatives. Such a team also should include representatives of any community agency that is significantly involved with a school.

Beyond these stakeholders, it is advisable to add the energies and expertise of classroom teachers, noncertificated staff, parents, and older students.

Where creation of "another team" is seen as a burden, existing teams, such as student or teacher assistance teams and school crisis teams, have demonstrated the ability to do resource-oriented functions. In adding the resource-oriented functions to another team's work, great care must be taken to structure the agenda so sufficient time is devoted to the additional tasks. For small schools, a large team often is not feasible, but a two-person team can still do the job.

Full Integration Into School Improvement Planning and Decision Making

Resource-oriented mechanisms cannot be isolated entities. The intent is for them to connect to each other and be part of an integrated infrastructure at a school, for a family of schools, and at the district level. At a school, for example, a learning supports resource team should be a formal unit of a school's infrastructure. And, it must fully connect with the other infrastructure mechanisms (e.g., those associated with instruction and management-governance). Figure 2.4 illustrates an integrated infrastructure at a school level.

Resource-oriented mechanisms that are properly constituted, developed, and supported complement the work of the site's governance body through providing on-site overview, leadership, and advocacy for all activity aimed at addressing barriers to learning and teaching. Having an administrator for learning supports and a resource-oriented team provides necessary links with governance and administrative decision making and planning (e.g., related to program development and the allocation of budget, space, and staff development time). Such infrastructure connections are essential if student and learning supports are to be developed, maintained, improved, and increasingly integrated with classroom instruction.

Beyond the School

It can be invaluable to link schools to maximize their use of limited resources and achieve economies of scale. Schools in the same geographic or catchment area have a number of shared concerns. Furthermore, some programs and personnel already are or can be shared by several

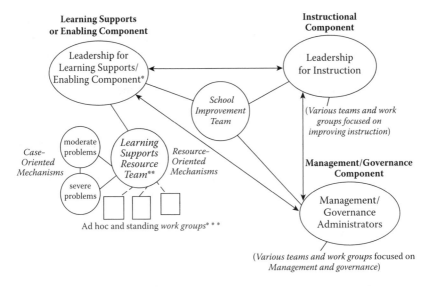

Figure 2.4 Example of an Integrated Infrastructure at the School Level

Within the figure:

Learning Supports or Enabling Component

Instructional Component

Leadership for Learning Supports/Enabling Component*

Leadership for Instruction

School Improvement Team

(*Various teams and work groups focused on improving instruction*)

Case-Oriented Mechanisms

moderate problems

*Learning Supports Resource Team***

Resource-Oriented Mechanisms

severe problems

Management/Governance Component

Management/Governance Administrators

Ad hoc and standing *work groups****

(*Various teams and work groups focused on Management and governance*)

---

*Learning Supports or Enabling Component Leadership consists of an administrator and other advocates/champions with responsibility and accountability for ensuring the vision for the component is not lost. The administrator meets with and provides regular input to the Learning Supports Resource Team.

**A Learning Supports Resource Team ensures component cohesion, integrated implementation, and ongoing development. It meets weekly to guide and monitor daily implementation and development of all programs, services, initiatives, and systems at a school that are concerned with providing learning supports and specialized assistance.

***Ad hoc and standing work groups – Initially, these are the various "teams" that already exist related to various initiatives and programs (e.g., a crisis team) and for processing "cases" (e.g., a student assistance team, an IEP team). Where redundancy exists, work groups can be combined. Others are formed as needed by the Learning Supports Resource Team to address specific concerns. These groups are essential for accomplishing the many tasks associated with such a team's functions.

For more on this, see

>http://smhp.psych.ucla.edu/pdfdocs/infrastructure/anotherinitiative-exec.pdf
>http://smhp.psych.ucla.edu/pdfdocs/studentsupport/toolkit/aidk.pdf

Adapted from various public domain documents written by Adelman and Taylor.

neighboring schools, thereby minimizing redundancy, reducing costs, and enhancing equity.

A group of schools can benefit from a *multisite resource mechanism* designed to provide leadership, facilitate communication and connection, and ensure quality improvement across sites. For example, what we call a *learning supports resource council* consists of a high school and its feeder middle and elementary schools. It brings together 1–2 representatives from each school's resource *team*. The council meets about once a month to further (a) coordinate and integrate programs serving multiple schools, (b) identify and meet common needs for capacity building, and (c) create linkages and collaborations among schools and with community agencies.

More generally, a multisite council provides a mechanism for leadership, communication, maintenance, quality improvement, and ongoing development of a comprehensive continuum of programs and services. Natural starting points for councils are the sharing of needs assessments, resource maps, analyses, and recommendations for reform and restructuring. Specific areas of initial focus are on local, high-priority concerns, such as addressing violence and developing prevention programs and safe school and neighborhood plans.

By providing a mechanism for a "family of schools" to coalesce resources in cost-effective ways, a multisite team can be especially useful for integrating and streamlining the efforts of high schools and their feeder middle and elementary schools. This clearly is important in addressing barriers with families who have youngsters attending more than one level of schooling in the same cluster. It is neither cost-effective nor good intervention for each school to make separate contacts in instances where several children from a family are in need of special attention. In addition, in connecting with community resources, multischool councils are especially attractive to community agencies that do not have the time or personnel to make independent arrangements with every school and that want to maximize distribution of scarce resources in ways that are efficient, effective, and equitable.

Representatives from learning supports resource councils also can be invaluable members of school–community planning groups (e.g., service planning area councils and local management boards). They bring information about specific schools, clusters of schools, and local neighborhoods, and do so in ways that underscore the value of school–community partnerships.

At the district level, the need is for administrative leadership and capacity-building support that help maximize the development of a comprehensive approach to addressing barriers to learning and teaching at each school (Center for Mental Health in Schools, 2007). Everyone at a school site should be aware that they have the support of someone at the district level who is responsible and accountable for providing leadership for the development of a school's enabling or learning supports component. And, it is crucial that such leadership is established at a high enough level to be at key decision-making tables when budget and other fundamental decisions are made.

The creation of resource-oriented mechanisms at schools, for families of schools, and at the district level is essential for weaving together existing school and community resources and developing a full continuum of interventions over time. Such mechanisms enable programs and services to function in an increasingly cohesive, cost-efficient, and equitable way. By doing so, they contribute to reducing marginalization and fragmentation of student and learning supports.

Getting From Here to There: The Problem of Systemic Change

Based on the available literature and our own policy and program analyses, we find widespread deficiencies in policy and practice with respect to how desired changes in schools are pursued. In particular, we find little evidence of sophisticated strategic planning for major systemic changes (Center for Mental Health in Schools, 2005e; Elmore, 2004; Fullan, 2005; Glennan, Bodilly, Galegher, & Kerr, 2004; Thomas, 2002).

The Implementation Problem and the Diffusion of Innovation

The problem of introducing new practices at schools has been widely called the *implementation problem*. Early research on the implementation problem has focused on concerns about and barriers to matters such as dissemination, readiness for and fidelity of implementation, generalizability, adaptation, sustainability, and replication to scale (Addis, 2002; Elliott & Mihalic, 2004; Franklin, DeRubeis, & Westin, 2006; Schoenwald & Hoagwood, 2001; Spoth & Redmond, 2002; Stirman, Crits-Christoph, & DeRubeis, 2004). All of these matters obviously are important.

Unfortunately, the trend has been to analyze and approach the matter with too limited a *procedural framework* and with too little attention to *context*. This has resulted in the tendency to skip these two core considerations. The deficiencies become apparent when the implementation process is conceived in terms of the complexities of (1) *diffusing innovations* and (2) doing so in the context of *organized settings* with well-established institutional cultures and infrastructures that must change if *effective* widespread application is to take place.

Those concerned with improving schools need to view the implementation problem from the vantage point of the growing bodies of literature on diffusion of innovations and systemic change. As the available research emphasizes, the work in these two overlapping arenas yields a broader and essential perspective for moving prototypes for school improvement into regular practice (Adelman & Taylor, in press-b; Greenhalgh, Robert, Macfarlane, Bate, & Kyriakidou, 2004; Magnabosco, 2006; Rogers, 2003; Senge, 1999; Sherry, 2003).

From this perspective, the implementation problem needs to be framed as a process of diffusing innovation through major systemic change. This encompasses the complexities of facilitating systemic changes that lead to the appropriate and effective adoption and adaptation of a prototype at a particular site and the added complexities of sustainability and replication to scale.

Enabling Systemic Change

Fullan (2005) stressed that effective systemic change requires leadership that "motivates people to take on the complexities and anxieties of difficult change." We would add that such leadership also must develop a sophisticated understanding of how to facilitate systemic change (Adelman & Taylor, 1997b, 2003, 2006a, 2006b; Taylor, Nelson, & Adelman, 1999).

Figure 2.5 highlights the ways in which major elements involved in implementing empirically supported innovative practices in an institutional setting are logically connected to considerations about systemic change. That is, the same elements can frame key intervention concerns related to implementing the practice and making systemic changes, and each is intimately linked to the other. The elements are conceived as encompassing the

- vision, aims, and underlying rationale for what follows.
- resources needed to do the work.
- general functions, major tasks, activities, and phases that must be pursued.
- infrastructure and strategies needed to carry out the functions, tasks, and activities.
- positive and negative results that emerge.

Strategic planning for implementing the specific innovative practices should account for each of these elements. This must be done with respect

Key considerations with respect to both the diffusion and systemic change processes:

>What is the vision, long-term aims, and underlying rationale?
>What are the existing resources that might be (re)deployed and woven together to make good progress toward the vision?
>What general functions, major tasks, activities, and phases need to be implemented?
>What infrastructure and strategies are needed to carry out the functions, tasks, and activities?
>What short-term indicators will be used as process benchmarks, what intermediate outcomes will indicate progress toward long-range aims, and how will negative outcomes be identified ?

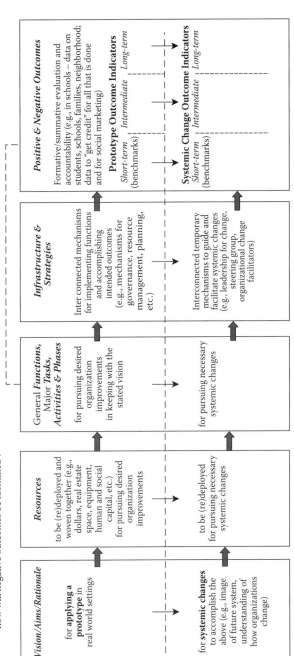

Adapted from various public domain documents written by Adelman and Taylor.

Figure 2.5   Linking Logic Models for Designing Diffusion of an Innovation and Related System Change

to accomplishing essential systemic changes for both (1) implementing the prototype in a given setting and (b) facilitating prototype replication and scale-up. (Each of the above elements as it relates to systemic change is described in Adelman & Taylor, in press-b; Center for Mental Health in Schools, 2005e.)

Elsewhere (e.g., Adelman & Taylor, 1997b), we have highlighted the nature and scope and the four overlapping phases of systemic change involved in prototype implementation and eventual scale-up. These are (a) *creating readiness*: increasing a climate or culture for change through enhancing both the motivation and the capability of a critical mass of stakeholders; (b) *initial implementation*: change is phased in using a well-designed infrastructure for providing guidance and support and building capacity; (c) *institutionalization*: this is accomplished by ensuring there is an infrastructure to maintain and enhance productive changes; and (d) *ongoing evolution and creative renewal*: through the use of mechanisms to improve quality and provide continuing support in ways that enable stakeholders to become a community of learners who creatively pursue renewal. At any time, an organization may be involved in introducing one or more innovations at one or more sites; it may also be involved in replicating one or more prototypes on a large scale. Whether the focus is on establishing a prototype at one site or replicating it at many, the systemic changes involve all four phases.

The nature and scope of a prototype are major influences on the diffusion process. For example, the broader the scope, the higher the costs; and the narrower the scope, the less the innovation may be important to an organization's overall mission. Both high costs and low valuing (e.g., marginalization) obviously can work against implementation and sustainability.

Whatever the nature and scope of the work, key facets include social marketing; articulating a clear, shared vision for the work; ensuring there is a major policy commitment from all participating partners; negotiating partnership agreements; designating leadership; enhancing and developing an infrastructure based on a clear articulation of essential functions (e.g., mechanisms for governance and priority setting, steering, operations, and resource mapping and coordination; and strong facilitation related to all mechanisms); redeploying resources and establishing new ones; building capacity (especially personnel development and strategies for addressing personnel and other stakeholder mobility); and establishing standards, evaluation processes, and accountability procedures. All of this requires careful planning based on sound intervention fundamentals.

Clearly, the many steps and tasks involved in diffusing innovations through systemic change call for a high degree of commitment and relentlessness of effort. Moreover, time frames for building the capacity to accomplish desired institutional changes must be realistic. Major systemic changes are not easily accomplished. Awareness of the myriad political and bureaucratic difficulties involved in making such institutional changes, especially with limited financial resources, leads to the caution that the process is not straightforward, sequential, or linear. Rather, the work proceeds, and changes emerge in overlapping and spiraling ways. In addition, those leading the way need to be opportunistic.

We need not belabor all this. Our point simply is to make certain that there is a greater appreciation for and more attention paid to the problems of systemic change as efforts are made to end the marginalization of mental health in schools and diffuse innovations such as those described throughout this chapter. To do less is to maintain an unsatisfactory status quo.

Concluding Comments

In looking to the future, it seems clear to us that any effort to enhance interventions for children's mental health must involve schools. Schools already provide a wide range of programs and services relevant to mental health and psychosocial concerns. However, schools can and need to do much more if the mandates of the No Child Left Behind Act and the Individuals With Disabilities Education Act and the recommendations of the President's New Freedom Commission on Mental Health are to be achieved.

At the same time, it is clear that the field of mental health in schools is in flux. There is widespread agreement that a great deal needs to be done to improve what is taking place. The call is for much more than expanded services and full-service schools. It encompasses movement toward developing comprehensive approaches that strengthen students, families, schools, and neighborhoods. Moreover, it involves the full integration of mental health concerns into a school's efforts to provide students with learning supports. Mental health in schools must be embedded into the basic mission of schools. This means developing well-integrated, comprehensive, multifaceted support systems that enable students to learn in ways that assure schools achieve their mandates.

Given the current state of school resources, the work must be accomplished by rethinking and redeploying how existing resources are used and by taking advantage of the natural opportunities at schools for countering psychosocial and mental health problems and promoting personal and social growth. Every school needs to commit to fostering staff and student resilience and creating an atmosphere that encourages mutual support, caring, and sense of community. Staff and students need to feel good about themselves if they are to cope with challenges proactively and effectively. For example, a welcoming induction and ongoing support are critical elements both in creating a positive sense of community and in facilitating staff and student school adjustment and performance. Schoolwide strategies for welcoming and supporting staff, students, and families at school *every day* are part of creating a mentally healthy school—one where staff, students, and families interact positively and identify with the school and its goals.

A major shift in policy and practice is long overdue. We must rethink how schools, families, and communities can meet the challenge of addressing persistent barriers to student learning and at the same time enhance how all stakeholders work together to promote healthy development.

All this, of course, involves major systemic changes. Such changes require weaving school-owned resources and community-owned resources together over time at every school in a district and addressing the complications stemming from the scale of public education in the United States.

The next decade must mark a turning point for how schools and communities address the problems of children and youth. In particular, the focus must be on initiatives to reform and restructure how schools work to prevent and ameliorate the many learning, behavioral, and emotional problems experienced by students. This means reshaping the functions of all school personnel who have a role to play in addressing barriers to learning and promoting healthy development. There is much work to be done as public schools across the country strive to leave no child behind and as the mental health field undergoes transformation.

References

Addis, M. E. (2002). Methods for disseminating research products and increasing evidence-based practice: Promises, obstacles, and future directions. *Clinical Psychology: Science and Practice, 9*, 421–424.

Adelman, H. S. (1995). Education reform: Broadening the focus. *Psychological Science, 6*, 61–62.

Adelman, H. S. (1996). Restructuring education support services and integrating community resources: Beyond the full service school model. *School Psychology Review, 25*, 431–445.

Adelman, H. S., & Taylor, L. (1994). *On understanding intervention in psychology and education.* Westport, CT: Praeger.

Adelman, H. S., & Taylor, L. (1997a). Addressing barriers to learning: Beyond school-linked services and full service schools. *American Journal of Orthopsychiatry, 67*, 408–421.

Adelman, H. S., & Taylor, L. (1997b). Toward a scale-up model for replicating new approaches to schooling. *Journal of Educational and Psychological Consultation, 8*, 197–230.

Adelman, H. S., & Taylor, L. (1998). Reframing mental health in schools and expanding school reform. *Educational Psychologist, 33*, 135–152.

Adelman, H. S., & Taylor, L. (1999). Addressing barriers to student learning: Systemic changes at all levels. *Reading and Writing Quarterly, 15*, 251–254.

Adelman, H. S., & Taylor, L. (2003). On sustainability of project innovations as systemic change. *Journal of Educational and Psychological Consultation, 14*, 1–26.

Adelman, H. S., & Taylor, L. (2006a). *The school leader's guide to student learning supports: New directions for addressing barriers to learning.* Thousand Oaks, CA: Corwin.

Adelman, H. S., & Taylor, L. (2006b). *The implementation guide to student learning supports: New directions for addressing barriers to learning.* Thousand Oaks, CA: Corwin.

Adelman, H. S., & Taylor, L. (2008). Best practices in the use of resource teams to enhance learning supports. In A. Thomas & J. Grimes (Eds.), *Best practices in school psychology V.* Bethesda, MD: National Association of School Psychologists.

Adelman, H. S., & Taylor, L. (2007). Systemic change for school improvement. *Journal of Educational and Psychological Consultation, 17*, 55–77.

Anglin, T. M. (2003). Mental health in school: Program of the federal government. In M. Weist, S. Evans, & N. Lever (Eds.), *Handbook of school mental health programs: Advancing practice and research.* Norwell, MA: Kluwer Academic.

Center for Mental Health in Schools, University of California, Los Angeles. (2004). *Addressing barriers to student learning & promoting healthy development: A usable research-base.* Los Angeles: Author. Retrieved March 12, 2008, from http://smhp.psych.ucla.edu/pdfdocs/briefs/BarriersBrief.pdf

Center for Mental Health in Schools, University of California, Los Angeles. (2005a). *School improvement planning: What's missing?* Los Angeles: Author. Retrieved March 12, 2008, from http://smhp.psych.ucla.edu/whatsmissing.htm

Center for Mental Health in Schools, University of California, Los Angeles. (2005b). *Addressing what's missing in school improvement planning: Expanding standards and accountability to encompass an enabling or learning supports component.* Los Angeles: Author. Retrieved March 12, 2008, from http://smhp.psych.ucla.edu/pdfdocs/enabling/standards.pdf

Center for Mental Health in Schools, University of California, Los Angeles. (2005c). *About infrastructure mechanisms for a comprehensive learning support component.* Los Angeles: Author. Retrieved March 12, 2008, from http://www.smhp.psych.ucla.edu/pdfdocs/infrastructure/infra_mechanisms.pdf

Center for Mental Health in Schools, University of California, Los Angeles. (2005d). *Developing resource-oriented mechanisms to enhance learning supports (continuing education modules).* Los Angeles: Author. Retrieved March 12, 2008, from http://smhp.psych.ucla.edu/pdfdocs/contedu/developing_resource_oriented-mechanisms.pdf; also available from http://smhp.psych.ucla.edu/pdfdocs/enabling/standards.pdf

Center for Mental Health in Schools, University of California, Los Angeles. (2005e). *Systemic change for school improvement: Designing, implementing, and sustaining prototypes and going to scale.* Los Angeles: Author. Retrieved March 12, 2008, from http://smhp.psych.ucla.edu/pdfdocs/systemic/systemicreport.pdf

Center for Mental Health in Schools, University of California, Los Angeles. (2006). *The current status of mental health in schools: A policy and practice analysis.* Los Angeles: Author. Retrieved March 12, 2008, from http://smhp.psych.ucla.edu/currentstatusmh.htm

Center for Mental Health in Schools, University of California, Los Angeles. (2007). *Toward a school district infrastructure that more effectively addresses barriers to learning and teaching.* Los Angeles: Author. Retrieved March 12, 2008, from http://smhp.psych.ucla.edu/pdfdocs//briefs/toward a school district infrastructure.pdf

Center for Mental Health in Schools, University of California, Los Angeles. (N.d.). Where's it happening? School Mental Health Project. Retrieved June 23, 2008, from http://smhp.psych.ucla.edu/summit2002/wheresithappening.htm

Dryfoos, J. G. (1994). *Full-service schools.* San Francisco: Jossey-Bass.

Elliott, D. S., & Mihalic, S. (2004). Issues in disseminating and replicating effective prevention programs. *Prevention Science, 5,* 47–53.

Elmore, R. F. (2004). *School reform from the inside out: Policy, practice, and performance.* Cambridge, MA: Harvard Educational Publishing Group.

Foster, S., Rollefson, M., Doksum, T., Noonan, D., Robinson, G., & Teich, J. (2005). *School mental health services in the United States, 2002–2003* (DHHS Pub. No. [SMA] 05-4068). Rockville, MD: Center for Mental Health Services, Substance Abuse and Mental Health Services Administration. Retrieved March 12, 2008, from http://www.mentalhealth.samhsa.gov/media/ken/pdf/SMA05-4068/SMA05-4068.pdf

Franklin, M. E., DeRubeis, R. J., & Westin, D. (2006). Are efficacious laboratory-validated treatments readily transportable to clinical practice? In J. C. Norcross, I. E. Beutler, & R. F. Levant (Eds.), *Evidence-based practices in mental health* (pp. 375–401). Washington, DC: American Psychological Association.

Fullan, M. (2005). *Leadership & sustainability: System thinkers in action.* Thousand Oaks, CA: Corwin.

Gardner, S. L. (2005). *Cities, counties, kids, and families: The essential role of local government.* Lanham, MD: University Press of America.

Glennan, T. K., Bodilly, S. J., Galegher, J., & Kerr, K. A. (Eds.). (2004). *Expanding the reach of education reforms: Perspectives from leaders in the scale-up of educational interventions.* Santa Monica, CA: RAND.

Greenhalgh, T., Robert, G., Macfarlane, F., Bate, P., & Kyriakidou, O. (2004). Diffusion of innovations in service organizations: Systematic review and recommendations, *Milbank Quarterly, 82*, 581–629.

Iowa Department of Education. (2004). *Developing our youth: Fulfilling a promise, investing in Iowa's future: Enhancing Iowa's systems of supports for learning and development.* Des Moines, IA: Author. Retrieved June 20, 2008, from http://smhp.psych.ucla.edu/pdfdocs/iowasystemofsupport.pdf

Kutash, K., Duchnowski, A. J., & Lynn, N. (2006). *School-based mental health: An empirical guide for decision-makers.* Retrieved March 12, 2008, from http://rtckids.fmhi.usf.edu/rtcpubs/study04/index.htm

Lim, C., & Adelman, H. S. (1997). Establishing school-based collaborative teams to coordinate resources: A case study. *Social Work in Education, 19*, 266–277.

Magnabosco, J. L. (2006). Innovations in mental health services implementation: A report on state-level data from the U.S. Evidence-Based Project. *Implementation Science, 1*(13). Retrieved November 22, 2006, from http://www.implementationscience.com/content/1/1/13

Marx, E., & Wooley, S. F. (Eds.). (1998). *Health is academic: A guide to coordinated school health programs.* New York: Teachers College Press.

Rogers, E. M. (2003). *The diffusion of innovations* (5th ed.). New York: Free Press.

Rosenblum, L., DiCecco, M. B., Taylor, L., & Adelman, H. S. (1995). Upgrading school support programs through collaboration: Resource coordinating teams. *Social Work in Education, 17*, 117–124.

Schoenwald, S. K., & Hoagwood, K. (2001). Effectiveness, transportability, and dissemination of interventions: What matters when? *Psychiatric Services, 52*, 1190–1197.

Senge, P. (1999). *The dance of change: Mastering the twelve challenges to change in a learning organization.* New York: Doubleday.

Sherry, L. (2003). Sustainability of innovations. *Journal of Interactive Learning Research, 3*, 209–236.

Spoth, R. L., & Redmond, C. (2002). Project Family prevention trials based in community-university partnerships: Toward scaled-up prevention interventions. *Prevention Science, 3*, 203–221.

Stirman, S. W., Crits-Christoph, P., & DeRubeis, R. J. (2004). Achieving successful dissemination of empirically-supported psychotherapies: A synthesis of dissemination theory. *Clinical Psychology: Science and Practice, 11*, 343–359.

Taylor, L., Nelson, P., & Adelman, H. S. (1999). Scaling-up reforms across a school district. *Reading & Writing Quarterly, 15*, 303–326.

Thomas, R. M. (2002). *Overcoming inertia in school reform: How to successfully implement change.* Thousand Oaks, CA: Corwin.

U.S. Department of Education. (1996). *Putting the pieces together: Comprehensive school-linked strategies for children and families.* Washington, DC: Author.

Web Site Resource

In addition to the above references, many resources related to this chapter are accessible through the Web site of the Center for Mental Health in Schools at the University of California, Los Angeles: http://smhp.psych.ucla.edu.

3

Building Resilience in Schools
A Focus on Population-Based Prevention

Katherine Brehm

Beth Doll

School success is a cornerstone of life success in the 21st century. Those who do not graduate from high school are significantly more likely than those who do graduate to be unemployed, live in poverty, be on public assistance, or be involved in crime (Boisjoly, Harris, & Duncan, 1998; Caspi, Wright, Moffit, & Silva, 1998; Freeman, 1996). Those who proceed on to higher education, completing a 4-year college degree or graduate education, will be rewarded with a lifetime of higher earnings and greater professional success (Miller, Mulvey, & Martin, 1995). Cumulative research from the past 60 years has established that the best predictors of school failure are demographic descriptors of students' families and communities, including poverty, minority status, and poor mastery of the English language (Velez & Saenz, 2001); and the proportion of public school students who are poor, speaking English as a second language, or socially marginalized is rising rapidly (Federal Interagency Forum on Child and Family Statistics, 2007). This defines the dilemma that faces 21st-century schools: How can they maintain and even increase the academic success of a student population that is increasingly at risk for school failure? It is no wonder, then, that schools are interested in the phenomenon of resilience.

What is Resilience?

Like many prominent educational terms, *resilience* is defined in multiple ways, and each variation has important implications for school practices.

Webster's (1983) described *resilience* as "the capacity to recover readily from illness or depression," a definition consistent with the term's historical meaning of a capacity to "return to the original shape or position after being bent, compressed or stretched." Used in this way, to describe a characteristic of disadvantaged children, Benard (1995) described resilience as "a set of qualities that foster a process of successful adaptation and transformation despite risk and adversity." These qualities have been very nicely summarized in Werner's (2006) comprehensive review of the developmental resilience research. Some qualities of resilient children are individual attributes that cannot be easily modified: individual intelligence, temperament, or emotional reactivity. Still, other qualities are more malleable and can provide a roadmap for school mental health services: positive self-concept, achievement motivation, internal locus of control, impulse control, planning and foresight, or helpfulness.

In a second variation on the term's definition, *resilience* can refer to any child's personal competence, as when Freiberg (1994) described resilience as children's capacity "to learn from and seek out the positive elements of their environment." Within this definition, resilience ought to be nurtured in all children, even if they have not yet been tested by adversity, so that they will successfully weather future trauma and tragedy with aplomb. Empirical investigations have provided sound descriptions of the knowledge, behaviors, attitudes, and emotional competence that promote children's developmental success. For example, Prince-Embury (2007) argued that students' personal capacity for coping with adversity can be understood as the interface between their capacity for effective relationships and their sense of autonomy (both strengths) and their incapacity to regulate their emotional reactions (a weakness). Still, Werner (2006) noted that the developmental resilience research has not yet clearly established whether the same factors that promote the success of vulnerable children might also be important for the success of children who have not experienced substantial adversity in their lives.

In these first two definitions, resilience has been treated as a characteristic of children; within the third definition, resilience is also considered to be a characteristic of the caretaking environments within which children develop. Resilience turns out to be an amazingly ordinary process in which characteristics and skills of the individual child, and the quality of the caretaking environment, come together to create an adaptive response to adversity (Masten, 2001). In our earlier work (Doll, Zucker, & Brehm, 2004), we use this third definition to argue that schools could be called resilient when the school environment made it possible for children to be successful despite the adversity imposed upon them in other domains of their life. In particular, we have argued that the characteristics of effective schools factor into two important groups—those that support strong interpersonal relationships of children with adults and their classmates, and those that strengthen the children's sense of autonomy and self-regulation. Indeed, children are never resilient in their own right without communities that care for and support them. Consequently, it makes most sense to speak of the resilience of children-in-schools, children-in-communities, and children-in-families. Outside of families, schools are the most prominent caretaking settings within which children develop personal competence and strength, and children's trajectories into developmental competence clearly demonstrate that social and psychological characteristics of schools are highly predictive of the academic success of high-risk children (Rutter & Maughan, 2002).

Debates over these conceptual definitions of resilience are at the center of an important sociopolitical deliberation about who is responsible for overcoming risk. If children are expected to "pull themselves up by their own bootstraps," then the goals of school mental health programs should be to help children develop the individual competencies that will make it possible for them to overcome adversity. However, if children-in-schools are expected to succeed, then school mental health programs should be promoting the practices and policies that predict success in high-risk children. Alternatively, if the capacity of schools to support the success of high-risk children is a product of the political and policy context afforded by the community, then state and local governments are charged with providing resources and support systems (both within and outside of schools) so that no child is left behind and all children have an equal chance of success.

This chapter is predicated on the position that resilience is a systemic phenomenon in that all of these contexts—families, schools, peers, and communities—co-act in dynamic ways to promote children's competence and resilience (Christenson & Anderson, 2002; Pianta & Walsh, 1996). Thus, student success reflects a continuous reciprocal interaction among individual characteristics of the child and characteristics of the school, family, and community contexts. Using this conceptual framework, the chapter will address three questions in turn: What makes it possible for children to succeed in school despite the odds? How do prevention programs promote resilience? And what are the promising interventions that promote resilience in schools? We will close with a brief discussion of the steps that school mental health practitioners should take to promote resilience.

What allows children to succeed in school despite the odds?

Engaged Families

There is good evidence that 80% of the variance in children's school success is attributable to home and family factors (Rutter & Maughan, 2002). In reviewing over 200 studies of school success, Christenson and Peterson (1998; as cited in Christenson & Anderson, 2002) identified a common set of familial influences that are important for children's high academic performance and motivation. Families of academically successful children had consistent home routines and provided age-appropriate monitoring of the children's daily activities and behavior. They supported children's learning in a variety of ways, held high expectations for the children's academic performance, established consistent and reasonable consequences for meeting those expectations, and communicated regularly with each other and the school about the children's learning progress. They provided ongoing guidance, interest, and verbal support for the children's school progress, an extension of the warm, friendly, encouraging, and respectful relationship that they had with their children. Families believed in the value of education and in the importance of their own involvement in children's schooling.

Optimally, schools will foster strong partnerships with such families, and they will work together to map out a protective pathway that will ameliorate the risk posed by adversities in children's lives. Together, adults in schools and adults in families will establish high performance expectations for the children and will create the situations that facilitate children's school success. Christenson and Anderson (2002) referred to this as the schools' "affordance value," which is "how the learning context facilitates or impedes child adaptation to challenges and demands of schooling" (p. 379). Vulnerable families sometimes need help in planning ways to work with schools to create these learning contexts. Some families are not available to collaborate at all in such partnerships. However, even when options for partnering with families are limited, it is still possible for schools to foster classroom and school environments that support the success of children at risk.

Effective Schools

Schools' role in this dynamic system has often been called their *climate*. Schools with inviting climates actively engage children and their families in opportunities for learning. A small portion of this climate is due to the school's safe, clean, and orderly physical environment. To a larger extent, the climate is readily apparent in the relationship that children and families have with their teachers, and in the children's academic success and social development (Esposito, 1999). Resilient schools also provide families with enrichment and extracurricular activities to stimulate their children's interests (Christiansen, Christiansen, & Howard, 1997). Adults in the school make note of children's special interests or talents, find ways for them to develop these talents further, and recognize the children's participation in school-based activities (Christiansen et al., 1997). When supportive adults are missing in children's lives, resilient schools can provide adult mentors to form one-to-one relationships with vulnerable children.

An essential component of students' success in schools is the psychological experience of "belonging." Belonging has been variously described as a sense of relatedness, membership, and community (Osterman, 2000). Children who have this connectedness with their school have more positive attitudes about school, are more engaged in their learning, and participate in more activities such as sporting events (Elias & Weissberg, 2000; Osterman). They demonstrate stronger emotional self-regulation and are less likely to engage in substance abuse, precocious sexual activity, and violence (Resnick, Bearman, & Blum, 1997).

Resilient Classrooms

Classrooms, too, can be characterized as resilient whether they exist within highly resilient schools or as islands of excellence within less effective schools. Resilient classrooms are places where even vulnerable children can be successful academically, socially, and personally (Doll et al., 2004). These classrooms excel in two respects: in providing the interpersonal relationships (with adults and peers) that children need to flourish, and in providing the sociopsychological scaffolding necessary for children to develop autonomy and self-regulation.

The importance of interpersonal relationships to classroom success has been broadly recognized, including relationships between students and their teachers (Pianta, 1999), between students and their peers (Doll, 1996), and between students' families and the teacher (Christenson & Sheridan, 2001). Teachers foster these relationships when they establish clear and firm boundaries for student and teacher behavior, and model respectful and supportive interactions (Dirling, 1999). By communicating caring, teachers promote children's emotional attachment to themselves and school (Elias and Weissberg, 2000). Simultaneously, effective interactions with classmates provide students with caring, assistance, company, and simple enjoyment (Johnson, Johnson, Buckman, & Richards, 1998). These relationships can be captured in anonymous student surveys that describe high rates of peer friendships and social inclusion, and competent management of social conflicts that occur between classmates (Doll, Murphy, & Song, 2003). Their peers can empower students to express themselves, take risks in the service of learning, and join fully into relationships. Finally, in effective classrooms, communication between families and the classroom is frequent and comfortable, and supports a shared understanding of children's responsibilities for learning. When families and schools interact effectively, children are more actively engaged in schooling and consequently are more successful (Anguiano, 2004; Hill et al., 2004).

The resilience of classrooms also emerges from the classroom motivational climate, including routines and practices that promote students' self-efficacy, self-control, and goal orientation (Doll et al., 2004). Contributing to this climate are mastery goals that charge students with learning the material that is presented, in contrast to performance goals in which students compete to learn more than their classmates. Within a mastery classroom, all students can potentially succeed in meeting their learning goals, reinforcing students' beliefs that their success is a function of the amount of effort they put into learning tasks (Ames, 1992). In this sense, mastery goals are interdependent with students' self-efficacy for learning, or their expectations that they can be successful in the classroom. Self-efficacy is also a product of teachers' expressed confidence in students and their encouragement of effort and understanding (Ryan, Gheen, & Midgley, 1998). Classmates, too, contribute by modeling their confidence in themselves and expectations of success for each other. Finally, an effective classroom environment facilitates multiple "turning point events" (Christiansen et al., 1997, p. 87) that allow students to work for and attain a higher standard of behavior or achievement. Sometimes these turning point events can be as simple as teachers observing and commenting on a student's work.

Effective Recess and Playgrounds

Although classrooms are generally teacher-controlled space, playgrounds and the unstructured playtime of recess belong to the children (Thomson,

2005). Indeed, in this age of latchkey families, computer games, and widespread concerns about children's safety, recess may provide the only opportunity many children have to freely socialize with peers (Council on Physical Education for Children, 2001; Jarrett, 2002; Pellegrini, Blatchford, Kato, & Baines, 2004). Unstructured peer interactions challenge children's capacities for cognitive reasoning; provide children with authentic and highly motivating models of social cooperation, negotiation, and affiliation; and educate children in the values of modern society (Pellegrini, 2005).

Still, within the current climate of high-stakes testing and academic standards, schools are confronting powerful demands that recess be sacrificed in order to increase academic learning time. Pellegrini (2005) has confronted these demands with equally strong theoretical and empirical arguments for the importance of recess for children's academic and social success. He noted that children become increasingly inattentive in the classroom as recess deprivation increases. For example, one study found that fourth graders were more on task and less fidgety when they were able to take a recess break after 2.5 hours of classroom instruction than if they took no break and were in class for 4 hours (Jarrett et al., 1998). Some researchers have suggested that it is the physical activity of recess that provides children with release, but more recent studies have shown that postrecess attention improves even when children spent most of the recess time socializing rather than engaging in physical activity (Jarrett et al.; Pellegrini, 2005). Other research has shown that recess may help children learn self-control and may reduce the anxiety that they experience due to competitive classroom practices (National Association of Early Childhood Specialists in State Departments of Education, 2002).

Recommendations for strengthening school recess practices generally stress policies and procedures that reduce playground aggression such as running, hitting, yelling, and interfering with the play of others (Colvin, Sugai, Good, & Lee, 1997; Lewis, Colvin, & Sugai, 2000). In fact, only 2% of children's playground behavior is verbally or physically aggressive (Pellegrini, 1995). Instead, recess holds more value as a time when adults can strengthen positive social interactions by prompting social problem solving, modeling mediation, challenging children to actively listen to and compromise with one another, and praising and encouraging prosocial helping behaviors. Other unstructured school settings such as hallways, lunchrooms, and entryways provide similar opportunities to promote social competence.

Competent Children

Children's contributions to their own resilience must be judged against the backdrop of what makes a child competent. Competent children adapt successfully and naturally in their environments because of interactions among three central protective processes: the presence of sensitive and responsive caretakers; the cognitive capacity to successfully engage with their environment; and the ability to self-regulate attention, emotions, and behavior (Masten & Coatsworth, 1998). Resilient children are those who maintain this competence, even when faced with severe adversity, or when one or more of these central protective processes are absent or malfunctioning. For example, Alvord and Grados (2005) described resilient children as having a proactive orientation rising out of beliefs that taking initiative in their lives will put them on the road to success. Additionally, children who have strong prosocial skills (such as sharing, compliance with social rules, and positive relationships with peers) will be predisposed to form strong connections and attachments with family and friends. Academic resilience, defined by passing grades, graduation, and good scores on standardized tests, is associated with children's internalized self-efficacy and their participation in engagement behaviors, such as coming to class on time, participating in class work, putting effort into completing assignments, and resisting the temptation to imitate disruptive peers (Finn & Rock, 1997).

How Can Preventive Interventions Promote Resilience?

It is the task of preventive interventions to foster competence and prevent damage in children who are struggling against adversity. An emphasis on prevention has been integral to school mental health since Cowen (1977, 1997) began his work in primary prevention in the schools. At that time, conventional definitions included primary prevention (intervening before any evidence of disturbance), secondary prevention (intervening when disturbance was first evident), and tertiary prevention (intervening once disturbances qualified as psychiatric disorders.) More recently, the National Institute of Mental Health's Workgroup on Mental Health Disorders Prevention Research recommended revised terminology to describe a continuum of mental health services extending from prevention services to maintenance services (Institute of Medicine, 1994). They parsed prevention into three types: universal prevention, or services directed toward the general population; selective prevention, or services directed toward a portion of the population whose risk of developing a disorder is high; and indicated prevention, or services directed toward people whose risk of disorder is high and who are already showing detectible signs or markers of the disturbance. An accompanying priority statement reinforced the importance of funding early preventive interventions as part of the larger program of mental health services.

This chapter organizes preventive interventions according to the familiar three-tiered models of service such as that described in the National Association of School Psychologists' Blueprint III (Ysseldyke et al., 2006). Within the first tier, universal mental health services are provided to promote psychological wellness and to prevent disturbance. Tier 1 (universal) interventions have as their basic goals to increase resources and competencies. Although they are less intensive than selective or indicated interventions, their lower per pupil cost makes them an efficient use of existing resources (Grant, Van Acker, Guerra, Duplechain, & Coen, 1998). Advantages to delivering prevention and intervention programs on a schoolwide or classroom-wide basis accrue when students remain in their typical environment and are exposed to modeling of skills by their high-functioning peers, and when their teacher is an active partner in the intervention process (Merrell, 2002).

At the second tier, selective mental health services are provided to students with early evidence of adjustment disturbances or high rates of demographic risk (i.e., evidence of poverty, family violence, or other characteristics that predict poor outcomes). A third tier of services is provided for students whose disturbance is pronounced and who are not able to benefit from schooling without substantial accommodations. Tier 2 and Tier 3 services are already provided in most schools, but a common practice has been to select a single high-risk behavior (e.g., gang involvement or substance abuse), study the risk and resilience factors associated with it (Stoiber & Good, 1998), and design and deliver a program to prevent it (e.g., the W.I.T.S. Program; Leadbeater, Hoglund, & Woods, 2003). Adelman and Taylor (2006) cautioned that such isolated efforts may produce programmatic silos—distinct interventions to address separately several different disturbances, despite the fact that these disturbances actually share common causes and solutions. A more appropriate practice is to provide a coordinated, comprehensive intervention program that simultaneously addresses the collected risk behaviors as a group. In many cases, these preventive efforts are most powerful when they strengthen the naturally occurring features of schools that mediate risk–outcome relationships in children, because these natural sources of support are easier to maintain over time.

It is common for references to suggest that 1–5% of a school's students generally require Tier 3 services, and 15–20% of the school enrollment will benefit from Tier 2 services (Osher, Dwyer, & Jackson, 2004; Walker et al., 1996). However, there are little data to document these proportions, and particular schools may have striking differences in the prevalence as well as the nature of targeted services that are needed (Baker, Kamphaus, Home, & Winsor, 2006). Both demographic and functional risk are not evenly distributed across all school communities but instead tend to concentrate into niches of very high risk, particularly in distressed urban schools or very isolated rural communities (Pianta & Walsh, 1996). The growing interest in population-based school mental health services is due, in part, to these models' emphasis on systematic needs assessment to identify the nature of mental health needs within a school's enrollment and to plan for an array of mental health services that matches those needs (Doll & Cummings, 2008).

In one more extension of the school mental health service continuum, Adelman and Taylor (2006) argued that there should be a fourth tier of services—services to build the infrastructure necessary to maintain an effective program of preventive interventions over time. Often, schools already have viable program components in place that could be woven together into an effective prevention effort, but these services lack impact unless they are organized and coordinated into a comprehensive effort by the school to address barriers to learning (Adelman, 1996; Adelman & Taylor, 2008). School-based collaborative teams, also called *resource coordinating teams*, are one means to organize and coordinate existing school-owned programs and personnel (Adelman, 1996; Adelman and Taylor, 1994; Lim & Adelman, 1997; Rosenblum, DiCecco, Taylor, & Adelman, 1995). These teams consist of personnel involved in educational support services (such as school psychologists, nurses, school social workers, or counselors), bilingual and Title I coordinators, an administrative representative such as an assistant principal, and representatives of community agencies with whom the school has an ongoing relationship. Unlike traditional prereferral teams, which put the onus on the child and teacher to change through accommodations and modifications, resource coordinating teams build capacity at the level of decision making and resource allocation and facilitate alignment of schools' social, emotional, and academic goals (Osher et al., 2004). In this way, the team can reduce the isolation of school and community mental health professionals and eliminate piece-meal interventions that are costly and inefficient (Adelman, 1993).

Preventive Interventions That Build Resilience

Over the past decade, a gradual consensus has emerged that school men-tal health interventions should meet empirical standards for effectiveness before they are implemented (Chambless & Hollon, 1998; Kratochwill & Stoiber, 2002). Still, the call for evidence-based interventions has not yet been reconciled with the realities of school mental health practices. For example, early insistence on random-assignment treatment-and-control studies has been moderated with the realization that such designs are dif-ficult to achieve with prevention programs, where the outcomes of an inter-vention may stretch across years or even decades, and where the targets of universal prevention programs may be large samples or even populations. Moreover, careful examination of many identified evidence-based inter-ventions shows that existing studies have been conducted primarily with White and middle-class participants. Consequently, we have highlighted the following interventions that have promising evidence of their impact even though none have met the most rigorous standards for effectiveness. Ultimately, decisions about whether a prevention program is sufficiently evi-dence based for use will rest with a school's mental health planning team.

Interventions to Reduce Disruptive Behaviors

A primary concern of teachers is reducing disruptive behavior of stu-dents in classrooms. Although teacher-centered classroom strategies can produce improved student behavior and achievement, there are impor-tant long-term benefits to teaching students to control their own behav-ior, thus increasing their ability to function autonomously in any setting (Bear, 2008). A framework for behavioral self-control can be built out of classroom expectations for behavior, developed cooperatively with stu-dents early in the school year, and the routines and rules that convey these expectations to students (Doll et al., 2004). Proactive behavior manage-ment principles applied universally throughout a school provide even more support for autonomous student functioning. Specific techniques to teach behavioral expectations, routines, and rules include using posi-tive and negative examples of the routine, engaging students in role-play practice of the routine, arranging opportunities for practice in authentic settings, and monitoring student performance and providing reinforcement or corrective feedback (Sugai, Horner, & Gresham, 2002). Scripts applying this coaching model to 20 pragmatic classroom routines can be found in Witt, LaFleur, Naquin, and Gilbertson (1999).

By definition, universal prevention programs target students in general education classrooms. Students with and without disabilities can support each other's appropriate behavior using classwide peer-assisted self-management (CWPASM; Mitchem, Young, West, & Benyo, 2001). CWPASM teaches students self-management skills, social skills, self-monitoring, and self-reinforcement. Then, at regular intervals, students rate themselves and a partner on their behavioral self-control. Peer ratings include criteria such as being on task, following directions, and obtaining teacher attention appropriately. CWPASM led to improvements in the social competence of all students as well as improvements of at-risk students with high rates of disruptive behavior. Teachers described the program as highly feasible and acceptable, and students found the program to be acceptable, likeable, and effective.

The Metropolitan Area Child Study (MACS) project (Grant et al., 1998) uses universal and selective school and classroom interventions to instill beliefs and norms that discourage school violence, aggression, and extreme examples of disruptive behavior. Selective prevention strategies, in the form of peer and family interventions, work to reduce aggressive behavior in an at-risk sample of students. Interactive teacher workshops strengthen universal classroom management skills by creating schoolwide routines that reinforce prosocial behavior and establish consistent consequences for problem behavior. Then, teacher collaborators model lessons and provide follow-up support to classroom teachers. At the same time, all students participate in a 2-year, manualized social problem-solving curriculum called "Yes I Can" during the second and third grades, and again in the fifth and sixth grades. Student scores on a measure of aggression showed that the school and classroom components of the intervention were most effective for students at the highest demographic risk.

Students who are actively engaged in learning are less disruptive. Instructional activities that promote academic engagement include those that are interesting, are well paced to avoid wasting time, require frequent responses from students, and take advantage of independent and one-on-one instructional groupings (Greenwood, Maheady, & Delquadri, 2002). For example, classwide peer tutoring (Greenwood, Delquadri, & Hall, 1989; Greenwood et al., 2002) uses structured tutor–tutee pairs to increase self-control behaviors such as "raising hands" and "academic talk." Other programs use peers as effective mediators of both academic and behavioral tasks. Reciprocal peer tutoring (Fantuzzo & Rohrbeck, 1992) uses student-set academic goals, interdependent group reward contingencies, and reciprocal peer tutoring to improve elementary students' academic achievement and classroom behavior.

Interventions to Strengthen Relationships

James Comer (1998) has said, "Relationships are to child development what location is to real estate." Multicomponent prevention programs that alter the relational climate of the school are essential to resilient schools and have long-term impact on the success of students. The following four examples describe the kinds of relational interventions that reduce risk factors and increase protective factors.

Structuring schools as moral communities promotes the development of caring relationships that underlie resilience (Edwards, 2000). Moral communities include students and their teachers as members and encourage meaningful, adult-guided dialogue between students and adults about issues that concern them. Through moral communities, the needs, interests, and capacities of students are supported and used to strengthen the school as a whole. For example, in a moral community, students could be given a voice in curriculum and school operation. Problems can be prevented and solved when students feel they belong in the school and their decision-making skills are developed and utilized in ways that match their maturity and experience.

When students feel that they belong in a school, they are said to be bonded or attached to their school. School bonding reflects an attachment between students and their school that is formed through close emotional relationships with people at school, signified by a committed investment in school, and expressed by a strong motivation to achieve (Catalano, Haggerty, Oesterle, Fleming, & Hawkins, 2004). The Seattle Social Development Project (SSDP; Catalano et al., 2004) promotes bonding to school by changing the behavior of socializing agents in the school and altering the climate to increase prosocial behavior and peer acceptance. Teachers at each grade level received training in interactive teaching, cooperative learning, and classroom management strategies, including how to give feedback and contingent praise, to promote academic achievement and bonding. A parent component focused on improving child bonding to parents through training in positive praise and feedback, parent family management skills, and, when the children reached adolescence, support for children's use of refusal skills. Ultimately, the SSDP sought to reduce the risk of antisocial behavior during adolescence.

Whereas the SSDP targeted the relationship characteristics of environments longitudinally, Coping With the Middle School Transitions (CWMST; Lochman & Wells, 2002) uses universal prevention strategies at specific developmental crossroads for students. The CWMST embeds an indicated intervention for students at moderate to high risk for aggressive antisocial behavior within a universal intervention designed to prevent substance abuse and social problems for all students transitioning from elementary to middle school. Fifth grade teachers received inservice training in strategies to promote home–school involvement and strengthen the social competence of transitioning students. Parents of all fifth and sixth graders participated in parenting meetings to discuss their concerns about the transition to middle school, acquaint them with ways to promote positive peer relationships, and provide strategies to address other developmental issues and tasks of their children. Students in the CWMST classrooms experienced greater social acceptance and fewer social problems than students in control classrooms. Concurrent with the universal CWMST intervention, a small group of aggressive students from those classrooms participated in the Coping Power program, during which they were instructed in anger management and social problem solving. Parents of the aggressive students were instructed in ways to support their children's Coping Power skills and received additional training in stress management and parenting. Children in the Coping Power group reported that their social competence with peers increased; their teachers reported improvements in anger management and social problem-solving skills. Lochman and Wells noted that pairing the Coping Power intervention with the universal CWMST intervention made the classroom a less stressful environment for the aggressive students to practice and develop their new skills.

As an additional example of an intervention to strengthen classroom relationships, effective behavioral supports (EBS; Sprague et al., 2001) combined a resource-coordinating team and universal interventions to improve the safety and social competence of elementary and middle school students. The program focused on clarifying behavioral expectations and rules, teaching positive alternative behaviors, and using incentives to motivate the practice of new skills. The EBS used the Second Step violence prevention program (Grossman et al., 1997) to teach social skills such as anger control, problem solving, and empathy. At the same time, a team of administrators, teachers, and related services professionals met monthly to monitor the intervention's implementation and support the teachers. At the end of the year, office discipline referrals in EBS schools were reduced relative to non-EBS schools and to baseline referral data from the EBS schools. Moreover, EBS students at all grade levels demonstrated higher scores on a written test of skill definition and described more appropriate responses to social problems posed in Second Step vignettes. Results of the EBS evaluation showed that improvements on meaningful measures of school safety and student social skill knowledge can be made in a relatively short period of time and at relatively little expense.

Playground Interventions

On the playground, student problem behaviors can be reduced by increasing adults' active supervision and precorrecting students regarding school rules (Colvin et al., 1997; Lewis et al., 2000). *Active supervision* is defined as moving around the area being supervised, scanning both near and distant areas, and talking with students both informally and to give warnings of rule violations or to praise appropriate behavior. How active supervisors are is more important in promoting students' appropriate behavior than how many supervisors are present. Precorrection includes reminding students of rules and behavior expectations just before they enter the playground or transition into or out of the school building. Together, these two strategies are efficient and require little training time.

Students can monitor and structure play for each other. For example, Play Fair Squad students, some of whom had been previously identified as bullies, were trained to organize and monitor noncompetitive, inclusive playground games in one elementary school (Chuoke & Eyman, 1997). The rotating squad members chose the games for the day, monitored the games to minimize competitiveness, and reminded participants of the rules. Peer conflict declined on the playground and, reflecting a change in school climate, in classrooms as well. In variations on this strategy, older students could organize games and activities for younger students, and student council representatives could be playground problem solvers (Butcher, 1999).

Another approach was taken by the staff of an elementary school who improved students' self-management skills on the playground by teaching recess routines and expectations (Todd, Haugen, Anderson, & Spriggs,

2004). At the beginning of the year, teachers and their students participated in two recess workshops. The 45-minute outdoor recess workshop involved walking the playground boundaries, receiving instruction and practice in how to use the various playground equipment and game areas, and watching a demonstration of self-management skills and behavior rules. The 30-minute indoor recess workshop focused on classroom routines for free play, including a brief indoor recess to practice the routines. The workshops were repeated once during the school year at the request of teachers. Office-managed discipline referrals during recess decreased by 80% the second year of the intervention.

Another approach to promoting resilient playgrounds is through playground games and the interpersonal interactions that the games support. Pellegrini et al. (2004) observed that simple games, such as chase games and races that can be played by even the youngest children, "scaffold" social interactions. With their simple rules, familiarity, and routinized formats, such games provide a template for peers to interact and enjoy each other's company even when they do not know each other well or lack the higher level social skills to play more complex games. As children become more mature and familiar with each other, their play can shift to more complex games, such as ball games.

Several universal interventions prevent playground problems and increase cooperative play by teaching children game-related social skills, providing them with organized games to play, and then supervising their game play. Classroom teachers taught their elementary school students specific play-related social skills, such as how to join a game and how to win and lose gracefully, as well as rules and routines for specific activities and games, such as tetherball, four square, and kickball (Lewis, Powers, Kelk, & Newcomer, 2002). In addition, playground supervisors gave students plastic loops to put on their wrists when they were seen complying with targeted social skills. When the students in a classroom had collected enough loops, they could vote as a group on a reward. Decreases were seen in physical aggression, misuse of play equipment, name calling, and arguing. As a result, school personnel were able to focus more attention on specific students and problem areas of the playground and reinforce students who were behaving appropriately.

Leff, Costigan, and Power (2004) examined the role of playground supervision and organized games (such as hopscotch, relay races, and jump ropes) on cooperative play and problem behaviors. Children were able to move freely between these games as playground supervisors actively facilitated their play. Providing the organized games increased the children's

cooperative play and interaction and decreased incidences of rough physical play, even when adult supervisors were not present. However, the presence of adult supervisors was important to increase interactions between
children of different ethnic backgrounds. Similar results were reported by
Reumann-Moore and Suess (2006), who also found that organized games
and social skill instruction reduced injury and increased enjoyment during recess time. Games that allowed for different levels of participation
for children (e.g., actor, audience, and referee) increased the inclusiveness
of playgrounds and reduced the inappropriate behavior that sometimes
results from having nothing better to do (Murphy, Hutchinson, & Bailey,
1983). Finally, preschool teachers who led their students in both cooperative and competitive games observed that their students displayed fewer
cooperative behaviors and more aggressive behaviors during competitive
games (Bay-Hinitz, Peterson, & Quilitch, 1994). Moreover, free play was
influenced by the type of game the children had played the day before.

Competence-Building Preventive Interventions

Although the previous interventions strengthened the interpersonal
environment of the school and classroom, individual child competence
may also be the mediator of resilience. In particular, resilience is attributable to children's social-emotional competence including five core skills:
learning to recognize and manage one's emotions, developing empathy
and understanding of the perspective of others, making responsible decisions, establishing rewarding relationships, and handling interpersonal
problems effectively (Collaborative for Academic, Social, and Emotional
Learning [CASEL], 2003; Greenberg et al., 2003). The Collaborative for
Academic, Social, and Emotional Learning (2003) has spearheaded an
effort to promote social-emotional learning interventions and to dissemi-
nate information about their effectiveness (descriptions and ratings of
social-emotional learning interventions are available at the CASEL Web
site, http://www.CASEL.org, as a monograph entitled *Safe and Sound:
An Educational Leader's Guide to Evidence-Based Social and Emotional
Learning Programs*).

A highly regarded classroom-based social-emotional learning program
is Second Step (Frey, Hirschstein, & Guzzo, 2000). Second Step targets
three areas of competence in children from prekindergarten through
the ninth grade: empathy, social problem solving, and anger management. In 15–25 weekly or biweekly lessons, children learn to identify and

understand emotions, control impulsiveness, choose positive behaviors, and maintain emotional and cognitive control in difficult situations. A six-session workshop trains parents to reinforce the Second Step skills taught to their children, and a schoolwide interdisciplinary team supports implementation and generalization of the program. In a rigorous randomized control study, Grossman et al. (1997) showed that Second Step prompted decreases in second and third graders' verbal and physical aggression and increases in their prosocial behavior in school classrooms, playgrounds, and lunchrooms. The effects were still evident after 6 months.

Results of two studies with low-income children suggest that Second Step may be better at strengthening positive behaviors than decreasing negative ones. First, Taub (2001) showed that Second Step increased social competence (e.g., following rules, demonstrating leadership skills, staying calm in problem situations, and interacting positively with peers) in third through fifth grade students from an impoverished rural community. At the same time, antisocial behaviors of Second Step and control students increased, suggesting that it takes longer to unlearn negative patterns of behavior than acquire positive ones. A similar pattern was reported by McMahon and Washburn (2003) for African American fifth through eighth graders in a high-poverty urban community. The Second Step students' empathy and prosocial behavior increased over time, but there was no significant decrease in the students' aggressive and impulsive behavior.

Promoting alternative thinking strategies (PATHS) is a universal competence-building intervention that strengthens the self-regulation, self-determination, and problem-solving skills of students in both general education and special education classrooms (Kam, Greenberg, & Kusche, 2004). PATHS lessons integrate affect, behavior, and cognition to teach self-control and coping, emotional self-management, positive self-esteem, peer relationships and communication, and interpersonal problem-solving skills for children in kindergarten through the fifth grade (Greenberg, Domitrovich, & Bumbarger, 2001). Older students are encouraged to apply program skills to academic content areas with lessons on study skills and work habits, attention, and academic goal setting. The generalization of PATHS to academic performance was demonstrated in an action research report from Kelly, Longbottom, Potts, and Williamson (2004). The written work of their 9- and 10-year-old students who received 1 year of PATHS instruction became richer in content and more descriptive. A modified PATHS curriculum reduced internalizing and externalizing behaviors and self-reported depression of first through third grade children in self-contained special education classrooms (Kam et al., 2004). Lessons were simplified to focus on basic skills of self-control and emotional understanding. The intervention lasted for 1 year, and the impact was sustained over a 2-year follow-up period. Internalizing and externalizing behaviors continued to decrease for the intervention group, whereas they increased for the control group. In addition, students in the intervention group more readily understood their own emotions and those of others, and were more likely to use self-control strategies to deal with problems.

PATHS has also been implemented as a universal intervention within a multicomponent indicated prevention program (Fast Track) that targets children with early-onset conduct problems (Conduct Problems Prevention Research Group, 1999, 2004). In a randomized clinical trial of PATHS with first grade children from high-risk schools, diminished aggression and improved self-control and on-task behavior were demonstrated through pre- and postintervention interviews with teachers; peer sociometric measures of aggression, disruptiveness, and social status; and classroom observations by naïve observers. The fidelity of teachers' implementation of PATHS was more critical to intervention effectiveness than the number of lessons taught.

Another universal intervention to promote child competence is the Social Decision Making and Problem Solving Program (SDM-PSP; Elias & Weissberg, 2000). The program curriculum includes 25–40 weekly lessons that teach students in general and special education to use their emotions to effectively solve problems inside and outside the classroom. Lesson content is sequenced to start at early elementary grades with basic skills of self-control and social awareness, establishing a foundation for instruction in an eight-step thinking strategy to facilitate social decision making in upper elementary and middle school. Teachers are also provided with applications of the SDM-PSP skills for academics and other classroom situations. In a study of its effectiveness (Elias, Gara, Schuyler, Branden-Muller, & Sayette, 1991), students in an experimental group received 2 years of SDM-PSP at two levels of fidelity (high and moderate) when they were in the fourth and fifth grades, whereas a control group received no intervention. After the students entered middle school, SDM-PSP students were better able to manage the stress of middle school and used social decision-making strategies to mediate social problems. Without booster sessions or additional intervention, these same SDM-PSP students in the 11th grade showed significantly higher social competence and self-efficacy, scored higher than control students on a national achievement test, and demonstrated significantly lower rates of substance abuse and antisocial behavior and higher self-efficacy scores. Finally, although the SDM-PSP students as a group showed significantly higher social competence scores, girls in the high-fidelity group benefited most.

Another well-known universal intervention, I Can Problem Solve (ICPS; Shure & Spivak, 1988), uses games, didactic discussion, and group interaction to teach interpersonal problem solving (alternative solution generation, consequential thinking, and nonviolent conflict resolution) to children in preschool through the fifth grade. In the sixth grade, students are taught refusal skills by their teachers to reduce their vulnerability to drug abuse and negative peer pressure. A parent curriculum is also available (Shure & Digeronimo, 1995). Self-report measures collected from the first through 12th grades showed higher levels of academic achievement and reduced school problems (violence, drug abuse, and risky sexual behavior) for ICPS students but not for students in control groups. Although a 2-year program is most effective for preschool and kindergarten children, preventive effects of the intervention have been demonstrated after 1 year (Shure & Spivak, 1979). Shure and Healey (1993) compared the effects of ICPS and a parallel intervention using cognitive problem-solving training without the interpersonal application. Students in an inner-city school were exposed to ICPS or the cognitive-only intervention three times a week for 4 months in either the fifth grade only or in both the fifth and sixth grades. The ICPS group demonstrated significant improvement in interpersonal cognitive problem solving and prosocial behavior over the cognitive-only group after 1 year, and showed reductions in negative, impulsive behavior after a second ICPS intervention in the sixth grade. Students in the cognitive-only group became more impulsive over the course of the intervention. In particular, students' ability to generate problem solutions appeared to be the most significant mediator of behavior change and prosocial skill development.

An abbreviated ICPS intervention may also be effective. In two separate studies, 7- and 8-year-old students received two ICPS lessons a week for 4 weeks, whereas a control group received no intervention. ICPS students showed significant improvements in their ability to generate alternative solutions and think consequentially, as well as in their sociometric status in the classroom (Erwin & Ruane, 1993; Rixon & Erwin, 1999). In one of these studies (Rixon & Erwin), playground observations showed that ICPS students engaged in significantly fewer social isolation behaviors (playing alone or interacting passively in a group) than controls, but no improvement in student sociometric status was found in either study.

A fourth competency-building intervention for elementary school students is the Unique Minds School Program (UMSP; Stern, 1999; see also Linares et al., 2005). The manualized curriculum provides lessons for kindergarten through fifth grade students to enhance their self-efficacy, problem-solving, and social-emotional functioning. Additional lessons in self-management, self-monitoring, and mind–body connections are introduced in the fourth and fifth grades, A parent component generalizes the UMSP skills to the home, and suggestions are made for generalizing the concepts and skills to academic instruction and less structured school settings, such as playgrounds. Fourth grade students who received 2 consecutive years of UMSP demonstrated higher self-efficacy for learning, better prosocial problem-solving skills, and higher report card grades in math compared to a control group.

The Positive Action (PA) program (Flay, Allred, & Ordway, 2001) is a wellness-oriented program that teaches students in kindergarten through the 12th grade to self-assess, set, and work toward self-improvement goals. Parent and community involvement materials are also available. In two school districts where PA was widely implemented for 3 or more years, district archival data showed increased student self-concept, reduced problem behaviors, and improved school performance for PA relative to control schools. In another study, Flay and Allred (2003) again used matched controls and district archival data to examine the effects of PA elementary schools that had implemented the program for at least 8 years. At the elementary school level, fourth grade students who had received at least 2 years of PA showed significant improvement over other students and matched controls on standardized state reading achievement tests. At the middle school level, schools with more PA graduates scored higher on reading and math achievement tests than schools with fewer PA graduates. At the high school level, schools with more PA graduates had lower dropout rates, fewer disciplinary referrals, and a higher percentage of high school graduates who continued their education.

Steps to Promoting Resilience

By now, it should be clear that the promotion of children's resilience is an enormous task. First, the goals that underlie resilience (belonging, caring relationships, active supervision, and self-regulation) are broad and ambitious, and cannot be easily achieved with brief, one-shot interventions. Moreover, there are multiple and complicated interconnections among and between resilience, risk, social support, and family well-being, such that intervention programs must be comprehensive and well integrated if they are to have meaningful impact on children's lives. At the same time, it is reassuring to realize that even very simple steps, like refining playground games and supervision or adding some caring adults to a child's community, can shift a child's developmental trajectory toward success and away from failure.

Efforts to promote the resilience of high-risk children in schools must be guided by clear decisions, including decisions about the purpose of the programs, the grade levels at which a particular program is best implemented, the optimal dosage for a program (e.g., the number and length of lessons), and the ideal duration of the program across grades and school years. In particular, it will be important for school efforts to be guided by a priori descriptions of program success. These descriptions should specify the differences in children's behaviors, achievements, and affects, or related schoolwide outcomes that will be convincing and meaningful evidence of program impact.

Comprehensive step-by-step procedures for implementing schoolwide and district-wide interventions can be found in Doll and Cummings (2008). Here, we will describe a few pragmatic guidelines for resilience promotion:

Guideline 1.   Consider what already exists in the school that is resilience promoting. Indeed, most schools have multiple programs and practices already in place that strengthen children's wellness and developmental competence. An important first step is to take stock of these existing resources with consideration to how broadly these are implemented, the fidelity with which they are delivered, the depth and strength of school support for them, and their apparent impact on children and the school as a whole. Programs that are broadly supported and effective can be integrated into a resilience promotion program, whereas those that are haphazard or ineffective might be modified or refined.

Guideline 2.   Survey existing data in the school that describe children's social and developmental needs, the nature and extent of adversity and protective factors in the community, and the nature and degree of success that children are experiencing. Comprehensive and objective needs assessment data can be invaluable in designing a resilience promotion program, but the collection and management of such data can also be quite costly in time and other resources. An important and often overlooked alternative is to mine existing data within the school to inform critical decisions about program purposes and impact.

Guideline 3.   When selecting interventions for a resilience-promoting program, balance their costs and impact. The most logical interventions are inexpensive programs that have strong and meaningful effects, especially when these impact large numbers of students. Alternatively, interventions can be avoided when they are very expensive and have relatively little effect, especially when they impact only a few students. Amazingly, even these very logical rules are frequently violated when schools select programs without regard to their cost or their impact. More difficult, once these obvious decisions are made, are decisions about programs that are costly but effective for a small subset of students, or those that are highly effective but for less important outcomes. It will be important for the school leaders to set clear priorities for the costs and purposes of the interventions that should be selected.

Guideline 4. Never skimp on duration or dosage. Even very simple interventions can have large potential impact when they are done well. Conversely, the most ambitious interventions may have very limited utility if they are inappropriately shortened or diluted. In many cases, these critical decisions are made at the time the interventions are selected—it is important to restrict a program to those interventions that a school can reasonably implement given a realistic assessment of the available resources. Once selected, a small amount of consistent attention will be important to ensure that an intervention stays vital and effective. Even effective practices can become unreliable and ineffective if neglected.

Guideline 5. Document, document, document. Resilience-promoting programs stretch across months and years, making it difficult to trust memory alone to describe what happened during the intervention, who participated and for how long, how the intervention was revised and refined, and what the results of the intervention were. These kinds of simple records will make it easy to describe the cost and benefit of the intervention at some future date, and may be instrumental in securing administrative or community support for the continuation of effective programs.

Guideline 6. Link the intervention to the basic academic goals of a school district. As more and more educational leaders emphasize the core responsibilities of schools, it is critically important that the relation between children's resilience and their academic success be made explicit. This relation is obvious to most school mental health professionals, and is implicitly supported by many classroom teachers, but the central importance of developmental competence to academic achievement is not readily apparent to many policy makers in schools. Making this connection explicit for school and community leaders can be essential to their ongoing support for an intervention, and ultimately to the availability of resources for the intervention's implementation.

Guideline 7. Market program successes out loud and at length. Successes do not count if they are not noticed, so it is important that the success of schools' resilience promotion programs be deliberately advertised. Key audiences include the policy makers who make decisions about school resource allocations, the community members who vote on school funding proposals, the families whose children participate in the programs, the teachers who implement the programs, and the children themselves. Above all, the audiences need to know that the program exists, serves an important purpose in the school, strengthens the success of children in the school, and is worthy of continued school and community support.

References

Adelman, H. S. (1993). School-linked mental health interventions: Toward mechanisms for service coordination and integration. *Journal of Community Psychology, 21*, 309–319.

Adelman, H. S. (1996). *Restructuring education support services: Toward a concept of an enabling component.* Kent, OH: American School Health Association.

Adelman, H. S., & Taylor, L. (1994). *On understanding intervention in psychology and education.* Westport, CT: Praeger.

Adelman, H. S., & Taylor, L. (2006). *The school leader's guide to student learning supports: New directions for addressing barriers to learning.* Thousand Oaks, CA: Corwin.

Adelman, H. S., & Taylor, L. (2008). School-wide approaches to addressing barriers to learning and teaching. In B. Doll & J. A. Cummings (Eds.), *Transforming school mental health services: Population-based approaches to promoting the competency and wellness of children* (pp. 277–306). Thousand Oaks, CA: Corwin Press in cooperation with the National Association of School Psychologists.

Alvord, M. K., & Grados, J. J. (2005). Enhancing resilience in children: A proactive approach. *Professional Psychology: Research and Practice, 36*, 238–245.

Ames, C. (1992). Classrooms: Goals, structures, and student motivation. *Journal of Educational Psychology, 84*, 261–271.

Anguiano, R. P. V. (2004). Families and schools: The effect of parental involvement on high school completion. *Journal of Family Issues, 25*, 61–85.

Baker, J. A., Kamphaus, R. W., Home, A. M., & Winsor, A. P. (2006). Evidence for population-based perspectives on children's behavioral adjustment and needs for service delivery in schools. *School Psychology Review, 35*, 31–46.

Bay-Hinitz, A. K., Peterson, R. F., & Quilitch, H. R. (1994). Cooperative games: A way to modify aggressive and cooperative behaviors in young children. *Journal of Applied Behavior, 27*, 435–446.

Bear, G. (2008). School-wide approaches to behavior problems. In B. Doll & J. A. Cummings (Eds.), *Transforming school mental health services: Population-based approaches to promoting the competency and wellness of children* (pp. 103–142). Thousand Oaks, CA: Corwin Press in cooperation with the National Association of School Psychologists.

Benard, B. (1995). *Fostering resilience in children* (Accession No. EDO-PS-95-9). Washington, DC: ERIC Clearinghouse on Elementary and Early Childhood Education.

Boisjoly, J., Harris, K., & Duncan, G. (1998). Initial welfare spells: Trends, events, and duration. *Social Service Review, 72*, 466–492.

Butcher, D. (1999). Enhancing social skills through school social work interventions during recess: Gender differences. *Social Work in Education, 21*, 249–262.

Caspi, A., Wright, B. E., Moffit, T. E., & Silva, P. A. (1998). Childhood predictors of unemployment in early adulthood. *American Sociological Review, 63*, 424–451.

Catalano, R. F., Haggerty, K. P., Oesterle, S., Fleming, C. B., & Hawkins, J. D. (2004). The importance of bonding to school for healthy development: Findings from the Social Development Research Group. *Journal of School Health, 74*, 252–261.

Chambless, D. L., & Hollon, D. S. (1998). Defining empirically supported therapies. *Journal of Consulting and Clinical Psychology, 66*, 7–18.

Christenson, S. L., & Anderson, A. R. (2002). Commentary: The centrality of the learning context for students' academic enabler skills. *School Psychology Review, 31*, 378–393.

Christenson, S. L., & Peterson, C. J. (1998). *Family, school, and community influences on children's learning: A literature review.* Minneapolis: All Parents Are Teachers Project (formerly Live & Learn), University of Minnesota Extension Service.

Christenson, S. L., & Sheridan, S. M. (2001). *Schools and families: Creating essential connections for learning.* New York: Guilford.

Christiansen, J., Christiansen, J. L., & Howard, M. (1997). Using protective factors to enhance resilience and school success for at-risk students. *Intervention in School and Clinic, 33*, 86–89.

Chuoke, M., & Eyman, B. (1997). Play fair—and not just at recess. *Educational Leadership, 54*, 53–55.

Collaborative for Academic, Social, and Emotional Learning. (2003). *Safe and sound: An educational leader's guide to evidence-based social and emotional learning programs.* Retrieved June 24, 2007, from http://www.casel.org

Colvin, G., Sugai, G., Good, R. H., III, & Lee, Y. Y. (1997). Using active supervision and precorrection to improve transition behaviors in an elementary school. *School Psychology Quarterly, 12*, 344–363.

Comer, J. (1998, July). Families and schools together: Building relationships. A keynote address presented at the U.S. Department of Education, Office of Special Education and Rehabilitative Services, Washington, DC.

Conduct Problems Prevention Research Group. (1999). Initial impact of the Fast Track prevention trial for conduct problems: II. Classroom effects. *Journal of Consulting and Clinical Psychology, 67*, 648–657.

Conduct Problems Prevention Research Group. (2004). The effects of the Fast Track program on serious problem outcomes at the end of elementary school. *Journal of Clinical Child and Adolescent Psychology, 33*, 650–661.

Council on Physical Education for Children. (2001). *Recess in elementary schools: A position paper from the National Association for Sport and Physical Education.* Retrieved July 25, 2007, from http://www.aahperd.org/naspe/pdf_files/pos_papers/current_res.pdf

Cowen, E. L. (1977). Baby-steps towards primary prevention. *American Journal of Community Psychology, 5*, 1–22.

Cowen, E. L. (1997). On the semantics and operations of primary prevention and wellness enhancement (or will the real primary prevention please stand up?). *American Journal of Community Psychology, 25*, 245–255.

Dirling, J. (1999). Inclusion: Enhancing resilience. *Preventing School Failure, 43*, 125–128.

Doll, B. (1996). Prevalence of psychiatric disorders in children and youth: An agenda for advocacy by school psychology. *School Psychology Quarterly, 11*, 20–46.

Doll, B., & Cummings, J. (2008). *Transforming school mental health services: Population-based approaches to promoting the competency and wellness of children.* Thousand Oaks, CA: Corwin Press in cooperation with the National Association of School Psychologists.

Doll, B., Murphy, P., & Song, S. (2003). The relation between children's self-reported recess problems, and peer acceptance and friendships. *Journal of School Psychology, 41*, 113–130.

Doll, B., Zucker, S., & Brehm, K. (2004). *Resilient classrooms: Creating healthy environments for learning.* New York: Guilford.

Edwards, C. S. (2000). Moral classroom communities and the development of resilience. *Contemporary Education, 71*, 38–41.

Elias, M. J., Gara, M. A., Schuyler, T. F., Branden-Muller, L. R., & Sayette, M. A. (1991). The promotion of social competence: Longitudinal study of a preventive school-based program. *American Journal of Orthopsychiatry, 61*, 409–417.

Elias, M. J., & Weissberg, R. P. (2000). Primary prevention: Educational approaches to enhance social and emotional learning. *Journal of School Health, 70*, 186–190.

Erwin, P. G., & Ruane, G. E. (1993). The effects of a short-term social problem solving programme with children. *Counseling Psychology Quarterly, 6*, 317–325.

Esposito, C. (1999). Learning in urban blight: School climate and its effect of the school performance of urban, minority, low-income children. *School Psychology Review, 28*, 365–377.

Fantuzzo, J. W., & Rohrbeck, C. A. (1992). Self-managed groups: Fitting self-management approaches into classroom systems. *School Psychology Review, 21*, 255–263.

Federal Interagency Forum on Child and Family Statistics. (2007). America's children in brief: Key national indicators of well-being, 2006. Retrieved July 12, 2007, from http://www.childstats.gov/americaschildren/index.asp

Finn, J. D., & Rock, D. A. (1997). Success among students at risk for school failure. *Journal of Applied Psychology, 82*, 221–234.

Flay, B. R., & Allred, C. G. (2003). Long-term effects of the Positive Action program. *American Journal of Health Behavior, 27*(Suppl., 1), 6–21.

Flay, B. R., Allred, C. G., & Ordway, N. (2001). Effects of the Positive Action program on achievement and discipline: Two matched-control comparisons. *Prevention Science, 2*, 71–90.

Freeman, R. (1996). Why do so many young American men commit crimes and what might we do about it? *Journal of Economic Perspectives, 10*, 25–42.

Freiberg, H. J. (1994). Understanding resilience: Implications for inner-city schools and their near and far communities. In M. C. Wang & E. W. Gordon (Eds.), *Educational resilience in inner-city America: Challenges and prospects* (pp. 151–165). Mahwah, NJ: Lawrence Erlbaum

Frey, K. S., Hirschstein, M. K., & Guzzo, B. A. (2000). Second Step: Preventing aggression by promoting social competence. *Journal of Emotional and Behavioral Disorders, 8*, 102–112.

Grant, S. H., Van Acker, R., Guerra, N., Duplechain, R., & Coen, M. (1998). A school and classroom enhancement program to prevent the development of antisocial behavior in children from high-risk neighborhoods. *Preventing School Failure, 42*, 121–127.

Greenberg, M. T., Domitrovich, C., & Bumbarger, B. (2001). The prevention of mental disorders in school-aged children: Current state of the field. *Prevention and Treatment, 4*(1).

Greenberg, M. T., Weissberg, R. P., O'Brien, M. U., Zins, J. E., Fredericks, L., Resnik, H., et al. (2003). Enhancing school-based prevention and youth development through coordinated social, emotional, and academic learning. *American Psychologist, 58*, 466–474.

Greenwood, C. R., Delquadri, J. C., & Hall, R. V. (1989). Longitudinal effects of classwide peer tutoring. *Journal of Educational Psychology, 81*, 371–383.

Greenwood, C. R., Maheady, L., & Delquadri, J. C. (2002). Classwide peer tutoring programs. In M. R. Shinn, H. M. Walker, & G. Stoner (Eds.), *Interventions for academic and behavior problems II: Preventive and remedial approaches* (pp. 611–649). Bethesda, MD: National Association of School Psychologists.

Grossman, D. C., Neckerman, H. J., Koepsell, T. D., Liu, P., Asher, K. N., Beland, K., et al. (1997). Effectiveness of a violence prevention curriculum among children in elementary school. *Journal of the American Medical Association, 277*, 1605–1611.

Hill, N. E., Castellino, D. R., Lansford, J. E., Nowlin, P., Dodge, K. A., Bates, J. E., et al. (2004). Parent academic involvement as related to school behavior, achievement, and aspirations: Demographic variations across adolescence. *Child Development, 75*, 1491–1509.

Institute of Medicine. (1994). *Reducing risks for mental disorders: Frontiers for preventive intervention research.* Washington, DC: National Academy Press.

Jarrett, O. S. (2002). *Recess in elementary school: What does the research say? ERIC Digest.* Champaign, IL: ERIC Clearinghouse on Elementary and Early Childhood Education.

Jarrett, O. S., Maxwell, D. M., Dickerson, C., Hoge, P., Davies, G., & Yetley, A. (1998). Impact of recess on classroom behavior: Group effects and individual differences. *Journal of Educational Research, 92,* 121–127.

Johnson, D. W., Johnson, R. T., Buckman, L. A., & Richards, P. S. (1998). The effect of prolonged implementation of cooperative learning on social support within the classroom. *Journal of Psychology, 119,* 405–411.

Kam, Chi-Ming, Greenberg, Mark T., Kusché, Carol A. (2004). Sustained Effects of the PATHS Curriculum on the Social and Psychological Adjustment of Children in Special Education. *Journal of Emotional and Behavioral Disorders, 12,* pp. 66–78.

Kelly, B., Longbottom, J., Potts, F., & Williamson, J. (2004). Applying emotional intelligence: Exploring the Promoting Alternative Thinking Strategies curriculum. *Educational Psychology in Practice, 20,* 221–240.

Kratochwill, T. R., & Stoiber, K. C. (2002). Evidence-based interventions in school psychology: The state of the art and future directions. *School Psychology Quarterly, 17*(Special issue), 341–389.

Kusche, C. A., & Greenberg, M. T. (1994). *The PATHS (Promoting alternative thinking strategies) curriculum.* Deerfield, MA: Channing-Bete.

Leadbeater, B., Hoglund, W., & Woods, T. (2003). Changing contexts? The effects of a primary prevention program on classroom levels of peer relational and physical victimization. *Journal of Community Psychology, 31,* 397–418.

Leff, S. S., Costigan, T. E., & Power, T. J. (2004). Using participatory research to develop a playground-based prevention program. *Journal of School Psychology, 42,* 3–21.

Lewis, T. J., Colvin, G., & Sugai, G. (2000). The effects of pre-correction and active supervision on the recess behavior of elementary students. *Education and Treatment of Children, 23,* 109–121.

Lewis, T. J., Powers, L. J., Kelk, M. J., & Newcomer, L. L. (2002). Reducing problem behaviors on the playground: An investigation of the application of school-wide positive behavior supports. *Psychology in the Schools, 39,* 181–190.

Lim, C., & Adelman, H. S. (1997). Establishing school-based collaborative teams to coordinate resources: A case study. *Social Work in Education, 19,* 266–278.

Linares, L. O., Rosbruch, N., Stern, M. B., Edwards, M. E., Walker, G., Abikoff, H. B., et al. (2005). Developing cognitive-social-emotional competencies to enhance academic learning. *Psychology in the Schools, 42,* 405–417.

Lochman, J. E., & Wells, K. C. (2002). The coping power program at the middle school transition universal and indicated prevention effects. *Psychology of Addictive Behaviors, 16*(4), S40–S54.

Masten, A. S. (2001). Ordinary magic: Resilient processes in development. *American Psychologist, 56,* 227–238.

Masten, A. S., & Coatsworth, J. D. (1998). The development of competence in favorable and unfavorable environments. *American Psychologist, 53,* 205–220.

McMahon, S. D., & Washburn, J. J. (2003). Violence prevention: An evaluation of program effects with urban African-American students. *Journal of Primary Prevention, 24,* 43–62.

Merrell, K. W. (2002). Social-emotional intervention in schools: Current status, progress, and promise. *School Psychology Review, 31,* 143–147.

Miller, P., Mulvey, C., & Martin, N. (1995). What do twin studies reveal about the economic returns to education? A comparison of Australian and U.S. findings. *American Economic Review, 85,* 586–599.

Mitchem, K. J., Young, R., West, R. P., & Benyo, J. (2001). CWPASM: A classwide peer-assisted self-management program for general education classrooms. *Education and Treatment of Children, 24,* 111–140.

Murphy, H. A., Hutchinson, J. M., & Bailey, J. S. (1983). Behavioral school psychology goes outdoors: The effect of organized games on playground aggression. *Journal of Applied Behavior Analysis, 16,* 29–35.

National Association of Early Childhood Specialists in State Departments of Education. (2002). Recess and the importance of play. Retrieved July 25, 2007, from http://naecs.crc.uiuc.edu/position/recessplay.pdf

Osher, D., Dwyer, K., & Jackson, S. (2004). *Safe supportive, and successful schools: Step by step.* Longmont, CO: Sopris West.

Osterman, K. F. (2000). Students' need for belonging in the school community. *Review of Educational Research, 70,* 323–367.

Pellegrini, A. D. (1995). *School recess and playground behavior.* Albany: State University of New York Press.

Pellegrini, A. D. (2005). *Recess: Its role in education and development.* Mahwah, NJ: Lawrence Erlbaum.

Pellegrini, A. D., Blatchford, P., Kato, K., & Baines, E. (2004). A short-term longitudinal study of children's playground games in primary school: Implications for adjustment to school and social adjustment in the USA and the UK. *Social Development, 13,* 107–123.

Pianta, R. C. (1999). *Enhancing relationships between children and teachers.* Washington, DC: American Psychological Association.

Pianta, R. C., & Walsh, D. J. (1996). *High risk children in schools: Constructing sustaining relationships.* New York: Routledge.

Prince-Embury, S. (2007). *Resiliency scales for children and adolescents.* San Antonio, TX: Harcourt Assessments.

Reddy, L. A., & Richardson, L. (2006). School-based prevention and intervention programs for children with emotional disturbance. *Education and Treatment of Children, 29,* 379–404.

Resnick, M. D., Bearman, P. S., & Blum, R. W. (1997). Protecting adolescents from harm: Findings from the National Longitudinal Study on Adolescent Health. *Journal of the American Medical Association, 278*, 823–832.

Reumann-Moore, R., & Suess, G. (2006). *Children at play: An evaluation of EW/NSCC's socialized recess program* (ERIC document ED 490194). Philadelphia: Education Works and National School and Community Corps.

Rixon, R., & Erwin, P. G. (1999). Measures of effectiveness in a short-term interpersonal cognitive problem-solving programme. *Counselling Psychology Quarterly, 12*, 87–93.

Rosenblum, L., DiCecco, M. B., Taylor, L., & Adelman, H. S. (1995). Upgrading school support programs through collaboration: Resource coordinating teams. *Social Work in Education, 17*, 117–124.

Rutter, M., & Maughan, B. (2002). School effectiveness findings, 1979–2002. *Journal of School Psychology, 40*, 451–475.

Ryan, A. M., Gheen, M. H., & Midgley, C. (1998). Why do some students avoid asking for help? An examination of the interplay among students' academic efficacy, teachers' social-emotional role, and the classroom goal structure. *Journal of Educational Psychology, 90*, 528–535.

Shure, M. B., & Digeronimo, T. F. (1995). *Raising a thinking child workbook: Teaching young children how to resolve everyday conflicts and get along with others.* Champaign, IL: Research Press.

Shure, M. B., & Healey, K. N. (1993, August). Interpersonal problem solving and prevention in urban schoolchildren. Paper presented at the American Psychological Association annual meeting, Toronto, Canada.

Shure, M. B., & Spivak, G. (1979). Interpersonal cognitive problem solving and primary prevention: Programming for preschool and kindergarten children. *Journal of Clinical Child Psychology, 8*, 89–94.

Shure, M. B., & Spivak, G. (1988). Interpersonal cognitive problem solving. In R. H. Price, E. L. Cowen, R. P. Lorion, & J. Ramos-McKay (Eds.), *Fourteen ounces of prevention: A casebook for practitioners* (pp. 69–82). Washington, DC: American Psychological Association.

Sprague, J., Walker, H., Golly, A., White, K., Myers, D. R., & Shannon, T. (2001). Translating research into effective practice: The effects of a universal staff and student intervention on indicators of discipline and school safety. *Education and Treatment of Children, 24*, 495–511.

Stern, M. B. (1999). *Unique Minds School Program.* Unpublished manual. (Available from Ackerman Institute for the Family, 149 East 78th Street, New York, NY 10021)

Stoiber, K. C., & Good, B. (1998). Risk and resilience factors linked to problem behavior among urban, culturally diverse adolescents. *School Psychology Review, 27*, 380–397.

Sugai, G., Horner, R. H., & Gresham, F. M. (2002). Behaviorally effective school environments. In M. R. Shinn, H. M. Walker, & G. Stoner (Eds.), *Interventions for academic and behavior problems II: Preventive and remedial approaches* (pp. 315–350). Bethesda, MD: National Association of School Psychologists.

Taub, J. (2001). Evaluation of the Second Step violence prevention program at a rural elementary school. *School Psychology Review, 31,* 186–200.

Thomson, S. (2005). "Territorialising" the primary school playground: Deconstructing the geography of playtime. *Children's Geographies, 3,* 63–78.

Todd, A., Haugen, L., Anderson, K., & Spriggs, M. (2004). Teaching recess: Low-cost efforts producing effective results. *Journal of Positive Behavior Interventions, 4,* 46–52.

Velez, W., & Saenz, R. (2001). Toward a comprehensive model of the school leaving process among Latinos. *School Psychology Quarterly, 16,* 445–467.

Walker, H. M., Horner, R. H., Sugai, G., Bullis, M., Sprague, J., Bricker, D., et al. (1996). Integrated approaches to preventing antisocial behavior patterns among school-age children and youth. *Journal of Emotional and Behavior Disorders, 4,* 194–209.

Webster's desk dictionary of the English language. (1983). New York: Gramercy.

Werner, E. (2006). What can we learn about resilience from large-scale longitudinal studies? In S. Goldstein & R. Brooks (Eds.), *Handbook of resilience in children* (pp. 91–105). New York: Springer.

Witt, J., LaFleur, L., Naquin, G., & Gilbertson, D. (1999). *Teaching effective classroom routines.* Longmont, CO: Sopris West.

Ysseldyke, J., Burns, M., Dawson, M., Kelly, B., Morrison, D., Ortiz, S., et al.. (2006) *School psychology: A blueprint for training and practice III.* Bethesda, MD: National Association of School Psychologists.

4

Building Schoolwide Positive Behavior Supports

Anne F. Farrell

A school psychologist receives a request for assistance from a middle school team. The teachers express frustration about the behavior of two students, one of whom carries a classification of learning disability. The other student, although bright and capable, has demonstrated escalating attention and behavior problems. He is teasing other students, interrupting, and becoming angry and insulting when redirected. The other student, who is socially awkward and isolated, is his frequent victim, and storms out of the classroom one day. The teachers report loss of instructional time associated with managing behavior and conclude that their present strategies are ineffective. Hoping to circumvent further difficulties, they ask the school psychologist to observe and assist.

The principal of a diverse urban high school faces growing concern about chronic conduct problems. The staff and faculty feel overwhelmed by the number of discipline referrals, and there have been some episodes of violence. The school's graduation rate is dropping, particularly among students with disabilities. Despite the problems, there are many high-achieving students. The principal notes that there are discipline problems occurring within individual classes and particularly in common areas. There is growing community pressure to address problems.

These two scenarios are quite different from each other but represent a realistic range of problems facing today's school personnel. They raise both distinct and overlapping issues, among them the availability of human and material resources and supports and the accessibility of knowledge and expertise for addressing problem behavior—from mildly distracting to potentially dangerous. Today's educators report problem behavior and classroom management among their top concerns (Farkas,

Johnson, & Foleno, 2000; Imbimbo & Silvernail, 1998; Mitchell & Arnold, 2004; National Center for Education Statistics, 1999). What behaviors do they find challenging? The type, frequency, and severity of problem behavior vary greatly, but typical problems include distracting and disruptive behaviors (verbal or nonverbal interruptions), noncompliance (silent or vocal), aggression (verbal and nonverbal), tantrums and outbursts, self-injury, and theft. Although it is difficult to pinpoint the instructional time lost on behavior management, Scott and Barrett (2004) placed it at 6,000 hours over 1 year in one school.

Is it conceivable that a single technology could address problems at both the individual and systems levels? The field of positive behavior support (PBS) shows promise and success in managing such a range of problems in schools. Emerging from a behavior analytic tradition and framed in a public health perspective, PBS offers comprehensive methods and strategies. Yet, PBS cannot be effectively implemented without the talents, commitment, training, and support of virtually all members of the instructional community. To the extent that effective PBS interventions entail systemic change, their success is also dependent on the careful coordination of resources from academics to mental health.

Does that mean that no PBS initiative can be successful outside a comprehensive, "top-to-bottom" school reform? Not exactly, but lasting change in complex organizations is most often the result of ambitious, multiyear initiatives. As discussed in this chapter, contemporary PBS involves multitiered efforts with universal prevention strategies, interventions for students at risk, and comprehensive supports for students with demonstrated problems. Implementation of all three levels—universal, targeted, and individualized supports—may require both overlapping and unique skill sets (Carr, 2006; Crimmins & Farrell, 2006). By virtue of their training, school psychologists often possess a number of competencies that are key to the success of PBS.

The purpose of this chapter is to provide an overview of the foundations, assumptions, and features of PBS. It begins with a brief review of the historical, scientific, legislative, and philosophic origins of PBS and describes what is known about the organizational support, staff training, and related infrastructure required for implementation. Primary, secondary, and tertiary levels of intervention are discussed and delineated, and the emerging empirical base for these facets is briefly reviewed. The chapter concludes with mention of future directions for PBS. Although this is not intended to provide a complete review of the PBS literature or substitute for training in PBS, the reader will find ample reference to existing curricula and published literature. This chapter presupposes that the reader is somewhat conversant with the principles of operant conditioning and applied behavioral analysis (ABA).

Foundations of PBS: Scientific, Policy, and Philosophical Roots

PBS has its roots in history, policy, and scientific progress of the 20th century, including behaviorism, education, and the American civil rights movement. A number of contemporaneous and interrelated developments across those areas gave rise to what is now the field of positive behavior support. The foundational concepts of PBS are embedded in this discussion.

Historical and Policy Influences

Through the 1970s, students with disabilities were educated in segregated settings, outside the mainstream. Following the 1954 U.S. Supreme Court decision that forced the dismantling of racial segregation in schools (*Brown v. Board of Education*), some questioned the logic behind the segregation of students with disabilities. The passage of the Education of All Handicapped Children Act (EAHCA; PL 94-142) in 1975 permanently altered the landscape of American education, mandating individualized supports for students with disabilities in ways that are still very much with us today. Prior to EAHCA, schools engaged in two main forms of discrimination (Turnbull, Turnbull, & Leal, 1999): completely excluding students with disabilities, in which case they remained mostly in institutions, and failing to provide a proper education to admitted students.

A related historical development was the decline of institutionalization and the rise of the independent living movement, which began in the late 1950s, but is not fully realized even today (Fleischer & Zames, 2001). Arguing from the same civil rights premise, members of the independent living movement asserted that institutions unduly abridged the freedoms of their residents and provided substandard care that did not prepare children or adults to live independently. Although individuals with disabilities led the independent living movement, it was chiefly parents who insisted that children should be educated in community public schools rather than segregated residential ones. In fact, lawsuits filed by parents provided an important impetus for landmark federal legislation to protect the due process rights of students and ensure free, appropriate public education (Turnbull et al., 1999). EACHA was subsequently amended and became the Individuals With Disabilities Education Act (IDEA; 1990).

A philosophic legacy of the inclusion and independent living movements is person-centered planning (PCP; Kincaid & Fox, 2002). PCP includes themes such as seeing students as "people first" rather than primarily through the lens of diagnostic labels or disability classification, using ordinary language, capitalizing on the individuals' strengths and capacities, and strengthening the role of the student and family (Lyle O'Brien & O'Brien, 2002). PCP and self-determination can currently be described as having moved from philosophy to practice.

Scientific Groundwork: Operant Conditioning and Applied Behavioral Analysis

Pivotal groundwork for PBS lies in the field of ABA. B. F. Skinner's work (1953) in operant conditioning began in the 1950s and was applied increasingly over the following decades. As a technology for understanding and changing human behavior, operant conditioning demonstrated great promise across the fields of education, mental health, and disabilities. Space does not permit discussion of the evolution of Skinnerian conditioning into the field of ABA, but perhaps the inaugural issue of the *Journal of Applied Behavioral Analysis* in 1968 marks the genesis of the specialty. In that issue, Baer, Wolf, and Risley (1968) provided a definition of ABA that included five key components: (a) the importance of behavior to be altered, (b) the quantification of behavior and its change, (c) careful specification and analysis of the experimental manipulations (interventions) contributing to change, (d) how effective those interventions were in promoting sufficient change, and (e) the generality of the change.

Early demonstrations of the effectiveness of ABA, although compelling, were also problematic. Within a Skinnerian paradigm, problem behaviors were subject to punishment and desired behaviors were reinforced. The prime consideration was the functional relationships contained in the "three-term contingency": discriminative stimulus, operant behavior, and punishment or reinforcement. Stimuli that followed a behavior and served to reduce its future probability were defined as *punishers*, and those that increased future probability were labeled *reinforcers*. Rarely did these early demonstrations consider the function of behavior, attend to social validity, or plan for maintenance and generalization (Wagner, 2002). Put simply, interventionists delivered reinforcers in the form of food and other tangibles and provided unpleasant consequences for challenging behavior. The use of "aversives" was common.

Horner et al. (1990) noted that the technical definition of *aversive* includes any stimulus that produces an avoidance or escape reaction; in practice, ABA often involved painful or humiliating aversives such as electric shock, slapping, restraint, pepper spray, and loud noises. Beginning in the late 1970s, there was considerable debate regarding the ethics of so-called aversive therapies, particularly when the aversives delivered seemed out of proportion to problem behaviors (Singer, Gert, & Koegel, 1999). Their diminishing use would follow sustained, vocal community debate and require the emergence of effective alternatives.

From within the field of ABA, there came increasing emphasis on the functional relation between problem behavior and the environment; this functional analysis was critical in the move toward positive procedures. For example, Durand (1990) and others (Carr & Durand, 1985; Durand et al., 1989; Meyer & Janney, 1989) demonstrated that identifying the communicative function of problem behaviors aided in their reduction and that data-based decision making in schools led to meaningful outcomes. Increasingly, the field viewed "conventional" behavioral approaches as hampered by their nonfunctional orientation (Carr, Robinson, & Palumbo, 1990), reactive approach, short-term focus, and inability to create lifestyle change (Bambara & Kern, 2005).

Once clinical and empirical demonstrations indicated that nonaversive procedures could reduce problem behavior, the aversives debate quelled somewhat. In 1990, Horner et al. proposed a new technology labeled "positive behavioral support" as an alternative to aversive procedures. These authors emphasized several themes of PBS: lifestyle change, functional analysis, multicomponent interventions, manipulation of setting events and antecedents, teaching adaptive behavior, environments with effective consequences, minimal use of punishment, and distinguishing crisis intervention from proactive programming. They further asserted social validation and human dignity as defining elements. Even if they are not fully realized, these themes and values are very much part of PBS today (Snell, 2005).

Wagner (2002) and others (Anderson & Freeman, 2000; Koegel, Koegel, & Dunlap, 1996) have credited ABA as pivotal to the shift from medical to developmental-educational models and a corresponding individualization of supports. At its origins, ABA was intended to produce *socially important* change that requires that interventions are justifiable only when the change produced is meaningful. This refers to social validity (Haynes

& O'Brien, 2000), the extent to which the focus or intended outcomes are relevant and appropriate in the context of the student's environment, and relates to ecological validity, the degree to which results are evidenced or generalized across contexts (Haynes & O'Brien).

PBS's early successes occurred mostly in the segregated educational settings and were demonstrated primarily with individuals with severe disabilities (Safran & Oswald, 2003). As PBS gained empirical support (e.g., the publication of a monograph synthesizing over 100 published articles that produced data on 230 participants and over 350 outcomes; Carr et al., 1999) and community acceptance, its dissemination and transfer to more inclusive settings, including schools, became more common. Over time, and in response to policy mandates, PBS has been applied with students with high-incidence disabilities (such as emotional and behavioral disorders), with students at risk, and with general student populations. The term *PBS* was coined in 1990 (Horner et al.); in 1994, Bambara and Mitchell-Kvacky described PBS as "emerging." Since that time, the field has witnessed the establishment of a journal devoted to PBS (1999), an international organization (the Association for Positive Behavior Support), and an annual conference inaugurated in 2003 (Dunlap & Koegel, 2004). In 15 years, PBS moved from emerging to established. Although the field has come far, there is still much work to be done and many contributions that have yet to be fully realized.

In sum, PBS emerged as an applied scientific endeavor encompassing a range of philosophical and historical influences. Among its aims was improving the education and inclusion of students with disabilities; however, recent developments include universal applications encompassing entire classes, schools, and districts. The succeeding sections detail assumptions and components of PBS and the three-tiered schoolwide model.

Assumptions of PBS

The historical and philosophical underpinnings of PBS foretell its assumptions: full inclusion of students with disabilities; methods derived from ABA, in particular a functional approach to problem behavior, dual focus on decelerative and accelerative change, and emphasis on proactive approaches; person-centered planning; collaborative team approaches; and emphasis on socially valid long-term change.

Inclusion

A major goal of PBS is the inclusion of individuals with disabilities in regular education (Bambara & Kern, 2005; Lucyshyn, Horner, Dunlap, Albin, & Ben, 2002). Historically, problem behavior has led to the exclusion and segregation of individuals with disabilities, as well as the use of aversives. Prior to PBS, the lack of adequate means to address challenging behavior resulted in lost opportunities for inclusion and lifestyle enhancement. Students with disabilities remain less likely than their peers to graduate from high school; within the population of students with disabilities, those with emotional and behavioral disorders are even less likely to experience academic success (U.S. Department of Education, 2001).

ABA Methods

Applied behavior analysis frequently employs the single-case design as the method for investigating the efficacy of a given intervention, and this approach characterized many of the early PBS demonstrations. (The reader is referred to Alberto & Troutman, 2006; Crimmins, Farrell, Smith, & Bailey, 2007; Didden, Korzilius, van Oorsouw, & Sturmey, 2006; and John, 2008, this volume, for more detailed discussions of behavior analysis in PBS and behavior modification.) Single-case designs are employed quite usefully within both research and community applications. One of their main advantages is in the ability to test a hypothesis about the function served by problem behavior.

Functional Approach to Problem Behavior

PBS assumes that problem behaviors emerge because they serve functions for individuals, even if behaviors meet with responses that superficially appear discouraging or punitive. The functional behavioral assessment (FBA) has been a core ABA procedure for decades, but its use became much more widespread after 1997 (Ervin, Ehrhardt, & Poling, 2001). Gable et al. (2004) stated that "the logic behind FBA is disarmingly simple—namely, that practically all student behavior is purposeful; it satisfies a need and is related to the context in which it occurs" (p. 75). Understanding what motivates behavior is key to meeting its underlying need—and ultimately to rendering it unnecessary.

Durand and Crimmins (1992) proposed four main communicative functions for problem behavior: attention, escape, sensory, and tangible. Although acknowledging that motivations may be multiple (and can also include habit), these authors presupposed that individuals with substantive observational knowledge of behavior can often glean underlying motivations through the functional behavioral assessment. These functions have been validated (Bihm, Kienlen, Ness, & Poindexter, 1991). Dunlap, Harrower, and Fox (2005) noted that employing the terms *motivation* and *purposeful behavior* does not imply that the student is aware of the maintaining consequences, or that the behavior is intentional or premeditated.

When the function of behavior is understood, the corresponding intervention is poised to move beyond suppressing problem behavior to teaching new skills that bring the desired outcome. In essence, a functional approach assumes that behavior is communication; problem behaviors are not inherent deficits but individual responses used to achieve specific ends (Bambara & Mitchell-Kvacky, 1994).

Positive Approaches

Punishment is delivered following a behavior and is designed to reduce its frequency. Although it can be effective in reducing behavior, change is usually short-lived and requires close monitoring (Crimmins et al., 2007; Netzel & Eber, 2003). Punishment is a reactive approach: One waits for problem behavior to occur and responds in a way that discourages it. In schools, punishment may take the form of redirection, verbal correction, loss of privilege, or formal discipline procedures. When reactive procedures predominate, as is the case in most schools (Jackson & Panyan, 2002), recurring problem behaviors may be punished either consistently or intermittently. In any case, if consequences fail to curtail problem occurrence, the student is likely to experience repetitive and escalating punishments.*

Under these circumstances, the student may habituate to consequences or even find them reinforcing. For example, a student who is removed from the classroom for highly disruptive behavior may find the experience

---

* Note the technical use of the term *punishment* here; a consequence that reduces problem behavior is punishment, but it does not have to be demeaning or punitive. See Crimmins et al. (2007) for further discussion of the roles of punishment and reinforcement.

embarrassing initially. Over time, the student not only habituates to this consequence but also comes to experience relief from the frustration or tedium of task demands. A consequence that was intended to reduce (punish) the problem behavior now inadvertently reinforces it by providing escape. Further, the student does not have opportunity to acquire, utilize, or experience reward for alternative coping behaviors. The teacher may appreciate a break from managing the student's behavior, thus removal from the class is negatively reinforced. (Removing the student is associated with the withdrawal of stress: Once the student leaves, stress is reduced and classroom management becomes easier.) Classmates may reinforce unruly behavior by attending to it and may also experience relief at its cessation.

This underscores the deficiency of punishment that is delivered in the absence of instructional or corrective procedures. As Crimmins et al. (2007) pointed out, students with problem behavior do not possess "viable alternatives" and can be "stuck" in an escalating sequence of punishments without legitimate support for more adaptive responses. In contrast, positive interventions do not rely primarily on punishment (whether highly aversive or mild) but instead focus on the development of viable, sustainable alternatives to problem behavior.

Another positive approach practiced within PBS is accommodation, the practice of making environmental or contextual alterations in an attempt to avoid triggering problem behavior. Accommodations are alternations in routines, tasks, and environments that consider the common precursors of challenging behavior (Horner, Sugai, Todd, & Lewis-Palmer, 1999–2000).

Dual Focus on Decelerative and Accelerative Change

Rather than effectively reducing problem behavior, punishment has been associated with increases in truancy, dropout, vandalism, and other antisocial behaviors (March & Horner, 2002; Mayer, 1995; Sulzar-Azaroff & Mayer, 1991; Skiba & Peterson, 2000). Understanding that sustainable change requires the development of alternative behaviors, PBS focuses on both deceleration of problem behavior and acceleration of acceptable alternatives. The ultimate objective of the activities involved in the implementation of PBS surpasses amelioration of problem behavior; it entails locating, developing, teaching, coaching, and reinforcing replacement skills that will serve the student in a range of future circumstances.

Identifying the function of problem behavior allows the team to generate functionally equivalent, socially acceptable alternatives.

Collaborative Team Approaches

Two or more individuals working together toward a common goal comprise a team (Bambara, Nonnemacher, & Koger, 2005), and school teams can involve as few as two individuals or many more. Much has been written about the benefits of team approaches in the fields of education and disabilities (Hanft, Rush, & Sheldon, 2004; Snell, 2005). Crimmins et al. (2007) offered three main reasons for teaming in PBS: the value of multiple perspectives and contexts, collective advocacy for resources, and shared burdens and rewards. Bambara et al. (2005) stated that the PBS process "mandates" the collaboration of people who are integrally involved with the student in different contexts.

Snell and Janney (2000) distinguished "core" and "extended" team members, but both can include family members, regular and special education teachers, teaching assistants and aides, related service providers, administrators, school psychologists, guidance counselors, and any other individuals who spend significant time with the child. Family input is crucial to obtaining valid assessment data (Dunlap, Newton, Fox, Benito, & Vaughn, 2001; Lucyshyn, Dunlap, & Albin, 2002). Problem behaviors (at the individual and group levels) are multidetermined and overlearned; therefore, the involvement of individuals from a range of settings and who possess complementary perspectives and expertise is optimal to creative problem solving. Not all team members need possess expertise in PBS; however, it is essential that at least one person is a PBS specialist (some teams use PBS coaches in this role).

Person-Centered Planning

Wehmeyer (2000) referred to the "confluence" of PCP and self-determination in describing the mutual influences of these constructs and their role in education. In short, these two concepts form a vision of education in which instructional programs are student directed, in contrast to the traditional view of students as mere recipients of services.

Because self-determination incorporates student (and family) preferences, capabilities, and choices, it requires individualization—designing the plan around the student rather than simply placing the student in a pre-conceived program. Effective PBS entails moving beyond simply valuing family input to respecting students and families as partners in assessment and planning. The same standards of human dignity and respect afforded to individuals without disabilities or problem behavior are applied to students with difficulties (Bambara & Mitchell-Kvacky, 1994). This value is appealing and straightforward, yet the frustration of managing problem behavior can strain interaction; few educators reach the classroom with explicit training in family partnerships.

Socially Valid Long-Term Change

The aim of intervention in PBS is meaningful, durable change that affects quality of life and increases choice making and control (Meyer & Evans, 1989). Maintaining and extending change require investment of resources well past the initial intervention. Assessment and intervention are ongoing, closely related activities. Plans that lack monitoring of accelerative and decelerative change are neglected plans, because initial reductions in problem behavior are unlikely to be maintained and generalized in the absence of replacement behaviors. Thus, the benefits of behavior change will not accrue, and corresponding improvements in quality of life are not possible (Carr et al., 2002; Meyer & Evans).

Components and Features of PBS

PBS involves three main components: examining problem behaviors in broad life contexts, sampling the educational, social, and physical environments; as practicable, modifying environments to accommodate learner needs; and instruction and support for emerging alternatives to problem behavior (Crimmins & Farrell, 2006). These components are subsumed into the process of conducting functional behavioral assessments and developing behavior intervention plans, which are core activities in PBS, and also characterize universal, schoolwide approaches. Components of schoolwide PBS practices are discussed below, but aspects relating to systems change are included as features for the purposes of this discussion.

Functional Behavioral Assessment

The functional behavioral assessment (FBA) is conducted in order to determine proximal and distal influences on problem behavior. The FBA process involves a series of steps designed to arrive at a statement regarding the function of problem behavior, including an understanding of how contextual factors contribute to problem behavior and how consequences reinforce or maintain it. There are ample comprehensive resources on individualized PBS (IPBS; e.g., Bambara, Dunlap, & Schwartz, 2004; Bambara & Kern, 2005; Blakeslee, Sugai, & Gruba, 1994; Crimmins et al., 2007; Crone & Horner, 2003; Dunlap et al., 2005; Fox & Davis, 2005; Gresham, 2004; Gresham, Watson, & Skinner, 2001; Jackson & Panyan, 2002; Lohrmann-O'Rourke, Knoster, & Llewellyn, 1999; Lucyshyn et al., 2002; Watson & Steege, 2003). Due to space constraints, methods and issues of assessment and intervention planning are not addressed here.

Three main steps comprise the FBA: gathering information in order to develop a hypothesis about the underlying function of behavior, testing the hypothesis by manipulating the putative controlling variables, and developing an intervention plan based on the results of the hypothesis test. The hypothesis test is basically a single-case design examining the effects of specific conditions and consequences on the occurrence of behavior. Updating the behavioral paradigm, Dunlap et al. (2005) referred to the "four term contingency": setting events (slow triggers), antecedents (fast triggers), problem behavior, and maintaining consequences. The goal of the FBA is to arrive at a confirmed hypothesis regarding these terms.

Technically, the environmental conditions that influence the likelihood of a behavior are termed *setting events* or *establishing operations*. Setting events ("slow triggers") are distal factors that increase the potential for behavior to occur, but do not necessarily cause or immediately precede it. Examples of setting events include physiological conditions (e.g., fatigue and illness), cognitive and emotional factors (such as symptoms of a mental health disorder, or relationship disruptions resulting in emotional distress), aspects of the physical environment (e.g., routines, and change in a classroom seating pattern), and social influences (patterns of socialization in the classroom or school). Antecedents are more commonly known because of their association with the "three term contingency" of antecedent–behavior–consequence (A–B–C); these are immediate triggers, or "fast triggers," that precede the occurrence of problem behavior. The distinguishing feature of antecedents is that their presence is required to elicit the target behavior.

The consequences that follow a behavior most likely maintain it (Dunlap et al., 2005), even if they are not readily apparent. Viewed this way, the behavior of the disruptive student (mentioned earlier) appears logical. It is motivated and maintained by escape from task demands. If the student can work independently in math but struggles greatly in reading, the team might hypothesize that writing is an antecedent to problem behavior. They alter task demands (independent writing work versus none) and examine whether the frequency and intensity of problem behavior fluctuate accordingly. To assess the hypothesis that escape maintains the behavior, the team schedules 2-minute breaks following 10 minutes of seatwork. If taking breaks prevents or significantly alters the frequency of disruptive behavior, the second hypothesis is supported. Because they establish the functional relationships among antecedents, behaviors, and consequences, both hypothesis tests have the potential to inform useful, valid antecedent interventions. If the hypothesis testing does not confirm presumed functional relationships, the team may reassess its understanding of the problem behavior, and can do so before intervention.

Within school teams, FBAs involve a range of time and activity commensurate with the frequency and intensity of problem behavior. Published reports regarding the amount of time required to conduct an FBA vary greatly (Crimmins & Farrell, 2007; Kern, Hilt, & Gresham, 2004; Reid & Nelson, 2002). Although some studies do not specify the amount of time required to conduct FBAs, it appears that data collection procedures may take as little as 3 and as long as 60 hours. Periods of observation range from 3 to 20 days. In Ervin, Ehrhardt, et al.'s (2001) review of more than 100 studies, school personnel and experimenters collaborated on hypothesis tests less than 20% of the time. Because so many published reports reference procedures and time estimates conducted under the leadership of expert researchers, it is impossible to ascertain how representative they are of typical school procedures, which themselves may vary depending on the problem history, nature, severity, and frequency; staff preparedness; and other context factors such as administrative support and family involvement (Crimmins & Farrell, 2006).

Behavior Intervention Plan

Once functions and maintaining behaviors are identified, school staff are in a position to develop a behavior intervention plan (BIP). The BIP is based on information gleaned during the FBA, namely, an understanding of the function of problem behavior. The effective BIP has multiple components (Horner et al., 1999–2000) that address accelerative and decelerative goals. It demonstrates understanding of the problem behavior and stipulates stimulus-based and reinforcement-based procedures, the individuals responsible for monitoring and intervention, and thresholds above and below which the plan requires modification. Prevention may take the form of instructional or environmental accommodations designed to prevent some occurrences of problem behavior (Horner et al., 1999–2000). Kern and Clarke (2005) noted a number of antecedent and setting event interventions that are matched to function and may serve to prevent problem behavior. Contingency management procedures such as differential reinforcement of alternative behaviors, interspersal, and extinction are frequently included (Carr et al., 1999; Ervin, Radford, Bertsch, Ehrhardt, & Poling, 2001). As stated earlier, BIPs include student-centered interventions designed to teach adaptive alternatives.

In developing BIPs, there is an array of strategies and skills from which to choose, among them functional communication training (Durand, 1990), social skills training (Goldstein, 1999; Gresham, Sugai, & Horner, 2001), coaching self-management and self-regulation (Ninness, Ellis, Miller, Baker, & Rutherford, 1995; Perry, VandeKamp, Mercer, & Nordby, 2002), social stories (Gray, 2000), academic skills, and assertiveness training (Alberti & Emmons, 1995). Thus, when alternative behavior is identified, the literature from ABA, behavior therapy, cognitive behavior therapy, school psychology, and education serves as intervention resources. (Many of the approaches and strategies that are detailed in chapters 6 through 12 can be utilized effectively within behavior support plans.) The contributions of school psychologists can be enormously valuable at this stage. Whereas other team members may be intimidated at the range of skills needed to enact plans, many fall within the professional repertoire of the school psychologist: operationalizing outcomes; completing task analyses; formulating plans to prompt specific behaviors; assessing when to fade cues or reinforcers; programming for generalization; and providing training or coaching in social skills, discrimination, relaxation, or anger management.

Systems Change Features

Sugai and Horner (2002a) suggested that effective PBS practices can only be sustained if they are integrated into systems; this requires understanding and applying principles of organizational management and redesign. If inadequate support and infrastructure exist, emerging practices will not be institutionalized and change attempts will likely fail. Sugai and Horner stated that PBS incorporates four systems-level elements. First, desired outcomes must be specified. Second, data systems must be available to capture meaningful information about change. Third, evidence-based practices are necessary to achieve maximal gain. Finally, administrative and other systems must be created and maintained in support of activities and outcomes. These features apply to all PBS applications.

Legislative Support and Mandates

By the time IDEA was amended in 1997 (P.L. 105-17), the problems of acute and chronic school violence were near the forefront of national debate. As such, IDEA 1997 was intended to promote overall school safety and included provisions relating to student discipline. There was also growing recognition that students with disabilities were disproportionately subject to school discipline procedures and were deprived of individual education program (IEP) services under IDEA when they were removed from the classroom or school, even temporarily. To remedy this, Congress embedded specific procedures pertaining to the discipline of students with disabilities.

IDEA 1997 amounted to a legislative mandate for individualized PBS. It required schools to conduct functional behavioral assessments and behavior intervention plans when the behavior of classified students led to 10 or more days of suspension or consideration of an alternative (more restrictive) educational setting. IDEA 1997 did not specify the exact triggers, contents, or format of the FBA and BIP. It required a manifestation determination to establish whether problem behavior was caused by the student's disability. As a consequence, FBA and BIP procedures, initially demonstrated with the small proportion of students with severe disabilities and persistent behavior problems, were now the required and preferred interventions for classified students with impeding behaviors (Crimmins & Farrell, 2007; Scott, Nelson, & Zabala, 2003; Turnbull, Wilcox, Stowe, and Turnbull, 2001). Before that time, the use of PBS in schools was scattered. Complying with IDEA required all schools to train instructional and support staffs in PBS procedures.

The reauthorization of IDEA in 2004 preserved the core requirements of manifestation determination and FBA and BIP when suspension or reconsideration of placement is at issue. By this time, schoolwide applications of PBS had demonstrated both promise and success. Accordingly, IDEA 2004 supported the broader use of PBS in schools, endorsing systemic school interventions and professional preparation in positive behavior interventions and supports. Rare yet appalling episodes of violence in U.S. schools also had relevant impact on policy. Schools developed "zero-tolerance" policies that required disciplinary procedures regardless of context or circumstance. Some warned that this may again marginalize students with disabilities (Markey, Markey, Quant, Santelli, & Turnbull, 2002); others noted that schools were once again asked to "do more" (Horner, Sugai, Todd, & Lewis-Palmer, 1999–2000). Over the last 15 years, schools have experienced increasing pressure to improve overall achievement, address achievement gaps, address difficult behavior, and reduce or prevent episodes of violence.

Schoolwide PBS

Schoolwide positive behavior support (SWPBS) emerged more recently than the individualized approach discussed above; SWPBS encompasses individualized PBS within a linked hierarchy of activities described in the paragraphs that follow. SWPBS arose out of three trends and concerns. First, although it was clear that PBS had demonstrated success at managing problem behavior with individual students, it was also apparent that the vast majority of students (approximately 80%, according to Sugai & Horner, 2002b) do not present problems. Second, the PBS literature established that contextual variables operating within the classroom, hallway, playground, and cafeteria all influenced student behavior. This led to explicit recognition of school climate as an intervening variable in the development, maintenance, and remediation of problem behavior. Third, although the vast majority of students display no more than occasional difficulties, and only about 1% require intensive supports, approximately 15% are at risk for developing problems. (Risk refers to the appearance of an empirically demonstrated predictor of poor outcome. In community health, this might refer to smoking; and in schools, accumulating incidences of mild infractions are associated with future disciplinary action.)

Walker et al. first applied the U.S. Public Health Service's model of prevention to antisocial behavior in 1996. They cited alarming statistics on the rise of youth violence, reiterated existing concerns about reactive approaches in schools, and suggested that schools conceive of and manage problem behavior within a public health model. This paradigm presupposes that preventing disorders is often more efficient, less costly, and more humane than awaiting their appearance and treating them. In medicine, general and developmental surveillance (screening and wellness visits) rest on the assumption that when risk factors and early symptoms are identified, treatment can be initiated promptly, and outcomes improve. The three tiers consist of primary, secondary, and tertiary prevention, and are depicted in Figure 4.1.

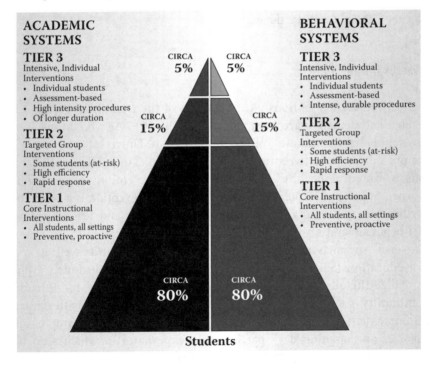

Figure 4.1 PBS applies prevention logic to both academic and behavioral systems within schools and complements response-to-intervention (RTI) Models. (Used with permission from OSEP Technical Assistance Center for Positive Bahavioral Interventions and Support.)

Figure 4.1 presents three levels of intervention within academic and behavioral systems. The recent inclusion of academic systems is of particular importance given the emergence of response-to-intervention (RTI; Brown-Chidsey & Steege, 2005) and positive youth development (Greenberg et al., 2003) models in education. Much concept development for SWPBS occurred through the Office of Special Education Programs (OSEP) Center on Positive Interventions and Supports (n.d.; http://www. pbis.org), and the past few years have seen increasing demonstrations of SWPBS success in diverse settings and regions (Irvin, Tobin, Sprague, Sugai, & Vincent, 2004; Lohrmann & Talerico, 2004; Lohrmann-O'Rourke et al., 1999; Luiselli, Putnam, & Sunderland, 2002; Nelson, Martella, & Galand, 1998; Nersesian, Todd, Lehmann, & Watson, 2000; Netzel & Eber, 2003; Sugai & Horner, 2002b; Taylor-Greene & Kartub, 2000; Todd et al., 2002). Much of the current summary derives from the work of Sugai and Horner, and the reader is referred to Horner et al. (2005) and Sugai and Horner (2002a) for more detail.

Universal Interventions

The universal interventions (at the bottom of the triangle in Figure 4.1) reach all students but are most germane to the 80–90% who do not have problem behavior and are unlikely to develop it. Universal interventions are preventive, proactive strategies that are parallel to public health campaigns aimed at healthy lifestyles—primary prevention. According to Horner, Sugai et al. (2005), the aim of universal prevention is a coherent, predictable, reinforcing school culture that models and teaches prosocial behavior and also responds promptly and predictably to problems. Universal supports are applicable to general education as well as special education (Sailor et al., 2006). In essence, universal models aspire to realize the alternate pathway model for all members of the learning community, such that appropriate, desired behaviors meet with natural reinforcement and undesirable ones go unrewarded. For example, one involves an "opening day" participatory experience in which students generate behavioral expectations with instructor support (Taylor-Green et al., 1997). Procedures for recognizing positive behavior and correcting undesirable behaviors are agreed upon and shared with all members of the learning community (all staff, including bus drivers, cafeteria employees, and custodians, as well as teachers and families).

Targeted Group Interventions

The midsection of the triangle in Figure 4.1 involves targeted group interventions for students who are identified as at risk, approximately 5 to 10% of the school population. These interventions are delivered with high efficiency and monitoring, involve ongoing feedback, and are intended to support students with emerging problem behaviors.

These are students whose backgrounds often include academic failure, poverty, limited family and community support, disability, and association with deviant peers. Research suggests that the presence of these factors, especially in the absence of protective buffers (quality health and educational supports, stable child care, healthy role models, etc.), increases the likelihood of problems. Examples of secondary or targeted interventions include check-in, check-out systems; daily report cards; classroom-wide self-monitoring and self-management systems; and dyadic peer behavior monitoring (Crone, Horner, & Hawkins, 2004; Hawken & Horner, 2003; Lewis, Colvin, & Sugai, 2000; March & Horner, 2002; Norris, 2003; Turnbull et al., 2002). Similar to the earlier point regarding the availability of ample resources and curricula to support BIP development for individuals, there are scores of group interventions available for use in targeted interventions. This might suggest that group and universal interventions are not novel, and to some extent PBS does represent a synthesis of existing technologies and knowledge. Distinct to PBS is a systems orientation to identification, management, tracking, and analysis, and a long-term approach.

Individual Interventions

The top of the triangle in Figure 4.1, 1–5% of the school population, does not respond to universal or targeted interventions, and requires the individualized supports. IPBS is mandated and enforceable under IDEA (Crimmins & Farrell, 2006), as opposed to universal and targeted interventions, which are endorsed but not enforceable under federal law. This level of intervention represents the most durable focus of research and perhaps has the most support (Carr, 2006; Horner, Carr, Strain, Todd, & Reed, 2002; Scott & Eber, 2003).

Organizational Support and Infrastructure

It is beyond the scope of this chapter to present a comprehensive explanation of the study, processes, procedures, and resources required to develop effective SWPBS. Published reports to date, however, converge to endorse the systems change features proposed by Sugai and Horner (2002b). As described by several others (Horner et al., 2005; Office of Special Education Programs [OSEP], 2004; Turnbull et al., 2002), developing SWPBS requires a multiyear commitment. Table 4.1 details some of the tasks involved, and Figure 4.2 depicts an example of how individualized, targeted-group, and universal interventions might interrelate. SWPBS consists of four blended components: outcomes, practices, systems, and data use (Horner et al., 2005). Accumulating evidence regarding SWPBS is cited above and discussed briefly below.

The State of PBS: Current Practices and Their Support

It is clear that PBS, although relatively young among the behavior interventions, has become accepted as a technology for intervening in a range of school problems. Despite data supporting several practices and elements, there is much work to be done to articulate and establish standards of practice, address the reliability and validity of PBS elements, and ensure that the workforce is prepared and supported in conducting interventions at all three tiers of PBS. This section briefly recaps current knowledge regarding current practices, existing support for them, and directions for future inquiry.

Individualized PBS

As stated earlier, there are scores of publications documenting the success of IPBS, yet at the same time, the field lacks consensus and requires further inquiry into a number of key issues with the potential to affect the adoption of PBS. Crimmins and Farrell (2006) conducted a review of the IPBS literature and examined trends regarding the resources and components required for IPBS. They found general agreement about the effectiveness of FBA procedures but could extract no consensus regarding the "core" procedures that comprise IPBS. That is, experts did not agree about

TABLE 4.1   Activities for Implementation of Schoolwide PBS Efforts

Phase	Activities and Steps	Outcomes and Implications
Initial Planning	Solidify foundation for collaboration and operations: • Establish planning group. • Decide on initial goals. • Secure PBS expertise. • Communicate plans. • Recruit PBS advisory council. • Prepare for needs assessment.	Establish systems (structure, leadership, resources, and priorities): • Recruit input from all stakeholders. • Encourage diverse council membership reflecting community characteristics. • Assess human and other resources required. • Coordinate various PBS elements. Secure "buy-in" from key constituent groups: • Seek input from faculty, staff, families, students, and community members. • Plan for and allocate resources in support of staff training and commitment.
Needs Assessment	Conduct and review needs assessment: • Analyze existing data. • Conduct interview and observations. • Use existing surveys or devise own. • Determine data management needs. • Analyze initial data.	Understand trends in problem behavior, including the following: • Type, setting, severity, and frequency. • "Hot spots" or problem contexts. • Students with multiple incidents and risk factors. Anticipate ongoing data collection and management needs: • Design or procure data management system. • Ensure staff capacity and expertise to collect and manage data.
Implementation	Analyze needs assessment: • Review data from observations, checklists, and interviews. • Identify strengths and opportunities for improvement; establish goals. • Prioritize desired outcomes. Develop detailed workplan and practices: • Address preventable, high-frequency, and/or urgent incidents first.	Feasible workplan constructed: • Based on priorities, desired outcomes are articulated; realistic targets are established. • Schoolwide behavioral expectations are defined, taught, encouraged, and monitored. • Ongoing staff involvement and training are planned and communicated; meetings are limited, strategic, and useful. • Steps are communicated clearly, so efforts are predictable and transparent.

TABLE 4.1   Activities for Implementation of Schoolwide PBS Efforts (Continued)

Phase	Activities and Steps	Outcomes and Implications
	Enact workplan: • Develop or revise positive behavior expectations using a collaborative, multiple-constituent approach. • Ensure communication of behavior standards, rewards, and consequences. • Develop specialized initiatives for high-risk students; ensure coordination with universal and individualized PBS. • Ensure that universal initiatives are accessible to students with disabilities. • For students with established difficulties, coordinate with behavior support workgroup or student support team. • Select, coordinate, and integrate curricula for health, behavior, and risk.	Constructive change occurs when the following are in place: • Behavior expectations are clear, positive behavior is recognized and rewarded, and all students benefit from primary prevention efforts. • Prevention efforts may result in a fairly immediate reduction in incidents. • Plan capitalizes on existing strengths. • Students at risk and those with demonstrated difficulties are identified and receive targeted supports. • Policies, procedures, and resources serve at-risk youth and their families. • School staff coordinate targeted and universal efforts. • Youth support efforts are integrated, with an emphasis on skills and themes (e.g., self-regulation, social values, and decision making).
Program Evaluation	Ongoing data collection and analysis: • Monitor implementation. • Assess outcomes in relation to objectives and benchmarks. • Identify new or changing "hot spots." • Develop specialized initiatives for high-risk students. • Revise benchmarks, objectives, and implementation steps in response to change.	Assessment of implementation and outcomes results in the following: • Ineffective strategies are revised or replaced. • New initatives are developed in response to ongoing data analysis. • Leaders track both reduction in incidents and improvement in quality-of-life indicators. • Students at risk and with persistent difficulties receive individualized supports in wraparound model. • IPBS and targeted and schoolwide interventions are modified in keeping with quantitative and qualitative data

Source: Adapted from Crimmins, Farrell, Smith, and Bailey (2005).

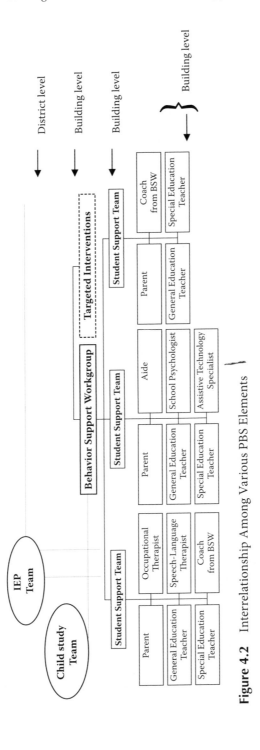

Figure 4.2 Interrelationship Among Various PBS Elements

the conditions that should trigger the FBA and its minimal components (assessment methods, hypothesis testing, and matching FBA and BIP components; Scott, Meers, & Nelson, 2000). If the literature suggests that the FBA is commonly employed, its results are less frequently addressed in the BIP. Because IDEA does not require tracking of IPBS, there are essentially no national or statewide data on compliance (Gresham, Watson et al., 2001), let alone on whether FBA–BIP procedures are affording their intended benefits.

With respect to personnel preparation in IPBS, essential and recommended elements have been offered (Dunlap et al., 2000; Heineman & Dunlap, 2000; Weigle, 1997), and several authors have suggested training models that engage school teams as opposed to relying on external consultants (Crone & Horner, 1999–2000; Hanft et al., 2004; McCormick, 2006; Scott & Nelson, 1999). Currently, it is not possible to characterize the amount or type of training required for staff competence in IPBS. Published estimates of training time typically involved in-service duration equivalent to one full week of training and subsequent field-based follow-up, or 9 semester hours of classroom training. Crimmins and Farrell (2006) also noted the absence of IDEA-based competencies (including PBS) among some of the accreditation criteria for teacher preparation programs.

Among their observations regarding gaps in the IPBS literature were the absence of attention to family and student involvement in IPBS procedures; the continuing reliance of trained school personnel on reactive, punitive, consequence-based approaches to problem behavior; the use of strategies already in place in schools (instead of turning to novel intervention and support strategies); the relatively frequent exclusion of students; and insufficient attention to external and social validity in IPBS research—factors likely to inhibit increased diffusion of PBS as a technology. Some have been critical of the paucity of field research undertaken and have exhorted others to provide more than "one-shot" training that does little more than increase staff familiarity with PBS procedures instead of developing competence (Conroy, Clark, Fox, & Gable, 2000; Gable, 1996). On the other hand, existing research suggests that trained school staff are better able to validate hypotheses about function, consider function in the development of replacement behaviors, and examine outcomes (Van Acker, Boreson, Gable, & Potterton, 2005).

Thus, although there is ample support for the use and effectiveness of IPBS procedures, especially in restrictive settings, there is still much work to be done. Field research needs to examine the type and amount of training necessary for personnel of various backgrounds to attain minimal and optimal competence in planning, collaboration, and delivery. For example, Crone, Hawken, and Bergstrom (2007) examined the effectiveness of a staff-training initiative utilizing the effective behavior support model (Lewis & Sugai, 1999). Participants from 10 school teams demonstrated increased (pre and post) knowledge about the FBA–BIP process and effectively applied it with individual students. Similar work, especially if conducted on a broader scale, can be effective in addressing important questions about IPBS and also has the potential to inform the field about the interrelated elements of SWPBS. A nearly ubiquitous concern in the FBA training literature is the balance between economic and practical feasibility and the need to maintain conceptual and procedural integrity (fidelity). Nevertheless, before the reliability, validity, and utility of school practices can be improved or best practices can be fully articulated, more information about current practice needs to be available. This normative base can serve as a benchmark for comparison and improvement. Because SWPBS emerged relatively recently, there is less extant research evaluating primary and secondary interventions; a brief review of notable achievements and future directions follows.

Targeted Group Interventions

Targeted or secondary interventions aim to diminish the impact of apparent risk or early signs of problem behavior. When employed effectively, they have the potential to avert negative outcomes for groups and individuals. Following the public health model, this may produce economic efficiencies in addition to reducing the time, effort, and human cost absorbed by challenging behavior. Owing to the potentially large numbers of students involved, Scott and Eber (2003) suggested that secondary assessment and intervention practices be based on both empirically validated practice and local data, as well as consider logic and efficiency. The secondary intervention team includes teachers, parents, students, school psychologists, and others who may contribute professional or personal expertise. Both secondary and tertiary interventions can effectively address both behavioral and academic concerns.

To date, secondary interventions have been shown to increase positive adult–student contact to help reduce dropout (Sinclair, Christenson, Evelo, & Hurly, 1998), improve social skills and reduce anger problems (Freeman et al., 2006; Lane et al., 2003), improve behavior during transitions (Turnbull et al., 2002) and improve academic outcomes (Freeman et al.). Although the sheer number of publications regarding secondary interventions would appear unimpressive, it is arguable that secondary interventions represent a continuing effort to implement empirically validated initiatives in schools. As such, research endorsing interventions and approaches such as the PREPARE curriculum (Goldstein, 1999), and universal screening and intervention programs for depression and suicidality (Commission on Adolescent Suicide Prevention, 2005) may be considered support for the inherent model, if not the content, of secondary PBS initiatives.

Universal Supports

Comprehensive SWPBS initiatives have demonstrated important success, particularly within the last several years. Although space does not permit a thorough review of these successes, some attainments are noted here. Horner et al. (2004) demonstrated that SWPBS could be implemented with fidelity. Employing an implementation assessment tool, these authors found that 11 of 13 schools met or surpassed an 80% implementation benchmark within 2 years. Lohrmann-O'Rourke et al. (1999) found significant reductions in office discipline referrals, a convenient and commonly employed outcome. McCurdy, Mannella, and Eldridge (2003) achieved reductions in discipline referrals as well as student assaults. Lewis et al. (2000) demonstrated reductions in problem behavior associated with "hot spots" such as the playground. Scott and Barrett (2004) reported very large reductions in student discipline and recorded impressive time savings for faculty and staff following SWPBS adoption. Addressing the sustainability in the absence of extensive researcher involvement, Horner et al. (2004) reported ongoing school implementation for 6 years in one setting. In a 3-year SWPBS endeavor in Chicago, Bohanon et al. (2006) achieved decreases in discipline referrals and found that demands on staff time diminished over the course of implementation.

Recently there has been scholarly discussion over the extent to which SWPBS can capably address the needs of all three tiers of the triangle in Figure 4.1. (The reader is referred in particular to a special issue on severe disabilities and school-wide positive behavior support, introduced by Bambara & Lohrmann, 2006.) SWPBS is intended to increase the overall competence of school staff in PBS methods, so it is ironic that it is criticized for a relative lack of emphasis on the needs of students with significant disabilities. For example, Sailor et al. found no data on academic improvements for students receiving special education and further concluded that most universal interventions were driven by general education objectives. Recently, there have been promising demonstrations of a "trickle down" from primary and secondary SWPBS interventions to individual students. For example, Tobin and Martin (2001) reported decreases in office discipline referrals for students with problem behavior following team-based training on FBA–BIP procedures. Hawken and O'Neill (2006) offered suggestions for including students with severe disabilities in all levels of SWPBS. To paraphrase Reinke, Herman, and Tucker (2006), the leap from preventing problems or reducing risk in individual cases to reducing the incidence and prevalence of a particular problem is a formidable one, but one that future research needs to address.

Future Directions

Scale-Up Studies of Training and Implementation

In 2003, Rotholz and Ford stated, "It is a simple task to provide examples of existing literature on positive behavior support. It is considerably more difficult to pinpoint the widespread implementation of these methods at the local level or systems that promote and support them" (p. 355). Although important progress has been made and is underway, the need for coordinated, scale-up studies of all three levels of PBS remains. In particular, future initiatives should examine how primary, secondary, and tertiary interventions can be optimally interlaced to benefit the majority of students without problem behavior, as well as their counterparts who are at clear risk and those who have established difficulties. Similar endeavors are required to better understand how the content and methods of various training curricula and models interact with participant, school, and setting characteristics and other contextual variables to influence the uptake of PBS in the community. Constituent-focused research that addresses the perceived social validity of PBS (by educators, families, and students) is needed. Current research efforts are incremental indicators, yet demonstrations using more rigorous, controlled (randomized) designs would be a ringing endorsement of the SWPBS model.

Coordinating PBS and Other Systems of Support

PBS shares an underlying prevention logic with response-to-intervention models currently required under IDEA and No Child Left Behind. McIntosh, Chard, Boland, and Horner (2006) implemented a three-tier intervention for both reading and behavior support and attributed its success to the number of shared critical features across the two systems. Although RTI has yet to be fully defined, localized, and implemented, a common infrastructure across behavioral and academic systems is feasible. Effective delivery will require training of current school personnel and improvements to preservice preparation.

PBS has potentiated the effects of two additional systems of support, wraparound models (Scott & Eber, 2003) and school efforts to promote child and adolescent mental health (Adelman & Taylor, this volume; Romer & McIntosh, 2005). Wraparound is a positive model of support that involves constructive, defined, and cross-system planning for individual students and their families (Eber, Sugai, Smith, & Scott, 2002; Stroul & Freidman, 1986). It is most appropriate for students with complex, significant needs and those who are involved with multiple service systems (education, health, mental health, disability, child welfare, juvenile justice, etc.). Like PBS, school-based mental health initiatives involve successive levels of prevention, identification, and direct care. Coordinated research across these models can effectively demonstrate the ability to reduce the prevalence and severity of problems.

The application of SWPBS and its integration with wraparound models enhance the likelihood of proactive interventions across the contexts of the student's life (home, school, and community) and have demonstrated success in both avoiding restrictive placement and improving achievement (Eber et al., 2002). In addition, although schools have traditionally been reluctant to address student needs outside the conventional academic domains, the social, mental, and behavioral health needs of children and adolescents comprise a principal public health concern. Because learning is a fundamentally social endeavor (Jackson & Panyan, 2002), comorbidity across these functional domains is a major impediment to learning and learning environments (refer to chapter 2 for further discussion of mental health in schools and chapter 5 for a rationale on the importance of fostering social competence in schools). Systematically addressing these issues will require abandonment of existing "silo" paradigms and systems, careful allotment of resources within schools and across school systems, and the commitment of key school personnel with the vision and competence to achieve meaningful, lasting change. As such, the field of positive behavior supports offers an opportunity for school psychologists to contribute meaningfully to individual student outcomes, intervention for students at risk, and school reform efforts.

References

Alberti, R. E., & Emmons, M. L. (1995). *Your perfect right: A guide to assertive living.* Atascadero, CA: Impact.

Alberto, P., & Troutman (2006). *Applied Behavior Analysis for Teachers (7th ed).* New York: Prentice-Hall.

Anderson, C. M., & Freeman K. A. (2000). Positive behavior support: Expanding the application of applied behavior analysis. *Behavior Analyst, 23,* 9–14.

Baer, D., Wolf, M., & Risley, R. (1968). Some current dimensions of applied behavior analysis. *Journal of Applied Behavior Analysis,* 1(1), 91–97.

Bambara, L., Dunlap, G., & Schwartz, I. S. (Eds.). (2004). *Positive behavior support: Critical articles on improving practice for individuals with severe disabilities.* Austin, TX: Pro-Ed and TASH.

Bambara, L. M., & Kern, L. (2005). *Individualized supports for students with problem behavior: Designing positive behavior plans.* New York: Guilford.

Bambara, L., & Lohrmann, S. (2006). Introduction to special issue on severe disabilities and school-wide positive behavior support. *Research and Practice for Persons with Severe Disabilities, 31,* 1–3.

Bambara, L., & Mitchell-Kvacky, N. A. (1994). Positive behavior support for students with severe disabilities: An emerging multicomponent approach for addressing challenging behaviors. *School Psychology Review, 23,* 263–279.

Bambara, L. M., Nonnemacher, S., & Koger, F. (2005). Teaming. In Bambara, L. M., & Kern, L. (Eds.) *Individualized supports for students with problem behaviors: Designing positive behavior plans* (pp. 71–106). New York, NY: Guilford Press.

Bihm, E. M., Kienlen, T. L., Ness, M. E., & Poindexter, A. R. (1991). Factor structure of the Motivation Assessment Scale for persons with mental retardation. *Psychological Reports, 68,* 1235–1238.

Blakeslee, M. A., Sugai, G., & Gruba, J. (1994). A review of functional assessment use in data-based intervention studies. *Journal of Behavioral Education, 4,* 397–413.

Bohanon, H., Fenning, P., Carney, K. L., Minnis-Kim, M. J., Anderson-Harriss, S. A., Moroz, K. B., et al. (2006). Schoolwide application of positive behavior support in an urban high school: A case study. *Journal of Positive Behavior Interventions, 8,* 131–145.

Brown, F., & Michaels, C. A. (2006). School-wide positive behavior support initiatives and students with severe disabilities: A time for reflection. *Research and Practice for Persons With Severe Disabilities, 31,* 57–61.

Brown-Chidsey, R., & Steege, M. W. (2005). *Response to intervention: Principles and strategies for effective practice.* New York: Guilford.

Carr, E. G. (2006). SWPBS: The greatest good for the greatest number, or the needs of the majority trump the needs of the minority? *Research and Practice for Persons With Severe Disabilities, 31,* 54–56.

Carr, E. G., Dunlap, G., Horner, R. H., Koegel, R. L., Turnbull, A. P., Sailor, W., Anderson, J. L., Albin, R. W., Koegel, L. K., & Fox, L. (2002). Positive behavior support: Evolution of an applied science. *Journal of Positive Behavior Intervention, 4,* 4-16.

Carr, E. G., & Durand, V. M. (1985). Reducing problem behavior through functional communication training. *Journal of Applied Behavioral Analysis, 18,* 4–16.

Carr, E. G., & Durand, V. M. (1985). Reducing behavior problems through functional communication training. *Journal of Applied Behavior Analysis, 18,* 111–126.

Carr, E. G., Horner, R. H., Turnbull, A. P., Marquis, J. G., Magito McLaughlin, D., McAtee, M. L., Smith, C. E., Anderson Ryan, K., Ruef, M. B., & Doolabh, A. (1999). *Positive behavior support for people with developmental disabilities: A research synthesis.* Washington, DC: American Association on Mental Retardation.

Carr, E. G., Robinson, S., & Palumbo, L. W. (1990). The wrong issue: Aversive versus nonaversive treatment. The right issue: Functional vs. nonfunctional treatment. In A. C. Repp & N. N. Singh (Eds.), *Perspectives on the use of nonaversive and aversive interventions for persons with developmental disabilities* (pp. 361–380). Sycamore, IL: Sycamore.

Commission on Adolescent Suicide Prevention. (2005). Targeted youth suicide prevention programs. In Commission chairs of the Annenberg Foundation Trust at Sunnylands' Adolescent Mental Health Initiative, D. L. Evans et al., (Eds.). *Treating and preventing adolescent mental health disorders: What we know and what we don't know* (pp. 445–462). New York, NY: Oxford University Press.

Conroy, M. A., Clark, D., Fox, J., & Gable, R. A. (2000). Building competence in FBA: Are we headed in the right direction? *Preventing School Failure, 44,* 169–174.

Crimmins, D., & Farrell, A. F. (2006). Individualized behavioral supports at 15 years: It's still lonely at the top. *Research and Practice for Persons With Severe Disabilities, 31,* 31–45.

Crimmins, D., Farrell, A. F., Smith, P. W., & Bailey, A. (2007). *Positive strategies for students with problem behavior.* Baltimore: Paul H. Brookes.

Crone, D., Hawken, L., & Bergstrom, M. K. (2007). A demonstration of training, implementing, and using functional behavioral assessment in 10 elementary and middle school settings. *Journal of Positive Behavior Interventions, 9*, 15–29.

Crone, D. A., & Horner, R. H. (1999–2000). Contextual, conceptual, and empirical foundations of functional behavioral assessment in schools. *Exceptionality, 8*, 161–172.

Crone, D. A., & Horner, R. H. (2003). *Building positive behavior support systems in schools.* New York: Guilford.

Crone, D., Horner, R., & Hawken, L. (2004). *Responding to problem behavior in schools: The Behavior Education Program.* Guilford Press.

Didden, R., Korzilius, H., van Oorsouw, W., & Sturmey, P. (2006). Behavioral treatment of challenging behaviors in individuals with mild mental retardation: Meta-analysis of single subject research. *American Journal on Mental Retardation, 111*, 290–298.

Dunlap, G., Harrower, J., & Fox, L. (2005). Understanding the environmental determinants of problem behaviors. In L. Bambara & L. Kern (Eds.), *Individualized supports for students with problem behaviors* (pp. 25–46). New York: Guilford Press.

Dunlap, G., Hieneman, M., Knoster, T., Fox, L., Anderson, J., & Albin, R. W. (2000). Essential elements of inservice training in positive behavior support. *Journal of Positive Behavior Interventions, 2*, 22–32.

Dunlap, G., & Koegel, R. L. (2004). Editorial. *Journal of Positive Behavior Interventions, 6*, 194.

Dunlap, G., Newton, J. S., Fox, L., Benito, N., & Vaughn, B. (2001). Family Involvement in Functional Assessment and Positive Behavior Support. *Focus on Autism and Other Developmental Disabilities, 16*, 215–221.

Durand, V. M. (1990). *Severe behavior problems: A functional communication training approach.* New York: Guilford.

Durand, V. M., & Crimmins, D. B. (1992). *The Motivation Assessment Scale administration guide.* Topeka, KS: Monaco & Associates.

Durand, V. M., Crimmins, D. B., Caulfield, M., & Taylor, J. (1989). Reinforcer assessment I.: Using problem behavior to select reinforcers. *Journal of the Association for Persons with Severe Handicaps, 14*, 113–126.

Eber, L., Sugai, G., Smith, C. R., & Scott, T. M. (2002). Wraparound and positive behavioral interventions and supports in the schools. *Journal of Emotional and Behavioral Disorders, 10*, 171–180.

Ervin, R. A., Ehrhardt, K. E., & Poling, A. (2001). Functional assessment: Old wine in new bottles. *School Psychology Review, 30*, 173–179.

Ervin, R. A., Radford, P. M., Bertsch, P., Ehrhardt, K. E., & Poling, A. (2001). A descriptive analysis and critique of the empirical literature on school-based functional assessment. *School Psychology Review, 30*, 193–210.

Farkas, S., Johnson, J., & Foleno, T. (2000). *A sense of calling: Who teaches and why.* New York: Public Agenda.

Fleischer, D. Z., & Zames, F. (2001). *The disability rights movement: From charity to confrontation.* Philadelphia, PA: Temple University Press.

Fox, J., & Davis, C. (2005). Functional behavior assessment in schools: Current research findings and future directions. *Journal of Behavioral Education, 14,* 1–4.

Freeman, R., Eber, L., Anderson, C., Irvin, L., Horner, R., Bounds, M., et al. (2006). Building inclusive school cultures using school-wide PBS: Designing effective individual support systems for students with disabilities. *Research and Practice for Persons With Severe Disabilities, 31,* 4–17.

Gable, R. A. (1996). A critical analysis of functional assessment issues for researchers and practitioners. *Behavioral Disorders, 24,* 249–252.

Gable, R. A., Quinn, M. M., Rutherford, R. B., Howell. K., Hoffman, K., & Butler, C. J. (2004). *Conducting a functional behavioral assessment and developing a positive behavioral intervention plan.* Washington, DC: American Institutes for Research.

Goldstein, A. (1999). *The PREPARE curriculum: Teaching prosocial competencies* (Rev. ed.). Champaign, IL: Research Press.

Gray, C. (2000). *The new social story book: Illustrated edition.* Arlington, TX: Future Horizons, Inc.

Greenberg, M. T., Weissberg, R. P., O'Brien, M. U., Zins, J. E., Fredericks, L., Resnik, H., & Elias, M. J. (2003). Enhancing school-based prevention and youth development through coordinated social, emotional, and academic learning. *American Psychologist, 58,* 466–474.

Gresham, F. M. (2004). Current status and future directions of school-based behavioral interventions. *School Psychology Review, 33,* 326–343.

Gresham, F. M., Sugai, G., & Horner, R. H. (2001). Interpreting outcomes of social skills training for students with high-incidence disabilities. *Exceptional Children, 67,* 331–344.

Gresham, F. M., Watson, T. S., & Skinner, C. H. (2001). Functional behavioral assessment: Principles, procedures, and future directions. *School Psychology Review, 30,* 156–172.

Hanft, B. E., Rush, D. D., & Sheldon, M. (2004). *Coaching families and colleagues in early childhood.* Baltimore: Paul H. Brookes.

Hawkens, L. & Horner, R. (2003). Evaluation of a targeted group intervention within a school-wide system of behavior support, *Journal of Behavioral Education, 12,* 225–240.

Hawkens, L. S., & O'Neill, R. E. (2006). Including students with severe disabilities in all levels of school-wide positive behavior support. *Research and Practice for Persons with Severe Disabilities, 31,* 46–53.

Haynes, S. N. & O'Brien, W. H. (2000). *Principles and Practice of Behavioral Assessment.* New York, NY: Kluwer Academic/Plenum Publishers.

Hieneman, M. & Dunlap, G. (2000). Factors affecting the outcomes of community-based behavioral support: I. Identification and description of factor categories. *Journal of Positive Behavior Interventions, 2*(3), 161–169.

Horner, R. H., Carr, E. G., Strain, P. S., Todd, A. W., & Reed, H. K. (2002). Problem behavior interventions for young children with autism: A research synthesis. *Journal of Autism and Developmental Disorders, 32,* 423–446.

Horner, R. H., Dunlap, G., Koegel, R. L., Carr, E. G., Sailor, W., Anderson, J., et al. (1990). Toward a technology of "nonaversive" behavioral support. *Journal of the Association for Persons with Severe Handicaps, 15,* 125–132.

Horner, R. H., Dunlap, G., Koegel, R. L., Carr, E. G., Sailor, W., Anderson, J., Albin, R. W., & O'Neill, R. E. (2005). Toward a technology of "nonaversive" behavioral support. *Research and Practice for Persons for Severe Disabilities, 30,* 3–10.

Horner, R. H., Sugai, G., Todd, A. W., & Lewis-Palmer, T. (1999–2000). Elements of behavior support plans: A technical brief. *Exceptionality, 8,* 205–215.

Horner, R. H., Sugai, G., Todd, A. W., & Lewis-Palmer, T. (2004). School-wide positive behavior support: An alternative approach to discipline in schools. In L. Bambara & L. Kern (Eds.), *Individualized supports for students with problem behaviors: Designing positive behavior plans* (pp. 359–390). New York: Guilford Press.

Imbimbo, J., & Silvernail, D. (1998). *Prepared to teach? Key findings of the New York City Teacher Survey.* New York: New Visions for Public Schools.

Irvin, L. K., Tobin, T. J., Sprague, J. R., & Vincent, C. G. (2004). Validity of office discipline referrals measures as indices of school-wide behavioral status and effects of school-wide behavioral interventions. *Journal of Positive Behavior Interventions 6,* 131–147.

Jackson, L., & Panyan, M. V. (2002). *Positive behavioral support in the classroom: Principles and practices.* Baltimore: Paul H. Brookes.

Kern, L., & Clarke, S. (2005). Antecedent and setting event interventions. In Bambara, L.M., & Kern, L. (Eds.) *Individualized supports for students with problem behaviors: Designing positive behavior plans* (pp. 201–236). New York, NY: Guilford Press.

Kern, L., Hilt, A. M., & Gresham, F. (2004). An evaluation of functional behavioral assessment process used with students with or at risk for emotional and behavioral disorders. *Education and Treatment of Children, 27,* 440–452.

Kincaid, D., & Fox, L. (2002). Person-centered planning and positive behavior support. In S. Holburn & P. M. Vietze (Eds.), *Person-centered planning: Research, practice, and future directions* (pp. 29–50). Baltimore: Paul H. Brookes.

Koegel, L. K., Koegel, R. L., & Dunlap, G. (Eds.). (1996). *Positive behavioral support: Including people with difficult behavior in the community.* Baltimore: Paul H. Brookes.

Lane, K. L., Wehby, J., Menzies, H. M., Doukas, G. L., Munton, S. M., & Gregg, R. M. (2003). Social skills instruction for students at risk for antisocial behavior: The effects of small-group instruction. *Behavioral Disorders, 28,* 229–248.

Lewis, T., Colvin, G., & Sugai, G. (2000). The effects of precorrection and active supervision on the recess behavior of elementary students. *Education and Treatment of Children, 23,* 109–121.

Lewis, T. J., & Sugai, G. (1999). Effective behavior support: A systems approach to proactive schoolwide management. *Focus on Exceptional Children, 6,* 1–24.

Lohrmann, S., & Talerico, L. (2004). Anchor the boat: A classwide intervention to reduce problem behavior. *Journal of Positive Behavior Interventions, 6*(2), 113–120.

Lohrmann-O'Rourke, S., Knoster, T., & Llewellyn, G. (1999). Screening for understanding: An initial line of inquiry for school-based settings. *Journal of Positive Behavior Interventions, 1*(1), 35–42.

Lucyshyn, J. M, Dunlap, G., & Albin, R. W. (Eds.). (2002). *Families and positive behavior support: Addressing problem behaviors in family contexts.* Baltimore: Paul H. Brookes.

Lucyshyn, J. M, Horner, R. H., Dunlap, G., Albin, R. W. & Ben, K. R. (2002). Characteristics and Context of Positive Behavior Support with Families in *Families and Positive Behavior Support: Addressing problem behaviors in family contexts.* Baltimore: Paul H. Brookes.

Lyle O'Brien, C., & O'Brien, J. (2002). The origins of person-centered planning: A community of practice perspective. In S. Holburn & P. M. Vietze (Eds.), *Person-centered planning: Research, practice and future directions.* Baltimore: Paul H. Brookes.

March, R. E., & Horner, R. H. (2002). Feasibility and contributions of functional behavioral assessment in schools. *Journal of Emotional and Behavioral Disorders, 10,* 158–170.

Markey, U., Markey, D. J., Quant, B., Santelli, B., & Turnbull, A. (2002). Operation Positive Behavior Change: Positive behavior support in an urban context. *Journal of Positive Behavior Interventions, 4,* 218–230.

Mayer, G. R. (1995). Preventing antisocial behavior in the schools. *Journal of Applied Behavioral Analysis, 28,* 467–478.

McCormick, L. (2006). Professional and family partnerships. In M. J. Noonan & L. McCormick (Eds.), *Young children with disabilities in natural environments.* Baltimore: Paul H. Brookes Publishers.

McCurdy, B. L., Mannella, M. C., & Eldridge, N. (2003). Positive behavior support in urban schools: Can we prevent the escalation of antisocial behavior? *Journal of Positive Behavioral Interventions, 5,* 158–170.

McIntosh, K., Chard, D. J., Boland, J. B., & Horner, R. H. (2006). Demonstration of combined efforts in school-wide academic and behavioral systems and incidence of reading and behavioral challenges in early elementary grades. *Journal of Positive Behavior Interventions, 8,* 146–154.

Meyer, L. H., & Evans, I. M. (1989). *Nonaversive intervention for behavior problems.* Baltimore: Paul H. Brookes.

Meyer, L., & Janney, R. (1989). User-friendly measures of meaningful outcomes: Evaluating behavioral interventions. *Journal of the Association for Persons with Severe Handicaps, 14,* 263–270.

Mitchell, A. & Arnold, M. (2004). Behavior management skills as predictors of retention among South Texas Special Educators, *Journal of Instructional Psychology, 31*(3), 214–219.

National Center for Education Statistics. (1999). *Teachers' Feelings of Preparedness, Teacher Quality: A Report on the Preparation and Quality of Teaching.* Retrieved at http://nces.ed.gov/surveys/frss/publications/1999080/6.asp on September 28, 2005.

Nelson, J. R., Martella, R., & Galand, B. (1998). The effects of teaching school expectations and establishing a consistent consequence on formal office disciplinary actions. *Journal of Emotional and Behavioral Disorders, 6*(3), 153–162.

Nelson, J. R., Roberts, M. L., Rutherford, R. B., Sarup, R. M., & Aaroe, L. A. (1999). A statewide survey of special education administrators and school psychologists regarding functional behavioral assessment. *Education and Treatment of Children, 22,* 267–279.

Nersesian, M., Todd, A. W., Lehmann, J., & Watson, J. (2000). School-wide behavior support through district-level system change. *Journal of Positive Behavior Interventions, 2,* 244–248.

Netzel, D. M., & Eber, L. (2003). Shifting from reactive to proactive discipline in an urban school district: A change of focus through PBIS implementation. *Journal of Positive Behavior Interventions, 5,* 71–79.

Ninness, H. A. C., Ellis, J., Miller, W. B., Baker, D., Rutherford, R. (1995). The effect of a self-management training package on the transfer if aggression control procedures in the absence of supervision. *Behavior Modification, 19,* 464–490.

Norris, J. A. (2003). Looking at classroom management through a social and emotional learning lens. *Theory Into Practice, 42,* 313–318.

Office of Special Education Programs (OSEP) Center on Positive Behavior Interventions and Supports. (N.d.). Welcome to the National Technical Assistance Center on Positive Behavioral Interventions and Supports (PBIS). Retrieved June 24, 2008, from http://www.pbis.org

Perry, N. E., Van de Kamp, K. O., Mercer, L. K., & Nordby, C. J. (2002). Investigating teacher student interactions that foster self-regulated learning. *Educational Psychologist, 37,* 5–15.

Reid, R., & Nelson, R. (2002). The utility, acceptability, and practicality of functional behavioral assessment for students with high-incidence problem behaviors. *Remedial and Special Education, 23,* 15–23.

Reinke, W. M., Herman, K. C., & Tucker, C. M. (2006). Building and sustaining communities that prevent mental disorders: Lessons from the field of special education. *Psychology in the Schools, 43,* 313–329.

Rotholz, D. A., & Ford, M. E. (2003). Statewide system change in positive behavior support. *Mental Retardation, 41,* 354–364.

Safran, S. P., & Oswald, K. (2003). Positive behavior support: Can schools reshape discipline practices? *Exceptional Children, 69,* 361–373.

Sailor, W., Zuna, N., Choi, J. H., Thomas, J., McCart, A., & Roger, B. (2006). Anchoring schoolwide positive behavior support in structural school reform. *Research and Practice for Persons With Severe Disabilities, 31,* 18–30.

Scott, T. M., & Barnett, S. B. (2004). Using staff and student time engaged in disciplinary procedures to evaluate the impact of school-wide PBS. *Journal of Positive Behavior Interventions, 6,* 21–27.

Scott, T. M., & Eber, L. (2003). Functional assessment and wraparound as systemic school processes: Primary, secondary and tertiary systems examples. *Journal of Emotional and Behavioral Disorders, 5,* 131–143.

Scott, T. M., Liaupsin, C., Nelson, C. M., & McIntyre, J. (2005). Team-based functional behavior assessment as a proactive public school process: A descriptive analysis of current barriers. *Journal of Behavioral Education, 14,* 57–71.

Scott, T. M., Meers, D. T., & Nelson, C. M. (2000). Toward a consensus of functional behavioral assessment for students with mild disabilities in public school contexts: A national survey. *Education and Treatment of Children, 23,* 265–285.

Scott, T. M., & Nelson, C. M. (1999). Using functional behavioral assessment to develop effective intervention plans: Practical classroom applications. *Journal of Positive Behavior Interventions, 1,* 242–251.

Scott, T. M., Nelson, C. M., & Zabala, J. (2003). Functional behavior assessment training in public schools: Facilitating systemic change. *Journal of Positive Behavior Interventions, 5,* 216–224.

Sinclair, M. F., Christenson, S. L., Evelo, D. L., & Hurley, C. (1998). Dropout prevention for youth with disabilities: Efficacy of a sustained school engagement procedure. *Exceptional Children, 65*(1), 7–21.

Singer, H. S., Gert, B., & Koegel, R. L. (1999). A moral framework for analyzing the controversy over aversive behavioral interventions for people with severe intervention. *Journal of Positive Behavior Interventions, 2,* 88–100.

Skiba, R. J., & Peterson, R. (2000). School discipline at a crossroads: From zero tolerance to early response. *Exceptional Children, 66,* 335–347.

Skiba, R. & Peterson, R. (2000). School discipline at a crossroads: From zero tolerance to early response. *Exceptional Children, 32,* 200-216.

Skinner, B. F. (1953). *Science and human behavior.* New York: Macmillan.

Snell, M. E. (2005). Fifteen years later: Has positive programming become the expected technology for addressing problem behavior? A commentary on Homer [sic] et al. (1990). *Research and Practice for Persons with Severe Disabilities, 30,* 11–14.

Snell, M. E. (2006). What's the verdict: Are students with severe disabilities included in school-wide positive behavior support? *Research and Practice for Persons with Severe Disabilities, 31,* 54–56, 62–65.

Snell, M. & Janney, R. (2000). Teachers' guide to inclusive practices: Social relationships and peer support. Baltimore: Paul H. Brookes Publishing.

Stroul, B. A., & Freidman, R. (1986). *A system of care for severely emotionally disturbed children and youth.* Washington, DC: CASSP Technical Assistance Center.

Sugai, G., & Horner, R. (2002a). The evolution of discipline practices: School-wide positive behavior supports. *Child and Family Behavior Therapy, 24*, 23–50.

Sugai, G., & Horner, R. H. (2002b). Introduction to the special series on positive behavior supports in schools. *Journal of Emotional and Behavioral Disorders, 10*, 130–135.

Sulzar-Azaroff, B., & Mayer, G.R. (1991). *Behavior analysis for lasting change.* Orlando: FL: Holt, Rinehart and Winston, Inc.

Taylor-Greene, S., Brown, D., Nelson, L., Longton, J., Gassman, T., Cohen, J., et al. (1997). School-wide behavioral support: Starting the year off right. *Journal of Behavioral Education, 7*, 99–112.

Taylor-Greene, S. J., & Kartub, D. T. (2000). Durable implementation of school-wide behavior support: The high five program. *Journal of Positive Behavior Interventions, 2*(4), 233–235.

Tobin, T., & Martin, M. (2001). Can discipline referrals be reduced by functional behavioral assessment. Paper presented at the Annual Meeting of the Council for Exceptional Children, Kansas City, MO.

Todd, A., Haugen, L., Anderson, K., Spriggs, M. (2002). Teaching recess: Low cost efforts producing effective results. *Journal of Positive Behavior Interventions, 4*(1), 46-52.

Turnbull, A., Edmonson, H., Griggs, P., Wickham, D., Freeman, R., Guess, D., et al. (2002). A blueprint for schoolwide positive behavior support: Implementation of three components. *Exceptionality, 68*, 377–402.

Turnbull, A., Edmonson, H., Griggs, P. Wickham, D., Sailor, W. Freeman, R., Guess, D., Lassen, S., et al. (2002). A blueprint for schoolwide positive behavior support: Implementation of three components. *Exceptional Children, 68*, 2002.

Turnbull, A., Turnbull, R., & Leal, D. (1999). *Exceptional lives: Special education in today's schools.* Upper Saddle River, NJ: Merrill.

Turnbull, H. R., Wilcox, B. L., Stowe, M., & Turnbull, A. P. (2001). IDEA requirements for use of PBS: Guidelines for responsible agencies. *Journal of Positive Behavior Interventions, 3*, 11–18.

U.S. Department of Education. (2001). *Twenty-third annual report to Congress on the implementation of the Individuals with Disabilities Education Act.* Washington, DC: Author.

Van Acker, R., Boreson, L., Gable, R. A., & Potterton, T. (2005). Are we on the right course? Lessons learned about current FBA/BIP practices in schools. *Journal of Behavioral Education, 14*, 35–56.

Vaughn, B. (2006). The wave of PBS: Who is left behind? *Research and Practice for Persons with Severe Disabilities, 31*, 66–69.

Wagner, G. A. (2002). Person-centered planning from a behavioral perspective. In S. Holburn & P. M. Vietze (Eds.), *Person-centered planning: Research, practice and future directions.* Baltimore: Paul H. Brookes.

Walker, H. M., Horner, R. H., Sugai, G., Bullis, M., Sprague, J. R., Bricker, D., et al. (1996). Integrated approaches to preventing antisocial behavior patterns among school-age children and youth. *Journal of Emotional and Behavioral Disorders, 4,* 194–209.

Watson, T. S., & Steege, M. W. (2003). *Conducting school-based functional behavior assessments: A practitioner's guide.* New York: Guilford.

Wehmeyer, M. L. (2002). The confluence of person-centered planning and self-determination. In S. Holburn & P. M. Vietze (Eds.), *Person centered planning: Research, practice, and future directions.* Baltimore, MD: Paul H. Brookes Publishers.

Weigle, K. L. (1997). Positive behavior support as a model for promoting educational inclusion. *Journal of the Association for Persons with Severe Handicaps, 22,* 36–48.

5

Fostering Social Competence in Schools

Barry Barbarasch

Maurice J. Elias

High-stakes tests. Substance abuse. Suicide. Academic standards. Delinquency. Media and technology. Teacher retention. Interpersonal violence. Dropouts. Changes in families. The list of issues facing today's educators and students is daunting. But genuinely effective schools—those that prepare students not only to pass tests at school but also to pass the tests of life—are finding that social-emotional competence and academic achievement are interwoven and that integrated, coordinated instruction in both areas maximizes students' potential to succeed in school and throughout their lives. Schools are now seen as "an important if not central arena for health promotion [and] primary prevention ... in addition to the education of students" (Roeser, Eccles, & Samoroff, 2000, p. 467). These findings are not surprising, as shown in the work of Wang, Haertel, and Walberg (1997). They examined 28 categories of influences on learning, which they based on reviews of 179 handbook chapters, 91 research syntheses, and surveys of 61 national experts. Wang et al. (1997) found that 8 of the 11 most influential categories involved social and emotional factors (e.g., student–teacher social interactions, classroom climate, and peer group). Further, according to the National Center for Education Statistics (2002), among the major reasons cited for dropping out of school, several involve social and emotional factors: not getting along with teachers or peers (35.0% and 20.1%, respectively), feeling left out (23.2%), and not feeling safe (12.1%; National Center for Education Statistics, 2002). Thus, it is understandable that Wang et al. concluded that "direct intervention in the psychological determinants of learning promises the most effective avenues of reform" (p. 210), which supports providing social and emotional learning in schools.

Social and Emotional Learning Defined

In simple terms, social and emotional learning (SEL) is the capacity to recognize and manage emotions, solve problems effectively, and establish positive relationships with others, competencies that clearly are essential for all students. Thus, SEL targets a combination of behaviors, cognitions, and emotions. As described by the Collaborative for Academic, Social, and Emotional Learning (CASEL), SEL is the process of acquiring and effectively applying the knowledge, attitudes, and skills necessary to recognize and manage emotions; developing caring and concern for others; making responsible decisions; establishing positive relationships; and handling challenging situations capably. Similar to the way students learn academic skills, they learn, practice, and apply SEL skills by engaging in positive activities in and out of the classroom. Initial skills that they have learned become enhanced, nuanced, and better integrated over time to address the increasingly complex situations children face in terms of academics, social relationships, citizenship, and health (Collaborative for Academic, Social, and Emotional Learning [CASEL], 2003; Elias et al., 1997).

SEL largely evolved from research on prevention and social competence (Consortium on the School-Based Promotion of Social Competence, 1994), social learning theory, and emotional competence (Elias, Parker, Kash, Weissberg, & O'Brien, in press), and interest in SEL ignited in the mid-1990s with the publication of Goleman's *Emotional Intelligence* (1995) and Gardner's *Multiple Intelligences* (1993). A high level of interest continues over a decade later, with research showing an increasing number of positive outcomes of SEL and states and school districts adopting requirements for teaching SEL (Zins, Weissberg, Wang, & Walberg, 2004). Indeed, growing numbers of educators and parents recognize the relationships between academic and social-emotional learning, particularly within the context of schools' systems of support.

SEL also fits well with the response-to-intervention (RTI) model utilized to identify children with disabilities. This is a three-tiered model, in which each level represents an increased intensity and frequency of service (Burns & Coolong-Chafflin, 2006). SEL programs are a particularly good fit with Tier I programming. Tier I has been conceptualized as the tier in which all children receive programming involving teaching children social skills that all students are expected to display. It consists of schoolwide expectations, rules, procedures, as well as lesson plans to teach them. It is seen as a preventive approach that not only teaches but also reinforces students for displaying these behaviors. SEL approaches may also be utilized for Tier II and Tier III interventions. Students at Tier II have been identified as requiring additional support. Interventions may include social skills groups, group counseling, and mentoring. Students at Tier III require a more in-depth assessment regarding their educational and social emotional needs. Data from students functioning at Tier I, and the response to Tier II interventions, would provide valuable information. Functional behavioral assessments and/or behavior rating scales could be utilized and serve as the basis for a behavior improvement plan (BIP; Sandomierski, Kincaid, & Algozzine, 2007). SEL would provide continuity, and serve as the basis for the assessment and intervention process. An RTI approach applied to social competence emphasizes universal interventions as well as classroom and schoolwide implementation. This not only makes SEL an ideal approach for facilitating the development of social competence but also provides baseline data for children who may develop the need for more intensive services.

Systems of Support

Instruction in SEL is provided in the context of caring, safe, well-managed, and participatory classroom, school, and other learning environments. Those learned skills are then reinforced in the school, home, and community. Social-emotional instruction thereby benefits all children, not only those who are at risk but also those beginning to engage in negative behaviors and those already displaying significant problems. The focus of most SEL programs is universal prevention and promotion—that is, preventing behavior problems by promoting social and emotional competence. Smaller numbers of students may require moderate to intensive treatment that focuses on social-emotional competence, but SEL programming is intended to enhance the growth of all children, to help them develop healthy behaviors, and to prevent their engaging in maladaptive and unhealthy behaviors. This also fits well with the Tier I interventions of RTI described above, with its focus on universal programming and promotion of social competencies.

Such efforts should be viewed within the context of a system of support that provides a comprehensive continuum of services based on student needs. The continuum involves three system levels that support the academic and social-emotional development of all students. Additionally, the costs associated with providing the necessary support at each level are spread out across many students at the prevention and promotion level, which results in a relatively small cost per student; however, the costs rise as the intensity of the support increases. Hence, the cost per student is much higher for early intervention and treatment, particularly for the latter.

As a system of support, SEL is a unifying concept for organizing, coordinating, and integrating school-based prevention and promotion programs that minimizes fragmentation and reduces marginalization of these efforts. The most effective, sustained approaches involve students, parents, educators, and community members as partners in planning, implementing, and evaluating SEL efforts. Systematic social and emotional education begins in preschool, continues through high school, is intentionally linked to academics, and is an integral component of the school curriculum (CASEL, 2003; Elias et al., 1997).

Problems and Implications

In today's society, children face countless situations that can have a negative effect on their social-emotional and academic development and ultimately on their happiness in life. For example, the United States arguably is more deeply divided and confused today than it has been since the civil rights and Vietnam War eras, as we grapple with issues such as preemptive war, civil liberties, personal freedoms versus national security, abortion, the definition of marriage, affirmative action, and immigration. Inequities between the richest and poorest households continue to widen and are the widest since these data were first recorded in the 1960s (Wollman et al., 2003). In the past, menaces to world peace were well known; now they may be anonymous, fanatical terrorists who don't discriminate between soldiers and civilians, who hide within the general populace, and who might be the person sitting next to you on a plane or walking by you at the mall, which can lead to a generalized sense of insecurity and fear.

Fifty years ago, social institutions and political leaders were highly respected and influential. Children did not pick up the morning paper to learn about sexual abuse by religious leaders or the lurid details of political figures' sexual indiscretions. The evening television news was not filled with stories of business executives and cultural icons being sent to prison because of their unethical, illegal behavior that betrayed and harmed the future of thousands of their employees and investors, nor was it saturated with nightly discussions of war and terror on a world scale with impending implications on our doorsteps.

Previous generations of parents did not have to be Internet savvy. "Dangerous strangers" supposedly lurked around the corner or on the other side of town, but they did not exist in children's bedrooms or the family room via Internet chat rooms and easily accessible pornographic Web sites. Video games, such as Grand Theft Auto and Halo 3, had not been invented, and the media were not as notorious about delivering messages that encourage unhealthy behaviors. In the past, children's sporting events were not scheduled every day of the week and from morning to late in the evening on weekends, thereby putting tremendous pressures on families and their values. Today, many role models are tarnished, unethical behavior seems commonplace, and new opportunities to develop and engage in negative behaviors abound. More than ever, students are faced with uncertainty in their daily lives and in their futures, and many feel a sense of insecurity, disenfranchisement, disillusionment, and even fear. For all of these reasons, SEL is perhaps more important than ever as an essential component of school reform (Zins, Walberg, & Weissberg, 2004).

Actions for Prevention and Promotion

Why Students Should Be Taught SEL

Developing social-emotional competence is a key to success in school and in life. We know that emotions affect how and what we learn, that caring relationships provide the foundation for lasting learning, and that important SEL skills and knowledge can be taught. Research shows that SEL has positive effects on academic performance, benefits physical health, improves citizenship, is demanded by employers, is essential for lifelong success, and reduces the risk of maladjustment, failed relationships, interpersonal violence, substance abuse, and unhappiness (Elias et al., 1997; Zins et al., 2004).

Many of today's prevention and promotion initiatives are fragmented, which does not contribute to their collective effectiveness. Schools nationally implement a median of 14 practices (among them, metal detectors, advisory periods, recreational activities, architectural features of the school, school change management practices, and informational posters and brochures) to prevent problem behavior and promote safe environments (Gottfredson & Gottfredson, 2001), so it is easy to understand why such efforts may not be coordinated. The result is lost opportunities to reinforce skills across programs and activities, as well as competition for resources. However, SEL can serve as the organizing framework for a broad array of prevention and promotion efforts (Elias et al., 1997). As noted above, a number of school professionals, such as school psychologists, have expertise in the areas of program development and implementation, and therefore, they can play an integral role in the planning and implementation of SEL programs that are coordinated within and across grade levels and schools.

Key Components of Effective SEL

Five key SEL competencies are taught, practiced, and reinforced through SEL programming (CASEL, 2003):

- *Self-awareness*: Identification and recognition of one's own emotions, recognition of strengths in self and others, sense of self-efficacy, and self-confidence
- *Social awareness*: Empathy, respect for others, and perspective taking
- *Responsible decision making*: Evaluation and reflection, and personal and ethical responsibility
- *Self-management*: Impulse control, stress management, persistence, goal setting, and motivation
- *Relationship skills*: Cooperation, help seeking and providing, and communication

As noted earlier, these competencies are taught most effectively within caring, supportive, and well-managed learning environments. Development of autonomy, self-discipline, and ethics is more likely in environments in which mutual respect, cooperation, caring, and decision making are the norm (Bear, 2005). Such contexts are structured in ways that encourage students to explore and try new learning activities, provide them with easily accessible opportunities to address their personal needs and problems, and support them in establishing positive relationships with peers and adults. As a result, students feel safe and secure and are not fearful of making mistakes. Ultimately, a reciprocal relationship exists between SEL skills and school climate. A positive school environment promotes SEL, and SEL facilitates a supportive climate. Because social, emotional, and academic growth are interdependent, the result is synergistic progress in all of these areas.

TABLE 5.1 Outline of Effective Social and Emotional Learning (SEL) Instruction

- Based on theory and research and carefully planned
- Interactively teaches SEL skills for applications to daily life
- Builds connections to school through caring, engaging classroom and school practices
- Promotes developmentally and culturally appropriate instruction
- Leads to coordinated, integrated, and unified programming linked to academic outcomes
- Enhances school performance by addressing emotional and social dimensions of learning by engaging, and interactive methods
- Involves school–family–community partnerships
- Establishes organizational supports and policies that foster success
- Provides high-quality staff development and support
- Addresses key implementation and sustainability factors, including continuous improvement, outcomes evaluation, and dissemination factors

Source: Based on Elias et al. (1997); and Collaborative for Academic, Social, and Emotional Learning (2003).

A comprehensive list of 37 guidelines for developing SEL can be found in *Promoting Social and Emotional Learning: Guidelines for Educators* (Elias et al., 1997). These guidelines, which are summarized in 10 major points in Table 5.1, describe in detail what effective SEL instruction entails. For example, it must be systematic, provided over multiple years, integrated with the academic curriculum, and supported by school–family–community partnerships and a caring supportive environment. In addition, in recent years, SEL programming has been linked with the development of a positive school climate. Joe Zins pioneered this work with the Ohio Department of Education. Together, they developed nine useful guidelines specific to school climate, which are presented in Table 5.2 (Zins & Elias, 2006).

SEL programming should be approached from a risk and resilience perspective. In other words, children may acquire risk processes, such as school failure, involvement with antisocial peers, or family poverty, that make it more likely that they will develop problem behaviors. The more risk processes they have, the higher their relative risk, although having risk processes does not guarantee that a student will develop problems, and many of them do not. On the other hand, protective mechanisms or the development of competencies—such as bonding to school, learning to consider the perspectives of others, and possessing adequate social decision-making skills—keeps children from harm's way or buffers them from the negative effects of such harms, and thus leads to more successful

TABLE 5.2   Ohio Guidelines for School Climate

Guideline 1. Operational principles for local schools that are grounded in best practices for academic achievement and are espoused by the community will produce effective systems.

Guideline 2. School–community partnerships enable the provision of comprehensive services for students and staff.

Guideline 3. Regular, thorough assessment and evaluation result in continuous improvement.

Guideline 4. High-quality staff development and administrative support lead to effective program implementation.

Guideline 5. Addressing real and perceived threats to safety and security enables students to focus on learning and teachers to focus on instruction.

Guideline 6. A student's sense of belonging in the classroom encourages classroom participation, positive interactions, and good study habits.

Guideline 7. Engagement of parents and families in school–home learning partnerships maximizes the potential for effective instruction and student learning.

Guideline 8. Youth engagement in forming school policy and procedures integrates an essential perspective into proposed solutions.

Guideline 9. High-quality food service supports improvements in academic performance and behavior.

Source: From Center for Students, Families, and Community (2004).

adaptation. These positive, health-promoting processes may be found within the child and at the family and community levels.

Evidence-Based SEL

Research Support

The past two to three decades have seen great progress in educational researchers' and practitioners' knowledge of how to prevent social-emotional and other problems, and in how to promote competence and health-enhancing behaviors. A growing number of programs, strategies, and techniques are available for promoting healthy development and preventing negative outcomes, and a stronger empirical base has emerged in the SEL field (Greenberg et al., 2003). Thus, a number of evidence-based SEL curricula and programs are available that lead to outcomes such as the prevention of substance abuse and interpersonal violence and to the promotion of mental health, positive youth development, and academic achievement (e.g., Catalano, Berglund, Ryan, Lonczak, & Hawkins, 2002; Durlak & Wells, 1997; Elias & Arnold, 2006; Gottfredson & Wilson, 2003; Tobler et al., 2000;

Zins, Weissberg, et al., 2004). Many of the positive outcomes found to be associated with SEL interventions are summarized in Table 5.3.

Although many research and practice issues still need to be addressed, the empirical investigations behind current SEL evaluation efforts include better study designs, use of manualized and readily replicable interventions, more analyses of longitudinal data leading to a better understanding of the operation of risk and protective processes, and improvements in knowledge of pathways and stages associated with development of maladaptive behaviors (Elias, Mitchell, & Haynes, in press; Greenberg, 2004; Mrazek & Haggerty, 1994). Consequently, the quality of the research support for school-based preventive interventions is substantially stronger (i.e., more than 60 randomized controlled trials) than four other areas of educational research (e.g., math education and staff development) examined by the U.S. Department of Education's Institute for Education Sciences (Whitehurst, 2003). A number of organizations have identified, reviewed, and rated evidence-based programs, and these are monitored by the Collaborative for Academic, Social, and Emotional Learning (www.CASEL.org); in addition, a National Registry of Effective Programs and Practices (NREPP; see http://modelprograms.samhsa.gov) has been established that includes the category of general substance abuse and treatment programs.

Costs

Evidence shows that effective SEL programs can provide a good return for their costs; that is, the value of their benefits exceeds their costs (Aos, Lieb, Mayfield, Miller, & Pennucci, 2004). For instance, providing the Seattle Social Development Program (Hawkins, Smith, & Catalano, 2004) costs $4,590 per student served annually, but its benefits were $14,426, or $3.14 per dollar spent per student. Likewise, the Child Development Project (now known as Caring School Community; Schaps, Battistich, & Solomon, 2004) has benefits of $28.42 for each dollar spent, and Life Skills Training (Botvin, 1998, 2002) has $25.61 in benefits. Examples of demonstrated benefits include improved educational outcomes (e.g., test scores and graduation rates), reduced crime, lowered substance abuse, and decreased teen suicide attempts. However, such programs do not result in positive benefits across the board, as some generate more costs than benefits. For example, Drug Abuse Resistance Education (D.A.R.E.) costs $99 per student served but has resulted in no benefit according to the criteria used (Aos et al., 2004). As with other areas of education, SEL programs must be examined carefully before being adopted.

TABLE 5.3   Examples of SEL Outcomes Related to Success in School and Life

Attitudes

Higher sense of self-efficacy

Better sense of community (bonding) and view of school as caring

Stronger commitment to democratic values

More positive attitudes toward school and learning

Improved ethical attitudes and values

Higher academic motivation and educational aspirations

Greater trust and respect for teachers

Improved coping with school stressors

Increased understanding of consequences of behavior

Behaviors

More prosocial behavior

Fewer absences and suspensions; maintained or improved attendance

More likely to work out own way of learning

Reductions in aggression, disruptions, and interpersonal violence

Fewer hostile negotiations, lower rate of conduct problems, and better conflict resolution skills

More classroom participation and higher engagement

Greater effort to achieve, and more frequent reading outside of school

Better transitions

Less drug, tobacco, and alcohol use and delinquent behavior

Decreases in sexually transmitted diseases, HIV/AIDS, and suicide

More involvement in positive activities (e.g., sports)

Performance

Improved math, language arts, and social studies skills

Increases in achievement over time (elementary to middle school)

Higher achievement test scores and no decreases in scores

More progress in phonological awareness

Improved learning-to-learn skill

Better problem solving and planning

Improved nonverbal reasoning

Source: Reprinted from "Facilitating Success in School and in Life Through Social and Emotional Learning," by J. E. Zins, M. J. Elias, and M. T. Greenberg, 2003, *Perspectives in Education,* 21(4), pp. 59–60. Copyright 2003 by *Perspectives in Education.* Reprinted with permission. See also Consortium on the School-Based Promotion of Social Competence (1994); Elias et al. (1997); Fredericks (2003); U.S. Department of Health and Human Services (2002); and Wilson, Gottfredson, and Najaka (2001).

Use

Evidence-based practices are not used as widely and effectively as they could be (Biglan, Mrazek, Carnine, & Flay, 2003), and we do not know enough about how to influence teachers, educational leaders, and schools to adopt and maintain such practices (Glasgow, Vogt, & Boles, 1999). As discussed later, the manner in which social-emotional instruction is delivered is also important (e.g., with fidelity to how it was planned), and we need to learn more about what reinforces the adoption of, adherence to, and sustainability of these interventions (Elias, Zins, Graczyk, & Weissberg, 2003). Significant "person power" issues also exist; far fewer personnel have been trained in SEL approaches than are needed for widespread dissemination. Although some progress is being made in making SEL part of the preparation of professionals such as school psychologists, counselors, and educators, efforts in these directions must be more extensive if they are to touch the many children who need them (Elias & Arnold, 2006; Zins, 2001).

The Implementation Process

This section contains a brief overview of key implementation issues. The following are examples of activities for school psychologists and other support staff members who wish to be involved in implementation efforts (these are discussed in more detail in Elias et al., 2003). Here, they may be best thought of as alternative starting points from which connections to other activities listed can be made. Much of the initial role of school mental health practitioners is to generate interest through action and enlist collaboration among others in the school until a "tipping point" is reached and momentum toward comprehensive attention to promoting children's social competence becomes a shared priority.

- *Conduct school and community risk and needs assessments for program planning.* Determine the need and readiness for social-emotional programming. Identify specific issues that could be addressed, examine what already is in place, and create forums for discussion of these issues.
- *Consult with school personnel.* Assist in exploring, adopting, implementing, and continuing SEL programming. Support educational leaders who are involved in implementing and integrating SEL-related efforts into the school culture and organizational routines.
- *Be a champion for SEL.* Be a leader, and promote the case for SEL instruction. Create specific examples in your schools of how SEL can

lead to safe, caring learning environments in classrooms or building-wide, with parents, and/or via after-school programming.

- *Promote organizational support.* Help develop policies and practices that will enhance SEL so that adequate support and resources are devoted to those efforts. Encourage the adoption of SEL in district curriculum standards by showing how other settings similar to yours have done this effectively.
- *Act as a liaison to coordinate and integrate school–family–community SEL efforts.* Work with parent groups and municipal and community organizations to ensure continuity and coordination of prevention messages and services.
- *Help ensure maintenance and sustainability.* Examine the integrity with which SEL programs are adopted, and monitor the adaptations that occur to promote high quality. Create the sense that SEL programs do work but, like most things, may require adjustment to be the right fit for your particular context. This can only occur through proper and ongoing evaluation efforts. Doing so will ensure that support and resources will continue to be devoted to these efforts.
- *Share findings publicly.* Assess the extent and quality of SEL program implementation using identified benchmarks, evaluate formatively and summatively whether goals are attained, and plan appropriate modifications to improve the quality of service delivery, the receptivity among staff and students, and the effectiveness of the efforts, all of which are interconnected.

Before examining more specific implementation issues, we must express two caveats. First, the field is a long way from systematically preparing school-based professionals to engage in the activities that make up SEL programs. Even with qualified personnel, the process of implementation takes time. It is common for adoption and institutionalization to take 3 to 5 years, so expectations about outcomes must be tempered based on that reality (Elias et al., 1997; Lippitt, Langseth, & Mossop, 1985).

Readiness and Sanction
To begin, how does a school know if it is ready to devote more efforts and resources to SEL, and if it is ready to adopt specific programming? The school will have many considerations, but among the first is to understand its organizational motivations and the need for change, as well as the outcomes it hopes to achieve. A first step is to perform an organizational analysis, involving interviews, observations, questionnaires, rating scales, examination of permanent products and records, and so forth, and that targets staff members, students, parents, and community members. The data collected will help the participants understand issues such as

organizational climate and health, communication processes, boundaries, roles, leadership styles, and external influences. Of particular importance at this early stage is an understanding of current related efforts and how new programming might help to better meet identified needs by either supplementing or replacing what is being done (Lippitt et al., 1985; Zins & Illback, 1993).

Once participants determine the school's readiness, they should identify program goals and reach consensus about which goals to address. In addition, sanction for implementation must be gained at the administrative, staff, and parent–community levels. Having champions of the cause within the organization is important, but beyond those individuals, the position taken by educational leaders, such as principals, is critical to ensuring sufficient support for role changes, ongoing staff development and coaching, scheduling, program monitoring and evaluation, and resource allocation. Ongoing staff development and coaching, for instance, are likely to lead to high-quality programming, fidelity, and sustainability.

Programming

Among the challenges at this point is to select appropriate evidence-based programming from the myriad of potential approaches. Fortunately, several program reviews are available that include ratings of effectiveness. These reviews help promote standards for quality SEL programming and enable educators to compare and select appropriate programs, based on the match between local needs and program effectiveness, goals, intervention techniques, strengths and limitations, costs, and so forth.

An excellent resource for ratings is *Safe and Sound: An Educational Leaders' Guide to Evidence-Based Social and Emotional Learning (SEL) Programs* (CASEL, 2003). The guide contains reviews and comparisons of 80 programs across 17 variables of interest, including the five key SEL skills listed earlier. To be included in the review, programming had to be school based and pertain to general education; consist of multiyear, sequenced instruction or an organizational structure to promote lessons beyond the first year; be systematic and comprehensive; have at least eight lessons in one program year; and be nationally available. The programs were rated on outcome effectiveness; how well the five key SEL skills are addressed; the availability of student assessment measures; if it includes support for schoolwide, family, and community involvement; and whether professional development is offered. Of this group, 21 were identified as *select* because they met CASEL standards for high-quality SEL instruction, ongoing professional development support, and evidence of effectiveness based on well-designed evaluations. Within the programs that included methods to promote the integration of SEL with academic curricula and teaching practices, an impressive 83% produced academic gains.

The core, active elements of the intervention (i.e., specifically what will be implemented, what are negotiable versus nonnegotiable aspects of program integrity, and how can differences compared with current practices, systems, and values be resolved) must be well understood by those seeking to adopt a program. Visiting a site to see the program operating, or talking with current users, usually provides insights that cannot be obtained elsewhere. Furthermore, all programs have limitations; schools must be wary of programs that are oversold by overzealous champions who build unwarranted expectations for them. Rather, by being aware of the strengths and limits of programs, and being able to predict many roadblocks and sources of resistance, schools often can learn to manage and address these problems (e.g., resistance, fear of failure, changing roles, scaling up too rapidly, and more ecological intrusion that results in unanticipated challenges) so that implementation may proceed more smoothly. School psychologists, who are trained in the areas of program planning and implementation, can be a valuable resource in making these determinations.

Ownership

Programs have associated values that must be supported by and compatible with relevant school policies, practices, and goals if they are to succeed. Buy-in from constituencies at different organizational levels, including parents and the community, must be ascertained, and their commitment established. School leadership and high-status individuals need to be involved early in the implementation process, and, ultimately, ownership needs to be created among all constituencies.

Roles and functions of stakeholders may be altered, but SEL program planners should recognize that the same job could be done in different ways. For instance, school psychologists do not have to spend the majority of their time conducting psychoeducational assessments and developing individual interventions. Instead, they may focus more energy on systems change by implementing SEL programs, which may decrease the press for direct services (Zins, 2001). Parents too can be true partners in deciding how SEL programming is delivered to their children, rather than being uninvolved or passive recipients.

Another implementation challenge is dealing with competing agendas. Elements of the organization may have different priorities, but consensus must be achieved to avoid battles over resources and direction of efforts, because such competition increases fragmentation and marginalization. The organization should review potential areas of conflict and fragmentation, such as for resources, roles of staff, boundaries, time allocation, priorities, and overlap (Novick, Kress, & Elias, 2002). Likewise, when the staff overspecializes or focuses too much on one area, such as on positive behavioral interventions and supports or on conflict resolution, rather than being broad based, too much energy may inadvertently be devoted to providing services rather than empowering individuals within the school.

Application

Numerous opportunities exist for the application of SEL concepts, such as the following (see Zins, Weissberg, et al., 2004):

- Adopt specific SEL curricula (e.g., the Second Step program).
- Infuse SEL activities into regular academic curricula (e.g., literacy and history).
- Develop supportive, caring learning environments (e.g., improve the school climate).
- Alter instructional processes (e.g., cooperative learning).
- Reinforce SEL skills as part of the informal curriculum (e.g., at lunch and in the playground).
- Promote school–family–community partnerships.
- Engage students actively and experientially in the learning process (e.g., via service learning).
- Reflect SEL in behavior management and discipline practices and policies.
- Integrate SEL methods into extracurricular activities (e.g., sports).

One of the more common concerns about adopting SEL programming is how it will fit into an already packed school day. As seen in the list above, the options require a range of adaptations, from relatively minor to more substantial changes in the school ecology. Introducing a specific SEL curriculum may be difficult in some schools, but using SEL principles to guide school discipline and behavior management practices may be less intrusive to organizational routines and resources. The goal is to infuse SEL into ongoing activities and program delivery systems in schools and communities to make the intervention sustainable. Likewise, organizational processes and structures must be established to ensure high-quality implementation and to promote sustainability (Greenberg, 2004). Without such safeguards, programs can easily drift from what was planned and intended, and core program elements inadvertently may be omitted because of time concerns. Such deviations from the program may affect outcomes. Often, the core, active elements of the intervention are not clear, so practitioners, researchers, and program developers must work together to identify them. Fortunately, many schools have successfully navigated these dilemmas and can serve as models for organizations embarking on this work (Elias & Arnold, 2006; Elias, Arnold, & Hussey, 2002; Elias et al., 1997; Lantieri, 2002).

Because implementing a program will usually involve making adaptations, even with highly structured, manualized interventions, one way to view this issue is to examine the quality and nature of the changes. Support staff members and classroom teachers should work together to anticipate and plan for modifications while they work to ensure that core program elements are maintained. Some adaptations are beneficial in terms of improving outcomes and facilitating ownership (and thus durability), whereas others harm program integrity. Furthermore, programs need to be tailored culturally to ethnic and racial minority children to maximize the programs' effectiveness (Botvin, 2004). In other words, the better the cultural fit is, the more likely that buy-in and perceptions of the program's relevance will occur.

Finally, systems to support SEL must be integrated across levels of prevention/promotion and treatment services (e.g., universal to indicated prevention and treatment; Adelman & Taylor, 2000), across student developmental levels, and across school, family, and community systems, as shown in Figure 5.1. The fragmentation and marginalization that characterize the educational and mental health systems today largely result from a lack of coordination and integration (Illback, Cobb, & Joseph, 1997); however, the system-wide adoption of SEL can reduce fragmentation and be a unifying conceptual scheme (Elias et al., 1997, 2003). School psychologists, with their knowledge of schools and school systems, and in how they interface with other systems, can take a strong leadership role in facilitating the integration of SEL programs.

Standards and Accountability

More attention should be devoted to state department of education instructional standards that include teaching SEL to further institutionalize and sustain such efforts. For example, in 2003, Illinois passed the Children's Mental Health Act (Public Act 93-0495), in which social and emotional development are defined as integral to schools' mission and essential to

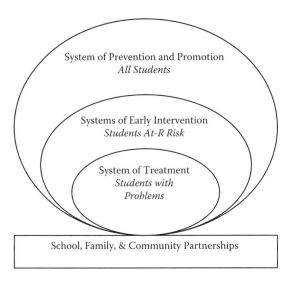

Figure 5.1   Integrated and Coordinated Systems to Support the Development of All Children

students' academic readiness and school success. The act is intended to ensure that schools incorporate the following:

- Regard social and emotional development as integral to their mission and a critical component of student academic readiness and school success.
- Take concrete steps to address their students' social and emotional development.
- Have the flexibility to include social and emotional learning in their school improvement plans.
- Develop a policy for incorporating social and emotional development into the district's educational program, including assessing social and emotional skills.
- Develop a policy for responding to children with social, emotional, or mental health problems that affect learning.

Social and emotional development standards are now included as part of the Illinois Learning Standards, which means that children's social-emotional development must be addressed in the curriculum. Consequently, all students in the state receive such instruction. One result of the Illinois legislation is that it has made paramount the need to measure social-emotional skills because every district must have a policy for incorporating social-emotional development into the district's educational program. That policy includes not only teaching and assessing SEL for all students but also responding to children who have social, emotional, or mental health problems that affect their learning. Likewise, it requires schools to be accountable for conducting valid and reliable assessments of social-emotional, academic, and health-related outcomes, as well as of school climate, based on input obtained from multiple constituencies (e.g., students, parents, teachers, and community members).

In addition, the Ministry of Education in Israel has mandated that all students in grades 1–9 nationwide in religious, secular, and mixed schools receive one hour of "Kishurai Chaim" ("Life Skills") each week for the entire school year. Further, the ministry is supporting this financially and programmatically, by creating a comprehensive and integrated social competence promotion curriculum to be used for this purpose, delivered by the teachers with training, consultation, and support provided by school psychologists and counselors (see Shadmi & Noy, 2002, for an early version of this plan; current information can be obtained from hshadmi@netvision.co.il).

Thus, SEL assessment is one area in need of further development and may be of special interest to many school-based mental health professionals. For purposes of accountability and acceptability, we need to determine that SEL has value-added outcomes for student learning, and we need to be able to assess the quality of the SEL instruction that occurs in the classroom. Although some school-based mental health professionals are involved in developing measures, others could examine indicators of competence, health, and the like to see how well they align with SEL constructs. There is no reason to delay making SEL part of standard assessment processes using the best measures available.

Summary

Students today must be prepared not only to pass tests at school but also to pass the tests of life. Social-emotional competence and academic achievement are highly related, and effective schools are focusing efforts on integrated, coordinated instruction in both areas to maximize students' potential to succeed in school and throughout their lives. A growing body of research demonstrates that evidence-based SEL interventions are associated with academic achievement, health, and citizenship, so a major challenge for schools is how to make SEL a core element of the curriculum and how to implement relevant programming with fidelity and in ways that are sustainable. SEL is also consistent with the provision of Tier I services for those utilizing response to intervention in addressing students' behavioral and social needs. These Tier I services can then be built upon in Tiers II and III to provide greater synergy and continuity than when different models are used at each level. Tremendous opportunities exist for school-based mental health professionals, including school psychologists, to assist schools in these endeavors, and additional training opportunities must be made available to prepare them for such roles.

Recommended Resources

Books and Other Printed Material

Elias, M. J., Zins, J. E., Weissberg, R. P., Frey, K. S., Greenberg, M. T., Haynes, N. M., et al. (1997). *Promoting social and emotional learning: Guidelines for educators.* Alexandria, VA: Association for Supervision and Curriculum Development. The authors define the field of social and emotional learning. They draw upon the most recent scientific studies, the best theories, site visits carried out around the country, and their own extensive experiences to describe effective approaches to SEL. The discussion is framed by 39 concise guidelines for promoting SEL.

Greenberg, M. T., Weissberg, R. P., O'Brien, M. U., Zins, J. E., Fredericks, L., Resnik, H., et al. (2003). Enhancing school-based prevention and youth development through coordinated social and emotional learning. *American Psychologist, 58,* 466–474. In this article, the authors make the case for the widespread implementation of beneficial prevention programming. They advocate for research-based, comprehensive school reform models that improve social, health, and academic outcomes; school policies that demand accountability for fostering children's overall development; professional development related to helping educators implement programs effectively; and ongoing monitoring and evaluation to guide school improvement.

Zins, J. E., Weissberg, R. P., Wang, M. C., & Walberg, H. J. (Eds.). (2004). *Building academic success on social and emotional learning: What does the research say?* New York: Teachers College Press. This comprehensive book contains a concise review of the field of social and emotional learning (SEL), with a specific examination of its effect on academic achievement and school success. Relevant outcomes from a number of the best SEL programs nationally are reviewed, leading the editors to conclude that "there is a growing body of scientifically based research supporting the strong impact that enhanced social and emotional behaviors can have on success in school and ultimately in life" (p. 19).

Web Sites

Collaborative for Academic, Social, and Emotional Learning (CASEL; http://www.casel.org): CASEL is a major national organization whose mission is to enhance children's success in school and in life by promoting coordinated, evidence-based social, emotional, and academic learning as an essential part of education from preschool through high school. CASEL's three primary goals are to advance the science of SEL; expand coordinated, evidence-based practice; and build a sustainable and collaborative organization to accomplish its mission.

Center for Social and Emotional Education (CSEE; http://www.csee.net): CSEE is an educational and professional development organization dedicated to supporting effective social-emotional learning, teaching, and leadership in K–12 schools. It integrates research and best practices in education, including risk prevention, health promotion, mental health, effective citizenry, character education, and social-emotional learning to promote students' ability to learn and develop in healthy ways.

Substance Abuse and Mental Health Services Administration (SAMHSA), U.S. Department of Health and Human Services (http://www.samhsa.gov): SAMHSA's mission is to build resilience in and facilitate recovery for people with or at risk for substance abuse problems and mental illness. Its vision is a life in the community for everyone, and it supports a variety of school-based prevention efforts.

School Mental Health Project (SMHP), University of California, Los Angeles (http://smhp.psych.ucla.edu): The mission of the SMHP is to improve outcomes for young people by enhancing the field of mental health in schools. It connects mental health and psychosocial concerns with school reform and improvement by integrating health and related concerns into a broad perspective that includes addressing barriers to learning and promoting healthy development.

References

Adelman, H., & Taylor, L. (2000). Moving prevention from the fringes into the fabric of school improvement. *Journal of Educational and Psychological Consultation, 11,* 7–26.

Aos, S., Lieb, R., Mayfield, J., Miller, M., & Pennucci, A. (2004). *Benefits and costs of prevention and early intervention programs for youth.* Olympia: Washington State Institute for Public Policy.

Bear, G. G. (with Cavalier, A., & Manning, M.). (2005). *Developing self-discipline and preventing and correcting misbehavior.* Boston: Allyn & Bacon.

Biglan, A., Mrazek, P., Carnine, D. W., & Flay, B. R. (2003). The integration of research and practice in the prevention of youth problem behaviors. *American Psychologist,* 5i8, 433–440.

Botvin, G. J. (1998). Preventing adolescent drug abuse through Life Skills Training: Theory, methods, and effectiveness. In J. Crane (Ed.), *Social programs that work* (pp. 225–257). New York: Russell Sage Foundation.

Botvin, G. J. (2002). *Life skills training.* White Plains, NY: Princeton Health Press.

Botvin, G. J. (2004). Advancing prevention science and practice: Challenges, critical issues, and future directions. *Prevention Science, 5,* 69–72.

Burns, M. K., & Coolong-Chaffin, M. (2006). Response to intervention: The role of and effect on school psychology. *School Psychology Forum: Research and Practice, 1*(1), 3–15. Retrieved July 9, 2007, from http://www.nasponline.org/publications/spf/issue1/burns.pdf

Catalano, R. F., Berglund, M. L., Ryan, J. A. M., Lonczak, H. S., & Hawkins, J. D. (2002). Positive youth development in the United States: Research findings on evaluations of positive youth development programs. *Prevention & Treatment, 5,* Article 15. Retrieved September 8, 2003, from http://journals.apa.org/prevention/volume5/pre0050015a.html

Center for Students, Families, and Community. (2004). *Ohio guidelines for school climate.* Columbus, OH: Author.

Collaborative for Academic, Social, and Emotional Learning. (2003). *Safe and sound: An educational leader's guide to evidence-based social and emotional learning (SEL) programs.* Chicago: Author.

Consortium on the School-Based Promotion of Social Competence. (1994). The promotion of social competence: Theory, research, practice, and policy. In R. J. Haggerty, L. Sherrod, N. Garmezy, & M. Rutter (Eds.), *Stress, risk, resilience in children and adolescents: Processes, mechanisms, and interaction* (pp. 268–316). New York: Cambridge University Press.

Durlak, J. A., & Wells, A. M. (1997). Primary prevention mental health programs for children and adolescents: A meta-analytic review. *American Journal of Community Psychology, 25,* 115–152.

Elias, M. J., & Arnold, H. A. (Eds.) (2006). *The educator's guide to emotional intelligence and academic achievement: Social-emotional learning in the classroom.* Thousand Oaks, CA: Corwin.

Elias, M. J., Arnold, H., & Hussey, C. (Eds.). (2002). *Leadership practices for caring and successful schools.* Thousand Oaks, CA: Corwin.

Elias, M. J., Gara, M., Schuyler, T., Branden-Muller, L., & Sayette, M. (1991). The promotion of social competence: Longitudinal study of a preventive school-based program. *American Journal of Orthopsychiatry, 61,* 409–417.

Elias, M. J., Parker, S. J., Kash, V. M., Weissberg, R. P., and O'Brien, M. U. (In press). Social and emotional learning, moral education, and character education: A comparative analysis and a view toward convergence. In L. Nucci & D. Narvaez (Eds.), *Handbook on moral education*. New York: Taylor & Francis.

Elias, M. J., Zins, J. E., Graczyk, P. A., & Weissberg, R. P. (2003). Implementation, sustainability, and scaling up of social–emotional and academic innovations in public schools. *School Psychology Review, 32*, 303–319.

Elias, M. J., Zins, J. E., Weissberg, R. P., Frey, K. S., Greenberg, M. T., Haynes, N. M., et al. (1997). *Promoting social and emotional learning: Guidelines for educators*. Alexandria, VA: Association for Supervision and Curriculum Development.

Elliott, D. S., & Mihalic, S. (2004). Issues in disseminating and replicating effective prevention programs. *Prevention Science, 5*, 47–53.

Fredericks, L. (2003). *Social and emotional learning, service-learning, and educational leadership*. Chicago: Collaborative for Academic, Social, and Emotional Learning.

Gardner, H. (1993). *Multiple intelligences: The theory in practice*. New York: Basic.

Glasgow, R. E., Vogt, T. M., & Boles, S. M. (1999). Evaluating the public health impact of health promotion interventions: The RE-AIM framework. *American Journal of Public Health, 89*, 1322–1327.

Goleman, D. (1995). *Emotional intelligence*. New York: Bantam.

Gottfredson, D. C., & Wilson, D. B. (2003). Characteristics of effective school-based substance abuse prevention. *Prevention Science, 4*, 27–38.

Gottfredson, G. D., & Gottfredson, D. C. (2001). What schools do to prevent problem behaviors and promote safe environments. *Journal of Educational and Psychological Consultation, 12*, 313–344.

Greenberg, M. T. (2004). Current and future challenges in school-based prevention. *Prevention Science, 5*, 5–13.

Greenberg, M. T., Weissberg, R. P., O'Brien, M. U., Zins, J. E., Fredericks, L., Resnik, H., & Elias, M. J. (2003). Enhancing school-based prevention and youth development through coordinated social and emotional learning. *American Psychologist, 58*, 466–474.

Hawkins, J. D., Smith, B. H., & Catalano, R. F. (2004). Social development and social and emotional learning. In J. E. Zins, R. P. Weissberg, M. C. Wang, & H. J. Walberg (Eds.), *Building academic success on social and emotional learning: What does the research say?* (pp. 135–150). New York: Teachers College Press.

Illback, R. J., Cobb, C. T., & Joseph, H. M., Jr. (Eds.). (1997). *Integrated services for children and families*. Washington, DC: American Psychological Association.

Lantieri, L. (Ed.). (2002). *Schools with spirit: Nurturing the inner lives of children and teachers*. Boston: Beacon.

Lippitt, G. L., Langseth, P., & Mossop, J. (1985). *Implementing organizational change: A practical guide to managing change efforts*. San Francisco: Jossey-Bass.

Mrazek, P. J., & Haggerty, R. J. (Eds.). (1994). *Reducing risks for mental disorders: Frontiers for preventive intervention research*. Washington, DC: National Academy Press.

National Center for Education Statistics. (2002). *Dropout rates in the United States 2000.* Washington, DC: U.S. Department of Education, Offices of Educational Research and Improvement.

Novick, B., Kress, J. S., & Elias, M. J. (2002). *Building learning communities with character: How to integrate academic, social, and emotional learning.* Alexandria, VA: Association for Supervision and Curriculum Development.

Roeser, R. W., Eccles, J. S., & Samoroff, A. J. (2000). School as a context of early adolescents' academic and social–emotional development: A summary of research findings. *Elementary School Journal, 100,* 443–471.

Ross, M. R., Powell, S. R., & Elias, M. J. (2002). New roles for school psychologists: Addressing the social and emotional learning needs of students. *School Psychology Review, 31*(2), 43–52.

Sandomierski, T., Kincaid, D., & Algozzine, B. (2007). Response to intervention and positive behavior support: Brothers from different mothers or sisters with different misters. *OSEP Technical Assistance Center on Positive Behavioral Interventions and Supports.* Retrieved July 9, 2007, from http://www.pbis.org/news/New/Newsletters/Newsletter4-2.aspx

Schaps, E., Battistich, V., & Solomon, D. (2004) Community in school as key to student growth: Findings from the Child Development Project. In J. E. Zins, R. P. Weissberg, M. C. Wang, & H. J. Walberg (Eds.), *Building academic success on social and emotional learning: What does the research say?* (pp. 189–205). New York: Teachers College Press.

Shadmi, C., & Noy, B. (2003). Promoting the social-emotional and intellectual well-being of students and the school as an ecosystem: From program to way of life. In M. J. Elias, H. A. Arnold, & C. S. Hussey (Eds.), *EQ + IQ = Best leadership practices for caring and successful schools.* Thousand Oaks, CA: Corwin.

Tobler, N. S., Roona, M. R., Ochshorn, P., Marshall, D. G., Streke, A. V., & Stackpole, K. M. (2000). School-based adolescent drug prevention programs: 1998 meta-analysis. *Journal of Primary Prevention, 20,* 275–337.

U.S. Department of Health and Human Services, Substance Abuse and Mental Services Administration. (2002). SAMHSA model programs: Model prevention programs supporting academic achievement. Retrieved January 23, 2003, from http://modelprograms.samsha.gov

Wang, M. C., Haertel, G. D., & Walberg, H. J. (1997). Toward a knowledge base for school learning. *Review of Educational Research, 63,* 249–294.

Whitehurst, G. R. (2003, October). Evidence-based safe and drug-free schools programs. Keynote address at Office of Safe and Drug-Free Schools National Conference, Washington, DC.

Wilson, D. B., Gottfredson, D. C., & Najaka, S. S. (2001). School-based prevention of problem behaviors: A meta-analysis. *Journal of Quantitative Criminology, 17,* 247–272.

Wollman, N., Yoder, B. L., Brumbaugh-Smith, J. P., Gross, H., Leiter, B. E., Fry-Miller, A. L., et al. (2003). *Poverty gaps in the U.S. between the races, age groups, and genders decreased steadily since 1995—but still a ways to go.* Retrieved July 3, 2008, from http://www.manchester.edu/links/violenceindex/NewsReleases/PovertyGapsInUS.pdf

Ysseldyke, J. E., Burns, M., Dawson, P., Kelly, B., Morrison, D., Ortiz, S., et al. (2006). *School psychology: A blueprint for training and practice III.* Bethesda, MD: National Association of School Psychologists. Retrieved July 9, 2007, from http://www.nasponline.org/resources/blueprint/FinalBlueprintInteriors.pdf

Zins, J. E. (2001). Examining opportunities and challenges for school-based prevention and promotion: Social and emotional learning as an exemplar. *Journal of Primary Prevention, 21*(4), 441–446.

Zins, J. E., & Elias, M. J. (2006). Social and emotional learning. In G. G. Bear & K. M. Minke (Eds.), *Children's needs III: Development, prevention, and intervention* (pp. 1-13). Bethesda, MD: National Association of School Psychologists.

Zins, J. E., Elias, M. J., Greenberg, M. T. (2003). Facilitating success in school and in life through social and emotional learning. *Perspectives in Education, 21*(4), 59–60.

Zins, J. E., & Illback, R. J. (1993). Implementing consultation in child services systems. In J. E. Zins, T. R. Kratochwill, & S. N. Elliott (Eds.), *Handbook of consultation services for children* (pp. 204–226). San Francisco: Jossey-Bass.

Zins, J. E., Walberg, H. J., & Weissberg, R. P. (2004). Getting to the heart of school reform: Social and emotional learning for school success. *NASP Communiqué, 33*(3), 35.

Zins, J. E., Weissberg, R. P., Wang, M. C., & Walberg, H. J. (Eds.). (2004). *Building academic success on social and emotional learning: What does the research say?* New York: Teachers College Press.

Section III

Targeted and Intensive Interventions

6

Applying Rational-Emotive Behavior Therapy in Schools

Ann Vernon

"What problem would you like to work on today?" the counselor asked the sullen young teenager sitting across the room staring at the floor.

"I don't know," he mumbled.

"Well, it's rather obvious that it wasn't your idea to pay me this visit," the counselor replied.

"You're right about that—this is the last place I'd rather be," he muttered.

"So tell me why you are here," encouraged the counselor.

"Because the stupid teacher said he would kick me out of class if I don't change. He's ticked at me because I haven't been turning in my homework and he says I'm lazy. He doesn't know what he is talking about.... I'm not lazy; I just hate his English class. Why should I write about dumb topics when I'm gonna be a mechanic and will never have to use this stuff?"

"I see," the counselor replied. "You're angry with the teacher because he wants you to change and you don't think this is your problem. You just want him off your back."

School practitioners can most likely identify with this scenario: the resistant client; the teacher who expects you to wave a magic wand and turn this student into the most enthusiastic, prolific writer in the class; and the challenge to you as the professional. Amidst all of your other duties, your job is to find a way to connect with this client in order to help him own the problem, realize that the likelihood of changing the teacher is minimal, assist him in dealing with his negative feelings resulting from demands and overgeneralizations, and help him understand the short- and long-term consequences of his behavior. And you don't have the magic wand!

But what you can have is knowledge about rational-emotive behavior therapy (REBT) and how to apply it with school-aged students. This theory has a long history of application in the schools. As Albert Ellis himself stated, "I have always believed in the potential of REBT to be used in schools as a form of mental health promotion and with young people experiencing developmental problems" (Ellis & Bernard, 2006, p. ix). Ellis and Bernard noted that REBT and rational-emotive education (REE), the educational derivative, have been adopted by many mental health practitioners who have found this approach to be highly effective. Not only does it work with individual clients, but practitioners can also apply the concepts to students in small groups and classroom guidance, and in consultation with teachers, parents, and other school personnel.

The purpose of this chapter is to provide a brief overview of REBT, with specific emphasis on applications with school-aged clients. As Ellis and Bernard (2006) pointed out, one of the misconceptions about REBT is that when it is practiced with young clients, it is simply "a downward extension of REBT adult methods" (p. xi). In fact, there are many specific techniques that are tailored to the developmental levels of children and adolescents, helping them learn REBT in their "own language" through unique methods designed to help them apply the theoretical constructs to their own lives.

Another important focus of this chapter will be on applications with individuals and small groups, as well as classroom guidance in the form of a specific emotional education curriculum based on REBT. A case study illustrating how to apply the theory, as well as a review of the effectiveness of REBT with children and adolescents for treating a variety of childhood disorders, will also be addressed.

Overview of Rational-Emotive Behavior Therapy

Brief History of REBT

As previously noted, REBT has a long-standing history of application with children, starting in the mid-1950s when Ellis pioneered this form of treatment with children as well as with their parents. In fact, Bernard, Ellis, and Terjesen (2006) pointed out that for the most part, REBT was the only cognitive-restructuring approach used with school-aged children throughout the 1950s and 1960s. In 1971, Ellis established the Living School to help young people learn rational principles that were introduced along with their regular elementary curriculum. During the 5-year existence of this school, teachers found that by deliberately teaching REBT principles, students improved their mental health. The school closed in

1975 in an effort to make a greater impact on children's mental health through consultation. Consequently, the Rational-Emotive Education Consultation Service was established, providing in-service workshops for teachers and counselors and consultation to schools regarding implementation of REE curriculum materials (Bernard et al., 2006).

Based on the success of the Living School, which established that elementary students could learn rational-emotive concepts that would have a positive impact on their behavior and emotional adjustment, numerous studies (discussed later in this chapter) were conducted in the 1970s to verify the efficacy of this approach with young people. In the 1980s, Ellis and Bernard (1983) published *Rational-Emotive Approaches to the Problems of Childhood*, a very comprehensive book that specifically described how this theory could be applied to treat a variety of childhood disorders such as obesity, anxiety and phobia, conduct disorders, low frustration tolerance, underachievement, childhood sexuality, and impulsivity. An additional focus was on working with parents and teachers and implementing rational-emotive education in the classroom and in small groups. Throughout the 1980s and 1990s, other publications specifically targeted the school-aged population. Bernard and Joyce (1984) published *Rational-Emotive Therapy With Children and Adolescents*, which thoroughly discussed applications of this theory with young clients, parents, and teachers. Barrish and Barrish (1985, 1989) wrote two practical books about parenting, and Knaus (1974) and Vernon (1989a, 1989b, 1998a, 1998b, 1998c) published rational-emotive education curricula to assist students in learning REE principles to promote positive mental health. In addition, Bernard and DiGiuseppe (1991) contributed to the field by writing *Rational-Emotive Consultation in Applied Settings*, discussing applications of the theory with parents and teachers so they could learn to apply the principles with children. Other publications, too numerous to mention, documented the process and effectiveness of utilizing this theory with young people.

Theoretical Overview

The primary goal of REBT is to help clients develop a rational philosophy of life that they can employ with present as well as future problems in order to reduce emotional stress and self-defeating behavior. Specifically, counselors assist clients in accepting themselves as fallible humans who should not equate their self-worth with their performance or expect that they have to win others' approval in order to be worthwhile. They also try to help clients become less demanding and intolerant of others (Dryden, DiGiuseppe, & Neenan, 2003; Dryden & Ellis, 2001). In addition, counselors work with clients to develop high frustration tolerance so that they can cope more effectively with daily hassles and life's conditions and learn that they can stand things that are uncomfortable or difficult.

According to Ellis (2001a, 2001b), the best way to reduce the emotional distress that is created by irrational thinking in the form of demands on self (I must be perfect), others (others should treat me fairly and exactly as I want to be treated), and the world (the world and everything in it should be fair, and I shouldn't have to work too hard for anything or withstand discomfort) is to help people change their thoughts so that they can experience less intense negative emotions, behave in more self-enhancing ways that will help them attain personal goals and lead happier and more fulfilling lives, and think more rationally and functionally.

Ideally, a major goal for the REBT counselor is to help clients achieve philosophic change, which means that they relinquish irrational beliefs and replace them with rational beliefs. In essence, they adopt a rational philosophy about life (Dryden, 2002b). In reality, this is often difficult for some clients, particularly children and adolescents, given their cognitive limitations. DiGiuseppe and Bernard (2006) cautioned that although it is easier to help children change misperceptions and dispute inferences, this can also be problematic. They cited the example of a child who says his parents don't love him, which in fact may be true. Therefore, if the counselor verifies this, it is better to try to help the child deal with this reality rather than to try to challenge his perceptions, which may jeopardize the relationship and only temporarily help the child. It is critical for the counselor to carefully assess the beliefs and determine if philosophic change is feasible. If not, then counselors can encourage young clients to make behavioral changes and challenge inferences and automatic thoughts in order to correct distorted thinking so they can view situations more accurately.

Ellis developed the A–B–C model to conceptualize the major constructs of REBT, as well as the process of change (Dryden, 1999; Dryden & Ellis, 2001; Ellis, 2001b). According to this theory, people erroneously assume that an activating event (A), which may be real or perceived, causes their negative emotions and self-defeating behaviors (C). However, it is not the event itself; two people could experience the same event but respond differently because of how they think about it. Therefore, emotional and behavioral consequences (C's) are affected by beliefs (B's) that may be rational and lead to self-helping consequences, or may be irrational and result in self-defeating consequences (Ellis, 2001b). To reduce the negative impact of irrational beliefs, these beliefs must be disputed (D), resulting in effective new beliefs (E) and more moderate, healthy emotions (F).

It is important to discuss the role of the REBT counselor, specifically with regard to working with children and adolescents. REBT counselors are active and involved, educating clients and helping them develop more effective problem solving skills. Unfortunately, being active and directive has been associated with a major misconception of REBT, which is that in order to practice the theory you must emulate Ellis, who prefers a very directive style with a deemphasis on the therapeutic relationship (DiGuiseppe, 2002; Dryden, 2003). Although Ellis himself prefers a more active, directive therapeutic style with most clients (Ellis, 2002a; Ellis & MacClaren, 1998), he has acknowledged that the degree to which one is active and directive is a choice. Dryden (2002a, 2002b) noted that the REBT literature has underplayed the importance of the relationship and stressed that counselors must be flexible. According to Dryden (1999), "Effective rational emotive behavioral counselors vary their therapeutic styles and can adopt a variety of therapeutic styles to fit with the therapeutic requirements of different clients" (p. 20).

Varying the therapeutic style is particularly essential when working with children and adolescents. Patience, flexibility, and less directiveness are critical aspects of the counseling process. Vernon (2002b) developed the C.A.R.E. model that describes various ways of connecting with young clients, including self-disclosure, having a sense of humor, and being warm and genuine. She discussed the use of games, art techniques, and specific get-acquainted activities as effective ways to build rapport with this population.

DiGiuseppe and Bernard (2006) noted that a positive working relationship is essential in working with children, but added that this relationship will develop throughout the counseling process. For this reason, REBT counselors begin almost immediately to work on the problem, combining relationship building with assessment and possibly intervention in this first session.

Effectiveness With Young Clients

There are many compelling reasons why REBT is especially appropriate for children and adolescents. First, it incorporates many techniques and concepts that help children and adolescents move beyond their concrete thinking tendencies that can become problematic throughout their development. Through creative, developmentally appropriate strategies, children can learn to distinguish between facts and assumptions and identify dichotomous thinking and other cognitive distortions, which helps them gain perspective that reduces negative emotion and behavior. Consequently, children develop behavioral and emotional self-control as they learn the connection between thoughts, feelings, and behaviors. Another important reason for using this theory with school-aged populations is that it teaches them what they realistically can and cannot change in their lives. Given the high preponderance of dysfunctional families, the negative impact of this can be mitigated somewhat by helping children focus on what they can control, which are their thoughts, feelings, and behaviors. For this reason, the theory is empowering.

Because it is a briefer form of counseling, it is very effective with young clients whose sense of time is more immediate. Given their stage of development, often the problem they present with today might not be a relevant issue tomorrow, and for this reason, they need something to help them *now* (Vernon, 2004b). Furthermore, with an educative focus, children learn concepts that they can apply to present problems as well as future concerns. This preventative emphasis can help minimize the severity of problems because children can apply the rational principles they learned when dealing with a past issue. The fact that REBT counselors promote skill acquisition and help clients develop practical coping skills throughout the counseling process is another salient feature of this theory. Teaching clients how to *think* better, which enables them to not only feel better but also *get* better because they correct the faulty thinking that creates and perpetuates problems, is another reason this approach is so effective. The fact that it can be readily adapted to children of most ages, cultural backgrounds, and intelligence levels also lends to its applicability.

Finally, this theory takes into account the developmental level of the client. DiGiuseppe and Bernard (2006) and Vernon (2002a) stressed the importance of using concrete examples employing practices that take into account the fact that they are active learners and need to learn REBT concepts in a variety of ways, often that involve "doing" and "seeing" as much as "hearing" (DiGiuseppe & Bernard, p. 88). Emotive, behavioral, and cognitive techniques that take developmental levels into account will be described in the remainder of this chapter.

Assessment and Case Conceptualization

DiGiuseppe and Bernard (2006) described two stages of the assessment process. First is problem identification, which can involve both formal and informal methods to determine if there is a problem and who owns it. This is especially important in working with young clients who are often referred by parents or teachers, because a child's misbehavior, for example, may be the adults' lack of knowledge about appropriate discipline methods rather than the actual behavior of the child. The second stage of the assessment process is the problem analysis stage, which is ongoing throughout the counseling process. In this stage, the analysis focuses on identification of irrational beliefs as well as on disturbed emotions and behaviors.

Dryden et al. (2003) developed an 18-step treatment sequence that best illustrates the stages of the counseling process and how change occurs. A description of the assessment part of this sequence will be subsequently described, with specific examples of how to tailor it to the child's developmental level.

The first step is to ask the client what problem he or she would like to work on, which may be somewhat different when working with children or adolescents, for several reasons. First, they may not be able to articulate the problem clearly. Second, they may be referred by someone else and therefore don't see the problem as their problem. Third, they may be reluctant consumers, unsure and hesitant about the counseling process. Consequently, the counselor may need to spend more time developing rapport and use various developmentally appropriate strategies to elicit the target problem. For example, if the child is reluctant to talk about the problem, invite him or her to draw a picture of it or act it out. If the practitioner is aware ahead of time what the presenting problem is, he or she could select a children's book with a similar theme, and after the child reads it, ask him or her how the character's problem is similar to their own.

If the client discloses more than one problem, the second step would be to agree on which problem to work on first. At this point the counselor also helps the client distinguish between emotional and practical problems. For example, an adolescent may have a practical problem, not completing homework, but feels anxious and guilty, which is the emotional problem. The third step involves selecting a concrete, realistic, and attainable goal. For children, the goal should be relatively short term because their sense of time is so immediate.

Step 4 involves specificity, which is especially important when working with younger clients. It is often helpful to ask for a specific example
of the target problem: "Can you give me an example of when this recently
happened?" "If we pretended that we were watching a movie about this
problem, what exactly would we see?" These strategies help the counselor
more accurately assess the A, B, and C.

In step 5, the counselor assesses the emotional consequence or the activating event, depending on whether the client first describes an event or
a feeling. Typically children and adolescents present the activating event,
and if this is the case, the counselor actively listens to the client's description of the problem. Generally speaking, REBT counselors do not encourage the client to elaborate extensively on the activating event (Dryden,
2002b), but that may vary depending on the nature and severity of the
problem. This point is especially pertinent when working with young clients, who may need more "talk time" because they don't have others who
assume an active listening role with them.

If the activating event was assessed in step 5, step 6 is assessing the C,
emotional and behavioral consequences. This step involves asking the client to describe how he or she feels relative to the activating event. Because
this could be difficult for children or even adolescents whose feeling
vocabulary may be limited, the counselor should employ various strategies such as feeling word lists, role play, pantomime (Vernon, 2002a), feel
wheels (Vernon, 2006a), or activities such as *How Do You Feel?* (Vernon,
2006a, pp. 125–126) or *Feeling Finders* (Vernon, 2006a, p. 37). To identify the degree of emotional intensity, REBT counselors frequently use an
emotional thermometer (DiGiuseppe & Bernard, 2006). In keeping with
the theory, counselors should ask, "How do you feel about the situation"
as opposed to "How does that situation make you feel?" (Dryden et al.,
2003, p. 25), because the latter reinforces the idea that A causes C. It is also
important to assess how the child behaved relative to the activating event.
This is especially critical in working with younger clients because although
they may not accurately label the emotion, the behavioral response clues
in the counselor to what the child may have been feeling. "When you felt
mad, what did you do?" is a direct way to elicit the behavior, or you can
ask the child to show you how she acted or draw a cartoon about it if the
child isn't very verbal.

After the activating event and the emotional and behavioral consequences have been assessed, the counselor and client agree upon a goal
with regard to the assessed problem (step 7). This may involve helping the
client understand the consequences of the unhealthy negative emotion and

behavior so that there is more motivation to identify a goal, which should be realistic and specific. Helping the client understand the link between the problem as the defined goal and the problem as the assessed goal is the next step (step 8), which is followed by identifying and assessing any relevant meta-emotional problems (step 9) such as being depressed about being depressed, according to Dryden (2002b).

Step 10 is to teach the connection between feelings and behaviors (C) and beliefs (B). It is often helpful to use a specific example, such as asking the adolescent client to describe how she felt about not being chosen for the honor band. After ascertaining how she felt in this circumstance, ask the client if she knows of others who were rejected and if they felt the same way. After determining that different people feel differently about the same event, help her see that feelings are based on beliefs: If she took this rejection to mean she was a failure, she would be more upset than someone else who didn't view this as being a personal failure, but rather on the fact that there were lots of competent musicians vying for a limited number of spots.

When the B–C link is clear, step 11 is to assess the irrational beliefs, which is the major objective of the REBT assessment process. It is important to remember that not all beliefs are irrational. For example, if a child comes to counseling feeling very sad that his grandmother died, the counselor would probe for any irrational beliefs such as "This is so awful I will never be able to stand it" or "I can't go on living if my grandma isn't in my life," but it is also very likely that the child's beliefs are rational, in which case you would simply help the child deal with his grief. Identifying irrational beliefs can be more difficult with younger clients because they may not be conscious of their irrational thinking. Therefore, the counselor needs to employ various techniques such as using thought bubbles (empty clouds drawn over a head) to help elicit specific beliefs relative to an activating event, eliciting beliefs through puppets with younger children (Vernon, 2002a), and using open-ended questions such as "What was going through your mind?" or "Were you aware of any thoughts in your head?" (Walen, DiGiuseppe, & Dryden, 1992). DiGiuseppe and Bernard (2006) described the use of the instant replay technique ("Can you replay in your mind what happened last week when your mom got angry with you"), sentence completion ("When I have chores to do I think..."), and the expansion–contraction technique, where the client describes in his or her own words the thoughts about the problem and the counselor interjects prompts such as "What do you mean when you say you thought that ..." (p. 103). And, although it is important to search for the core

beliefs—self-demandingness, other-demandingness, and world-demand-
ingness (Dryden et al., 2003)—it is also appropriate when working with
younger clients to assess inferences and other distorted thinking patterns
such as tunnel vision, awfulizing and catastrophizing, overgeneralizing,
and dichotomous thinking because these also result in emotional disturbance. During the assessment process, it is important to identify the following specific irrational beliefs common to children (Waters, 1982):

1. It's awful if others don't like me.
2. I'm bad if I make a mistake.
3. Everything should always go my way; I should get what I want.
4. Things should come easy to me.
5. The world should be fair, and bad people must be punished.
6. I shouldn't show my feelings.
7. Adults should be perfect.
8. There's only one right answer.
9. I must win.
10. I shouldn't have to wait for anything. (p. 572)

Waters (1981) also enumerated irrational beliefs for adolescents:

1. It would be awful if my peers didn't like me. It would be awful to be a
   social loser.
2. I shouldn't make mistakes, especially social mistakes.
3. It's my parents' fault I'm so miserable.
4. I can't help it. That's just the way I am, and I guess I'll always be this
   way.
5. The world should be fair and just.
6. It's awful when things do not go my way.
7. It's better to avoid challenges than to risk failure.
8. I must conform to my peers.
9. I can't stand to be criticized.
10. Others should always be responsible. (p. 6)

Other age-appropriate techniques for assessing beliefs include playing
the game *Rational or Irrational* (Vernon, 2002a, pp. 48–49), which helps
adolescents learn to distinguish between rational and irrational beliefs so
that they can classify their own beliefs, or inference chaining (Vernon,
2002a, p. 49), where the counselor uses prompts such as "because ..." and
"and ..." to help the child with verbal expression ("When your teacher
doesn't call on you, you feel angry ... because ...?").

Applications in School Settings

The previous section addressed assessment of the activating event, the emotional and behavioral consequences, and irrational beliefs using the model developed by Dryden et al., (2003). The remaining steps in that model describe what occurs after assessment, although it is important to remember that this model may not be linear because assessment is ongoing even throughout the treatment phase.

Individual Counseling

Having assessed the irrational beliefs, step 12 is to connect the irrational beliefs to the emotional and behavioral consequence. It is preferable to elicit this from the client as opposed to telling the client that the connection exists. With children and adolescents, the counselor must use various approaches to teach this connection. Worksheets such as *I Think, I Feel* (Vernon, 2006b, pp. 115–116) or *Changing Thoughts, Changing Feelings* (Vernon, 2006b, pp. 221–223) or bibliotherapy selections from *Color Us Rational* (Waters, 1979) are effective strategies.

Step 13 is getting clients to question their beliefs; helping them see that their beliefs are unproductive, illogical, unrealistic, or self-defeating (Dryden et al., 2003). With children and adolescents, many different disputing techniques should be employed, such as the friend dispute (Dryden et al., 2003): "Suppose your best friend failed a test, would you think she was an all time stupid idiot? If not, then why do you think you are so stupid and idiotic if you don't perform well?" (p. 47). Other developmentally appropriate disputations include writing rational endings to stories, playing a game such as *Adios Anxiety* (Vernon, 2002a, pp. 85–86) in which clients identify rational coping-self statements to deal with anxiety before jumping ahead on a hopscotch board, or disputing self-downing beliefs through an intervention involving a metaphor: "Don't soak it up like a sponge" (Vernon, 2002a, p. 77).

Other age-appropriate disputations include having clients make rational posters: on one side, they list or illustrate irrational ideas, and on the other side, rational counterparts (Vernon, 2002a). Using worksheets such as *Erase the Irrational* (Vernon, 2006a, pp. 247–248), where the client replaces irrational beliefs with rational counterparts, or employing an activity such as *Challenging Irrational Beliefs* (Vernon, 2006b, pp. 53–55) that helps them learn how to challenge dysfunctional thoughts, are also effective disputing strategies.

After the irrational beliefs have been challenged, it is important to help clients deepen their conviction in rational beliefs by repeatedly questioning the irrational beliefs, which can be done through reverse role playing with younger clients, where the counselor plays the role of the irrational client and the client has to dispute the beliefs (Vernon, 2002a). This step (step 14) can also be accomplished through homework assignments such as having the client convince his or her parents why their rational beliefs are better than their irrational thoughts or by using a paradoxical intervention, where the client deliberately voices irrational thoughts for a 10-minute period of time and tape-records him or herself in order to hear how exaggerated these thoughts were when the tape is replayed.

Step 15 is to check the validity of the activating event because after questioning the irrational beliefs, it may be relevant to ask how realistic the A was, was there another way to view the situation, or were the inferences true. For example, if an adolescent's A was that she was a terrible student, and after engaging her in an activity designed to probe her overgeneralizations, she realized that she was good in most subjects but not all, the client would come to realize that she had in fact distorted the A, which will help her be more realistic about troublesome events in the future.

Homework is an integral part of the REBT counseling process, and step 16 is identifying relevant homework assignments that help the client continue to question the irrational beliefs and strengthen the rational beliefs. Homework assignments can be as creative as the counselor wishes and may include imagery assignments, emotive-evocative assignments, or cognitive assignments (Dryden et al., 2003). With younger clients who may have a negative connotation to the term *homework*, asking them to complete projects or experiments may yield more positive results. For example, they could interview their parents about mistakes they made to help them dispute the idea that everyone always has to be perfect. Other suggestions include writing rational songs, making rational bumper stickers or banners, or analyzing television shows for examples of rational thinking and behaving. These homework assignments should be checked at each session, which is step 17.

The last step of the counseling process is to facilitate the working-through process by helping clients repeatedly challenge and change irrational beliefs in order to integrate rational thinking into their emotional and behavioral repertoire.

Small Group Counseling

Ellis, who started using REBT in groups as early as 1959, maintained that it is generally more effective than using REBT individually (Ellis, 2002b). Terjesen and Esposito (2006) indicated that a distinctive feature of REBT groups is that they are more psychoeducational, where the goal is to educate group members about how to overcome their disturbing emotions and dysfunctional beliefs in order to develop more appropriate affective and behavioral responses.

REBT concepts can readily be incorporated into small-group counseling, and Vernon (2004b) described two types of REBT small groups: the problem-centered group and the preventive group. In the problem-centered group, members raise their current concerns and are taught to apply REBT principles to facilitate problem resolution by the group leader with assistance from group members, depending on their ability to do so. As Bergin (2004) noted, this type of group may be more appropriate for intermediate, junior high, or high school students who are better able to articulate their problems, understand the concepts, and help others apply them. The open-ended format allows group members to learn about how to solve their own problems, but they also gain perspective by observing how other members' problems are addressed. The group leader may use didactic methods to teach disputational skills, the ABC format, and problem-solving strategies as appropriate. Modeling rational thinking and helping group members apply rational principles to their everyday problems are the primary goals. In a problem-centered group, members typically volunteer to participate, although teachers or parents may recommend that they attend. Counselors may also invite members to join a group as a follow-up to individual counseling.

A variation of the problem-centered group is to select a specific topic that all participants are grappling with, such as anger, procrastination, perfectionism, low-frustration tolerance, transitions, or family issues. Group members frequently volunteer for this type of group because they identify with the particular topic, or they may be referred and requested to join. With this approach, the discussion is limited to the specific topic, and the leader helps members apply REBT concepts to deal with current issues relative to the topic. Although the leader assumes an active role, at least initially, group members are strongly encouraged to help each other. The group setting provides the opportunity for members to learn more about their issues, explore and express feelings, and learn how their thoughts affect their feelings and behaviors.

Another type of group is the developmental or preventative group. This group teaches children and adolescents to apply REBT concepts to help them deal with the typical challenges involved in growing up. The approach is similar to a classroom group in that the focus is on prevention, but the small group is limited to 6–10 children, thus allowing for more interaction and personalization of concepts. Typically a theme is chosen for a 6–8-week module, with a different aspect of the topic targeted at each session. Topics may include relationships with parents, peers, or teachers; communication and assertion; school success; problem solving and decision making; or self-acceptance. Or, the focus may be more specifically on teaching REBT concepts such as the ABC process, identifying and disputing irrational beliefs, and so forth. In the preventive group, the assumption is that participants do not have a particular problem but that they are learning skills.

It is imperative that the specific content of the sessions be developmentally and culturally appropriate. This approach is generally more didactic, and a variety of techniques are used to introduce concepts: role-playing, games, simulations, art and music activities, videos, or bibliotherapy, for example. The intent is to teach concepts and engage group members in discussions and activities that facilitate their understanding of rational principles that they can apply to present and future developmental concerns. Some of the topics may be similar to those presented in the general problem-solving groups, but there is not the assumption in forming these groups that students who volunteer or are asked to join have a significant problem; this approach is more appropriate for anyone and is more preventive than remedial.

Integrating REBT Into the School Environment

There are four basic approaches to implementing an REE program: the informal approach (teachable moment), structured emotional education lessons, learning centers, and integration into the curriculum (Vernon & Bernard, 2006). Although each of these approaches has merit, it is preferable to implement all four approaches, in addition to practicing and modeling REBT concepts in the environment.

The Informal Approach: Teachable Moment
The basic assumption of this approach is that teachers and parents will seize "teachable moments" to introduce and reinforce rational thinking concepts. There are numerous ways in which this can be done: with the entire class, individually, or with small groups of children. For example, after a basketball game, in which it was evident that the team captain was extremely upset with himself because they had lost the game, the coach could pull him aside and ask how he felt about losing and what he was thinking about this loss. He could ask such things as "What does this say about you if your team lost the game?" "Is there any evidence that says that you were the one solely responsible for losing the game?" and "How logical is it to assume that you will never win any games this year?" "And suppose you don't win another game—is that the worst thing that could ever happen to you?" Challenging his thinking in this way helps him stop the self-downing, awfulizing, and overgeneralizing. A next step could be to ask what he could have done, if anything, to improve, which could result in appropriate goal setting for the next game.

The informal approach can also be used with small groups. For instance, as the teacher was walking through the hall, she noticed a group of young adolescents arguing with each other. As she approached the group, she heard all sorts of accusations being directed at one individual: "You're a horrible, selfish friend ... you stole Marissa's boyfriend, and we will never forgive you for it. We know you are the one who started all the rumors about us, and we are going to turn all the other girls against you so that no one in this class will ever speak to you again." The teacher wanted to defuse the situation, so she pulled the group into an empty classroom and asked them to tell her more about the situation. As they talked, she began to challenge some of their assumptions: Where was the evidence that this girl had started all the rumors? Did they know for a fact that she "stole" another's boyfriend? Did they have so much power that they could turn *everyone* against her? Forever is a long, long time—do they really believe that they will *never* speak to her again, or is it possible that they will eventually get over being so upset? These disputations seemed to help deescalate their emotions and put the problem in better perspective, and eventually they reached a point where they could communicate more effectively about how they felt and listen to the other side of the story.

In each of these situations, if the coach or teacher had not intervened, the problems would have compounded themselves and interfered with children's ability to concentrate in school. Furthermore, until the underlying beliefs are addressed, the problems would have perpetuated themselves.

Nipping problems in the bud through this informal approach helps prevent this from occurring.

To use this approach, it is necessary to have a thorough understanding of the basic REBT principles and the disputation process. In addition, it is important to realize that although it might be easier to tell children how to feel or what to do to solve a problem, it is advisable that they be allowed to work things out for themselves, with proper guidance. Once they are able to dispute their irrational beliefs that will result in more moderate, healthy feelings, they are in a better position to look at alternatives and develop a plan to resolve the problem.

Structured REE Lessons

The second approach, the most structured of all, is a series of emotional education lessons that can be presented to a small group or to a total class of children. In contrast to subject matter lessons, these lessons are typically not graded because the emphasis is on personal application of concepts. However, in this age of accountability, teachers can develop effective ways to measure whether or not the concepts have been attained, because skill acquisition is also an inherent part of the lessons.

Rational-emotive education lessons are typically experiential, with a good deal of student involvement and group interaction, which increases the likelihood that children will be engaged in the activity. Understandings are deduced from the use of such methods as simulations, games, role-playing, art activities, bibliotherapy, guided discussions, and music and writing activities. In addition, time is spent debriefing the lesson so that, through guided questions, children master the content. REE lessons are developed around the following basic concepts: self-acceptance, feelings, beliefs, and disputing beliefs (Vernon, 2004c). It is critical that these concepts be presented in accordance with the developmental level of the child. For example, it is appropriate to use the terms *rational* and *irrational* with older adolescents, but with younger children, the terms *sensible* and *insensible* would be easier for them to grasp. Likewise, younger children will not understand the concept of disputing unless it is presented in a very concrete manner, such as with the use of puppets in a dialogue, with one puppet being insensible and the other being sensible. Similarly, whereas adolescents can more readily understand how irrational beliefs result in negative feelings and unproductive behaviors, younger children need to have these concepts presented in a very concrete method, such as making a paper chain to visually illustrate how insensible thoughts create negative feelings that result in poor behavioral choices.

It is also important to present the concepts in a sequential manner to assure greater mastery of the concepts. It is also best to introduce these concepts in units. For example, the first unit might be self-acceptance, and all concepts pertaining to that would be introduced, followed by those relating to beliefs, and so forth. It is also advisable to have a sequential progression of lessons within the specific units so that concepts can be introduced and expanded on. These lessons should actively engage students in a variety of different ways and be designed according to the following format (Vernon, 1998a, 1998b, 1998c, 2006a, 2006b).

First, identify one or two learning objectives, which are stated in behavioral terms such as "Students will be able to identify the connection between thoughts and actions" and should be developmentally appropriate. Second, develop a stimulus activity, which is the heart and soul of the lesson and should be engaging and creative. Art, music, games, role-playing, puppet plays, writing, and simulations are all appropriate formats to use in developing REE lessons. For example, an REE lesson on learning the difference between facts and beliefs can be conducted in a game format similar to that of tic tac toe (Vernon, 2006a, pp. 131–133). Experiential activities can also be very engaging. Elementary children can be divided into two groups, procrastinators and nonprocrastinators. They are to pretend that they are recruiting "members" to their club, so the procrastinators make a poster of all the good things about being a procrastinator, and the nonprocrastinators do the same. Discussion follows about the advantages and disadvantages of procrastination (Vernon, 2002a, p. 184). Adolescents can learn how to use rational thoughts to deal with depression by drawing around their hand, identifying self-defeating thoughts contributing to depression on the fingers, and writing disputes in between (Vernon, 2002, p. 131). An imagery activity helps young teens learn how to apply this strategy to help them identify effective problem-solving techniques (Vernon, 2006b, p. 71). It is advisable to use more concrete activities with younger children and gradually introduce more abstract lessons with adolescents. However, it is also important to be experiential and to use a wide array of activities to maintain their interest. The stimulus activity should take no more than half of the allotted time for the lesson, leaving time for discussion.

A third component in the lesson plan format is to ask content and personalization questions. Because a critical part of the lesson is the personal application of concepts, it is very important to allow sufficient time for discussion. Two types of questions provide the most effective debriefing: content questions, which focus on the cognitive concepts presented in the lesson, and personalization questions, which involve applying the concepts to the child's own life. For example, in a lesson on rational thinking, the objective was to learn how to distinguish between rational and irrational thinking. The activity, for high school students, involved a short lecturette on the difference between rational and irrational thinking, followed by a worksheet, where students were asked to identify irrational beliefs in statements such as "My parents never let me do anything—everyone else has more freedom than I do" and "I can't stand it if my boyfriend breaks up with me—I'll never find anyone like him again." The content questions asked students to describe the difference between rational and irrational thinking and examples of key irrational beliefs. The personalization questions asked students if they were generally rational or irrational thinkers, what they would need to do to change the way they think in order to handle situations more effectively, and how they can apply what they learned to their own lives (Vernon, 1998c).

Using this lesson plan format provides a basic structure, but at the same time allows for flexibility and creativity in the actual design of the activity. The inclusion of both content and personalization questions achieves the objectives of emotional education programs: to present mental health concepts and to help students personally apply these to their own lives. The primary focus is prevention, with the hope that these concepts will reduce the frequency and intensity of future problems.

It is very appropriate to ask students what they learned following a lesson or to assign homework as a follow-up to the lesson to help reinforce the concepts. After the lesson on facts and assumptions, for example, a homework assignment for younger children could involve having them be "fact detectives," where they attempt to identify facts versus assumptions in their interactions with peers or siblings. The reader is referred to Vernon's *The Passport Program: A Journey Through Emotional, Social, Cognitive, and Self-Development*, grades 1–5, 6–8, and 9–12 (1998a, 1998b, 1998c); and *Thinking, Feeling, Behaving: An Emotional Education Program*, grades 1–6 and 7–12 (2006a, 2006b), for specific examples of REE lessons. Bernard (2005) has also written an emotional education program targeting academic performance.

REE Learning Centers

Oftentimes elementary and middle school teachers establish learning centers, where students work independently on activities to reinforce concepts presented in class or to introduce new ideas. REE activities can easily be incorporated into this type of format through worksheets, writing, or games. Examples include having students write rational limericks or make rational posters for their rooms, make up silly songs to help them deal with sad feelings, write rational stories based on a problem they are experiencing, develop a feeling vocabulary by finding feeling words in a puzzle, or complete worksheets that address a variety of social-emotional-cognitive topics.

The teacher is limited only by his or her creativity in designing center activities. However, the center activities should be engaging and able to be completed independently.

Integration Into the Curriculum

Yet another approach to REE emotional education is to integrate the concepts into an existing subject matter curriculum. When teaching literature, teachers could select and discuss stories that present characters solving problems rationally or expressing feelings in a healthy manner. Topics for themes could be related to making mistakes, identifying strengths and weaknesses, and the prices and payoffs for perfection. Vocabulary and spelling lessons could include feeling-word vocabularies and definitions. Social studies lessons could focus on personal and societal values and on a rational understanding of the concept of fairness as it applies to societal groups or to law and order, for example.

Integration into the curriculum is less direct than a structured lesson, but it is a viable way of reinforcing rational concepts and making them an integral part of the school structure. Although it may seem awkward and forced initially, once teachers become more familiar with the REE concepts, they will find that integration becomes more natural.

Consultation

A final method of integrating REBT into the school setting is through consultation, a triadic process in which the professional works with other school personnel or parents, helping them learn to apply REBT concepts with their children. Ellis and Bernard (2006) characterized consultation as a collaborative problem-solving process that improves the functioning of parents and teachers relative to the young client. The reader is referred to Joyce (1990, 1994) for a thorough discussion of rational-emotive behavior consultation with parents.

The Effectiveness of REBT With School-Aged Populations

Gonzalez et al. (2004) pointed out that studies documenting the effectiveness of REBT with adults could not be assumed to hold true for children and adolescents, and for this reason, "investigating the efficacy of REBT with children and adolescents per se clearly is necessary if we wish to use this technique with this population" (p. 223). In addressing this issue, several meta-analyses have been conducted, the first by Bernard and Hajzler (1991). Their analysis focused on REE with school-aged children. They reviewed 21 studies, examining REE's effectiveness with anxious students, learning-disabled students, high-risk students, and students with low self-esteem, and some studies with a nonclinical population. In essence, they concluded that REBT had a positive impact. Gossette and O'Brien (1993) reviewed unpublished dissertations and four published reports. They questioned Bernard and Hajzler's (1991) exclusion of doctoral dissertations and questioned the use of REBT with school-aged children. Although they found that there was a significant change in irrationality, they posited that this could be due to learning new information as students do in classrooms rather than reflecting real change.

A later meta-analysis by Gonzalez and colleagues (2004) also focused on REBT with children and adolescents in order to assess the impact of treatment. Of the 46 studies that were included in refereed journals, a total of 19 met their specific selection criteria, which included the requisite that each study have a control group. Results of this meta-analysis concluded that REBT had the most significant impact on disruptive behaviors, which the researchers did not find surprising because this is one of the most frequently reported reasons why children are referred for therapy. They cautioned that the large effect size for disruptive behaviors may be an outcome of measures such as frequency counts used to assess the behavior.

Interestingly enough, REBT seemed to be as effective for children and adolescents who reported an identified problem as for those who did not, suggesting that REBT is useful for both intervention and prevention. In addition, REBT was more effective than alternative treatment and than a no-treatment control, and those receiving longer treatment had better results.

Another finding from the Gonzalez analysis was that the effects of REBT are strong, despite some methodological differences among studies. There are some limitations of the meta-analysis, including the small number of studies, the fact that dissertations were not included, and the fact that the authors compared effects across different dependent measures (Ellis & Bernard, 2006).

With regard to other research, Wilde (1996) conducted a study to ascertain whether elementary students could learn REBT concepts presented in a classroom guidance program. Wilde sampled 95 fourth graders from a rural public school. Lessons were conducted twice a week for 30 minutes for 2 weeks. Prior to initiating the lessons, students were pretested using the Idea Inventory, which has been reported to have good internal consistency, according to Wilde. Following the four-session intervention, the Idea Inventory was again administered, and the difference between pre- and posttests was significant at the .05 level. In three of the five classrooms, the t scores were also significant at the .05 level. Wilde concluded that the REE lessons led to an increase in rational thinking but indicated that a follow-up assessment would be advantageous in order to determine if this increase would continue over time.

In yet another study, Shannon and Allen (1998) sampled 56 11th grade students in an Upward Bound program in order to test the efficacy of an REBT training program designed to improve math scores. According to these researchers, students who participated in the REBT skills-training program received better scores on a standardized math achievement test than did the control group. In addition, they analyzed weekly homework assignments and classroom behavior, which clearly indicated that there were significant changes in the experimental group's math self-talk. Their conclusion was that teaching REBT in the classroom can enhance student achievement and may carry over to other aspects of their lives.

Katchman and Mazer (1990) investigated the efficacy of rational emotive education as a mental health prevention program. The population included 109 high school juniors and seniors taking psychology. Students were divided into an experimental and a control class. Pre- and posttests consisted of the Rational Behavior Inventory, the Defense Mechanism Inventory, and the Eysenck Personality Inventory. Students in the experimental group had 12 biweekly REE sessions. Results of this study, which also included an analysis of academic effort grades, grade point averages, and number of detentions, indicated that REE did not have a significant increase with regard to rationality, contrary to other studies (DiGiuseppe & Kassinove, 1976) that stated it did. Katchman and Mazer posited that adolescents' egocentrism could interfere with their ability to think rationally. However, there were indications that REE effectively reduces the use of aggressive maladaptive defenses and increases the use of more adaptive defenses, which they pointed out is in keeping with Ellis' contention that reducing self-blame and hostility is a goal of treatment. The researchers also found that the more adaptive responses were still prevalent 10 weeks after treatment, attesting to the efficacy of this approach.

Bernard, Ellis, and Terjesen (2006) cited several concerns relative to evidence-based research, including the fact that much of the research fails to report specific characteristics of the study, the setting, and the treatments employed. With this paucity of detail, it is difficult to determine what is effecting change. These authors also noted that treatment integrity and the lack of REBT training for therapists and supervisors conducting the research are major concerns. They pointed out that because of this, the accuracy and effectiveness of the therapeutic interventions must be called into question. Their recommendation is for greater attention to detail in conducting research and that researchers be trained in REBT.

The Case of Todd

According to the evaluation conducted by the school psychologist, Todd's academic is not problematic, nor is his externalizing behavior. Given this important background information, the REBT therapist would assume that the problem is related to performance anxiety and perfectionism and that these psychological problems are interfering with his ability to attain good grades as he has in past years. However, given that his behavior has changed considerably in recent months and that the declining grades may be a sign of depression, it would be important to do a further assessment to see if this is a significant concern.

The REBT school counselor would initially do some rapport building as needed with Todd, reassuring him that counselors routinely help youngsters with school-related problems and asking him if he has any questions or concerns about the counseling process. She would then begin the assessment procedure by clarifying the activating events (A). The counselor would first ask Todd what he sees as the problem, but if he is unable to do this, the counselor would share her understanding based on parent and teacher input: that he reports being stressed about doing his schoolwork, that he has not been turning in homework despite the fact that he is spending more time than needed on it, and that his grades have dropped. The counselor would ask Todd which of these problems he would like to work on first in order for him to feel as if he has some power in the therapeutic relationship. Once they have agreed on the issue (getting stressed about schoolwork), the REBT therapist would then ask him to describe the emotional consequences: how he feels and behaves relative to this problem. It is very likely that the counselor may need to employ some developmentally appropriate strategies such as word lists or drawing to help Todd express these feelings and behaviors because children are sometimes unable to do so. She also may have Todd rate on a 1–10 scale how anxious and/or worried he is about schoolwork by using an emotional thermometer, which is a concrete way for him to describe the intensity of his emotions.

After Todd has described the A and the C (emotional consequence), the counselor would then teach this client the B–C connection by asking if he thinks his classmates feel as worried as he does about doing their schoolwork, then pointing out that because many of them probably don't, it isn't just that doing schoolwork causes him to worry, but what he tells himself about it.

To make this more concrete, the counselor would ask Todd if he can describe one of the last times he felt worried about his schoolwork. She would draw a head on a sheet of paper with several thought bubbles stemming from it and ask Todd to describe what he is thinking when he gets worried about his schoolwork (that it is too hard, that he won't ever get it done right, that the teacher and his parents will think he is dumb if he doesn't get everything right, and that his classmates would make fun of him if they knew how dumb he was). If Todd has difficulty identifying his beliefs, the counselor can say something like "Other kids sometimes worry about pleasing others, doing it right, and so on" as a way of eliciting thoughts. As is typical for this age, some of these will be inferences rather than core irrational beliefs.

Once the beliefs have been identified, the counselor will engage Todd in the disputing process by asking questions such as "Where is the evidence that you will never get it right? How do you know your parents and teachers will think you are dumb if you don't get everything right? Do you think they always do everything perfectly?" She might adapt an intervention on perfectionism (Vernon, 2002a, p. 103), having him list all the advantages and disadvantages of having to do things perfectly to help him see that his insistence on being perfect is contributing to his anxiety.

Employing homework in the form of a behavioral experiment could be effective in this case. The counselor would first use imagery to help Todd imagine the worst thing that would happen if he turned in the homework he had worked so hard on, and after he has that image in his mind and feels the high anxiety, have him imagine that the worst does not happen and how that affects his level of anxiety. After he is able to see that the worst probably won't happen, ask if he is willing to experiment with turning the homework in this week and ask him to determine how many times he is willing to do this. Give him an index card so that each time he turns in homework he can record his teacher's response.

Checking homework in the following session should reinforce the rational thoughts: that the teacher did not yell at him or embarrass him in front of the whole class, for example, if he turned in less-than-perfect homework. In subsequent sessions the counselor would continue to work on disputing irrational beliefs using developmentally appropriate interventions. Helping Todd look at all of his strengths, not just focusing on his academic performance, might be effective. This could be done by having him draw a large circle on a sheet of paper and putting several small circles into the large one. He could then label each small circle with such things as *sports*, *music*, *chores*, *schoolwork*, and *Scouts*, and beside each circle put a number (1 = low, 5 = high) to signify how he sees his performance in these areas. Upon completion, the counselor could help him see that he is a child who is very good at some things and not as good in others, but that he cannot rate his total self as "bad" if he has strong areas as well as weak areas.

The counselor would also incorporate some skill building into the sessions: teaching relaxation techniques that Todd could employ before working on his homework and keeping a worry box, which involves having him write down all the anxious thoughts about doing schoolwork on individual strips of paper and putting them in a box. After he turns in his homework, he can go back to the box and review his worries: If they didn't come true, he could throw them away. This should help him see that much of what he worries about may not come true. Other strategies would involve helping him develop rational coping self-statements such as "Even if this schoolwork is frustrating, I can figure it out; it doesn't have to be perfect." Depending on an assessment of his study skills, it might be helpful to engage him in an intervention called *Road to Achievement* (Vernon, 2002a, pp. 202–203) that helps him differentiate between effective and ineffective study skills.

With young clients, it is important to reinforce rational principles in multiple ways, which can be done with interventions; functional, logical, and empirical disputes; and homework. These approaches should decrease anxiety and have a positive impact on problematic behaviors. Parent and teacher consultation should also be employed. Teaching these significant adults how to help Todd develop and use rational coping self-statements, practice relaxation techniques, and ease up on his self-imposed pressure by sharing their own imperfections should help this young client gain control over this problem.

Typically, a problem of this nature can be resolved in 3–5 sessions. Periodic follow-up with the client, parent, and teacher would be important.

Summary

The purpose of this chapter has been to describe specific applications of rational-emotive behavior therapy in schools. From its inception, REBT has championed an educative, preventative focus, which is particularly relevant for use in schools. Of primary importance is the fact that this approach is easily learned and can be employed not only with children and adolescents but also with their parents and school personnel. As previously noted, REBT has been applied to a wide variety of presenting problems, as well as typical developmental issues.

This theory also is very versatile because it can be implemented in small-group settings to help children apply rational concepts to issues impacting their lives in the present, as well as with skills for dealing with future problems. Furthermore, it can be introduced in the classroom in the form of emotional education lessons. The focus here is more preventative, involving teaching REBT concepts and skills so that students have "emotional tools" that they can use in dealing with present as well as future problems that are both developmental and remedial in nature. The importance of an emotional education curriculum cannot be stressed enough: It is strikingly apparent that today's youth have many stressors to contend with and, unfortunately, often lack the appropriate skills for dealing effectively with their issues, as evidenced by the rampant depression and high teen suicide rates (Vernon, 2006c), as well as a multitude of other prevalent issues. Because growing up has become increasingly complex, it is imperative that educators place primary importance on equipping young people with skills, and rational-emotive education is an approach that actively teaches them cognitive, emotive, and behavioral techniques for dealing with typical developmental problems as well as more serious concerns.

Recommended Readings

School-based practitioners are encouraged to learn more about this approach by taking training offered through the Albert Ellis Institute (http://www.rebt.org) and by reading and viewing tapes demonstrating applications of the theory, also available through the institute. The following sources are also pertinent to working with school-aged populations:

Ellis, A. E., & Bernard, M. E. (2006). *Rational-emotive behavioral approaches to childhood problems.* New York: Springer. This is a very comprehensive source on applications of REBT with children and adolescents.

Vernon, A. (2002). *What works when with children and adolescents: A handbook of individual counseling techniques.* Champaign, IL: Research Press. This book contains over 100 REBT interventions for internalizing and externalizing problems, as well as typical developmental problems.

The following two sources are emotional education curricula designed for classrooms and small groups:

Bernard, M. E. (2005). *Program achieve: A curriculum of lessons for teaching students to achieve and develop social-emotional-behavioral well being* (Vols. 1–6, 3rd ed.). Oakleigh, Australia, and Laguna Beach, CA: Australian Scholarships Group and You Can Do It! Education.

Vernon, A. (2006). *Thinking, feeling, behaving: An emotional education curriculum* (two curriculums: grades 1–6 and 7–12). Champaign, IL: Research Press.

References

Barrish, H. H., & Barrish, I. J. (1985). *Managing parental anger.* Shawnee Mission, KS: Overland.

Barrish, I. J., & Barrish, H. H. (1989). *Surviving and enjoying your adolescent.* Kansas City, MO: Westport.

Bergin, J. J. (2004). Small group counseling. In A. Vernon (Ed.), *Counseling children and adolescents* (3rd ed., pp. 355–390). Denver, CO: Love Publishing.

Bernard, M. E. (2005). *Program achieve: A curriculum of lessons for teaching students to achieve and develop social-emotional-behavioral well being* (Vols. 1–6, 3rd ed.). Oakleigh, Australia, and Laguna Beach, CA: Australian Scholarships Group and You Can Do It! Education.

Bernard, M. E. (Ed.). (1991). *Using rational emotive therapy effectively: A practitioner's guide.* New York: Plenum.

Bernard, M. E., & DiGiuseppe, R. (Eds.). (1991). *Rational emotive consultation in applied settings.* Hillsdale, NJ: Erlbaum.

Bernard, M. E., Ellis, A. E., & Terjesen, M. D. (2006). Rational-emotive behavioral approaches to childhood disorders: History, theory, practice, and research. In A. E. Ellis & M. E. Bernard (Eds.), *Rational emotive behavioral approaches to childhood disorders: Theory, practice, and research* (pp. 3–84). New York: Springer.

Bernard, M. E., & Joyce, M. (1984). *Rational emotive therapy with children and adolescents: Theory, treatment strategies, preventative methods.* New York: Wiley.

DiGiuseppe, R. (1999). Rational emotive behavior therapy. In H. T. Prout & D. T. Brown (Eds.), *Counseling and psychotherapy with children and adolescents: Theory and practice for school settings* (pp. 252–293). New York: John Wiley.

DiGiuseppe, R. (2002). Idiosyncratic REBT. In W. Dryden (Ed.), *Idiosyncratic rational emotive behaviour therapy* (pp. 32–45). Ross-on-Wye, UK: PCCS.

DiGiuseppe, R., & Bernard, M. E. (2006). REBT assessment and treatment with children. In A. E. Ellis & M. E. Bernard (Eds.), *Rational emotive behavioral approaches to childhood disorders: Theory, practice, and research* (pp. 85–114). New York: Springer.

DiGiuseppe, R., & Kassinove, H. (1976). Effects of a rational-emotive school mental-health program on children's emotional adjustment. *Journal of Community Psychology, 4,* 382–387.

Dryden, W. (1999). *Rational emotive behavioural counselling in action* (2nd ed.). London: Sage.

Dryden, W. (2002a). Idiosyncratic REBT. In W. Dryden (Ed.), *Idiosyncratic rational emotive behaviour therapy* (pp. 2–14). Ross-on-Wye, UK: PCCS.

Dryden, W. (2002b). *Fundamentals of rational emotive behaviour therapy: A training handbook.* London: Whurr.

Dryden, W. (Ed.). (2003). *Rational emotive behaviour therapy: Theoretical developments.* New York: Brunner-Routledge.

Dryden, W., DiGiuseppe, R., & Neenan, M. (2003). *A primer on rational emotive therapy* (2nd ed.). Champaign, IL: Research Press.

Dryden, W., & Ellis, A. E. (2001). Rational-emotive behavior therapy. In K. S. Dobson (Ed.), *Handbook of cognitive behavioral therapies* (pp. 295–348). New York: Guilford.

Ellis, A. E. (2001a). *Feeling better, getting better, staying better.* Atascadero, CA: Impact.

Ellis, A. E. (2001b). *Overcoming destructive beliefs, feelings, and behaviors.* Amherst, NY: Prometheus.

Ellis, A. E. (2002a). *Overcoming resistance: A rational emotive behavior therapy integrated approach.* New York: Springer.

Ellis, A. E. (2002b). REBT and its application to group therapy. In W. Dryden & M. Neenan (Eds.), *Rational-emotive behaviour group therapy* (pp. 30–54). Philadelphia: Whurr.

Ellis, A. E., & Bernard, M. E. (1983). *Rational emotive approaches to the problems of childhood.* New York: Plenum.

Ellis, A. E., & Bernard, M. E. (2006). Preface. In *Rational emotive behavioral approaches to childhood disorders: Theory, practice, and research.* New York: Springer.

Ellis, A. E., & MacClaren, C. (1998). *Rational emotive behavior therapy: A therapist's guide.* Atascadero, CA: Impact.

Gonzalez, J. E., Nelson, J. R., Gutkin, T. B., Saunders, A., Galloway, A., & Shwery, C. S. (2004). Rational emotive therapy with children and adolescents: A meta-analysis. *Journal of Emotional and Behavioral Disorders, 12,* 222–235.

Gossette, R. L., & O'Brien, R. M. (1993). Efficacy of rational emotive therapy with children: A critical re-appraisal. *Journal of Behavior Therapy and Experimental Psychology, 24,* 15–25.

Hajzler, D. J., & Bernard, M. E. (1991). A review of rational-emotive education outcome studies. *School Psychology Quarterly, 6*(1), 27–49.

Joyce, M. (1990). Rational-emotive parent consultation. *School Psychology Review, 19*(3), 304–314.

Joyce, M. (1994). Rational-emotive parent consultation. In M. E. Bernard & R. DiGiuseppe (Eds.), *Rational-emotive consultation in applied settings.* Hillsdale, NJ: Lawrence Erlbaum.

Katchman, D. J., & Mazer, G. E. (1990). Effects of rational-emotive education on the rationality, neuroticism and defense mechanisms of adolescents. *Adolescence, 25*(97), 131–144.

Knaus, W. J. (1974). *Rational-emotive education: A manual for elementary school teachers.* New York: Institute for Rational-Emotive Therapy.

Shannon, H. D., & Allen, T. W. (1998). The effectiveness of a REBT training program in increasing the performance of high school students in mathematics. *Journal of Rational-Emotive & Cognitive-Behavior Therapy, 16*(3), 197–209.

Terjesen, M. D., & Esposito, M. A. (2006). Rational-emotive behavior group therapy with children and adolescents. In A. E. Ellis & M. E. Bernard (Eds.), *Rational emotive behavioral approaches to childhood disorders: Theory, practice, and research* (pp. 385–414). New York: Springer.

Vernon, A. (1989a). *Thinking, feeling, behaving: An emotional education curriculum for children.* Champaign, IL: Research Press.

Vernon, A. (1989b). *Thinking, feeling, behaving: An emotional education curriculum for adolescents.* Champaign, IL: Research Press.

Vernon, A. (1998a). *The passport program: A journey through emotional, social, cognitive, and self-development* (Grades 1–5). Champaign, IL: Research Press.

Vernon, A. (1998b). *The passport program: A journey through emotional, social, cognitive, and self-development* (Grades 6–8). Champaign, IL: Research Press.

Vernon, A. (1998c). *The passport program: A journey through emotional, social, cognitive, and self-development* (Grades 9–12). Champaign, IL: Research Press.

Vernon, A. (2002a). *What works when with children and adolescents: A handbook of individual counseling techniques.* Champaign, IL: Research Press.

Vernon, A. (2002b). Idiosyncratic REBT. In W. Dryden (Ed.), *Idiosyncratic rational emotive behaviour therapy* (pp. 143–158). Ross-on-Wye, UK: PCCS.

Vernon, A. (2004a). Applications of rational-emotive behavior therapy with children and adolescents. In A. Vernon (Ed.), *Counseling children and adolescents* (3rd ed., pp. 140–157). Denver, CO: Love Publishing.

Vernon, A. (2004b). Using cognitive behavioral techniques. In B. Erford (Ed.), *Professional school counseling: A handbook of theories, programs, and practices* (pp. 91–99). Austin, TX: PRO-ED.

Vernon, A. (2004c). Rational emotive education. *Romanian Journal of Cognitive and Behavioral Psychotherapies, 4*, 23–37.

Vernon, A. (2006a). *Thinking, feeling, behaving: An emotional education curriculum for children* (Rev. ed.). Champaign, IL: Research Press.

Vernon, A. (2006b). *Thinking, feeling, behaving: An emotional education curriculum for adolescents* (Rev. ed.). Champaign, IL: Research Press.

Vernon, A. (2006c). Depression in children and adolescents. In A. E. Ellis & M. E. Bernard (Eds.), *Rational emotive behavioral approaches to childhood disorders: Theory, practice, and research* (pp. 212–232). New York: Springer.

Vernon, A., & Bernard, M. E. (2006). Applications of REBT in schools. In A.E. Ellis and M.E. Bernard (Eds.), *Rational emotive behavioral approaches to childhood disorders: Theory, practice, and research* (pp. 415–460). New York: Springer.

Walen, S. R., DiGiuseppe, R., & Dryden, W. (1992). *A practitioner's guide to rational-emotive therapy* (2nd ed.). New York: Oxford University Press.

Waters, V. (1979). *Color us rational.* New York: Institute for Rational Emotive Therapy.

Waters, V. (1981). *The living school. RET Work, 1*, 1–6.

Waters, V. (1982). Therapies for children: Rational-emotive therapy. In C.R. Reynolds & T.B. Gutkin (Eds.), *Handbook of school psychology* (pp. 37–57). New York: Wiley.

Wilde, J. (1996). The efficacy of short-term rational-emotive education with fourth-grade students. *Elementary School Guidance and Counseling Journal, 31*, (2), 131–138.

7

Cognitive-Behavioral Therapy Approaches in a School Setting

Ray W. Christner

Rosemary B. Mennuti

Loren M. Pearson

School settings can be a complex and difficult environment to establish and implement a number of mental health interventions. Often, there is a misconception that mental health services are far removed from goals established in schools, and additional barriers of time, scheduling difficulties, and caseloads make the implementation of these services difficult. Moreover, school systems are faced with ensuring that interventions used for children in schools are based on "evidence-based practices" and that the interventions used produce positive student outcomes.

Over the past several years, a number of excellent resources have been introduced that have supported the use of cognitive-behavioral therapy (CBT) with youth for individual and group interventions (Christner, Stewart, & Freeman, 2007; Friedberg & McClure, 2002; Kendall, 2000; Mennuti, Freeman, & Christner, 2006; Reinecke, Dattilio, & Freeman, 2003). In addition, others have highlighted the potential effectiveness of CBT approaches used specifically within a school setting (Christner, Forrest, Morley, & Weinstein, 2007; Kendall, 2000; Mennuti et al., 2006; Ollendick & King, 2004).

Although a number of therapeutic approaches may be used in schools, we believe that CBT is a natural fit within this setting. For instance, many components of CBT (e.g., psychoeducation, skill building, between-session work, and progress monitoring) parallel many of the already existing services within school, thus making it easier for educators to accept (Christner & Allen, 2003; Christner, Mennuti, & Stewart-Allen, 2004;

Mennuti & Christner, 2005; Mennuti et al., 2006). Given CBT's time-limited, present-oriented, solution-focused approach (Reinecke et al., 2003), it can be adapted to the intervention service delivery model commonly seen in schools (e.g., response to intervention, or RTI), which allows services to be delivered on multiple levels, as highlighted in chapter 1 of this book. Furthermore, CBT can be used to prevent difficulties and build resilience in students without overly relying on diagnosing specific pathology. This is consistent with recent expansions to child mental health literature focusing on approaches that incorporate the inclusion of building psychological wellness in youth (Doll, 2008; Suldo & Shaffer, 2008).

Although CBT can be applied at universal, targeted, and intensive levels of intervention (see Christner, Forrest et al., 2007; Mennuti et al., 2006; Smallwood et al., 2007), for this chapter we will specifically discuss the use of CBT at a targeted and intensive level, addressing the needs of small groups and individuals. We will offer a brief overview of the basic foundations of CBT and then provide information on interventions and strategies that can be used by school-based mental health providers.

Overview of Cognitive-Behavioral Therapy

In comparison to other approaches, CBT is a relatively young approach to treatment that evolved from a number of theories and philosophies. The works of Albert Ellis (1962) and Aaron T. Beck (1967; see also Beck, Rush, Shaw, & Emery, 1979) are thought of as the seminal works in CBT that formally established it as an approach. At that time, Ellis developed rational therapy (RET; now called rational emotive behavior therapy, or REBT) and Beck established cognitive therapy (CT). These have led to the development of a number of other therapeutic approaches (e.g., dialectical behavior therapy and schema-focused therapy), all of which are included under the "umbrella" of CBT and have a constant theme that our thoughts, feelings, and behaviors are interrelated.

This interaction and relationship between thoughts, feelings, and behaviors are not simplistic or linear, suggesting a cause–effect relationship. Instead, this connection is multidirectional and involves complex interactions between cognitions, physiology, emotions, situations, and behaviors. Having awareness of the situational factors (e.g., social aspects) that activate a student's belief system, being able to link the beliefs with the child's cognitive process, and translating these concepts into clear and helpful strategies for the child are essential for effective interventions.

Keep in mind that the same situation can produce different reactions from different children, as the way a child interprets the experience ultimately modifies the intensity of his or her emotional and behavioral reaction (Friedberg & McClure, 2002; Shapiro, Friedberg, & Bardenstein, 2006). For example, think of a student rushing through the hallway to get a drink of water at the water fountain, and slipping on water that was dripped onto the floor. Different students would interpret this in different ways. One may respond, "I am always making a fool of myself"; another may think, "This is going to make me late, and I am going to get detention and everyone will laugh at me"; and another may say to himself, "I can't wait to find the idiot who made this mess." Each of these thoughts will have specific accompanying emotions and behaviors. This highlights that the thoughts and corresponding responses rest within the individual, not the specific event.

When considering an individual's belief system, practitioners must go beyond the recognition of a person's initial surface-level thoughts. Cognition can occur at multiple levels, with each level being more in-depth and core to one's sense of self. It is around that core that all experiences are understood and reactions are derived. As described above, many situations have the potential to activate our *automatic thoughts*, which are the beliefs that quickly enter our mind following an event. For instance, a student who is about to take a math test may have the automatic thought, "I'm not prepared, and I'm gonna fail," which may produce feelings of test anxiety. This quick thought of potential failure may be the result of the core belief, "You have to be prepared to succeed." The *core belief* is a deeper level of thought from which we interpret specific events. The core belief and automatic thoughts are based on our own personal cognitive template or framework that goes across most events or situations in our lives, known as *schemas*. Thus, using this case, the student may be working from the schematic template, "Success defines self-worth." So, the reaction to one simple event is in fact not that simple, and represents a deeper process. Just having an individual change those surface thoughts may impact that one situation, but is likely not to offer the depth of intervention needed to promote further psychological wellness.

Within this cognitive process, there are different errors that affect one's responses to situations. Kendall and MacDonald (1993) identified two cognitive factors—*cognitive distortions* and *cognitive deficiencies*. Cognitive distortions involve the errors in thinking that lead the individual to misinterpret or misperceive a situation or event (Freeman, Pretzer, Fleming, & Simon, 2004). Table 7.1 offers examples of cognitive distortions

TABLE 7.1   Cognitive Distortions Common to Students

1. *Dichotomous thinking*: The student views situations in only two categories rather than on a continuum. The world is either black or white with no shades of gray. For example, "I'm either a good student or a failure."

2. *Overgeneralization*: The student sees a current event as being characteristic of life in general, instead of one situation among many. For example, "Because I failed that science test, I'll never graduate or make it in college."

3. *Mind reading*: The student believes he or she knows what others are thinking about him or her without any evidence. For example, "I just know that Mr. P. is angry at me."

4. *Emotional reasoning*: The student assumes that his or her feelings or emotional reactions reflect the true situation. For example, "I feel like no one likes me, so no one likes me."

5. *Disqualifying the positive*: The student discounts positive experiences that conflict with his or her negative views. For example, "I only did well on those quizzes because Mrs. Jones helped me and I got lucky."

6. *Catastrophizing*: The student predicts that future situations will be negative and treats them as intolerable catastrophes. For example, "I better not even try the assignment because I might screw it up, and that would be awful."

7. *Personalization*: The student assumes that he or she is the cause of negative circumstances. For example, "My teacher didn't smile at me this morning. I must have failed that test and made her unhappy."

8. *Should statements*: The student uses *should* or *must* to describe how he or she or others are to behave or act. For example, "I must always get A's, and I shouldn't make mistakes."

9. *Comparing*: The student compares his or her performance to that of others. Oftentimes, the comparison is made to higher performing or older students. For example, "Compared to my older brother, my work looks like a kindergartner did it."

10. *Selective abstraction*: The student focuses attention on one detail (usually negative), and ignores other relevant aspects. For example, "My teacher gave me an unsatisfactory on the last assignment, so this means I'm one of the worst students!"

11. *Labeling*: The student attaches a global label to describe him or herself rather than looking at behaviors and actions. For example, "I'm a loser" rather than "Boy, I had a bad game last night."

Source: Adapted from Christner and Stewart-Allen (2004, November).

commonly seen in school-aged students, which were originally described by Christner and Stewart-Allen (2004, November). On the other hand, cognitive deficiencies are a deficit in an individual's cognitive processing skills (Kendall & MacDonald). A student with cognitive deficiencies may have minimal problem-solving skills, which results in impulsiveness or increased frustration.

CBT also involves behavioral components, such as environmental influences and/or skill deficits (Mennuti et al., 2006). School-based practitioners must be aware of environmental influences and experiences (e.g., teacher or parent interactions, ineffective parenting, and past trauma), as these will help to conceptualize a student's problems. Additionally, changes to the environment will in some cases be the initial line of intervention (e.g., positive behavioral support, and token economies). However, there are other cases where a student's difficulties are the result of behavioral skill deficits (e.g., poor self-monitoring or underdeveloped social skills), and this will require interventions focusing on the acquisition and generalization of a new skill set.

Assessment and Case Conceptualization

The basic foundation of CBT suggests that therapy and intervention selection be based on an informed approach. That is, rather than using trial and error to identify interventions that work, practitioners using CBT collect data on a child and determine interventions that have the potential for success, based on a thorough understanding of the problems and uniqueness of the child. Essentially, the cycle of assessment, case conceptualization, progress monitoring, and revision (when needed) is at the core of the CBT model.

School-based practitioners have access to data collection and assessment opportunities from multiple sources. Assessment data can include school records, observations in natural settings (e.g., the playground and cafeteria), interviews, self-reports, standardized rating scales, functional behavioral assessments, curriculum-based assessments, and psychoeducational testing (e.g., cognitive, academic, motor, and social-emotional). A description of these tools goes beyond the scope of this chapter, yet there are a number of references available for practitioners (see Sattler, see also Reynolds & Kamphaus, 2002). In an effort to help students referred for counseling, school-based providers may tend to move quickly to the selection of interventions in an attempt to "fix" the problem. It must be recognized that just selecting interventions based on "problem areas" is insufficient to meet the needs of many children.

To move beyond a problem-focused approach to intervention selection, CBT attempts to use assessment data to conceptualize individual cases in a manner leading to a thoughtful selection of strategies and techniques. Case conceptualization is a flexible, dynamic plan that fosters the generation and testing of hypotheses about the student and the student's behaviors. These hypotheses lead to specific treatment goals and targeted strategies or techniques to be employed. Good case formulation looks beyond goals needing to be addressed, and it considers possible barriers to intervention and resiliency factors that allow for proactive response. As noted above, it is essential that this information drives the pace of intervention, as well as the criteria from which progress will be assessed.

Murphy and Christner (2006) offered a case conceptualization model for children, with a specific focus on school settings. Their model includes a list of problems, developmental considerations, working hypotheses, origins of working hypotheses, antecedents and/or precipitating factors, maintaining factors, protective and resiliency factors, and diagnostic impressions, which evolve into an intervention plan. In Table 7.2, we offer a modified view of elements that school-based practitioners should consider when formulating cases.

It is important to remember that the initial assessment identifies the list of specific problems a student may have, though these need to be explored further to establish an understanding of the global challenges that are at the root of the student's functioning. Also, practitioners must keep in mind that their initial hypotheses on a student may not be totally accurate. Progressing monitoring and ongoing work with the student may provide

TABLE 7.2   Elements of Cognitive-Behavioral Case Conceptualization With Youth

Demographic information

Child's interests

Child's assets (e.g., interpersonal, academic, and behavioral)

Child's challenges (problems across settings—home, school, and community)

Developmental considerations (e.g., language, motor skills, cognitive [concrete operations, etc.], and social)

Protective and resiliency factors

Risk factors (e.g., individual, family, and school)

Levels of cognition (e.g., automatic thoughts, core beliefs, and schema)

Precipitating factors

Maintaining factors

Consequences of actions

Readiness to change

Working hypotheses

Origins of working hypotheses

Diagnostic impressions and educational classifications

further clarity, which leads to modified hypotheses and interventions. Remember, case conceptualization is not a static view of an individual, but a flexible and dynamic process that we test and modify as needed to lead us to the most effective method to effect change. It is with case conceptualization that the school-based practitioner identifies goals for intervention and begins to select strategies and techniques that have the potential to be effective with a particular individual. Through the use of progress monitoring, we can measure the effectiveness of an intervention and adjust it as needed.

The Structure of Cognitive-Behavioral Therapy (CBT)

As with many approaches, the initial session within a CBT framework focuses on building and enhancing a therapeutic relationship with the child, a process that continues throughout all subsequent sessions. It further provides an opportunity to socialize the child to the psychotherapy in general, as well as to the basic tenets of CBT. Specifically, this involves introducing the student to the idea that a connection and reciprocal relationship exist between situations, thoughts, feelings, and behaviors. Several excellent reference books are available to assist the practitioner in selecting developmentally appropriate tools for teaching the CBT concepts to children and adolescents (Friedberg & McClure, 2002; Stallard, 2005; Vernon, 2002). When working with elementary-aged children, practitioners need to be more entertaining and hands-on, such as by using stories, picture-book formats, drawings, feelings charts, and the like. For example, the school-based practitioner could use a story and have the child draw a picture of what is being said, such as the following.

Let's talk about a boy named Lee. Lee and his family were at an amusement park, and Lee wanted to ride the bumper cars. Can you draw a picture of Lee standing next to the bumper cars? [Using a dry erase board]. Great; Lee asked his parents, and they told him he was allowed. What do you think went through Lee's head when he found out he was allowed? Let's write that in a thought bubble: "I can't wait to ride the cars!" Now, how do you think Lee is feeling right now? Draw his face on the picture. Now, what do you think Lee is going to do?

Working with adolescents is much like working with adults; however some older students prefer visual supports or charts to clarify the concepts.

TABLE 7.3   Example of a Thought Record for Youth

What Happened? (Situation)	How Did You Feel? (Emotion)	What Went Through Your Mind? (Thought)	What Did You Do? (Behavior)

Thought records are very useful tools in helping older students understand the situation–thought–feeling–behavior connection. Table 7.3 provides a sample of a thought record that can be used with youth.

Some aspects of CBT involve helping the student see that not all thoughts are accurate or functional. For instance, the use of Socratic questioning or guided discovery can assist in identifying and addressing a student's cognitive distortions (e.g., "You haven't been asked to the prom yet; what goes through your mind about that?" "If you don't get a date, what would that say about you?" and "What evidence do you have that no one likes you?"). By using a variety of techniques, the CBT clinician can help students reframe their faulty thinking and identify thoughts that are more adaptive. In addition, a number of behavioral strategies may be employed that could also serve to enhance a student's functioning. A number of cognitive and behavioral interventions exist, and there are many resources that discuss the details of these strategies, including *Clinical Practice of Cognitive Therapy with Children and Adolescents: The Nuts and Bolt* by Friedberg and McClure (2002); *Clinical Applications of Cognitive Therapy*, 2nd ed., by Freeman et al. (2004); and *What Works When with Children and Adolescents: A Handbook of Counseling Techniques* by Vernon (2002). A list of potential strategies is offered in Table 7.4.

Considering the short-term nature of CBT, it is necessary that sessions be structured in order to use the time effectively. Having a standard session structure not only provides a process for the clinician to follow but also offers some predictability for the student within the session. An example of a session structure may include the following steps:

1. Relational check-in (e.g., "How are we doing together?")
2. Collaborative agenda setting with the student

3. Brief review of between-session work (e.g., homework)
4. Discussion of student's functioning since the last session
5. Address agenda items
6. Summarize session
7. Assign new between-session work
8. Elicit feedback from the student regarding the session (e.g., "How was our session today for you?")

Between-session work (aka homework) is another important component of the CBT model. It allows the student to practice new skills throughout the time between sessions in real-time settings. Discussing the homework with the student provides a wealth of data for the practitioner to monitor progress and adjust interventions, and homework is more likely to be completed if it is reviewed. It is through the use of between-session work and continual monitoring that we will be able to start seeing the generalization of the behaviors and skills being addressed within the session. School settings are an ideal environment to practice new skills, and school-based practitioners often have more frequent feedback regarding a student's implementation and generalization of these behaviors.

Applications in the School Setting

As previously noted, the CBT model functions well in the educational system (Mennuti et al., 2006). It is cost- and time-effective, which is an important factor within the dynamics of education, especially with administration. By concentrating on teaching a student new skills to

TABLE 7.4 Examples of Behavioral and Cognitive Interventions in the School Setting

Behavioral Interventions	Cognitive Interventions
Social skills training	Thought records
Contingency management systems	Guided discovery
Relaxation training	Challenging cognitive distortions
Systematic desensitization	Examining the evidence
Activity scheduling	Reattribution
Role playing	Thought stopping
Problem-solving training	Decatastrophizing
Assertiveness training	Labeling distortions
Pleasure prediction and problem prediction	Scheduling worries

overcome difficulties, CBT is often seen as more acceptable than some other, less direct approaches to behavioral change. Given that CBT follows a problem-solving approach, it can easily dovetail with the collaborative problem-solving model already existing in schools and districts (Allen & Graden, 2005; Kratochwill, Elliot, & Callan-Stoiber, 2005; Rosenfield, 2005; Zins & Erchul, 2005).

A unique feature of mental health practice in schools is the need to work with several players (e.g., teacher, parents, reading specialist, principal, and social worker), who are all invested in addressing the needs of a student with academic or behavioral problems. Thus, services will most often not occur in isolation, but instead be integrated as part of an established problem-solving team (e.g., a child study team or student assistance team). Allen and Graden (2005) indicated that the collaborative problem-solving model is supported by research, and it is compliant with efforts to improve student outcomes. Steps of this model include (a) establishing collaborative relationships among team members, (b) identifying the problems, (c) conducting extensive problem analysis, (d) developing an intervention plan that defines specific roles and responsibilities, and (e) monitoring progress and evaluating intervention outcomes. Being part of the school's problem-solving team also enhances the school-based mental health practitioner's ability to make other professionals involved with a student aware of the difficulties, as well as the strategies being tried. This may help facilitate a continuum of services rather than relying solely on individual or small-group interventions. Teachers and other staff can be taught to use similar interventions. For instance, when working with a student with test anxiety, the school-based mental health practitioner may instruct the teacher in several relaxation strategies that can be used across settings.

Where's the Evidence in Evidence-Based Practice?

The term *evidence-based practice* generally gives the impression of a scientific seal of approval. Although there are varied interpretations of what the "evidence" in evidence-based practice constitutes, there is little dispute that school districts prefer to invest their limited resources in services that are proven to produce positive outcomes for their students. Hoagwood and Erwin (1997) reviewed 10 years of research and found cognitive-behavioral therapy to be one of only three interventions with empirical support for their effectiveness. McCellan and Werry (2003) reported that well-designed studies found cognitive-behavioral and behavioral interventions to be the best psychosocial interventions for children and adolescents with mood, anxiety, and behavioral disorders. CBT has also been demonstrated to be effective with bipolar disorder (Vieta & Colom, 2004). Compton et al. (2004) concluded the "evidence" found CBT to currently be the treatment of choice for anxiety and depressive disorders of children and adolescents. Burns (2003), in the article "Children and Evidence-Based Practice," reported results of a meta-analysis indicating that effective treatments for a variety of childhood and adolescent disorders are almost all either cognitive-behavioral or behavioral. The reader is referred to the Kazdin and Weisz (2003) book *Evidence-Based Psychotherapies for Children and Adolescents* to review the effectiveness of CBT interventions for both internalizing and externalizing behaviors. Another resource for practitioners is Kendall's (2006) book *Child and Adolescent Therapy: Cognitive-Behavioral Procedures*, which reviews further information on empirically supported treatments for children and adolescents. In spite of the growing base of evidence demonstrating positive outcomes when using a CBT approach with children and adolescents, there should be a continued pursuit on building its efficacy and effectiveness within a school setting.

Conclusion

Given the need for short-term and effective interventions for use within school settings, the CBT model offers an approach that is flexible and consistent with the existing organization of school systems. Although this chapter focuses on the use of CBT at a targeted level of service, it is important to recognize the possible contribution that CBT has to go beyond providing interventions to those with diagnosed disabilities and to provide intervention to those at risk as well as to the entire school population. There continue to be advancements in the research supporting the use of CBT with children and adolescents, and there is growing evidence on its use within school settings. Using CBT as a means of addressing students' problems will require a paradigm shift for many educators, as many inventions have involved primarily behavioral approaches. The change in service delivery may require not only a shift in thinking regarding the orientation of services, but also the need for schools and educators to expand their view toward a continuum of mental health services based on cognitive-behavioral principles.

The Case of Todd

ASSESSMENT

Todd was referred to the school-based intervention team and recommended for individual counseling because of his acute stress and frustration with schoolwork. An assessment by the school psychologist ruled out learning problems, based on his above-average cognitive abilities and average to high-average academic achievement scores. Although his externalizing behaviors provided indication of general signs of anxiety and worry, no evaluation was reported regarding possible depressive features. Therefore, further evaluation would be needed to determine any signs of social anxiety, depression, and obsessive tendencies. From a CBT model, assessment of each area would occur using different rating scales. Two possible scales include the Beck Youth Inventories, 2nd ed. (BYI-2; Beck, Beck, Jolly, & Steer, 2005), and the Multidimensional Anxiety Scale for Children (MASC; March, 1997). The BYI-2 assesses multiple areas, and it includes self-report ratings of anxiety and depression. The MASC focuses specifically on anxiety, and will provide a greater understanding of anxiety symptoms, including the social and potentially obsessive features for his presentation. There are other possible scales that could be used with Todd, and the school-based practitioner will need to select both broad-band and narrow-band instruments to determine the information needed. Additionally, various observations and ecological data (e.g., homework completion) can also be useful in conceptualizing the case.

CASE CONCEPTUALIZATION

As noted earlier in this chapter, CBT utilizes a case conceptualization approach, which helps to summarize the case and to inform treatment or intervention decisions. When all of the assessment information is collected, the school-based practitioner uses this information to develop working hypotheses about the student's behaviors, from which the goals are developed. Remember, the idea of hypotheses generation is that they are truly working hypotheses—that is, they are developed and are modified as necessary based on information that is gathered through the intervention process.

For Todd's case, three initial hypotheses could be generated. First, the main or underlying hypothesis centers on his anxiety, as this seems to be the primary feature of his presentation. His anxiety is performance based, and he is likely to have automatic thoughts and beliefs, as well as physical responses consistent with this. His automatic thoughts may include, "My work isn't good enough," "If I turn in poor work, my teachers will think I'm an awful student," and "If my work isn't perfect, no one should see it." These automatic thoughts and his feelings of anxiety may reflect an underlying belief: "I must be perfect for people to be proud of me." The physiological responses that are often associated with anxiety include body tenseness, shallow breathing, heart pounding, and the like.

The second hypothesis centers on his social skills or interactions. However, with the information, there are two possible reasons for his anxiety. First, it is possible that he has not been "socialized" with children, and thus, he does not have the necessary skills to interact well with same-age peers. If this is accurate, his social interaction difficulties are skill based. On the other hand, his poor social interactions could be subsequent to the effect of his anxiety. That is, he spends so much time focusing on his academics that he does not have time to interact with other students appropriately. No matter which reason is accurate, it would be appropriate to provide intervention to help with his performance in this area.

The final hypothesis centers on his study skills or time management. Although he has done well in the past, there is a question of whether the change in academic skills may be due to the increasing academic demands of a higher grade level. Accordingly, part of the intervention plan should include some skill training around study skills and time management. Although this is not primary, having a goal in this area offers intervention that will augment and support the primary focus of reducing his anxiety.

GOAL SELECTION

Given the data provided on Todd, including background information from the initial interview, it appears that he is experiencing performance anxiety and social isolation. Interventions would begin by developing mutually agreed-upon goals addressing these issues. It appears that an appropriate primary goal would be for Todd to learn to manage and cope with his anxiety. This could be accomplished through cognitive restructuring and relaxation training. Second, it would be helpful to provide Todd with skills to enhance his age-appropriate social interactions and interests. This could be achieved through assessing his interests and social activities and having him complete activity-scheduling tasks. Third, although Todd appears to have good academic skills, a goal would be developed to help him learn efficient and effective ways to study and manage his study time. This could be attained by working with Todd on study skills and time management. Each of these goals will be addressed; however, they are not looked at as mutually exclusive, and instead, they are integrated within the context of the individual and his environment. Although the primary goal of decreasing anxiety appears to be the underlying issue, the other behaviors must be addressed, as they seem to be serving a maladaptive function, and to some extent maintain his anxiety. The specific objectives for each goal would be written in a behavioral manner, therefore offering an opportunity for progress monitoring. The progress monitoring would be carried out by Todd and by significant adults in his life (e.g., his teacher and mother). An example of an intervention plan for Todd is provided in Figure 7.1.

CBT INTERVENTION

Consistent with CBT and most therapy approaches, the initial phase of intervention must include an opportunity to build a relational connection (see Shirk & Russell, 1996, for additional information). To accomplish this, Todd will be encouraged to share his experiences, and the practitioner will help him reframe his thinking with compassion and not criticism in order to appreciate his strengths and develop a positive view of himself. This approach will allow Todd to take an active and collaborative role in his treatment, which is often ignored when providing intervention to students in schools. Although for this case study, we developed the goals for treatment, in a real case the intervention plan would be designed mutually between Todd and the clinician, and in schools, there will also be the involvement of others, such as parents and teachers. The collaboration not only is used with goals, but also should be integrated throughout intervention, including goal and objective development, strategy selection, and progress monitoring. The level of collaboration may change depending on the age of the student (e.g., with an 8-year-old the collaboration may be 30/70 student to clinician, whereas with a 16-year-old the collaboration may be more 50/50).

For Todd, the treatment plan above offers a list of the strategies that would be used in his case. However, there are others that could be substituted based on the conceptualization developed in collaboration with Todd. Although the space of this chapter does not offer the opportunity to discuss all possible interventions, we would like to highlight several of the interventions most consistent with CBT. In the initial session, information about Todd's thoughts would be obtained

INTERVENTION PLAN

Name: <u>Todd</u>   Date: <u>February, 2009</u>

Complaint: <u>Stressed out and frustrated with schoolwork</u>

Hypothesis: <u>Performance Anxiety and Social Isolation</u>

Goal	Goal	Goal
Learn to manage performance anxiety	Develop age appropriate social skills and interests	Improve study skills
↓	↓	↓
Objectives	**Objectives**	**Objectives**
1. Todd will reduce his negative thoughts about his ability to perform academically in school to less than 1× per day. 2. Todd will perform "10 breaths" 2 times daily at school and prior to starting his homework. 3. Todd will practice a 10-15 minute relaxation session daily. 4. Todd's anxiety ratings will decrease by 3-5 intervals.	1. Todd will identify a list of at least 10 things he is interested in doing such as after school clubs, teams, lessons, etc. 2. Todd will develop a weekly activity schedule including one weekday social activity and at least 1 weekend social activity with family and 1 activity with friends.	1. Todd will gradually reduce his time spent on homework to 60-90 per evening. 2. Todd will turn in at least 85% of completed homework daily. 3. Todd will learn effective methods to study for tests.
↓	↓	↓
Interventions	**Interventions**	**Interventions**
Dysfunctional Thought Record (DTR for Children) Relaxation Training Worry Log	Fun journal Activity Scheduling (or Pleasant Event Scheduling)	Gradual exposure to shorter homework sessions Study skills training Relaxation training
↓	↓	↓
Progress Monitoring	**Progress Monitoring**	**Progress Monitoring**
Self Monitoring Feelings Thermometer (SUDS) Beck Youth Anxiety Scale (Bimonthly)	Weekly Goal monitoring Beck Youth Depression Scale (monthly)	Weekly Goal monitoring Teacher report of homework submission rate Grades

Figure 7.1   Intervention Plan for Todd

by doing a dysfunctional thought record (DTR). There are a number of variations of DTRs, but generally they all assess similar aspects—situations, thoughts, feelings, and behaviors. A sample of a DTR was offered earlier in this chapter. Todd would be asked to keep a DTR over the following week in order to obtain some information about his thought processes. It should be noted that prior to having a student do this, he or she should be introduced or socialized to the CBT model of how thoughts, feelings, and behaviors are connected. The entire second session would be spent further discussing the basic tenets of CBT by using the student's DTR to highlight this connection. By doing this, the clinician and Todd will be able to begin moving toward learning ways to reconstruct or reframe his cognitions. The use of DTRs would continue throughout future sessions as a way to monitor his thoughts and their effect on his feelings and behaviors.

In the middle sessions, in addition to continued exploration of Todd's thought–feeling–behavior connections around his experiences, he would be introduced to anxiety management techniques, mainly relaxation training. Relaxation training would begin by teaching Todd diaphragmatic breathing to help reduce his stress. For between-session work, Todd would be asked to practice on a daily basis and keep track using a relaxation log, and he would also be asked to teach the relaxation to someone else, preferably his mother or a significant adult. Other techniques that could be taught include progressive muscle relaxation, guided imagery, and "10 breaths."

Once Todd has shown a "mastery" of relaxation techniques, he could be provided with opportunities to be exposed gradually to anxiety-provoking situations. For example, he could have to turn in an assignment that has a mistake on it or be asked to reduce the time he spends on homework. It should be noted that having him do these things prior to learning ways to reduce anxiety could be counterproductive. However, once he has the relaxation skills in place, he will be better able to use them to increase the chance he will engage in the other interventions and pull on his other internal resources to problem-solve.

Progress Monitoring

As part of the empirical nature of CBT, progress monitoring is an essential component of treatment. In Todd's case, progress monitoring would include self-report information, as well as observed information. Self-reporting should occur each session, and should use a rating based on subjective units of distress. For instance, the clinician would have Todd rate his level of anxiety over the past week on a scale from 1 to 10, with 1 being no anxiety and 10 being the most anxiety he has felt. To engage Todd in this, it could be presented as a *feelings thermometer*, and he could color it to represent his level of anxiety for the week. In addition, every third session, Todd would be requested to complete a standardized scale, such as the anxiety subscale of the BYI-2, mentioned earlier.

Other progress monitoring could be collected by his teacher or mother. For instance, his teacher could be asked to track his percentage of assignments completed and turned in. His mother could provide a record of the amount of time he is spending on homework. Data can be collected and used in many ways; however, a key point to remember is to only collect data that you will use. The intervention plan provided in Figure 7.1 offers other suggestions of information that would be collected for Todd. As with other model of progress monitoring, the information can be graphed or charted in order to offer visual representation of a student's progress. The results of the outcome not only are meaningful to Todd but also should be used by the therapist to make adjustments in goals, objectives, and interventions.

CONCLUSION

In summary, given the information offered on Todd, his treatment intervention would most likely consist of 8 to 12 sessions over a 3- to 4-month period. The final phase of his intervention would be to develop a maintenance plan, and this could include periodic "booster" sessions to help maintain his progress. Because the case conceptualization and treatment plan are considered fluid documents, they will be revisited throughout the work with Todd, and modifications will occur as needed.

References

Allen, S. J., & Graden, J. L. (2005). Best practices in collaborative problem solving for intervention design. In A. Thomas & J. Gimes (Eds.), *Best practice in school psychology IV* (Vol. 1). Bethesda, MD: National Association of School Psychologists.

Beck, A. T. (1967). *Depression: causes and treatment*. Philadelphia, PA: University of Pennsylvania Press.

Beck, A. T., Rush, A. J., Shaw, B. F., & Emery, G. (1979). *Cognitive therapy of depression*. New York: Guildford Press.

Beck, J. S., Beck, A. T., & Jolly, J. B., Steer, R. (2005). *Beck Youth Inventories, Second Edition*. San Antonio, TX: Harcourt Assessment, Inc.

Burns, B. J. (2003). Children and evidence-based practice. *Psychiatric Clinics of North America, 26*, 955–970.

Christner, R. W., Forrest, E., Morley, J., & Weinstein, E. (2007). Taking cognitive-behavior therapy to schools: A school-based mental health approach. *Journal of Contemporary Psychotherapy, 37*, 175–184.

Christner, R. W., Forrest, E., Morley, J., & Weinstein, E. (2007) Applying cognitive-behavior therapy to school-based mental health. *Journal of Contemporary Psychotherapy, 37*(2). P. 71–78.

Christner, R. W., Mennuti, R. B., & Stewart-Allen, J. (2004). School-based cognitive-behavior therapy (CBT). *Pennsylvania Psychologist Quarterly*, *64*(8), 22–23.

Christner, R. W., & Stewart-Allen, J. (2004, November). *Using cognitive-behavioral interventions for school related problems*. Invited presentation at Intermediate Unit No. 1, Coal Center, PA.

Christner, R. W., Stewart, J., & Freeman, A. (Eds.). (2007). *Handbook of cognitive behavior therapy (CBT) groups with children and adolescents: Specific settings and presenting problems*. New York: Routledge.

Compton, S. N., March, J. S., Brent, D., Albano, A., Weersing, R., & Curry, J. (2004). Cognitive-behavioral psychotherapy for anxiety and depression disorders in children and adolescents: An evidenced-based medicine review. *Journal of the American Academy of Child & Adolescent Psychiatry*, *43*(8), 930–959.

Doll, B. (2008). The dual-factor model of mental health in youth. *School Psychology Review, 37*(1), p. 69–73.

Ellis, A. (1962). *Reason and emotion in psychotherapy*. New York: Lyle Stuart.

Freeman, A., Pretzer, J., Fleming, B., & Simon, K. (2004). *Clinical applications of cognitive therapy* (2nd ed.). New York: Kluwer Academic/Plenum Publishers.

Friedberg, R. D., & McClure, J. M. (2002). *Clinical practice of cognitive therapy with children and adolescents*. New York: Guilford.

Hoagwood, K., & Erwin, H. D. (1997). Effectiveness of school-based mental health services for children: A 10 year research review. *Journal of Child and Family Studies, 6*(4), 435–451.

Hoagwood, K., Burns, B., Kiser, L., Ringeisen, H., & Schoenwald, S. (2001). Evidence-based practice in child and adolescent mental health services. *Psychiatric Services, 52*(9), 1179–1189.

Kazdin, A., & Weisz, J. R. (Eds.). (2003). *Evidence-based psychotherapies for children and adolescents*. New York: Guilford.

Kazdin, A., Weisz, J. R., Kendall, P. C., Aschenbrande, S. G., & Hudson, J. L. (Eds.) (2003). *Child-focused treatment for anxiety. Evidenced-based psychotherapies for children and adolescents*. New York: Guilford Press.

Kendall, P. (2006). *Child and adolescent therapy: Cognitive-behavioral procedures*. New York: Guilford.

Kendall, P. C. (Ed.) (2000). *Child and adolescent therapy: Cognitive behavioural procedures* (2nd Ed.). New York: Guilford Press.

Kendall, P. C. & Macdonald, J. P. (1993). Cognition in the psychopathology of youth and implications for treatment. In K. S. Dobson & P. C. Kendall (Eds.), *Psychopathology and Cognition*. New York: Academic Press.

Kratochwill, T. R., Elliot, S. N. & Callan-Stoiber, K. (2005). Best practices in school-based problem-solving consultation. In A. Thomas & J. Grimes (Eds.) *Best practices in school psychology IV (4th Ed.)* p. 583–609. Bethesda, MD: National Association of School Psychologists.

March, J. S. (1997). *Multidimensional Anxiety Scale for Children*. San Antonio, TX: Harcourt Assessment, Inc.

McCellan, J., & Werry, J. (2003). Evidenced-based treatments in child and adolescent psychiatry: An inventory. *Journal of the American Academy of Child & Adolescent Psychiatry, 42*(12), 1388–1400.

Mennuti, R. B., & Christner, R. W. (2005). School-based cognitive-behavioral therapy (CBT). In A. Freeman (Ed.), *International encyclopedia of cognitive behavior therapy*. New York: Kluwer/Springer.

Mennuti, R. B., Freeman, A., & Christner, R. W. (2006). *Cognitive-behavioral interventions in educational settings*. New York: Routledge/Taylor & Francis.

Murphy, V. B. & Christner, R. W. (2006). A cognitive-behavioral case conceptualization approach for working with children and adolescents. In R. B. Mennuti, A. Freeman, & R. W. Christner (Eds.), *Cognitive behavioral interventions in educational settings: A handbook for practice*. New York: Routledge Publishing.

Ollendick, T. H., & King, N. J., (2004). *Handbook of interventions that work with children and adolescents: Prevention and treatment*. Barrett, P.M., & Ollendick, T. H., (Eds.). New Jersey: John Wiley and Sons, Ltd.

Reinecke, M. A., Dattilio, F. M., & Freeman, A. (Eds.) (2003). *Cognitive therapy with children and adolescents: A casebook for clinical practice*. New York: Guilford Press.

Reynolds, C. R. & Kamphaus, R. W. (2002). *The clinicians guide to the behavior assessment system for children*. New York: Guilford Press.

Rosenfield, S. R. (2005). Best practices in instructional consultation. In A. Thomas & J. Grimes (Eds.) *Best practices in school psychology IV (4th Ed.)* p. 609–625. Besthesda, MD: National Association of School Psychologists.

Sattler, J. M. (2001). *Assessment of children: Cognitive applications. Fourth Edition*. San Diego, CA: Jerome M. Sattler Publisher Inc.

Shapiro, J. P., Friedberg, R. D., & Bardenstein, K. K. (2006). *Child and adolescent therapy: Science and art*. New Jersey: John Wiley & Sons, Ltd.

Shirk, S. R. & Russell, R. L. (1996). *Change process in child psychotherapy: Revitalizing treatment and research*. New York: Guilford Press.

Smallwood, D. L., Christner, R. W., & Brill, L. (2007). Applying cognitive-behavior therapy groups in school settings. In R. W. Christner, J. L. Stewart, & A. Freeman (Eds.), *Handbook of cognitive-behavior group therapy: Specific settings and presenting problems* (pp. 89–105). New York: Routledge.

Stallard, P. (2005). *Think good-feel good: A cognitive behavior therapy workbook for children and young people*. New Jersey: John Wiley and Sons, Ltd.

Suldo, S. M., & Shaffer, E. J. (2008). Looking beyond psychopathology: The dual-factor model of mental health in youth. *School Psychology Review, 37*, 52–68.

Vernon, A. (2002). *What works when with children and adolescents: A handbook of counseling techniques*. Champaign, IL: Research Press.

Vieta, E., & Colom, F. (2004). Psychological interventions in bipolar disorder: From wishful thinking to an evidence based approach. *Acta Psychiatrica Scandinavica, 110*(422), 34–38.

Zins, J. E. & Erchul, W. P. (2005). Best practices in school consultation. In A. Thomas & J. Grimes (Eds.) *Best practices in school psychology IV (4th Ed.)* [p. 625-645]. Bethesda, MD: National Association of School Psychologists.

8

Applying Behavior Modification in Schools

Kirk John

This chapter explores the use of behavior modification as a therapeutic tool for school-based mental health professionals. Since the inception of behavior modification interventions in the schools in the 1950s, these techniques have been heralded as a breakthrough in the successful treatment of students with behavior problems. Conceptually, the theory behind behavior modification is straightforward and this practical approach quickly gained popularity in schools. However, by the 1970s controversies with regard to its effectiveness emerged. In this regard, mental health professionals need a thorough understanding of these operant conditioning techniques to provide effective treatment.

Overview of Behavior Modification

The basic tenets of this orientation are simple and concise: All behavior serves a purpose, and all behavior is learned. Hence, if the purpose or function of a maladaptive behavior could be identified, then a plan of action could be initiated to "unlearn" the unwanted behavior and to learn an alternative, more appropriate replacement behavior (Myers, 2008). It should be noted that in the behavioral sense, *purpose* refers to the ongoing environmental contingencies that maintain a behavior and not to some symbolic or unconscious psychological motivation.

Behavioral approaches to therapy come from the school of thought in psychology known as behaviorism, which is based on the work of pioneers in field of psychology such as Thorndike, Watson, and Skinner. Bahaviorism maintains that environmental factors are central to the behaviors that people engage in throughout their lives (Ettinger, 2004). In short, previous patterns of reward and punishment for one's actions set in motion future behavior. In this regard, behavior can be viewed as a function of its consequences. In other words, the consequence of a behavior, that which follows the behavior, determines the future of that behavior. For example, if a student is recognized by his or her teacher for calling out a correct answer, it would be predicted that the student will be more likely to call out answers in the future. On the other hand, if that student was ignored or punished for calling out an answer, it would be predicted that future calling out of answers in the classroom would decrease. Of course, other variables, including cognitive states, can come into play in determining behavior; however, despite the complexity encountered, virtually all behavior can be operationally defined, evaluated, and changed. Behavior modification techniques, like other forms of behavioral approaches to therapy, are based on the systematic application of principles of learning to the creation or alteration of behavior.

Determinants of Behavior

Positive Reinforcement

As previously stated, behavior is controlled by its consequences, and all consequences can be grouped into one of four categories: positive reinforcement, negative reinforcement, extinction, or punishment. Positive reinforcement is arguably the most powerful, influential consequence in the long run and is the technique of choice when developing behavior intervention plans (Gredler, 2005). The importance of selecting and appropriately using positive reinforcement cannot be overstated. By definition, *positive reinforcement* is anything that follows a behavior and maintains or increases the frequency of that behavior. Positive reinforcement, therefore, is something that the person is motivated to obtain. For example, a child who wants his teacher's attention will act in ways that gain the teacher's attention, the student wanting an "A" will study, and a person wanting money will go to work each day.

In this regard, behavior modification is as much a theory of motivation as it is a theory of learning. If we are to get someone to change their behavior, we must be able to motivate them to engage in the desired behavior by making the desired behavior payoff. Simply stated, without a powerful reinforcer most interventions will fail. And though countless positive reinforcers exist in our environments, the dilemma is in finding the right reinforcer(s) for each person in question.

Notwithstanding the vast number of potential reinforcers, positive reinforcers can be grouped into two broad categories: primary reinforcers and secondary reinforcers. Primary reinforcers are the foundation of all reinforcement as they are unlearned, natural, biologically reinforcing agents. Primary reinforcers would include things like food, water, physical activity, and novel stimulation. In complex environments, primary reinforcers often have limited direct application, yet through classical conditioning, they serve as the basis for secondary reinforcers, and create countless reinforcement possibilities (LeFrancois, 2006). Thus, although secondary reinforcers have no inherent biological reinforcing value, they have gained the power to reinforce by being associated with a primary reinforcer or some other secondary reinforcer. Money is an excellent example of a secondary reinforcer. Certainly, we are not born needing money in the physical sense, yet because money can obtain so many things it is quite the motivator for most people. Other examples of secondary reinforcers would be praise, grades, clothing, or privileges of any sort. So reinforcers abound, but the conundrum is finding the right reinforcer(s) for the child.

Finding a reinforcer should not simply be a guess but a formal planned search for a meaningful item. This can best be accomplished by asking the child, observing the child, or interviewing others who are very familiar with the child's preferences. Once a reinforcer has been selected, a determination must be made on when and how to deliver the reinforcement so as to maximize its effectiveness. When beginning a behavioral program, it is best to administer the reinforcer continuously. The connection between the behavior that is being targeted and the presentation of the reinforcer for that behavior must be concretely established. Therefore, every time the behavior occurs, it must be followed by reinforcement to ensure the connection.

Research (Gredler, 2005) has shown that the reinforcer must be given as soon as possible after the behavior occurs to ensure that the connection is made. If too long of an interval transpires, the connection will not be made or an incorrect association with some random behavior might result. This is believed to be the explanation for the development of superstitious behavior. Athletes often demonstrate such superstitious behavior in their game-day rituals such as wearing the same article of clothing that they wore on the day they won the big game or identifying a jersey number as critical to performance.

Once a behavior has been established, the reinforcement for the desired behavior should be switched from continuous to intermittent reinforcement. This is of value because intermittent reinforcement is economical and practical: Who has time to reinforce every behavior every time it occurs? The real world does not provide continuous reinforcement; consequently, it makes sense to begin to strive for the maintenance of the target behavior in a real-world manner. Intermittent reinforcement also minimizes the impact of satiation, a phenomenon that is encountered with some reinforcers. *Satiation* refers to a reinforcer temporally losing its reinforcing properties as the person becomes "satisfied" with the reinforcer. After all, how many pieces of chocolate might a child eat before he or she no longer wants more chocolate? However, the most important reason for switching to intermittent reinforcement is that behavior maintained on an intermittent schedule of reinforcement is more resistant to extinction than behavior that is maintained on a continuous schedule of reinforcement (Martin & Pear, 2007). So, if our goal is to build behavior that lasts, intermittent reinforcement is the best option.

Intermittent reinforcement can be delivered in several ways; however, the two basic formats of intermittent reinforcement are known as *interval schedules* and *ratio schedules* of reinforcement. An interval schedule of reinforcement is based on the passage of time, and reinforcement delivered in this manner can be done via a fixed or variable time period. With fixed intervals, the time interval is static and does not vary in that the reinforcer is delivered after the passage of a predetermined time limit (e.g., every 5 minutes). The reinforcement will always be available at the end of the designated time period. With a variable interval schedule, the exact time the reinforcement will be available is not known. Instead, the availability of reinforcement varies around a predetermined time interval. For example, an average time interval of 5 minutes could be chosen, and the delivery of reinforcement would fluctuate around this time period. Reinforcement might be available after 3 minutes for the first reinforcement period and not until 6 minutes for the next.

On ratio schedules, reinforcement becomes contingent on the number of responses given, not the passage of time. Again, a fixed or variable delivery format may be chosen. With fixed intervals, the child must engage in the behavior a fixed number of times before the reinforcement will be given. With variable ratio schedules, reinforcement will be administered around a given number of responses. For example, on a fixed ratio schedule of four, a student would have to complete four worksheets before reinforcement would be delivered, and then another four worksheets to earn the next reinforcement. On the variable ratio schedule, an average of four responses per reinforcement could be chosen, but the reinforcement would be given unpredictably around the average number chosen. For example, the reinforcement might be given the first time after two responses and then not again until seven responses have been emitted, and so on.

It must be understood that the schedule one chooses to use is very important and is related to the type of behavior to be modified. Different schedules produce different types of behavior patterns. If a teacher is interested in creating a high rate of response, he or she should choose one of the ratio schedules because reinforcement is based on the number of responses emitted. On the other hand, if you want a behavior to occur over time, then an interval schedule should be chosen. To illustrate this further, if a teacher wanted a student to practice his or her multiplication tables, a ratio schedule (e.g., after every three recitations of the six tables, you will earn a token) should be chosen, whereas if a teacher wanted to increase independent study behavior, an interval schedule would be the best choice.

Negative Reinforcement

Negative reinforcement, like positive reinforcement, is a technique that is used to increase the frequency of a behavior. However, with negative reinforcement, the motivation to behave is not to obtain something wanted (positive reinforcement) but to remove or prevent something unwanted from happening. A child who completes her homework to avoid losing her recess is being controlled by negative reinforcement. In this scenario, homework completion behavior is being increased so as to avoid the unpleasant consequence of detention. Everyday life is replete with examples of negative reinforcement such as taking aspirin to remove the pain of a headache, lying to avoid punishment, and continuing to take addictive drugs so as to stop the pain of physical or psychological withdrawal. In summary, any behavior that continues or increases to eliminate an aversive stimulus is under the influence of negative reinforcement.

Extinction

Sometimes we want to eliminate a behavior, not increase it, and extinction is one of two techniques that has such an effect. *Extinction* in operant conditioning terms means not to reinforce a behavior. Simply stated, a behavior that does not pay off will diminish in frequency, and possibly, it will be eliminated altogether. Generally speaking, an employer who does not pay his workers will soon have no workers. Likewise, children who raise their hand to respond but are never called on to answer by their teacher will soon stop raising their hand.

Extinction is a slow behavioral change process; consequently, it tends to be very difficult for individuals to apply it steadfastly and consistently. In this regard, extinction tends to work best in conjunction with the positive reinforcement of an alternative behavior to the behavior being decreased. It should also be explained to all parties involved with a child that behaviors placed on an extinction schedule will get worse before they get better. This phenomenon is known as an "extinction burst" and represents the individual's attempt to manipulate the situation so as to obtain what he or she wants.

Punishment

In addition to extinction, punishment is a method of behavioral control that is employed to decrease the frequency of a behavior. Punishment seeks to decrease unwanted behavior by making the punishment contingent on the occurrence of the unwanted behavior. To achieve this end, punishment can be implemented through the presentation of an aversive stimulus or by the removal of some form of positive reinforcement.

The presentation of an aversive stimulus is what most people think of when they think of punishment, and it is known by the following names: positive punishment (because something aversive has been "added" to the environment), presentation punishment, or Type I punishment. Paddling a child or hollering at a child as a consequence of unwanted behavior would be classic examples of positive punishment. Although positive punishment can be effective in decreasing behavior, it tends not to eliminate the undesirable behavior but to suppress it only temporally. The fabled "class clown" illustrates this point. Even though the class clown is repeatedly punished, he or she resumes the aberrant behavior the next day, if not sooner. If we opt to make the aversive stimulus intense so as to increase the effectiveness of the punishment, we may decrease the behavior but at the cost of unwanted side effects. Among other things, harsh punishment has been shown to produce aggression, fear, or anxiety, and to lead to escape and/or avoidance behavior. Moreover, positive punishment has limited instructive value as it only tells the person what they have done wrong but not what they should do instead of the punished behavior.

Consequently, it has been advocated (LeFrancois, 2006) that negative punishment should generally be used in place of positive punishment, if one is to use punishment.

Negative punishment, also known as removal punishment or Type II punishment, is the removal of positive reinforcement contingent on an unwanted behavior. Time out or taking away a privilege (response cost) would be examples of negative punishment, and this form of punishment tends to avoid the negative side effects associated with positive punishment.

Case Conceptualization

The development of a successful behavioral intervention plan must be a collaborative effort. At minimum, the collaboration is between the child and the therapist; however, typically, and especially in schools, the collaboration is a team process with several collaborators (e.g., teachers, support personnel, peers, and parents) involved in the therapeutic process. In any case, the therapeutic process must begin with a comprehensive behavioral assessment. The assessment results serve as the foundation for the development of a behavior intervention plan. The plan is basically a list of contingencies that will be put into effect based on the specific behavior exhibited by the child. Stated more simply, the intervention will clearly define the specific behavior and the reinforcements delivered for desired behavior. Oftentimes, a punishment is delivered for the unwanted behavior. However, it must be understood that the process will adhere to rigorous scientific methodology. The behavior therapist will be explicit in his or her hypotheses and data driven in decision making.

Identify and Analyze the Problem

The therapeutic intervention process will begin with a general statement of the problem. However, once the target behavior(s) has been identified, it must be operationally defined (Wielkiewicz, 1995). General or abstract descriptions of the behavior are not acceptable, as such descriptions are open to speculation and, thus, resistant to precise measurement or implementation. Generally speaking, the target behavior is observable and will be stated in such a manner that no additional elaboration is necessary when the behavior is described to someone else. To say we must change little Johnny's antisocial behavior would be an unacceptable definition as "antisocial" is a vague, general concept without specific meaning. Instead, we would have to state what is meant by antisocial, such as "Johnny hits, bites, or cheats other children at school."

In conjunction with the identification of the target behaviors, the team must examine in detail the environmental niches and supports of the target behaviors. Precipitating events, consequences, and function of the behaviors are essential events the team must uncover. When doing this, the team must look across all environments (e.g., home, school, and community) in which the child is experiencing the problem to examine the "before" and "after" of the behavior in question. The "before," clues to what set a behavior in motion, is commonly referred to as the *antecedents of behavior*. Obviously, if we can manipulate these triggers of behavior, significant advantage will be gained in controlling the behavior. More importantly, the consequences of the behavior must be identified with certainty. Knowing the consequences of a behavior is to know what drives that behavior and provides the avenue by which to change it and replace it.

This search for the antecedents and consequences of a behavior is commonly referred to as the *ABCs of behavior*. *A* stands for the antecedents, *B* stands for the behavior of interest, and *C* represents the consequence that the behavior yields. To understand the consequence fully, however, we must also determine the function of the behavior. Indeed, knowing the function of a behavior is critical to knowing the true consequence of the behavior. If we misinterpret the consequence, the behavior plan is immediately in jeopardy. Hence, the emphasis today is on "function" in behavioral assessments, and this has resulted in what is now known as a *functional behavior assessment* (FBA; Watson & Steege, 2003).

To understand the importance of function, clarification on the meaning of *function* as it relates to a behavior is in order. On first impulse, one might assume that there are a myriad of possible functions for each behavior. However, globally, all behaviors result from one of two purposes: to gain something wanted or to avoid something unwanted (Watson & Steege, 2003). In the first case, to gain something wanted, we are referring to the attainment of positive reinforcement (this would include self-stimulatory behavior). In the second case, we are talking about negative reinforcement.

To bring clarity to this point, and to highlight the importance of correctly identifying the function of a consequence, consider the following scenario. Let us assume that little Johnny has a behavior problem in art class. The last 20 minutes of every art class are devoted to having the students create, free hand, a drawing or painting to be on display in the art room for the upcoming week. Inevitably, Johnny engages in disruptive behaviors during this time in art class each week. He is frequently out of his seat, commenting on the artwork of others, calling himself the teacher, or, when he is working on his project, he simply scribbles or drops paint on paper and then refers to himself as being creative. Consequently, his teacher spends time each period trying to get Johnny to remain in his seat and to work on his project with effort. Sometimes, she even laughs at Johnny's comments while trying to keep him on task. In addition, his peers find his behavior humorous and encourage his antics.

Observation of this situation suggests on the surface that the inappropriate behavior brings Johnny a lot of attention (i.e., the consequence) and that the function of his disruptive behavior is positive reinforcement. Yet, when a behavior plan is developed to provide Johnny with attention from his peers and his teachers for appropriate behavior, his inappropriate behavior continues. A more comprehensive evaluation of Johnny is then undertaken that reveals poor visual-motor-spatial skills and a history of teasing from his siblings concerning his poor artistic capabilities. Based on the new information, it can be seen that Johnny's acting-out behavior was not attention seeking at all but an attempt to avoid the criticism of others. So it is vital that a comprehensive assessment be completed, assessing all relevant settings and sources of information, to assure the correct function is identified.

The comprehensive assessment must also include the identification of the child's strengths and the identification of replacement behaviors. Concerning strengths, if positive reinforcement is to be emphasized and appropriate behaviors are to become self-generating, we must focus on what the child is good at or likes. Likewise, replacement behaviors are needed. If the inappropriate behavior manifested by the child is being engaged in to meet a need, then to take it away leaves the person with an unmet need. If we do not provide the child with an appropriate alternative, then some other behavior will be adopted by the child to meet that need, and this substitute may be no better than the one just eliminated.

Data Collection and Measurement

Once the team has been assembled and the target behaviors have been clearly and operationally defined, the assessment process begins. First, target behaviors are to be measured at their free operant level to establish a baseline (i.e., frequency of occurrence before intervention). Establishing a baseline not only provides a robust picture of the child's current problem but also provides future reference for the effectiveness of treatment. After the collection of baseline data, the intervention can be formally developed and implemented. Progress monitoring will continue throughout the course of the intervention. In this sense, assessment and intervention are then intricately linked and continuous. That is, assessment leads to an intervention, intervention monitoring (a form of assessment) leads to intervention adjustments, and so on throughout the course of the treatment.

Primary assessment techniques can be grouped into two categories: direct or indirect (Watson & Steege, 2003). Indirect assessment of the behavior refers to reports of the behavior obtained from secondary sources. Interviews of parents or teachers would be examples of indirect assessment as would the collection of data through structured inventories such as questionnaires or rating scales. Having the child role-play behaviors of concern or self-monitor his or her behaviors would also fall within the realm of indirect assessment. Although these indirect assessment techniques can yield valuable information, they are subject to observer bias and, at times, misrepresentation. Therefore, it is best, if time and resources permit, that direct assessment of the behavior be combined with the indirect assessment data to provide a comprehensive understanding of the issues to be addressed and the individual needs of the child.

Methods of direct observation and behavioral recording are numerous, and the choice of method is dependent on the type of behavior to be observed. The most straightforward method is known as *event recording*, and it refers to the recording of the behavior every time it occurs. Such frequency recording, however, is not practical with high-rate behaviors. An alternative to event recording for high-rate behaviors would be to use interval recording. Interval recording is done by breaking the observation time into time units (e.g., every 2 minutes equal one unit) and recording the behavior only once within the interval no matter how many times it occurs.

If time is limited, time sampling can be used. Time sampling takes place only at predetermined time points throughout the day. For example, the observer would rate the behavior every hour on the hour throughout the observation time. Another form of assessment is duration recording. This type of assessment is the method of choice if one is interested in measuring how long a behavior lasts (e.g., a tantrum).

Applications and Cautions for Use in Schools

Behavioral techniques have a proven history of efficacy in a wide range of settings, including school settings (Gresham, Watson, & Skinner, 2001). Moreover, behavioral interventions possess certain qualities that provide advantages over other therapeutic interventions in school settings. For example, behavioral techniques can be used regardless of the intellectual, reasoning, or verbal capabilities of the child. Consequently, behavioral interventions can be applied to special needs populations (e.g., mentally retarded or autistic) that would otherwise be unable to participate in a therapeutic intervention because of their disability. Moreover, behavioral interventions do not require intrinsic motivation on the part of the child to effect change. This is a real advantage when working with oppositional children or adolescents who are not self-referred yet engage in behaviors harmful to themselves or others. Other laudable advantages include economy of time compared to insight therapies, implementation by nonprofessionals (e.g., teachers and parents) with appropriate supervision, and problem solving that occurs in the real world. However, the most important reason for the use of behavioral interventions is that when used correctly, they work!

The research substantiating the effectiveness of behavioral interventions is undeniable; however, success is not guaranteed (Martin & Pear, 2008). In some situations, critical environmental contingencies are beyond the control of the therapist. For example, when working with children, parental or teacher cooperation is often essential to program success but is unobtainable. Or, possibly, within the confines of a school setting a powerful reinforcer cannot be found. However, too often, inconsistent application of the behavioral plan or incomplete knowledge concerning the application of behavioral techniques is the impediment to a successful intervention. In this regard, some common errors in implementing behavioral programs will be mentioned.

Inconsistent application of the behavioral plan can happen for several reasons. Sometimes team members misunderstand or do not believe the principles of learning they have been taught. Sometimes it may be a lack of commitment to the program because of the long-term, detailed effort required to effect change. Hence, it is incumbent upon the therapist to educate the team fully on basic principles, to provide ongoing support and encouragement, and to monitor the performance of team members throughout the program to ensure proper implementation.

Concerning the development of the plan itself, care must be taken to guard against simple but fatal design flaws (Witt, VanDerHeyden, & Gilbertson, 2004). To begin with, the selection of a potent reinforcer is critical. Selection of the reinforcer must always be done from the child's point of view and not from the team's point of view (Ormrod, 2008). Thus, even though something may appear to have strong reinforcing value to the team, it will have no impact on increasing behavior if it is not coveted by the child. For example, let us assume we decide to offer a child the most popular video game on the market as determined by a national survey: Would it work, and would it be a powerful reinforcer? The answer, of course, is no if our child does not like video games. The reinforcer must always be chosen based on evidence of what the child likes and not what the team thinks.

Moreover, sometimes even when a reinforcer has been found, if it is not strong enough to overpower competing reinforcers, the program will not work. This is often the case in a school setting with an attention-seeking child. Teacher attention and privileges are made contingent on appropriate behavior, yet the misbehavior continues for peer recognition. So, if a program is not working, then the first thing to reexamine is the reinforcer being used.

Care must also be taken to guard against the inadvertent use of extinction. Extinction, like all operant processes, is at work at all times, even when it is not being formally applied. Consequently, we must remember to make any and all behaviors we want to continue to pay off. Behaviors that do not pay off and that do not meet a need undergo extinction. So establishing a behavior is not enough; it must be maintained through intermittent reinforcement, or it will extinguish and previous, unwanted behaviors that do pay off will reappear.

Classroom teachers sometimes inadvertently increase discipline problems in their classrooms because of the inadvertent use of extinction. If a teacher pays attention to students only when they misbehave, and does not recognize students when they are engaging in appropriate behavior, you can be sure that the teacher will see a decrease in appropriate classroom behavior and an increase in inappropriate behavior from children wanting the attention of their teacher.

The misuse of extinction can also lead to the creation of intense unwanted behaviors. The typical response to an extinction procedure is for the child to intensify his or her behavior. This is to be expected, and if the extinction procedure is adhered to the behavior will decrease. However, if the individual's demands are met when the behavior intensifies, the inappropriate behavior will be reinforced and continue at the more intense level. The child who has been told several times that he is not allowed to go to the mall with his friends continues to nag and does so in an angry, louder voice. If the parent relents at this point for whatever reason (e.g., peace, sympathy, or fear), the child learns that escalations of behavior result in payoff. Thus, in the future, the child will use this strategy again (i.e., escalate the behavior in hopes of getting what he or she wants). And if the parent acquiesces again, we will soon have a child who is out of control and potentially dangerous. So, if extinction is to be used, it must be consistently applied or else behaviors may get worse instead of better.

On punishment, negative punishment (taking away a positive reinforcer) is the technique of choice due to the disadvantages previously stated with the use of positive punishment (Ettinger, 2004). But for negative punishment to work, that which is removed from the child must be of significant value to the child. Not removing a significant enough reinforcer is a mistake commonly encountered with the negative punishment technique of "time out." Teachers and parents who have not been successful with the use of "time out" are quick to conclude that the technique does not work. They will say, "I sent Johnny to his room for the entire evening for an entire week, and his behavior did not improve." They fail to realize that for Johnny, being confined in his room is not aversive. In fact, it is reinforcing as he does not have Mom or Dad asking him to do chores, he has a cell phone to talk to friends, and he has a TV and a CD player in his room for entertainment. Such punitive exile is not punitive; it is reinforcing. For such a strategy to work, Johnny must be deprived of something he truly does not want to lose.

A final caution has to do with data collection. Accurate record keeping is essential to knowing if a program is working and/or if modifications to the plan are needed (Witt et al., 2004). Unfortunately, it is often difficult to get parents or teachers to do ongoing record keeping as its value is not immediately apparent and as it is relatively time intensive. Therefore, it is incumbent upon the mental health practitioner to impress on all involved parties the need and advantages of progress monitoring. Points to stress would include the motivating effects on participants of graphically displayed positive results, and the ability to know if progress is being made with slow-to-change or high-frequency behaviors.

Evidence Base

The history of behavior therapy is one of empirical validation; consequently, behavioral techniques have an extensive research base. For over 50 years, researchers and practitioners alike have conducted countless investigations with school, clinical, business, and medical populations. Hundreds of books have been written elucidating the behavioral approach, and over 20 journals are devoted to the dissemination of research in this area (Martin & Pear, 2008). Consequently, a comprehensive summary of the available literature in this area is beyond the scope of this chapter. Instead, a sampling of school-based studies will be presented, illustrating the flexibility of behavior modification in dealing with a wide array of educationally related problems.

Students with severe developmental disabilities such as mental retardation or autism were among the first to be studied regarding the efficacy of behavior modification. With these populations, a remarkable range of behavioral excesses or deficits has been investigated and modified. From academics to self-injurious behaviors, no behavior would seem to be beyond the scope of this approach. A study by Wolf, Birnbrauer, Lawler, and Williams (1970) underscores the remarkable reach of operant conditioning procedures. Wolf et al. (1970) investigated classroom vomiting behavior in a 9-year-old mentally retarded, brain-damaged girl named Laura. Within 3 months of placement in a special education class, Laura began to vomit on almost a daily basis during class. Medical exams ruled out medical factors, and medications were not successful in controlling her vomiting. It was noted, however, that whenever this child vomited, she would be returned to her residence hall.

Based on this information, it was suggested that Laura's vomiting behavior was being maintained by negative reinforcement. That is, her vomiting behavior continued because it led to her removal from class. To test this hypothesis, a treatment–reversal–treatment procedure was employed. In the first phase of the program, Laura was required to remain in class regardless of her vomiting (extinction). During the initial stages of this phase, her rate of vomiting was frequent, with a high of 21 times in 1 day. However, within 30 days her rate of vomiting had declined to zero. After maintaining a zero rate for several sessions, this phase was discontinued. Phase 2 reinstated the original contingency of Laura being sent to her residence hall upon vomiting in class. Eventually, under this condition, Laura's vomiting occurred and again became frequent. Finally, the extinction procedure was again implemented, and Laura's vomiting returned to near zero with only two vomits occurring during the final 9 weeks of class.

Dealing with a less dramatic behavior, Moore, Waguespack, Wickstrom, Witt, and Gaydos (1994) demonstrated the benefit of behavior modification principles in increasing homework completion. These researchers used intermittent reinforcement and performance feedback to increase homework completion significantly with students who had a history of low homework completion. Students were informed that if they completed their daily homework to performance specifications, they would be eligible to mark their weekly homework chart for that day. And, if that day on their chart was designated as a reinforcement day, they would be allowed to choose a reward from a reinforcement menu. One of the day squares on the weekly homework chart would not result in reinforcement, so there was some unpredictability in the availability of reinforcement.

Five students in a third grade classroom and four students in a fifth grade classroom were chosen for study. The average baseline homework completion rate was 64.9% for the third graders and was 70.1% for the fifth graders. After implementing the "unpredictable" reinforcement procedure, homework completion rates rose on average for the third graders to 89.4% and for the fifth graders to 80.8%.

Using a combination of operant procedures, Musser, Kehle, and Jenson (2001) significantly reduced the frequency of disruptive behaviors in a group of emotionally disturbed students. The intervention consisted of the following techniques: public posting of classroom rules, precision requests by teachers, a token economy with response cost, and unpredictable positive reinforcement. In essence, students were versed on the classroom rules and informed that for compliance with the rules over time, they could earn stickers that could be exchanged for a "mystery" reinforcer (i.e., a valued object that was not known to the child prior to receiving it) when a predetermined number of stickers had been earned. As well, for noncompliance with rules they could lose stickers (response cost). Within this reinforcement framework, the teacher was instructed to make requests according to program guidelines and to move about the room as he or she taught.

These procedures were applied to three students, ages 8, 9, and 10, in an alternative school for special needs students meeting placement criteria for serious emotional disturbance. Disruptive behaviors monitored included failure to comply with teacher requests, talking without permission, being out of seat, playing with objects, verbal aggression, physical aggression, and being off task. At baseline, these behaviors were recorded on average in 37% of the time intervals observed. After treatment, the average number of intervals in which disruptive behavior was observed fell to 10% and remained at that level on follow-up.

Behavior modification techniques have also been applied to the treatment of abstract motivational behaviors such as a fear of failure. Stamps (1973) developed a procedure that identified a group of students in fourth, fifth, and sixth grade with a high fear of failure, and measured their expectations of success on arithmetic problems. Then, a self-reinforcement procedure was implemented whereby the students could reinforce themselves for matching correctly their level of aspiration with their actual success over a course of 10 sessions. At the beginning of each session, the students could readjust their level of expected success. Results were promising in that group gains were noted that were statistically significant in terms of more realistic aspiration levels and lower fear-of-failure scores compared to a control group that did not receive any interventions.

The Case of Todd

Based on the background information provided, Todd presents as a well-mannered, achievement-oriented child who wants very much to please others so as to receive their recognition and praise. In this regard, his excessive behavior and his performance-based anxiety are generated by the fear of being devalued by significant others for his lack of academic success. Stated in more behavioral terms, the positive reinforcement that he values the most (i.e., the praise and admiration of significant others) has largely been obtained through his exemplary behavior in academic and social situations. Consequently, as his schoolwork became more demanding and complex (transition from the third to fourth grade) and his grades declined, he began to engage in excessive study behavior in an attempt to avoid failure and the subsequent loss of personal recognition. Consequently, this case is not about eliminating one or two undesirable behaviors but about changing unrealistic expectations and irrational beliefs. In this regard, cognitively based interventions would be particularly suited for this case and should be part of the treatment regime (see chapter 6). However, traditional behavior modification techniques also have much to offer in changing Todd's maladaptive behavior, including his self-perceptions.

The following general behavioral plan illustrates how operant conditioning techniques could be used to change unwanted behaviors and to create more success for Todd based on realistic goals. In turn, the ongoing success created by realistic goal setting should rekindle his sense of self-efficacy. As always, the plan is straightforward—reinforce behaviors you want to occur, and punish or ignore behaviors you want to eliminate.

STEP 1: IDENTIFY THE PROBLEM AND OPERATIONALLY DEFINE THE TARGET BEHAVIORS

Case formulation would begin with an indirect assessment of the problem through interviews with family members, teachers, and Todd. The initial interviews, of course, are directed at identifying the problem in the form of specific target behaviors. Once the target behaviors have been identified, they must be put into operational terms to allow accurate assessment and monitoring. Fact finding concerning antecedents, consequences, and settings in which the behaviors occur would be begun, as well as a discussion of Todd's strengths and any developmental, social, family, or health problems that would be pertinent.

Based on the case data presented for Todd, the following target behaviors were identified: excessive homework completion behavior, not turning in homework, tantrum behavior, and anxiety over academic performance. Operationally defining the first three behaviors listed above is relatively straightforward; however, operationally defining anxiety over academic performance is problematic. Using terms provided by his mother, *stressed out* or *frustrated* are as vague as the term *anxiety* itself and offer no benefit. We could define *anxiety* as some measurable physiological event such as increased blood pressure or increased respiration, yet these biological responses would be hard to monitor in a school setting. However, as anxiety can be related in this case to a fear of failure, we can monitor Todd's "anxiety" through indirect behavioral responses. That is, we can measure behaviors that Todd uses to escape or avoid academic threats (e.g., excessive studying, not turning in work, and tantrum behaviors), and we can also measure that which elicits his anxiety—marginal academic performance.

On academic performance, we must define this in terms of Todd's viewpoint as he is not failing in the traditional sense. For Todd, failure would seem to mean anything less than an A. He has been a straight-A student and has received ongoing positive reinforcement for such performance for years from significant others. Teachers have described him as "perfect," and his caretakers have had high praise for his work ethic and his organizational skills. From this perspective, his excessive or avoidant behavior in regard to academic tasks is an attempt to prevent the loss of personal recognition and is being maintained through negative reinforcement.

Moreover, as the expectations of others are central to his strong need to please, we will also need to monitor parental and teacher comments concerning Todd's academic performance. It must be determined if comments are being made that criticize work products that are satisfactory (e.g., "You earned a B, but you can do better"), as well as comments that support his unrealistic attempts to seek perfection (e.g., "You can make all A's if you try hard enough"). If such comments are uncovered, they will need to be addressed in the behavior plan.

In summary, the target behaviors for this case could be stated as follows:

1. Homework completed within 60 minutes (this time was chosen based on teacher estimates of the time needed to complete the assignments)
2. Homework handed in on time
3. Verbal combativeness when told to discontinue academic tasks (i.e., tantrums)
4. Critical comments by significant others for academic work that is 75% accurate or better
5. Academic work resulting in less than 75% accuracy (based on psychoeducational assessments, this would seem to be a minimally acceptable level of performance for Todd)

Step 2: Obtain Baseline Data

Once the behaviors of concern have been determined and operationally defined, they will be monitored for frequency of occurrence before any interventions are begun. Baseline data serve several valuable purposes. First, such data provide a yardstick by which to measure the success of our behavior plan. In addition, the direct assessment of the target behaviors provides information that will confirm or, sometimes, contradict data collected through indirect assessment (e.g., interviews). For example, in this case, if we find that Todd does hand in his homework on a routine basis, we could eliminate this objective from the plan. Finally, directly observing the identified behaviors over time provides important data in regard to the environmental circumstances (e.g., antecedents, consequences, reinforcers, and settings) maintaining the behaviors that might be important to the development of the behavior plan.

STEP 3: FORMULATE A BEHAVIORAL PLAN

For each target behavior, antecedents, consequences, function, and setting events are analyzed and then integrated into a comprehensive plan of action.

Target Behavior 1: Completing Homework Within 60 Minutes

It may be that excessive study only occurs for certain types of homework. Such information could have relevancy in the overall treatment picture, and baseline data would help us in making this determination. In any case, we want to reinforce Todd when he completes his assignments within the time limit. A token reward system would be a viable option to use; however, because personal attention is such a strong motivator for Todd, reinforcement should also be provided in the form of praise from his family. Negative punishment could also be used in this case, as Todd will likely resist following the rules at first. Therefore, Todd would also lose tokens for exceptions to the rules.

Rules established concerning the completion of his homework would specify that he is to do his homework at a predetermined time each day and that he is to stop once the end time is reached. In addition, his homework performance should be monitored, initially, at 20-minute intervals to provide verbal encouragement if his work is correct or to offer assistance if he is unsure of the task. This will help reduce his rumination over his work. If he refuses to discontinue, tokens would be lost and a note would be sent to his teacher indicating Todd's progress at the designated discontinue time.

Target Behavior 2: Handing in Homework on Time

Todd's behavior of not handing in homework would seem to be a strategy used to avoid being evaluated in a negative way by his teacher on difficult assignments. For this behavior, Todd would be given tokens for bringing home an assignment sheet and for handing in his homework on time regardless of accuracy. To ensure compliance with homework policies, collaboration between the home and school would be initiated. Every day, Todd would be required to bring home a homework assignment sheet from his teacher for his mother's signature. Even on days when there is no homework, the signature sheet must still be brought home and signed.

Target Behavior 3: Tantrum Behavior Defined as Verbal Combativeness When He Is Told to Stop Working on His Studies

Generally speaking, tantrum behavior is a person's attempt to control a situation to their advantage through the use of unacceptable behavior. If given into by others, tantrum behavior will persist and can become very difficult to extinguish. In this case, we will assume that Todd engages in argumentative behavior when he is instructed to discontinue his excessive study behavior. Again, let us assume that Todd engages in such behavior only when he has difficult homework that he is unable to complete without error.

The plan for this behavior would be to have Todd's caregivers ignore his complaints and not engage in arguing with him or trying to reason with him when the tantrum occurs. If he does not comply with the rule, he will lose tokens. If he does comply, he should be given verbal praise and tokens. In addition, a *replacement behavior* would be given to Todd to use in lieu of his arguing. Todd would be allowed to request an additional 15 minutes to complete his work with adult assistance. In this way, Todd may receive instruction in an area of need and have the opportunity to complete his homework successfully.

Target Behavior 4: Critical Comments by Family Members or Teachers for Acceptable Academic Performance

As Todd harbors unrealistic expectations concerning goal setting, it is likely that significant others have contributed to these unrealistic expectations. This may have occurred unintentionally, but it must be dealt with if we are to get Todd to have positive feelings about himself for appropriate, realistic behavior. Consequently, we would have family members and teachers self-monitor their comments toward Todd in regard to academic performance. If it is found that they are contributing to his irrational belief system through negative comments, they will be instructed to abstain from such unrealistic comments and to praise accomplishments based on ability.

More specifically, whenever Todd's academic performance is at acceptable levels, he is to receive praise and recognition from others. This is to occur for any performance above 75%, and significant caregivers are not to suggest that better performance is expected (e.g., he gets a B but is told he could have had an A if he tried harder). If he scores below the cutoff level, he is not to be criticized or personally demeaned but to be given remedial assistance and praised for his effort.

Target Behavior 5: Acceptable Academic Performance Defined as Work Evaluated to Be at or Above a 75% Accuracy Level

Because the function of Todd's excessive behavior appears to be the avoidance of failure and the resultant negative evaluations of others, we want to ensure success. Toward that end, baseline data would be collected on the frequency of below-level work completed by Todd to determine if a significant achievement problem is occurring and, if so, in what academic areas. If it is found that his work is commensurate with his ability, significant others will be instructed to provide positive recognition for his efforts. This is to occur for any performance at or above 75%. If he scores below the cutoff level, he is to receive support from caregivers or his teachers on the concept. If it is found that he consistently performs below his ability level, remedial support would be provided.

Summary

Behavior modification is a powerful and practical therapeutic approach. Voluminous data documenting treatment procedures and outcome effectiveness are readily available for virtually any psychological or behavioral disorder. And for use in schools, it is unrivaled in its overall advantages compared to other treatment choices. Major advantages include effectiveness with school-aged populations, cost-effectiveness in terms of mental health practitioner–child contact time, therapeutic concepts that are understandable and meaningful to laypersons, and ease of incorporation of support personnel into the treatment program.

Moreover, child variables that can severely limit the application of other therapeutic approaches do not preclude the use of behavior modification. Minimum levels of abstract reasoning ability, intellectual development, verbal adeptness, and/or motivation to change are not prerequisites for service delivery. Traditional insight therapies or even more cognitively based behavior techniques cannot make such claims. Furthermore, behavior modification can be used not only for psychological, emotional, or behavior problems but for academic interventions as well. Consequently, the value of training in the use of behavior modification principles cannot be overstated. Behavior modification is a systematic, logical approach to improving skills or solving problems, and it is fundamental to any behavior change endeavor as it is derived from basic learning principles.

Notwithstanding the advantages of behavior modification, there are, of course, limitations and concerns (Santrock, 2008). One of the common criticisms of the use of traditional behavior modification is its reliance on factors external to the person in effecting behavior change. Stated another way, it relies on extrinsic motivation (factors outside of the person) rather than intrinsic motivation (factors within the person). The argument is that if the environmental contingencies under which the behavior was modified are discontinued, the maladaptive behavior patterns will return because we have not changed the person but the circumstances. Although there is some truth to this statement, this typically occurs only in a poorly designed program. A good behavior program will plan for and include contingencies that promote self-control and contingencies that foster generalization of the program to all environments in which the person functions (Akin-Little, Lovett, & Little, 2004).

Control, itself, is a controversial topic with the use of this form of behavior therapy. But this is a false criticism, for environmental contingencies are always at work influencing our behavior whether we are aware of them or not or in control of them or not. Clearly, scientifically based attempts to control behavior to the positive advantage of a person are preferable to letting them flounder at the whim of a capricious environment. Thoughtful planning that puts people in a positive circumstance and that gives them control of their own life is consistent with all forms of therapy and with any helping profession.

Recommended Readings

For the interested reader, a wide range of sources are available for detailed information concerning the use and applications of behavior modification.

Introduction to Behavior Modification

Martin, G., & Pear, J. (2007). *Behavior modification: What it is and how to do it* (8th ed.). Upper Saddle River, NJ: Prentice Hall.

Behavior Modification in School Settings

Watson, T. S., & Steege, M. W. (2003). *Conducting school-based functional behavioral assessments: A practitioner's guide.* New York: Guilford.

Wielkiewicz, R. M. (1995). *Behavior management in the schools: Principles and procedures* (2nd ed.). Boston: Allyn & Bacon.

References

Akin-Little, K. A., Eckert, T. L., Lovett, B. J., & Little, S. G. (2004). Extrinsic reinforcement in the classroom: Bribery or best practice. *School Psychology Review, 33,* 344–362.

Ettinger, R. H. (2004). *Psychology: The science of behavior.* Reno, NV: Best Value Textbooks.

Gredler, M. E. (2005). *Learning and instruction: Theory into practice* (5th ed.). Upper Saddle River, NJ: Prentice Hall.

Gresham, F. M., Watson, T. S., & Skinner, C. H. (2001). Functional behavioral assessment: Principles, procedures, and future directions. *School Psychology Review, 30,* 156–172.

LeFrancois, G. R. (2006). *Theories of human learning: What the old woman said* (5th ed.). Belmont, CA: Thomson Wadsworth.

Martin, G., & Pear, J. (2007). *Behavior modification: What it is and how to do it* (8th ed.). Upper Saddle River, NJ: Prentice Hall.

Moore, L. A., Waguespack, A. M., Wickstrom, K. F., Witt, J. C., & Gaydos, G. R. (1994). Mystery motivator: An effective and time efficient intervention. *School Psychology Review, 23*(1), 106–118.

Musser, E. H., Bray, M. A., Kehle, T. J., & Jenson, W. R. (2001). Reducing disruptive behaviors in students with serious emotional disturbance. *School Psychology Review, 30*(2), 294–304.

Myers, D. G. (2008). *Exploring psychology* (7th ed.). New York: Worth.

Ormrod, J. E. (2008). *Human Learning* (5th ed.). Upper Saddle River, NJ: Prentice Hall.

Santrock, J. W. (2008). *Educational psychology* (3rd ed.). Boston: McGraw-Hill.

Stamps, L. W. (1973). The effects of intervention techniques on children's fear of failure behavior. *Journal of Genetic Psychology, 123,* 85–97.

Watson, T. S., & Steege, M. W. (2003). *Conducting school-based functional behavioral assessments: A practitioner's guide.* New York: Guilford.

Wielkiewicz, R. M. (1995). *Behavior management in the schools: Principles and procedures* (2nd ed.). Boston: Allyn & Bacon.

Witt, J. C., VanDerHeyden, A. M., & Gilbertson, D. (2004). Troubleshooting behavioral interventions: A systematic process for finding and eliminating problems. *School Psychology Review, 33*, 363–383.

Wolf, M., Birnbrauer, J., Lawler, J., & Williams, T. (1970). The operant extinction, reinstatement and re-extinction of vomiting behavior in a retarded child. In R. Ulrich, T. Stachnik, & J. Mabry (Eds.), *Control of human behavior: From cure to prevention* (Vol. 2). Glenview, IL: Scott Foresman.

9

Applying Reality Therapy Approaches in Schools

Robert E. Wubbolding

Reality therapy, widely accepted and used in schools, originated in a mental hospital and a correctional institution. From the very beginning, it focused on mental health as an entity distinct from mental disorders. Because of this emphasis, reality therapists attend less to diagnosis and psychopathology than to their alternatives. Clients demonstrating emotional distress, cognitive disorders, or unacceptable behaviors are led to alternative choices, especially action-centered plans. Their tactical and strategic plans aim at increasing their positive human relationships. In addressing mental health, Glasser (2005) stated, "You are mentally healthy if you enjoy being with most of the people you know, especially with the important people in your life such as family, sexual partners and friends" (p. 5). Thus, people are happy if they experience satisfying human relationships. For such people, life is enjoyable, and they appreciate others who think and act differently. The mentally healthy person rarely criticizes or attempts to control others. Glasser stated, "If you have differences with someone else you will try to work out the problem; if you can't you will walk away before you argue and increase the difficulty" (p. 6).

More specifically, Glasser (1986) described three regressive stages of mental health not as pathological but as ineffective behaviors aimed at satisfying genetic needs.

Stage 1. *I give up.* This person has attempted to fulfill human needs effectively, but has not been able to do so. The only alternative that appears reasonable is to cease trying, thereby exhibiting listlessness, withdrawal, and apathy. Most teachers are familiar with students at this stage. This temporary stage precedes the more identifiable second stage.

Stage 2. *Negative symptoms*. Clients see their choices, including the following behaviors, as their best efforts to fulfill their wants and needs. However, these symptoms lead to more frustration:

- *Actions*. Someone exhibiting this negative symptom chooses destructive actions harmful to self or others. These range from mild acting out to severe antisocial behavior such as murder, rape, or suicide.
- *Thinking*. Cognitive disturbances are also attempts to fulfill needs. And though such efforts often succeed in controlling others, they are harmful and self-destructive. The word *disturbance* is used in a wide sense to include negative cognition, ranging from the chronically pessimistic and negativistic thinker to a person with severe psychotic conditions.
- *Feelings*. Negative emotions include a spectrum ranging from mild to severe depression, from chronic annoyance to habitual anger or rage, and from the "worried well" (Talmon, 1990) to phobic disorders.
- *Physiology*. Other ineffective attempts to fulfill needs, used when other choices do not appear to be available to a person, include physical ailments. Many such maladies are best treated not only with good medical care but also through counseling or psychotherapy designed to help clients make better choices—that is, to choose positive symptoms. As with students in stage 1, teachers are all too familiar with stage 2 students.

Stage 3. *Negative addictions*. Negative addictions to drugs, alcohol, gambling, work, and other behaviors or substances represent another regressive stage of ineffective behaviors aimed at fulfilling needs. Addicted students and children of chemically dependent families are well known to educators.

These three stages of regressively ineffective behaviors are not rigid and exclusive of one another. On the contrary, they provide a way to conceptualize ineffective human behavior related to need fulfillment. They also represent the reverse of effective behaviors.

Positive Stages

The positive stages of mental health offer effective ways to fulfill human needs. They serve to balance the negative stages and can be presented to clients and students as characteristics of mental health and as goals for the counseling or therapy process as well as for the entire educational process (Wubbolding, 2006).

Stage 1. *I'll do it; I want to improve; I am committed to change.* Such explicit or implicit statements made by clients represent the first stage of effective choices. This stage, like its negative mirror image, is quite temporary.

Stage 2. *Positive symptoms.* The following behavioral choices are effectively need-fulfilling and lead to less frustration and pain.

- *Actions*. Effective choices aimed at fulfilling human needs include both assertive and altruistic behaviors. Healthy individuals know how to get what they want, yet they contribute to society through family life, employment, and community service, and in many other ways.

- *Thinking*. The mirror image of cognitive disturbance is rational thinking. Among the many rational thinking patterns implicit in reality therapy are a realistic understanding of what one can and cannot control, acceptance of what is unchangeable, and knowledge that one is responsible for one's own behavior. Therefore, reality therapists reject the view that all early childhood traumas must of their nature continue to victimize a person throughout life.

- *Feelings*. Patience, tolerance, sociability, acceptance, enthusiasm, trust, and hope are among the emotions that are positive behaviors and energizing goals in the practice of reality therapy.

- *Physiology*. Another symptom of an effective lifestyle is the effort to attend to one's physical needs. Care of one's body, proper diet, and reasonable exercise are symbols of effective need fulfillment.

Stage 3. *Positive addictions.* Glasser (1976) has identified activities that enhance mental health and are intensely need satisfying. Included are running and meditation. Such behaviors, as well as others that approach positive addiction, are the opposite of negative addictions. Rather than being self-destructive, positive addictions add to psychological development and increase feelings of self-worth and accomplishment. Such addictions are the result of habitually but noncompulsively choosing the behavior for 12 to 18 months, for a limited time such as 45 minutes per day (or at least on a regular basis), and in a noncompetitive way.

Like the negative stages, the stages of growth are not absolutely discrete categories. Human beings exhibit many characteristics and can float back and forth from the negative to the positive. No one lives entirely in a world of ineffective or effective choices. Even the most disturbed person occasionally chooses effective behaviors, just as even the most well-adjusted person makes unhealthy or ineffective choices at times.

In summary, the principles of reality therapy allow for applications to any stage of a person's chronological and psychological development. They are applicable to preschool, elementary, and secondary students. Reality therapists use these principles at every stage of adult development. For instance, the use of quality time (i.e., time spent together in a noncritical way) can be adapted to persons of any age or time of life. Furthermore, human development is seen as a series of choices leading to stages of regression or the stages of effective need satisfaction (Wubbolding & Brickell, 2001). In schools, teachers incorporate the need system of choice theory and the WDEP system of reality therapy or lead management to remediate and prevent problems as well as to facilitate mental health and personal growth.

Overview of the Therapeutic Approach

Gaining insight, seeing connections, and reaching a higher level of self-awareness are often the result of the effective use of reality therapy. Still, their achievement does not constitute the primary aim of reality therapy. The fundamental goal of reality therapy is not and has never been the resolution of unconscious conflicts. Rather, behavioral change and improved need satisfaction comprise the goal of reality therapy. Its use is generally short term, empathic, direct, focused, and outcome based.

The founder of reality therapy, William Glasser, developed the system in a mental hospital and in a correctional institution (Glasser, 1965). Trained in the theory and practice of psychodynamic therapy, he rejected his formal training when he noticed that many of the successful therapists held clients responsible for their behavior. Although they theoretically taught the psychoanalytic method, he noticed that what seemed to be effective was often closer to what he would subsequently call *reality therapy*. Encouraged and mentored by his nonanalytical teacher, G. L. Harrington, Glasser formalized reality therapy in the early 1960s (Glasser, 1960). O'Donnell (1987) described how Glasser presented his unorthodox beliefs to Harrington. Instead of reprimanding Glasser, Harrington shook his head and said, "Join the club!" A 7-year relationship ensued during which they formulated the ideas that would become reality therapy. Harrington, in turn, had been influenced by Helmuth Kaiser, with whom he had worked at the Menninger Clinic in the 1950s. Kaiser (1955) believed that the goal of psychoanalysis should be to help patients take responsibility for their actions. Thus, he also had begun a journey away from conventional analysis.

The publication of *Reality Therapy* (1965) marked a watershed in the beginning of the delivery system that later found its validating theory, now known as *choice theory*. At first, reality therapy appealed to social workers, counselors, and educators. Trained to help patients resolve unconscious conflicts, psychiatrists rejected the foundational principles of reality therapy: current motivation, responsibility for actions, and behavioral choice. Because of its action-centered method and its absence of conventional and sometimes off-putting psychological terminology, teachers began to use it in their classrooms. The ultimate result was the publication of the book *Schools Without Failure* (Glasser, 1968), which described the schoolwide application of reality therapy, the heart of which was the class meeting. Other applications to schools include classroom use (Glasser, 1993; Sullo, 2007), classroom management (Glasser & Wubbolding, 1997; Wubbolding, 1993, 1997), and organizational development in schools (Glasser, 1990). Significant extensions of the principles of choice theory include management (Wubbolding, 1996), spirituality (Wubbolding, 1992), and cultural adaptations (Wubbolding, 2007; Wubbolding, Brickell, Imhof, Kim, Lojk, and Al-Rashidi, 2004).

Choice theory provides the basis for the delivery system of reality therapy. Originally, it was called *control theory* or *control system theory* because of the fundamental purpose of human behavior: to gain a sense of internal control. Five principles constitute the foundation for assisting clients and students in maintaining and achieving mental health:

1. Human beings are motivated to fulfill needs and wants. Human needs are general and universal. Wants are specific and unique to each individual. From the point of view of choice theory, five genetic motivators are the driving forces of human nature. The need for belonging and love urges human beings to seek relationships with others. This need expresses itself in the family, at work, and in society. The slogan "People need people" is not a mere cliché but rather a profound truth. Even hermits need people—to stay away from. The second need, power or inner control, motivates people to achieve, gain recognition, maintain self-esteem, reach varying levels of competence, and compete. Clearly, this need is not limited to the spirit of competition. Rather, it focuses on a sense of inner control, self-regulation, and pride in accomplishment. Freedom, the third need, motivates people to make choices and to be independent. The fourth psychological need, fun or enjoyment, leads human beings to laugh, to see incongruities, and to enjoy their relationships, their talents, their time, their choices, and the satisfaction of their curiosity (i.e., their learning). The fifth inner motivator, self-preservation or survival, is the foundation for life. Because of the need to preserve their existence, human beings develop appropriate behaviors such as biological functions. The survival need expresses itself in many

ways. Self-preservation for a homeless person requires skills quite different from those needed by the executive in the boardroom of a thriving
business.

Human needs, although not specific, provide the basis for the development of specific wants of each need. Consequently, a person develops
a specific want or picture of an individual who can satisfy the need for
belonging, an activity addressing the need for inner control, specific
desired choices connected with the freedom need, and concrete pictures
of fun or enjoyment. Wubbolding (2008) stated, "Wants are unique
to each individual and develop from choices designed to satisfy needs
within the context of a person's family and cultural environment" (p.
369).

2. The discrepancy between what human beings want and what they
perceive they are getting from the world around them is similar to an
out-of-balance scale. This difference or gap between "a want and a got"
constitutes the proximate cause of behavior aimed at fulfilling specific
wants and thereby putting scales in balance. For instance, an adolescent wanting independence and expressing it with the often repeated
theme "I want to be left alone" generates behaviors designed to achieve
that purpose. Such a student has a clearly defined want and an intensely
out-of-balance scale in that he or she is virtually never left alone. Many
such students' interactions with adults result in mutual arguing, blaming, criticizing, demeaning, and efforts to scare the other party. Thus,
the student experiences a painful chronic condition of tilted scales.

3. Human behavior, a composite of action, cognition, emotions, and physiology, has a twofold purpose. It is designed to satisfy wants and close
the frustration gap between a want and the perception that the want is
unfulfilled. The student generates behaviors in an attempt to achieve
his or her purpose (i.e., to be left alone). The second purpose of human
behavior aims at communicating with the world around us. Behavior,
especially actions and language, sends a signal to the environment. The
rebellious and belligerent behavior of the uncooperative student not
only is an attempt to maneuver the world but also constitutes the closely
allied purpose of communicating, "I want to be left alone." In this case,
the effort fails, and the people around the student often perceive the
opposite message: "I want constant reprimands and negative attention."
Too often, adults willingly heed the implied request. Glasser and Glasser
(1999) stated, "Choice theory language helps us to work out problems
with one another; external control language increases them" (p. viii).
The idea of behavior as a language provides the foundation for the effective use of a reality therapy tool: asking students to evaluate their own
behavior, for example "Is the message you are sending getting you what
you want?" (Wubbolding & Brickell, 2005).

4. Human behavior is best seen as chosen. More precisely, the action or doing component of human behavior presents the most easily changed part of total behavior (action, cognition, emotions, and physiology). The choice to alter actions results in an eventual change in thinking and feelings. Therefore, action is the handle on the suitcase of behavior. When someone lifts a suitcase by the handle, the entire suitcase follows. However, choice does not imply total control over each component of behavior. Wubbolding (1999) stated, "Compulsions, phobias, and psychoses are not explicitly chosen, but they can be dealt with from the *as if* position—treated as if they are choices and thus can be lessened and improved, if not cured" (p. 61). Jay Haley (1973) has emphasized that conceptualizing cases based on theory need not imply that the theory fits every specific situation perfectly.

5. Human beings see the world through a perceptual system. Information received from the external world is filtered through a knowledge filter or a low level of perception and through a valuing filter or high level of perception. The low level of perception allows human beings to recognize facts, people, ideas, and other data without putting a positive or negative value on them. By means of the valuing filter or high-level perception, we place a positive or negative value or judgment on the filtered information. The excitable and aggressive student sees people and circumstances working against him or her, resulting in a negative value placed on the external world as perceived. Teachers and parents perceive the students' behavior from a high-level perception, placing a negative value on it. On the other hand, an apathetic and disengaged student perceives much of the world from a low-level perception. This student's motto might be "I don't care." Consequently, the goal of the mental health practitioner using reality therapy is sometimes to help students lower their levels of perception and at other times to raise their levels of perception.

Choice theory, the basis of reality therapy, embodies the principles of internal control psychology. It explains how human behavior originates from within human beings, and it is not thrust upon them from the outer world. Mental disorders and emotional disturbance are not the result of external coercion. Rather, they are the result of our inability to satisfy our genetic human needs effectively: love and belonging, power or inner control, freedom or independence, fun or enjoyment, and survival or self-preservation. Choice theory does not deny the relevance of external influences. In circumstances such as imprisonment, loss of health, extreme physical deprivation, and the like, the only behavior seemingly available to the sufferer could be mental withdrawal or aggression. The role of the user of reality therapy is to help clients and students realize that irrespective of circumstances, they have potentially empowering choices available to them, especially regarding their relationships. When relationships improve, painful circumstances become at least somewhat more bearable.

Assessment and case conceptualization

Absent from the use of reality therapy are scientifically validated assessment instruments based solely on choice theory. However, the delivery system for mental health counseling and for prevention of mental disorders, reality therapy, overflows with specific techniques and tools for use in education. These skills are divided into two general components: environment and procedures.

Environment

Creating an appropriate trusting atmosphere lies at the basis of reality therapy implementation in counseling and in the classroom. Trust is built on an atmosphere that is characterized by the three F's: firmness, fairness, and friendliness. Children know what to expect and understand that their choices have consequences, both positive and negative. Adults using reality therapy demonstrate flexibility and consistency in applying policies and rules. They show a friendly attitude even when imposing negative consequences. More specifically, educators avoid behaviors such as arguing and attacking, blaming and belittling, criticizing and coercing, demeaning, colluding with excuses, instilling fear, giving up, and holding grudges that destroy trust, diminish healthy relationships, and create a toxic atmosphere. In contrast, they utilize tonic behaviors that build trust, facilitate healthy relationships, and create a need-satisfying atmosphere. Among such healthful behaviors are listening, doing the unexpected, using humor, allowing consequences, creating a sense of anticipation and eagerness in the classroom, accepting only quality work, and increasing choices (Figure 9.1).

Because mental health is rooted in healthy human relationships, educators using reality therapy in schools focus on their relationships with other adults and with children. Glasser (2005) stated,

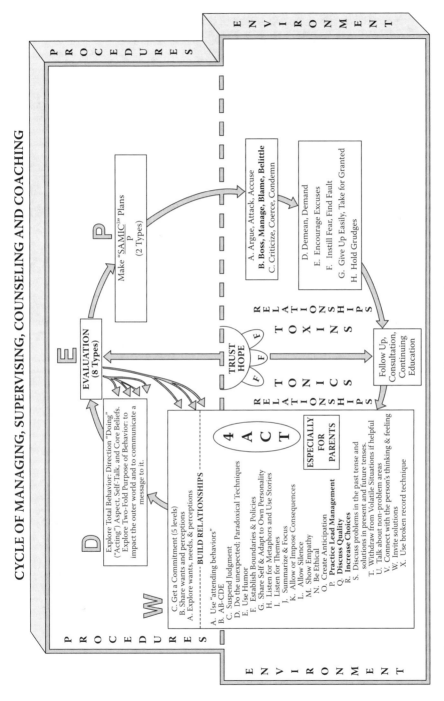

Figure 9.1 Cycle of Managing, Supervising, Counseling, and Coaching

SUMMARY DESCRIPTION OF THE
"CYCLE OF MANAGING, SUPERVISING, COUNSELING AND COACHING"

The Cycle is explained in detail in books by Robert E. Wubbolding:
Employee Motivation, 1996: Reality Therapy for the 21st Century, 2000
A Set of Directions for Putting and Keeping Yourself Together, 2001

Introduction:

The Cycle consists of two general concepts: Environment conducive to change and Procedures more explicitly designed to facilitate change. This chart is intended to be a **brief** summary. The ideas are designed to be used with employees, students, clients, as well as in other human relationships.

Relationship between Environment & Procedures:

1. As indicated in the chart, the Environment is the foundation upon which the effective use of Procedures is based.

2. Though it is **usually** necessary to establish a safe, friendly Environment before change can occur, the "Cycle" can be entered at any point. Thus, the use of the cycle does **not** occur in lock step fashion.

3. Building a relationship implies establishing and maintaining a professional relationship. Methods for accomplishing this comprise some efforts on the part of the helper that are Environmental and others that are Procedural.

ENVIRONMENT:

Relationship implies a close relationship is built on TRUST and HOPE through friendliness, firmness and fairness.

A. Using Attending Behaviors: Eye contact, posture, effective listening skills.
B. AB = "Always **B**e . . ." Consistent, **C**ourteous & **C**alm, **D**etermined that there is hope for improvement, **E**nthusiastic (Think Positively).
C. Suspend Judgment: View behaviors from a low level of perception, i.e., acceptance is crucial.
D. Do the Unexpected: Use paradoxical techniques as appropriate; Reframing and Prescribing.
E. Use Humor: Help them fulfill need for fun within reasonable boundaries.
F. Establish boundaries: the relationship is professional.

     4
     A
     C
     T

- Affirm feelings
- Accept
- Show affection
- Action consequences
- Conversation (WDEP)
- Time together

G. Share Self: Self-disclosure within limits is helpful; adapt to own personal style. Use stories.
H. Listen for Metaphors: Use their figures of speech and provide other ones.
I. Listen to Themes: Listen for behaviors that have helped, value judgments, etc.
J. Summarize & Focus: Tie together what they say and focus on them rather than on "Real World."
K. Allow or Impose Consequences: Within reason, they should be responsible for their own behavior.
L. Allow Silence: This allows them to think, as well as to take responsibility.
M. Show Empathy: Perceive as does the person being helped.
N. Be Ethical: Study Codes of Ethics and their applications, e.g., how to handle suicide threats or violent tendencies.
O. Create anticipation and communication hope. People should be taught that something good will happen if they are willing to work.
P. **Practice lead management, e.g., democracy in determining rules.**
Q. **Discuss quality.**
R. **Increases choices.**
S. Discuss problems in the past tense, solutions in present and future tenses.
T. Withdraw from volatile situations if helpful.
U. Talk about non-problem areas.
V. Connect with the person's thinking and feeling.
W. Invite solutions.
X. Use broken record technique.

Relationship Toxins:

Argue, **Boss Manage,** or Blame, Criticize or Coerce, Demean, Encourage Excuses, Instill Fear, or Give up easily, Hold Grudges.

Rather, stress what they **can** control, accept them as they are, and keep the confidence that they can develop more effective behaviors. Also, continue to use "WDEP" system without giving up.

Follow Up, Consult, and Continue Education:

Determine a way for them to report back, talk to another professional person when necessary, and maintain ongoing program of professional growth.

PROCEDURES:

Build Relationships:

WDEP

A. Explore **W**ants, Needs & Perceptions: Discuss picture album or quality world, i.e., set goals, fulfilled & unfulfilled pictures, needs, viewpoints and "locus of control."
B. Share Wants & Perceptions: Tell what you want from them and how you view their situations, behaviors, wants, etc. This procedure is secondary to A above.
C. Get a Commitment: Help them solidify their desire to find more effective behaviors.

Explore Total Behavior:

Help them examine the **D**irection of their lives, as well as specifics of how they spend their time. Discuss core beliefs and ineffective & effective self talk. Explore two-fold purpose of behavior: to impact the outer world and to communicate a message to it.

Evaluation – The Cornerstone of Procedures:

Help them evaluate their behavioral direction, specific behaviors as well as wants, perceptions and commitments. Evaluate own behavior through follow-up, consultation and continued education.

Make **P**lans: Help them change direction of their lives.

Effective plans are **S**imple, **A**ttainable, **M**easurable, **I**mmediate, **C**onsistent, **C**ontrolled by the planner, and **C**ommitted to. The helper is **P**ersistent. Plans can be linear or paradoxical.

Note: The "Cycle" describes specific guidelines & skills. Effective implementation requires the artful integration of the guidelines & skills contained under Environment & Procedures in a spontaneous & natural manner geared to the personality of the helper. This requires training, practices & supervision. Also, the word "client" is used for anyone receiving help: student, employee, family member, etc.

For more information contact:

Robert E. Wubbolding, EdD, Director

Center for Reality Therapy
7672 Montgomery Road, #383
Cincinnati, Ohio 45236

(513) 561-1911 • FAX (513) 561-3568
E-mail: wubsrt@fuse.net • www.realitytherapywub.com

The Center for Reality Therapy provides counseling, consultation, training and supervision including applications to schools, agencies, hospitals, companies and other institutions. The Center is a provider for many organizations which award continuing education units.

This material is copyrighted. Reproduction is prohibited without permission of Robert E. Wubbolding. If you wish to copy, please call.

Figure 9.2   Summary Description

You are mentally healthy if you enjoy being with most of the people you know, especially with the important people in your life … you lead a mostly tension-free life, laugh a lot, and rarely suffer from the aches and pains that so many people accept as an unavoidable part of living … it rarely occurs to you to criticize … if you have differences with someone you will try to work out the problem. (pp. 2–3)

Procedures

Wubbolding, (1991, 2000, 2006) has formulated the acronym WDEP, which stands for *wants, doing, evaluating,* and *plan,* and is useful for remembering and teaching specific reality therapy interventions with individuals and in the classroom. Each letter stands for a cluster of interventions springing from the five principles of choice theory enumerated above and epitomized in the foundational idea that human motivation is internal, with the corollary that human beings are responsible for their choices.

W

Define and clarify specific *wants.* When people interact with their environment, they accumulate a storehouse of specific wants or desires (i.e., specific pictures of what they want related to each need). Even with children demonstrating emotional disturbance or antisocial behavior, school personnel using the WDEP system enhance their relationships by helping students express their wants. Such effort does not imply that teachers can always accommodate the wants of students. Nevertheless, through the discussion of students' wants, teachers can deepen their relationship with students and thereby affect their mental health.

If counselors, social workers, psychologists, and administrators approach the students with consistency and with a similar school philosophy and vocabulary, students realize that the school is a safe place for them and one that provides opportunity for them to prosper emotionally and intellectually. This prosperity is the healthy alternative to emotional disengagement.

D

Explore total behavior with emphasis on action or *doing.* Users of the WDEP system emphasize discussion of actions over feelings in their interaction with the students. Emotions are important and need to be acknowledged. However, a change in actions accomplishes a change in feelings. An adult asks an angry child about actions after acknowledging his or her anger, resentment, or rage. A withdrawn child is often more willing to discuss actions rather than feelings of depression or isolation. Feelings are analogous to the lights on the dashboard of an automobile. They provide a vivid reminder to the driver that action should be taken. They are not the source of the problem or the problem itself.

Because behavior is total, cognition accompanies actions and feelings. In addition, although human beings have explicit control over actions more than other components of the behavioral system, they have some control over their thinking. Consequently, it is often useful to discuss with students their self-talk accompanying their actions. Wubbolding (2008) has identified both ineffective and effective internal language congruent with actions. Harmful or less effective actions are tied to such statements as the following:

1. "I have no control over my life. I have no choices. I am a victim."
2. "Nobody can tell me what to do. I can do anything I feel like doing."
3. "Even though what I'm doing is not helping me or other people, I'm going to continue to do it."
4. "Even though my wants cannot be fulfilled, I will continue to pursue their satisfaction."

It is often useful to ask clients about their thinking and to help them identify ineffective self-talk with the goal of helping them replace self-debilitating cognition and accompanying actions with positive and productive thoughts such as the following:

1. "I am in control of my life. I have choices and opportunities. I am a self-starter, not a victim."
2. "I am most effective when I live within reasonable boundaries. I recognize that the external world puts restrictions on my choices and that my choices have consequences."
3. "If what I am doing is ineffective—that is, not helping me or other people—I will choose another behavior."
4. "I will evaluate the realistic attainability of my wants and adjust them so that they are at least partially attainable."

Users of reality therapy do not shun discussions of feelings. On the contrary, they acknowledge emotions as paramount in mental health. If the most obvious and noticeable component of a student's behavior is a feeling, the counselor, therapist, or teacher acknowledges it but realizes that helping the child feel better means more than identifying and getting in touch with feelings. Wubbolding (1988) stated,

> Motivation is rooted in unresolved frustrations: the gaps between what we want and what we get which, when closed, result in need fulfillment. Thus feelings, an inseparable part of total behavior, are generated to close the gaps and fulfill needs ... human beings do not act *primarily* to feel better. They act, feel and think in order to get what they want. (p. 44)

The emphasis on actions makes reality therapy practical and appealing to teachers and school administrators. Although they do not identify themselves as mental health specialists, they deal with mental health issues on a daily basis. Therefore, users of reality therapy such as counselors, therapists, and other school personnel can be consistent in their interactions with students, thereby reinforcing the message given to students: "We are here to help you make better choices, especially action choices, with the result that you can feel good about school, about learning, and about your relationships with your peers and with adults. Moreover, you will learn what you need to know and maintain your mental health."

E

Self-*evaluation* provides the cornerstone for the WDEP mental health delivery system and constitutes the major prerequisite for change. No one alters a behavior or makes choices that are more effective before judging that current choices are ineffective, unhelpful, or destructive. Students not studying; wasting time by hanging out; demonstrating oppositional defiance, conduct disorders, or more serious pathology; or simply yielding to harmful impulses do not change their behavior until they clearly define their wants, study a range of choices, and firmly judge the desirability of their behavior. Professionals help school personnel (i.e., colleagues), parents, and students define what they want, help them connect their actions to their wants, and assist them in a courageous self-evaluation about the short- and long-term efficacy of their actions. This effort can be carried out in individual conferences, in group counseling, or with large groups in a classroom.

Wubbolding (2000, 2006) has enumerated 22 kinds of self-evaluation. Among the most significant issues are questions such as the following:

- Is your current behavior improving or diminishing your relationships with others?
- Have your recent actions resulted in the satisfaction of your wants, or have they resulted in undesirable consequences?
- How is your current behavior impacting other people? Is it helping or hurting them?
- Does it have a favorable or a destructive effect on their actions, thinking, or feelings?
- Are your current action choices against the law, the rules, or the school policies?
- Are your current action choices acceptable or unacceptable (i.e., against the unwritten norms of the school culture)?

- Are your wants attainable and realistically achievable?
- Are your wants really and truly good for you in the long run, not merely in the short run?
- You have expressed a level of commitment. Is it firm enough to accomplish the task?
- It is your perception that you have very little control over your life. Is it *really* true that you have little control over your actions and circumstances?
- You have made a plan. How likely is it to succeed? Does it contain the characteristics of an effective plan?

Users of the WDEP system help students and clients conduct a serious self-evaluation by asking relevant questions about various components of their motivational system: behavior, wants, and perceived locus of control. Often disturbed individuals, substance abusers, or children of chemically dependent families require a more guided approach. Similarly, the WDEP system should be used in a developmentally appropriate manner. It is often necessary to teach directly what works and what does not work, what is appropriate and inappropriate, what is acceptable and unacceptable, what facilitates and what prevents learning, and what serves and hinders the purpose of the school.

P

Discussions of current wants, behaviors, and self-evaluations usually precede a *plan* of action. Still, plans of action can be effective or ineffective and are subject to evaluation. Plans need not be grandiose or rapidly curative. But useful plans are SAMIC² plans:

Simple: uncomplicated and understandable.
Attainable: realistically doable and within the power of the planner.
Measurable: answers the question, "*When* will you do it?"
Immediate: carried out in the near future, not in the distant future.
Controlled: by the planner—not dependent on the behavior of other people.
    The plan is positive and is often called a *do plan* rather than a *stop plan*.
Consistent: repeated on a regular basis.

Although asking the question "What's your plan?" seems simple, an underlying metacommunication takes place. This simple question and other questions in the WDEP system impart a sense of hope and a belief in personal responsibility through implicit and sometimes explicit awakenings. "I need not be victimized by my own behavior or by emotional turmoil in my life." "Change is possible, and I can make it happen." "Other people can help me, and I cannot blame the external world for my plight."

Applications to School Settings

The WDEP system fosters mental health as well as remediates mental disorders. From the very beginning, reality therapy emphasized mental health (Glasser, 1960). Glasser stated that helping people with emotional disturbance meant assisting them to move from irresponsible to responsible behaviors. "Therapy is a special kind of teaching or training which attempts to accomplish in a relatively short and intense period what should have been established during normal growing up" (Glasser, 1965, p. 20).

The use of reality therapy in schools has reached beyond therapeutic interventions. The Schools Without Failure program introduced class meetings as a tool for enhancing mental health by satisfying students' needs, especially those of belonging and power or recognition (Glasser, 1968). The centrality of need satisfaction as an alternative to behavioral and mental problems is the core of the Glasser Quality School. In schools using the principles of choice theory and reality therapy, students elevate their levels of learning and their behavior.

Evidence Base

Reality therapy has been researched in a variety of settings. For instance, follow-up studies of former prisoners over a 12-year period found 84% of them completely or partially rehabilitated (Lojk, 1986). Using a single subject design with a client previously diagnosed with dysthymic disorder and somatization disorder and rediagnosed with posttraumatic stress disorder (PTSD), Prenzlau (2006) concluded that intervening with reality therapy reduced somatization and rumination behaviors often connected with PTSD. Chung (1994) studied the application of reality therapy to Hong Kong delinquent youth. Such youth are sometimes impervious to conventional counseling. She selected youth who demonstrated not only socially unacceptable behaviors but also low self-esteem. In the study, she found these youth significantly increased their self-esteem. Also, 55% increased their social communication, and 50% gained in self-confidence, ability to select friends, and problem solving. Finally, a resounding 65% even suggested that group therapy should extend from 12 weekly sessions to 20 sessions. In a meta-analysis of 43 studies conducted in Korea, Kim and Hwang (2006) found increases in self-esteem and locus of control of students in primary grades, junior and senior high school, and undergraduate school. Other studies conducted at Sogang University in Korea revealed a significant increase in a sense of inner control for students of both genders (Woo, 1998). A study of 313 students conducted by Bratter, Collabolletta, Gordon, and Kaufman (1999) at the John Dewey Academy, a residential school for alienated and angry adolescents, showed that 28% graduated and "100% of the graduates attend colleges of quality and 80% complete their higher education" (p. 11). The authors attributed the success to the confrontive, therapeutic, but nurturing orientation of the school. Lawrence (2004) studied the impact of reality therapy on persons with developmental disabilities who were randomly assigned to a support group or a reality therapy group. After six 1-hour treatment sessions, the reality therapy group showed statistically significant increases in self-determination compared with the control group.

Validating the implementation of choice theory through lead management and reality therapy is an ongoing effort. Research studies have shown that school interventions designed to enhance relationships as well as provide a firm, fair, and friendly school climate impact student achievement and behavior in a positive manner.

Edens and Smryl (1994) studied the effect of choice theory on disruptive behavior in a seventh grade class of 42 students: 22 White, 19 Black, and 1 Hispanic. The researchers stated, "The purpose of this study was to assess the effects of Glasser's Quality School principles and the use of reality therapy as a means of reducing disruptive behaviors in a middle school physical education class" (p. 40). Behavioral incidents lessened from 31 during the first week to 7 during the fourth week. The authors concluded,

> Using quality school concepts (choice theory, lead management, and reality therapy) entrusts students to make appropriate behavioral choices. When "ownership" of one's class is part of the class structure, middle school students respond favorably. They learn more, have more fun, and disruptive behaviors decline. (p. 44)

In some schools using choice theory and reality therapy, a time-out room is used when students demonstrate disruptive or excessively emotional behaviors. Often called a *responsibility room, planning room, connecting place,* or *time out center,* it serves as a retreat for students to reflect on their behavior and make choices that are more effective. Wubbolding (2000) stated, "Members of the William Glasser Institute debate the merits of using a responsibility room in school, with some instructors encouraging this structure and some opposing such rooms if choice theory is implemented throughout the entire school" (p. 221). In one school, the average number of students referred to the assistant principal's office was reduced from 30 a day to 2 or 3 per week. Griffith (private correspondence, June 27, 1999) stated that the faculty believed that the consistent use of the responsibility room as well as the safe and need-satisfying school atmosphere facilitated this dramatic improvement.

From the point of view of choice theory and reality therapy, mental health is the totality of the way human beings live, especially regarding their human relationships. A healthy lifestyle is the alternative to mental disorders. Students' healthy lifestyles focus on interactions with each other, achievements in school, and productive use of leisure time. When a school achieves the designation of a *Glasser Quality School*, it meets certain criteria established by the William Glasser Institute. These include eliminating toxic behaviors and substituting them with tonic behaviors or "caring habits," relationships based on trust, students doing quality work as well as faculty, students and parents learning and using choice theory, and the consensual perception of the school as a joyful place (Roth & Glasser, 2006). The first school achieving the designation *Glasser Quality School*, Huntington Woods in Wyoming, Michigan, established quality-centered goals from its very beginning (Ludwig & Mentley, 1997).

According to Ludwig (private correspondence, March, 1999), "Achievement scores on the Michigan Educational Assessment Program for reading and math consistently exceed averages for our state and district." Vandalism and acting-out behaviors are virtually nonexistent. Parent Janet Rea remarked,

> It's a thrill for me as a parent, first of all, to see that the kids are really learning and secondly to learn with them … the staff is very, very committed and as a result they get the parents involved right along with them. (p. 212)

Commenting on a change in school demographics, Andrea van der Laan (private correspondence, May 2006), the current principal, stated, "Our at-risk population doubled … we were not making the gains we wanted to see" (p. 20). Renewed efforts brought about a 28.2% increase in reading scores. "We took 11% more out of the bottom category. Science continues to be above the state average" (p. 20). She subsequently added, "When schools were first put on letter grades in 2004, Huntington was a C–. The second year we were B+ and the third year we were an A" (May 2006).

The achievements of Murray High School, a charter school in Virginia, illustrate the continuous and never ending journey to quality (Wellen & Abbott, 2005). According to the Virginia Department of Education Standards of Learning Test, in 2001, 67% of the students at Murray High School passed the English test; in 2005, 93% passed. In 2001, 69% of the students passed the science test; in 2005, 91% passed. The school had set a goal of 100% of the students graduating in June 2005. According to the *Report of the Status of Murray High School 2004–2005* (Murray High School, 2006), "All but one senior who was scheduled to graduate did so. All 35 seniors had sufficient verified credits to graduate. Two-thirds of the seniors participated in college-level classes, internships, and/or (other) programs. Of the 34 graduates, 85% had plans to attend college, two graduates went into the military, and three entered the workforce full time."

Hinton and Warnke (private correspondence, July 20, 2006) focused their research on the use of choice theory and the WDEP system in a suburban high school of 1,600 students. Choosing students with approximately the same grade average, they divided the freshman class into three teams, naming them *W*, *R*, and *B*. The W team experienced teachers using choice theory and the WDEP system, resulting in a failure of 44 classes, 29 of which were required. On the other hand, the B team failed 85 classes, 73 of which were required. Referrals for disrespect, disruption, and vulgarity numbered 29 times for the W team and 95 times for the B team. One teacher observed, "The overall difference was the work-it-out attitude established with the students."

Research on choice theory and reality therapy in education shows an increase in learning and a decrease in discipline problems. These studies point toward the utilization of choice theory and lead management (the WDEP system) as an effective tool for overall school improvement. Effective teaching and relationship building by educators increase the likelihood of students making effective educational and behavioral choices, the very essence of mental health.

Although evidence for the effectiveness of choice theory and reality therapy exists, more tightly controlled and long-term studies of at least a year are needed. Similarly, credibility for this system would dramatically increase if studies pinpointed specific mental health issues such as conduct disorder, attention deficit hyperactive disorder, depression, learning disabilities, Asperger's syndrome, oppositional defiant disorders, and other clinical diagnoses. Finally, researchers should insure that users of reality therapy, the WDEP system, have been adequately trained and continue to update their skills. Untrained practitioners and poor training serve to create invalid and unreliable conclusions, leading to misconceptions about theory and practice.

The Case of Todd

In applying reality therapy to Todd, several basic principles implicit in the theory and practice stand out.

- The successful use of reality therapy rests on the counselor's ability and skill in forming a relationship with the client. Figure 9.1 indicates that this relationship is "firm, fair, and friendly." The reality therapist understands and implements professional standards such as duty to warn, confidentiality, and informed consent. Clients are also treated fairly and offered high-quality services. *Friendliness* means that the therapist creates a safe atmosphere and demonstrates empathy and positive regard. This professional relationship serves as a basis for helping Todd improve his relationships with significant people at home and at school.
- The reality therapist realizes that successful therapeutic interventions include teaching the concepts of choice theory and reality therapy. However, this instruction is often indirect and subtle. It may consist of brief didactic discussions, but more often clients learn valuable lessons as a side effect of counseling.
- Reality therapy deals with both the presenting issues in a problem-solving manner as well as the underlying motivations of the client. The therapist will explore with Todd his study habits, temper tantrums, and other current behaviors. Even more importantly, Todd will be asked to discuss his perception of his behaviors; his relationships with classmates, teachers, and family; as well as his self-talk about his current action choices.
- Because of the pivotal place of relationships in the use of reality therapy, the therapist often consults with other people in the client's environment. Todd's mother and school personnel will be asked to provide information and to help improve their relationships with Todd.

Several initial therapy sessions will be devoted to discussions that, to the untrained observer, might seem like small talk. The conversation would focus on Todd's likes and dislikes, what he enjoys about school, and what he finds unappealing about it. Todd will describe what he does for fun, such as sports, hobbies, and games. Such questions include "How are you doing at home?" "Tell me a little about where you study and whether you do any chores around the house," "What kind of chores?" "What do you and your friends do together?" and "What's the most fun thing that you do?" Nevertheless, these conversations serve a therapeutic purpose. They facilitate the development of a relationship between the therapist and client, with the result that Todd slowly comes to the realization that the therapist is genuinely interested in him. The therapist's goal is to become part of Todd's quality world (i.e., Todd sees the counselor as someone who can truly help him in some manner, even a way yet to be defined). Another purpose of this conversation is to communicate indirectly to Todd that there is no hurry to solve the problem. Because Todd spends many anxious hours studying and puts a high value on his work ethic, it is possible that he would attempt to use the same intense behavior to overcome his problems. Yet, it could well be that new behaviors would be useful in dealing with Todd's frustrations.

The tentative treatment plan is to help Todd improve his relationships especially with his mother, family, and friends; to establish a pattern of enjoyable activities to be carried out daily; and to experience achievement either through schoolwork or at home. These plans are designed to get to the root of the problem of the presenting issues, thereby facilitating more effective fulfillment of his needs: belonging, inner control or achievement, and fun.

The WDEP system can be applied to Todd in many ways. In the above conversation, the counselor has already encouraged a discussion of current behavior (D). Further discussion of current *doing* behaviors would include descriptions of what other people (i.e., Todd's teachers, school counselor, and mother) have said about the amount of time spent compared with the quality of work habits applied to school assignments. Further discussion of current doing behaviors will center on Todd's self-talk. Is he telling himself, "If I do more of what is not working, I will get the result I'm seeking"? This kind of internal language is not as explicitly articulated as the preceding question, but it might be implied and concomitant with his potentially ineffective study habits. His current *feeling* behaviors also accompany his actions and thinking. The reality therapist would help him identify his anxiety and worries, discuss them, and choose to surrender at least some of the anxiety.

Todd and the therapist would discuss another symptom, temper tantrums. They would explore alternative options to choose when Todd begins to feel restless, anxious, irritable, or angry. More fundamental need-satisfying alternatives to the temper tantrums as well as excessive and anxious study would be the enhancement of relationships with friends through activities mutually satisfying such as hobbies, sports, and various kinds of exercise.

Integrated into the therapeutic interactions would be an exploration of Todd's wants (W). Specific questions for Todd would be "What do you want that you're not getting?" "Do you want to make any changes in what you are doing?" "Do you want to get rid of some of your unhappiness?" "Would you like to feel better about school or home or friends?" "Do you have a best friend?" "Tell me all about him," and "What do you like to do that you really enjoy?"

Self-evaluation plays a crucial role in reality therapy. All persons involved—Todd and other persons in his life—would be asked, "Are your current actions helping or hurting?" Many derivations of this question would be incorporated into the therapy sessions.

Because many problems are relationship issues, the therapist would seek to involve Todd's mother and even school personnel. Consultation with Todd's mother serves a twofold purpose: to explore the possibility of other problematic or excessively repetitive behaviors in order to determine his degree of absorption in frustrating activities, and to provide information and encouragement for Todd's mother as well as for school personnel.

Lying at the root of the symptoms described in the case could be major or minor dysfunctional relationships. Consequently, the reality therapist would encourage Todd's mother and teachers to avoid *toxic* behaviors, especially arguing, bossing, and criticizing. The therapist would strongly urge the mother to employ the alternative: quality or special time with Todd (Wubbolding & Brickell, 2001). Quality time, as seen in reality therapy, includes special time together that avoids or incorporates the following characteristics:

- No arguing
- No bossing or blaming
- No criticizing or creating conflict
- No discussing past misery or current problems
- Discussion of Todd's current positive and enjoyable activities
- Enjoyable to both parties
- Repetition: the activity is done on a daily basis or often

- Limited amount of time: the activity might last 15 minutes and should not be burdensome
- The activity should take effort: therefore, watching television together does not qualify as quality time

The skilled practitioner of reality therapy sees behavior as symptomatic of effective or ineffective need satisfaction. Todd's excessive focus on homework is symptomatic of unmet wants and needs. Through discussion with Todd and consultation with his mother and his teachers, the reality therapist will identify which specific needs to emphasize in treatment planning. The result will be positive plans focusing on several pathways or needs: choices that satisfy belonging, activities that satisfy power or inner control, and behaviors that help Todd have fun and replace his anxious and demanding self-expectations. Each of these pathways is chosen, and therefore Todd learns that he has control over his actions, thinking, and even feelings. At least he comes to the insight that he has more control than he thought he had. Moreover, paradoxically he learns effective control by surrendering ineffective control.

Summary

Developed in a mental hospital and a correctional institution, reality therapy has found a home in education. Because of the emphasis on personal responsibility, choosing behavior, and the central roles of current behavior and a clearly defined intervention system, educators (especially classroom teachers) have found the system practical and usable both for their classes and for the development of the school organization.

Five principles summarize choice theory, the basis for reality therapy: (a) Human motivation springs from internal needs and wants and is not determined by outside forces such as environment or early childhood. (b) The difference between what a person wants and has is the proximate cause of behavior. (c) All human behavior includes action, cognition, emotions, and physiology and is therefore called *total behavior*. (d) Human behavior, especially actions, is chosen (i.e., generated from within and purposeful). People need not remain victimized by the world around them. Mental health specialists assist clients to find personally satisfying choices. (e) Input or information received from the outside world is filtered through a perceptual camera in which human beings recognize the information and give it a value.

Reality therapy provides the vehicle for operationalizing choice theory. Summarized with the acronym WDEP, it allows school personnel to intervene in a system-wide and consistent manner. It has always been a mental health process rather than a method for merely remedying pathology. Whether used on a systemic basis, in the classroom, or in therapy, the goal of reality therapy is to enhance human relationships that are seen as the anchor for mental health. Educators create a firm, fair, and friendly environment for students, avoiding toxic behaviors such as arguing and attacking, blaming and bossing, and criticizing and creating conflict. They utilize tonic behaviors such as listening, supporting, negotiating differences, and implementing consequences. Furthermore, they help clients and students formulate and define their wants (W); become aware of their actions, that is, what they are doing (D); evaluate the effectiveness of their actions and the attainability of their wants (E); and make appropriate and realistically doable plans (P).

Reality therapy has been implemented cross-culturally in North America and around the world. There are now William Glasser Institutes in Europe, Asia, Australia, Africa, and South America. The system has enjoyed a slow but steady increase in respect as an effective intervention method. Although more research is necessary, studies have shown its efficacy in education, mental health, corrections, and many other settings.

Recommended Readings

Wubbolding, R. (2000). *Reality therapy for the 21st century*. Philadelphia: Brunner Routledge.

The most thorough and all-inclusive treatment of reality therapy. A 7-year project, this seminal book contains an overview of choice theory along with innovative applications and amplifications of the theory and practice. Chapter 9 contains major extensions of the procedures summarized in the practical and teachable acronym WDEP. In his cover endorsement, Gerald Corey stated, "I like this book and think it is a valuable resource to those who are interested in learning more about reality therapy."

A major contribution is its application to cross-cultural counseling: Japanese, Koreans, African Americans, Hispanics, Chinese, and others. Empowered by reality therapy, clients can choose alternatives to the victimology and oppression worldview often espoused by some multicultural writers. Chapter 12 presents a summary of research studies showing the effectiveness of reality therapy applied to addictions, education, delinquency, residential programs, and others.

Wubbolding, R., & Brickell, J. (2001). *Counselling with reality therapy*. Bicester, UK: Speechmark.

Written for international use and translated into Hebrew and Chinese, this book emphasizes relationship counseling in schools, applications to addictions, and integration into stages of group development. Paradoxical techniques are applied to resistance and dysfunctional behaviors, along with the use of metaphors, listening for themes, and the use of silence.

Wubbolding, R., & Brickell J. (2001). *A set of directions for putting and keeping yourself together*. Minneapolis, MN: Educational Media.

Practical, usable, hands-on source for self-help use with individual clients, students, and groups. Specific planning activities designed for each need: Belonging, achievement, fun, freedom, and health are presented in an easily manageable format. Ways to combat negative actions, thoughts, and feelings provide the reader with tools for self-help and for use with families.

Glasser, W. (1998). *Choice theory*. New York: Harper Collins.

A seminal and detailed exposition of choice theory as an internal control psychology. Marking a change in the name of the theory from *control theory* to *choice theory*, it contains chapters on marriage and family, education, the workplace, and the "quality community." It is a foundational book for students of reality therapy who desire an extended treatment of choice theory. In his cover endorsement, Robert Lefever, director of the PROMIS Recovery Centre, United Kingdom, stated, "It is in a class of its own in clarity and depth of understanding and is exceedingly helpful in clinical practice."

Glasser, W. (2005). *Defining mental health as a public health problem*. Chatsworth, CA: William Glasser Institute.

A challenge to the medical-pharmaceutical ideology, this 32-page booklet describes mental health as an entity separate from mental disorders. Controversial but persuasive, Glasser describes how most long-term psychological problems are at their root relationship issues. He challenges agencies and organizations to teach in a direct and comprehensive manner the art of establishing and maintaining human relationships as an alternative to mental disorders.

References

Bratter, T., Collaboletta, E., Gordon, D., & Kaufman, S. (1999). *The John Dewey Academy: Motivating unconvinced gifted self-destructive adolescents to use their superior assets.* Unpublished manuscript.

Chung, M. (1994). Can reality therapy help juvenile delinquents in Hong Kong? *Journal of Reality Therapy, 1*(1), 68–80.

Edens, R., & Smyrl, T. (1994). Reducing classroom behaviors in physical education: A pilot study. *Journal of Reality Therapy, 13*(2), 40–44.

Glasser, W. (1960). *Mental health or mental illness?* New York: Harper Collins.

Glasser, W. (1965). *Reality therapy.* New York: Harper Collins.

Glasser, W. (1968). *Schools without failure.* New York: Harper Collins.

Glasser, W. (1976). *Positive addiction.* New York: Harper Collins.

Glasser, W. (1986). *Basic concepts of reality therapy (chart).* Chatsworth, CA: William Glasser Institute.

Glasser, W. (1990). *The quality school.* New York: Harper Collins.

Glasser, W. (1993). *The quality school teacher.* New York: Harper Collins.

Glasser, W. (2005). *Defining mental health as a public health issue.* Chatsworth, CA: William Glasser Institute.

Glasser, W., & Glasser, C. (1999). *The language of choice theory.* New York: Harper Collins.

Glasser, W., & Wubbolding, R. (1997). *Beyond blame: A lead management approach reaching today's youth, 1*(4), 40–42.

Griffith, C. (1999, June 27). Responsibility room: Sturgis high school, Sturgis, Michigan. Private correspondence.

Haley, J. (1973). *Uncommon therapy.* New York: Norton.

Hinton, D., & Warnke, B. (2006, July 20). Choosing success in the classroom. Private correspondence.

Kaiser, H. (1955). The problem of responsibility in psychotherapy. *Psychiatry, 18,* 205–211. Reprinted in Fierman, B. (Ed.). (1965). *Effective psychotherapy.* New York: Free Press.

Kim, R-I., & Hwang, M. (2006). A meta-analysis of reality therapy and choice theory group programs for self-esteem and locus of control in Korea. *International Journal of Choice Theory, 1*(1), 25–30.

Lawrence, D. (2004). The effects of reality therapy groups counseling on the self-determination of persons with developmental disabilities. *International Journal of Reality Therapy, 23*(2), 9–15.

Lojk, L. (1986). My experiences using reality therapy. *Journal of Reality Therapy, 5*(2), 28–35.

Ludwig, S. (1999, March). The Wyoming Michigan quality school. Private correspondence.

Ludwig, S., & Mentley, K. (1997). *Quality is the key.* Wyoming MI: KWM Educational Services.

Murray High School. (2006). *Report on the status of Murray High School 2004–2005*. Murray, VA: Murray High School.

O'Donnell, D. (1987). History of the growth of the Institute for Reality Therapy. *Journal of Reality Therapy, 7*(1), 2–8.

Prenzlau, S. (2006). Using reality therapy to reduce PTSD-related symptoms. *International Journal of Reality Therapy, 25*(2), 23–29.

Roth, B., & Glasser, C. (2006). *Role-play handbook*. Beverly Hills, CA: Association of Ideas Publishing.

Sullo, R. (2007). *Activating the desire to learn*. Alexandria, VA: Association for Supervision and Curriculum Development.

Talmon, M. (1990). *Single session therapy*. San Francisco: Jossey-Bass.

Van der Laan, A. (2006, May). Huntington Woods Elementary School: Data. Private correspondence.

Wellen, C., & Abbott, W. (2005, Fall). A large comprehensive public high school heads down the quality school road. *William Glasser Institute Newsletter*, 17–21.

Woo, A. (1998). *A developmental study of a group social work program using reality therapy*. Unpublished Ph.D. dissertation, Department of Social Work, Yonsei University, Seoul, Korea.

Wubbolding, R. (1988). *Using reality therapy*. New York: Harper Collins.

Wubbolding, R. (1991). *Understanding reality therapy*. New York: Harper Collins.

Wubbolding, R. (1992). *You steer* (Audiocassette). Kansas City, MO: Credence Cassettes.

Wubbolding, R. (1993). *Managing the disruptive classroom* (Videotape). Bloomington, IN: Agency for Instructional Technology.

Wubbolding, R. (1996). *Employee motivation*. Knoxville, TN: SPC Press.

Wubbolding, R. (1997). The school as a system: Quality linkages. *Journal of Reality Therapy, 16*(2), 76–79.

Wubbolding, R. (2000). *Reality therapy for the 21st century*. Philadelphia: Brunner Routledge.

Wubbolding, R. (2006). *Reality therapy training manual*. Cincinnati, OH: Center for Reality Therapy.

Wubbolding, R. (2007). *Cultural adaptations of reality therapy: Round Table Discussion. (CD)*. Cincinnati, OH: Center for Reality Therapy.

Wubbolding, R. (2008). Reality therapy. In J. Frew & M. Spiegler (Eds.), *Contemporary psychotherapies for a diverse world* (pp. 360–396). New York: Lahaska.

Wubbolding, R., & Brickell, J. (2001). *Counselling with reality therapy*. Brackley, UK: Speechmark.

Wubbolding, R., & Brickell, J. (2005). Purpose of behavior: Language and levels of commitment. *International Journal of Reality Therapy, 25*(1), 39–41.

Wubbolding, R., Brickell, J., Imhof, L., Kim, R-I., Lojk, L., & A-Rashidi, B. (2004). Reality therapy: A global perspective. *International Journal for the Advancement of Counselling, 26*(3), 219–228.

10

Applying Family Systems Therapy in Schools

Heather K. Alvarez

An overarching theme across family therapy approaches is recognition that individuals are closely intertwined with their social environment and, in particular, are products of their nuclear family. It is important to note, however, that this shift from a focus on the individual to the acknowledgment of the system in which the individual functions is considered a revolutionary one in the field of psychology. Although the early work associated with the Child Guidance Movement of the 1920s recognized that the source of child symptoms may lie in tensions within the family, it was not for a number of decades before families were incorporated into the therapy process. Initially, families received consideration only in the context of therapy when they proved detrimental to the course of treatment (e.g., Jackson, 1959). In such cases, family members could be seen in conjunction with the client's own therapy. However, others found that the positive benefits of treatment for a target client could spread to other family members (Fisher & Mendell, 1958). Although there was some early debate about the relative impact of families in the context of therapy, by the 1950s there was no doubt that individuals' presenting problems and response to treatment were best understood in the context of their social and familial environment.

During the early developments of family therapy models and approaches, Murray Bowen, a psychiatrist primarily specializing in schizophrenia, offered a landmark contribution to the field that remains noteworthy among current research and practices. Specifically, Bowen emphasized the importance of theoretical foundations in the development of his clinical techniques with families. His approach, known as family systems therapy, is one of the most widely cited and utilized sources in the conceptualization and treatment of children and families across the field of family therapy. Bowen initiated his career in 1946 at the Menninger

Clinic, where he worked with schizophrenic patients and their mothers who resided at the clinic during their treatment. During his early work, Bowen recognized that traditional approaches that focused on the individual seemed to divide, rather than unify, families. In this regard, Bowen began to recognize that the family (rather than the individual) was the source of the disorder, and in 1955 he became the first among his colleagues to treat families together. Following his work at the Menninger Clinic, Bowen initiated a project at the National Institute of Mental Health (NIMH) where he hospitalized entire families of schizophrenic patients. He transitioned to Georgetown Medical School in 1959, where he served as a professor of psychiatry until his death in 1990. Later in his career, Bowen also included an additional component to his treatment model that proved both innovative and groundbreaking in the realm of clinical practice, namely, following personal struggles within the context of his own family. Bowen realized the merit of examining one's own family of origin as part of training in family therapy. Since the early 1970s, the study of the clinician's family of origin has become a principal foundation in family systems therapy. Additional defining features and concepts will be discussed in the next section.

Family System Therapy: Conceptual Foundations

Understanding "Systems" in Family Systems Therapy

The core foundations of family systems therapy can be traced back to general systems theory, which was later applied to families as part of family systems theory. General systems theory has guiding principles that apply to all kinds of systems, including business and industry, community organizations, schools, and families. These principles are relevant to understanding how families function and how families and communities interact. Families are recognized as systems as they display the core defining features of systems, including coherence, interdependence, and definable boundaries. Particular features of systems and the application to families are described in more detail below.

First, family members are thought to be the interrelated elements of the family system. As elements of a system, although family members have unique characteristics, the relationship among them is *interdependent* and predictable. Further, the individual family members as a group have a holistic quality that is "greater than the sum of its parts." In other words, characteristics of the family as a whole cannot be broken down to describe each of the individual family members in the same way. Describing individual family members does not describe the family system. Similarly, family members cannot be understood outside the context of their families. Any complete description of a family member has to consider patterns of interaction within the family and between the family and its social environment.

Family as systems experience pressure to maintain *homeostasis*, a steady, stable state that is maintained in the ongoing interaction system through the use of family messages and rules as well as feedback that reinforces stability (Krauss & Jacobs, 1990). The predictable nature of interactions among family members is considered a foundation to help maintain the family's stability (or equilibrium) and provide information to the family members about how they should function within the family system. These coherent patterns are also maintained by repetitive cycles of communication and behavior. These cycles involve messages and rules to influence, shape, and restrict family members' behavior. The content of messages and rules can assign or shift power among family members, control or limit behaviors, and are often self-perpetuating. Although some are explicit, most messages and rules are implicit—rarely openly stated or written down in more than a few words. Some will also take the form of behavior that contains both factual and relationship information about family systems (Krauss & Jacobs).

These relationships, in sum, are thought to create a semblance of a *structure* that defines membership in the system and boundaries between a family system and its outside environment. The boundaries between family systems fall on a continuum from opened to closed. Family systems that are more open will allow outside individuals and relationships to influence its patterns, whereas more closed family systems are more autonomous and resistant to external influences. This degree of flexibility required to adapt to external influences and internal change is referred to as *morphogenesis* (Krauss & Jacobs, 1990). Family systems will never be entirely closed or open; they all fall somewhere in the middle. In addition, individual families contain subsystems that consist of different small groups of two to three family members. Family subsystems include the spousal or partner subsystem, parent–child subsystems, and sibling subsystems. A family member's roles and functions are defined by their subsystems (Fine, 1992; Stafford & Bayer, 1993; Walsh, 1982). Each subsystem will have unique rules, boundaries, and characteristics that differentiate it from the family as a whole. Membership in subsystems will change over time as family members develop and have different experiences.

The interdependence within family systems is facilitated and maintained by the structural connectedness and interaction patterns described above. In this regard, when one family member in the family changes, reciprocal changes among other family members predictably follow. The level of interdependence will differ across families, and is generally thought to maintain function within the system. For instance, emotional interdependence can facilitate the cooperation necessary to meet basic survival needs (e.g., food and shelter) among family members. On the other hand, when one family member is experiencing distress, high levels of interdependence may lead to an exacerbation of distress among other family members.

Putting the pieces together, family systems theory is an application of general systems theory that views the family as a definable entity and uses systems thinking to describe the complex interactions in the family. Within the context of the family system, individual members are both unique contributions to, and interconnected with, other family members to create a holistic unit. This structure provides a foundation for emotional connections that are maintained through recursive patterns of communication. This conceptual framework formed the basis for the therapeutic approach described below.

Overview of Family Systems Therapy

Family systems therapy can be generally understood as an approach that emphasizes two forces working in balance within family relationships, namely, *individuality* and *togetherness*. With the interdependence among family members in mind, family members are thought to engage in behaviors that polarize each other through acts of pursuit and withdrawal that bring both closeness and distance among individuals. These relationships are also thought to remain potent throughout the course of one's life (not simply as part of childhood) and across multiple generations. According to Bowen, the success of families is related to the ability of family members to balance their fluctuating need for dependence and autonomy over the course of development.

Bowen viewed families as falling on a continuum of characteristics and dispelled the notion that families could be divided into different types. In this, Bowen introduced eight key descriptors of family system structure and processes: (a) differentiation of self, (b) triangulation, (c) nuclear family emotional processes, (d) family projection process, (e) multigenerational transmission process, (f) sibling position, (g) emotional cutoff, and (h) societal emotional process. Each is defined in greater detail below.

Differentiation of self refers to one's ability to separate one's experiences of feeling and thinking from those of others in the family. Given the presence of interdependence within families, family members are susceptible to conformity in an effort to reduce individual differences. The differences present between individuals reflect their differentiation of self. Family members who are undifferentiated also cannot separate their feelings from their thoughts. As a result, undifferentiated individuals think irrationally, and they cannot separate their own feelings from those of other family members and are more susceptible to their influence. In addition, undifferentiated individuals will try to control others as they are being controlled. Differentiation is described as the process of freeing oneself from one's family of origin, and in this, recognizing one's own contribution to problematic relationship systems and being able to remain emotionally related to family members.

Emotional triangles are the basic units of family relational systems. Dyads (e.g., marital couple) are inherently unstable as people in dyads vacillate between the poles of closeness and distance. When anxious or stressed, an individual may seek distance from his or her dyad partner and seek closeness from a third person in the family system to decrease the negative emotionality resulting from the presenting problem within the dyad. This is thought to "freeze" the system in place. In other words, as long as a third person is needed to reduce the anxiety or detract from the problem within the dyad, the problem will not be resolved. The poorer the functioning within a family, or the poorer the ability of an individual to cope with stress, the more likely the people in the system will *triangulate*.

A *triangle* is a family subsystem composed of three people. It is defined as the essential foundational unit of larger family systems as it is considered to be the smallest stable relationship subsystem possible. The person with the least differentiation of self will be most likely to get triangulated into some other dyad. Although a triangle is more stable than a dyad, it is viewed as tension producing as it singles out one individual within the triad as the "outsider," which is very difficult for one to tolerate. This is particularly the case when a member of the triad is experiencing anxiety about being the singled-out member of the subsystem. In triangulation, there is typically a minimal level of tension between the "outsider" striving to get closer to one of the two "insiders" and the insiders actively excluding the outsider. At times, tension will increase when one family member of the triangle is in conflict and two members are in harmony. In this context, triangulation, particularly for the "outsider," is thought to predict clinical problems for the individual family member.

Nuclear family emotional processes refer to the emotional patterns that exist in a family over years and across generations. This often involves a "fusion" or lack of differentiation or independence between family members. As a result, adult children may engage in an emotional cutoff from parents and form a fused or overly dependent relationship within the context of their marriage. Reactions to this family emotional process include four relationship patterns that govern where problems emerge in the family.

1. *Reactive emotional distance*: a pattern that occurs when family members distance themselves from each other to reduce the intensity of a dyadic relationship, but risk becoming too isolated.

2. *Physical or emotional dysfunction in one spouse*: occurs when a marital partner pushes the other to think and act in particular ways and the target spouse yields to the pressure. Although both marital partners work to maintain harmony in the family, one typically works harder than the other. This pattern is typically acceptable unless family tension is elevated, at which time the target spouse may experience increased distress because he or she has to yield more power and control to the other spouse. This situation can increase risk for the development of clinical problems within the target spouse.

3. *Marital conflict*: develops when family tension is elevated, causing marital partners to experience greater distress and anxiety. In this relationship pattern, spouses direct their distress and anxiety onto the marital relationship. This may include efforts to control the other spouse while simultaneously resisting the other's attempt to control him or her.

4. *Projection of problems onto one or more children*: this pattern occurs when a spouse externalizes his or her distress and anxiety on one or more of their children. In this, parents often experience a great deal of anxiety focused on the child and usually have an unrealistic, overly positive or negative view of the child. With this excessive focus, the target child will respond with greater reactivity and focuses on the parent. As a result, the child has more difficulty differentiating from the family and is at greater risk of experiencing elevated emotional or behavioral problems.

Nuclear family emotional processes operate across different types of nuclear family configurations, including intact, single-parent, and stepparent-led families. The intensity of these problems depends on the degree of difficulty with the original differentiation process.

Family projection process is the method by which emotional processes and differentiation are transmitted from one generation to the next. Although children learn the range of healthy and unhealthy emotional patterns in the context of parent–child relationships, certain children become more sensitive to the dynamics of family relationships during development. A child's elevated sensitivity to the family relationship leads to him or her experiencing greater anxiety about the family system and, as a result, increases his or her vulnerability to later emotional problems. The family projection process exacerbates this elevated sensitivity. The process involves three stages, namely, (a) a parent focuses his or her anxiety on a child in the family and perceives that there is something wrong with the child, (b) the parent interprets the child's reaction as a confirmation of his or her worry, and (c) the parent reacts to the child's behavior by treating him or her as if something is really wrong. The parent's reaction style shapes a child's behavior over time as the child starts to internalize the messages received from the parent. This process can place children within the family at greater risk for social and emotional dysfunction and impede their ability to differentiate from their family of origin. This process will, in turn, affect the child's interactions with his or her own spouse and/or children. Alternatively, children who are not targeted in the family projection process have healthier, more mature relationships with their parents and with family members later in life.

Although both mothers and fathers can participate in the family projection process, the mother is usually the primary caretaker and more at risk for projection through excessive emotional involvement with the children. The father typically occupies the outside position in triangles. The strength of the projection process is not related to the amount of time parents spend with their children.

Multigenerational transmission process is the process by which family emotional processes and differentiation are transferred and maintained over three generations. This is most often applied in explaining chronic and escalating distress or anxiety present across generations. Specifically, as differentiation decreases from one generation to the next, the level of anxiety is thought to increase. The transmission across generations occurs as a result of both explicit and implicit rules and messages communicated through family relationships. The multigenerational transmission process predictably follows as individuals within the family select mates with levels of differentiation of self that match their own. In turn, the individual and his or her mates will raise children who have a progressively more extreme level of differentiation relative to the individual.

Level of differentiation of self across generations can affect both individual and family functioning and is the foundation for the variation that can exist across members of a multigenerational family. The highly differentiated siblings and their children will have more stable nuclear families and contribute to a greater extent to the community, whereas siblings who are less differentiated are at greater risk for disorder and excessive reliance on others. This multigenerational transmission process predicts not only characteristics within individuals but also individuals' relationships with others.

Sibling position is thought to influence the development of personality characteristics during childhood such that personality results from strategies siblings use to interact and compete with each other. The basic premise of this concept is that children who grow up in the same sibling position have common individual characteristics and similar contributions to relationships. For instance, firstborn children are thought to be more likely to identify with power and authority. Further, children in different sibling positions complement each others' presenting characteristics. For instance, firstborn children tend to seek out leadership positions, whereas youngest children often prefer to be followers. This concept supports the notion of nonshared family experiences, such that each individual family member has a unique life experience. The concept of sibling position also highlights the multiple subsystems (e.g., dyads and triangles) within the overarching family system. The match between the sibling position and his or her family roles and expectations also relates to the way in which children respond to family relational patterns and their degree of differentiation in the family system. For example, a firstborn child who experiences increased anxiety and distress may be uncomfortable adopting a typical leadership role, and consequently may demonstrate greater dysfunction within the family system.

Emotional Cutoff
Emotional cutoff describes a reaction to undifferentiation in the family through separation by emotional or physical distance from the family of origin. Distancing can be achieved when individuals move away from their families and avoid going home, or when individuals stay in physical contact with their families but avoiding discussing sensitive issues. In this, although family members may look or feel independent from the family, he or she is not actually autonomous. The less differentiation within family systems, the more extreme emotional cutoff is displayed by the individual.

As part of this process, individuals try to reduce the tensions of family of origin interactions by emotionally cutting off. At the same time, they will often overvalue the importance of outside relationships (e.g., coworker relationships, or friends), which can lead to further tensions and conflict.

Societal Emotional Processes

The concept of societal emotional processes was developed to reflect the parallels between relationships in family systems and those within outside social systems. Bowen recognized that there are social and cultural influences on all systems (including family systems), including societal and community expectations about race, class, ethnic groups, gender, sexual orientation, and other social classifications. Shifts in social messages and rules both at the level of the family as well as across communities as a whole are thought to emerge as a result of these influences. Like family emotional processes, societal emotional processes are thought to exacerbate the direction of relational patterns with each generation until the consequences are strong enough to force shifts in the direction of progression. Further, the societal emotional process can have a certain degree of influence on the family emotional process depending on the family's level of differentiation. Specifically, the lower the level of differentiation, the more the family emotional process is influenced by societal emotional processes.

Therapy Goals

Therapy from a family systems model focuses on providing family members with an opportunity to learn more about themselves and their family relationships. An important aim of therapy is to help family members begin to take responsibility for their own problems and increase their differentiation in the family system. A principal therapeutic goal is to modify key triangles in the family, while maintaining emotional contact among family members, as other triangles will predictably change in relation to the first change. In order to accomplish this, the first step in therapy is often addressing the marital relationship, which is considered to be the most important triangle in the family. In this step, the therapist engages in the process of creating a therapeutic triangle with him or herself and the marital couple.

Bowen describes a series of four goals to be accomplished during this critical stage of the therapeutic process. First, the therapist aims to maintain an active and supportive emotional system among family members in order to avoid emotional reactivity during therapy. This is supported through the use of active questioning to both parents, eliciting each parent's reaction to what the other communicates to the therapist. This is done to prevent negative emotional exchanges between the parents and facilitate improved listening to each other's thoughts and concerns without the reactivity that can emerge during direct exchanges. This technique also promotes self-examination among family members in an effort to reduce emotional distress and increase problem solving. Second, the therapist remains emotionally neutral in order to encourage a *detriangulation*, so that the marital couple can resolve their marital conflict, manage their own anxiety, and support their emotional relationship. Third, the therapist aims to establish a more active, differentiated stance within the therapeutic relationship as a model for parents to begin to take the same stance with each other. The fourth goal is for the therapist to educate parents about the process of emotional systems and encourage them to work toward the differentiation of self in relation to their families of origin. This therapeutic technique improves the couple's ability to manage their children's behavior and improve relationships with families of origin.

According to Bowen, the overarching goal for the family is to promote healthy family functioning and family development as a function of (a) good emotional relationships with families of origin, (b) well-differentiated families, and (c) low anxiety among individual family members. More specifically, this model purports that normal family development involves families who adapt well to change influences from both within the family and outside, have a balanced sense of connection across generations while avoiding fusion and/or distance, acknowledge the importance of the family system while appreciating the differences among family members, and work to preserve a positive climate. Without this, family members are thought to repeat the dysfunctional cycles found in their own families of origin.

The context of therapy and the role of the therapist are specifically designed to promote the goals of therapy, including increasing self-focus among family members and decreasing negative emotionality in the family climate. First, as part of the therapy context, family members are often encouraged to engage in communication with the therapist individually rather than participate in family dialogue (which is thought to increase stress and negative emotionality). Further, according to this model, it is not necessary for all family members to be present in the therapy room. Instead, there is a focus on the most critical change agents (usually the parents) within the family system.

Therapy can also take place with a single individual parent or family member in isolation. In this context, the goals of therapy are slightly shifted to allow for more extensive self-exploration about one's role in the overall family system. Additionally, the family member focuses on learning how to examine his or her own emotional patterns in the parent subsystem and is guided in testing his or her self-perceptions in the context of family interactions outside therapy. Finally, the individual is encouraged to engage regularly in efforts to modify unhealthy relational patterns and negative emotional reactions.

Therapy Techniques

Primary techniques involved in family systems therapy include (a) the initial family assessment, (b) process questions, (c) relationship experiments, (d) detriangling, (e) coaching, (f) taking "I-positions," and (g) displacement stories. The initial family assessment will be discussed in detail as part of the next section. The remaining therapy techniques are described below:

- *Process questions*: Process questions are considered the key technique in the family systems therapy process. These are used by the therapist to actively engage family members and are intended to help reduce negative emotional reactions in the therapy context, slow down communication, and encourage the self-exploration process (particularly as it relates to the individual family member's contribution to presenting problems). Examples of process questions include "How are you connected to one another right now?" and "What did you hear him or her say?"
- *Relationship experiments*: Relationship experiments are used to help family members become aware of the emotional processes within their family system and recognize their contributing role in those processes. In this, family members accept experimental roles that challenge their current roles and examine the resultant effects. For instance, family members may switch roles to take each other's perspectives in discussing a particular concern or therapeutic goal.
- *Detriangling*: The technique of detriangling is to identify potential triangulation among every family member across all of their relationships and to move to a relationship pattern that includes emotional relating without gossiping, taking sides, or attacking others. This is aided by assessment activities (e.g., genograms) that enable the therapist and family members to map family relationships visually.

- *Coaching*: The therapist describes his or her role in therapy as a coach or consultant in order to emphasize a neutral stance within the family in order to avoid triangulation. In this role, the therapist concentrates on the process of family interaction patterns in an effort to help family members better express their ideas and concerns in a healthy manner. As a coach, the therapist also facilitates a climate that reduces anxiety among family members while engaging in therapeutic change during sessions.
- *Taking "I-positions"*: I-positions are established to help family members define positions as differentiated selves. The therapist emphasizes the autonomy among individual family members in an effort to help them define their own individual beliefs and ideas. This technique involves the therapist modeling I-positions early in therapy to demonstrate the actions to family members.
- *Displacement stories*: Displacement stories are used as a method for helping family members distance themselves from the emotional reactivity associated with their own family conflict in order to see their own roles and contribution to the conflict. This involves the discussion of stories about other families with similar presenting problems.

Assessment and Case Conceptualization

An important aspect to the conceptualization of presenting problems and treatment needs in the context of family systems therapy is that the family is viewed as the "client" and individual family member symptoms are viewed in the context of the family. In other words, there is an explicit focus on the family system as the unit of disorder, and family members each identify their unique contributions to this disordered system. More specifically, distress and disorder experienced by family members are thought of as a consequence of predictable patterns within the family system, including poor emotional differentiation between family members, increased negative emotionality and anxiety in the family, or a shift in triangulated relationship processes that have formerly maintained the stability of family subsystems. Conceptualization of family needs in the context of family systems therapy involves considering both structure (i.e., emotional triangles present within family relationships) and process (i.e., patterns of anxiety and emotional reactivity). The child with the symptoms is usually the one most affected by these family patterns and presents as the least differentiated and most isolated member of the family system. When a parent presents with the clinical symptoms, he or she is most likely in a dysfunctional relationship with a spouse.

Assessment within the context of family systems therapy involves an examination of an individual's current living situation, a person's life experiences, and the presenting problems within the family system (including the history of the problem and contributing factors) from the perspective of each individual participating in therapy. In this, a formal timeline is developed in order to connect key aspects of the trajectory of the presenting problem with events in the family life cycle. Historical information about the marital relationship and family is also collected. Particular attention is paid to the context surrounding notable developmental transitions within the family (e.g., dating or courtship, marriage, and child rearing).

Genograms
The core component of the assessment process in family systems therapy is the development of a *genogram*, a schematic depiction of family members, family structure, and emotional relationships—much like a comprehensive family tree. Typically, there is an index person (which may be the identified client or family member whose perspective is being assessed by the genogram). The genogram includes information about all family members as well, including age, dates of marriage, divorce, deaths, and geographical locations. Men and women are depicted by squares and circles, respectively, with demographic information presented inside or near the edge of the shape. Specifically, the genogram captures age, birth date, date of death (if applicable), and sexual orientation. Current location and annual income can also be included. Individual shapes can also be shaded using unique patterns to denote the presence of addiction, physical illness, or mental health issues. To further detail the family structure, lines are used in the genogram to connect each shape, with horizontal lines reflecting marital or partner relationships and vertical lines representing parent–child relationships. The characteristics of lines depicting family structure are also designed to reflect the nature of the structural relationship, including cohabitation among unmarried couples, divorce, and marital separation. A household is designated by encircling family members who are living together.

In addition, lines are drawn between family members to indicate the prevailing emotional relationship and interaction pattern. For instance, a wavy line reflects a conflictual relationship, whereas two parallel lines reflect a close relationship. More clinically significant relationship patterns can also be depicted, including a fused, enmeshed relationship (indicated by three solid lines) and abuse (indicated by a wavy line with an arrow pointing to the victim of the abuse).

The genogram provides a comprehensive view of family members across multiple generations within the family. It also offers a picture of repeated patterns of emotional relationships across family members over these generations. For some therapists, the genogram is collected only for the nuclear family. It is also helpful to gather information about extended family members as they relate to functioning within the nuclear family or the family of origin. Genograms can be drawn by hand, but there are also a number of computer programs available to assist with the process. The amount of detail included in this assessment depends largely on the information sought by the therapist and the needs or characteristics of the family.

Additional assessment techniques utilized by family systems therapists rely more heavily on ongoing examination of actual behavior in the context of sessions as opposed to extensive use of paper-and-pencil measures that rely on clients' subjective account of emotional experiences and family interactions. Indeed, in his early work, Bowen observed a difference between what individuals say they do and what they actually do.

Although self-report, paper-and-pencil assessment tools are available to assess a wide variety of individual and family characteristics, there is some continued concern about the accuracy of such instruments in understanding the complex dynamics of families.

Evidence Base

Although the status of family systems therapy in the field has historically related more to the merits of its theoretical foundations as opposed to its empirical foundations, recent researchers have advanced the investigation of this treatment modality. Early on, Bowen placed more emphasis on theory development through clinical observation and clinical training as opposed to well-constructed experimentation. Early studies of the effectiveness of family systems therapy utilized clinical observation to examine outcomes across families treated by Bowen. Outcomes of interest included an increase in self-references and signs of differentiation in the therapy setting, reductions in blaming, distinguishing thoughts from feelings, and increases in goal-directed actions. These early investigations showed support for Bowen's model as serving to change interaction processes in therapy. However, this work did not test whether changes in interaction processes had resultant positive outcomes following completion of treatment. Bowenian therapists often contend that those who strive to use controlled trials to investigate the effectiveness of family systems therapy are misguided in their efforts. Rather, much of the extension and advancement of this form of therapy has largely been through theoretical teachings and refining therapeutic techniques.

Early Investigations
Early investigations of family systems therapy foundations and techniques are detailed in Bowen's early writings published in the "Family Systems" journal (see Bowen, 1995). Specific empirical advances are described below.

Across the empirical work conducted in the testing of family systems therapy, Bowen and his successors have aimed to evaluate actual family member behavioral change as the critical measure of treatment outcome. As part of his original NIMH investigation, Bowen and his research team observed and recorded the behavior of 11 families treated in the inpatient unit and 7 families treated in the outpatient unit for as many as 24 hours a day. Bowen's research at the Menninger Foundation also supported his inclusion of families in the treatment of schizophrenia and alcohol use disorders. More specifically, he found that patients whose families worked with social workers during the treatment process demonstrated greater improvements relative to those without family participation. Bowen also studied the intensity of the mother–daughter relationship as a contributor to schizophrenia symptom severity among individuals being treated in a residential psychiatric ward. Two important advancements emerged from this early work. First, there was a shifting of focus of research on the family as a unit as opposed to on an individual family member. In fact, by 1956, parents and siblings became a focus of ensuing studies and started to be admitted into treatment with the identified client. Second, the first six concepts of Bowenian theory were based on his research observations of families living in the inpatient unit.

Contemporary Research
More recently, the field has witnessed a substantial increase in the empirical investigation of family systems therapy across a wide variety of settings and presenting problems, including health conditions such as reproductive functioning (Harrison, 1997) and chronic health conditions (e.g., Kerr, 1992), divorce (e.g., Gilbert, 2003), and parent immigrant status (Rauseo, 2003). In addition, the family systems model has been applied to the investigation of societal emotional processes within the workplace context (e.g., Comella, 2003). Finally, Dr. Michael Kerr has advanced the investigation of family systems therapy through his extensive work examining family processes.

Applications to School Settings

Family systems therapy is most commonly adapted for use in clinical settings and is unlikely to be administered in the context of the school setting. However, there are a number of considerations worth note in relation to school mental health and school settings. First, families often present to therapy following the onset of behavior problems among the children. School professionals often serve as the initial referral source in identifying the presenting behavior problems in the school setting and recognizing the need for intervention. School professionals may be asked to provide historical information about the presenting problem as part of the treatment process. Given the more objective stance that assessment respondents outside the family can provide in reporting about the child's behavior, this is an important resource for a therapist to fully understand presenting problems.

Second, from the standpoint of the family systems model, the presenting characteristics of individual family members are not considered outside the context of the family. School professionals can adopt this model in their own perception of student needs such that presenting behavior problems in the school context may be best explained by conflict or relational patterns within the family environment. This conceptualization is likely to support the communication, collaboration, and engagement with parents and other family members in best serving the needs of students (e.g., Taylor & Adelman, 2000). There is clear merit in drawing connections between parents and schools for the purpose of promoting school mental health efforts. Indeed, Kazdin and Wassell (1999) found that children respond better to treatment when parents perceive few negatives related to the intervention and its potential outcomes.

The Case of Todd

ASSESSMENT AND CONCEPTUALIZATION

From a family systems therapy perspective, Todd's presenting difficulties are conceptualized in the context of the family system. This family system is composed of three individuals: Todd, his biological mother, and his maternal grandmother. A number of key considerations in conceptualizing Todd's presenting needs may relate to family relational patterns.

First, the unique contributions of each family member must be considered, as the presence or absence of both functional and dysfunctional behavioral patterns may relate to Todd's current presentation. Further, his biological father and other extended family members do not live in the home, but their contributing role to Todd's current presentation may also be relevant. Second, Todd's family rules, norms, and routines should be examined as eliciting or maintaining factors of his presenting characteristics. Recurring patterns of poor emotional differentiation between Todd and his mother and/or grandmother are possible, given that he is the only child in the home and has reported the presence of both anxiety and some acting-out behaviors in the home. It is also possible that Todd's mother or grandmother are also experiencing increased negative emotionality and anxiety, which would further contribute to Todd's clinical and academic problems if it is being focused on Todd. Additionally, shifts in a previously stable triangulated relationship between the three family members are possible as Todd's behavior changes and over the course of his development more generally. For instance, Todd may seek greater independence from his mother and grandmother, who target a great deal of attention and worry toward his social, academic, and emotional functioning.

Assessment of Todd's presenting needs would involve an exploration of his family history using a genogram technique, which may elucidate the presence of learning or anxiety problems that cut across generations. In addition, family emotional relationships that support and/or impede Todd's academic and emotional functioning would be identified. Although little is known about the family history at this point, a genogram based on the available case information may utilize the foundation offered in Figure 10.1.

From the family systems perspective, there are both family structure and family process factors of note with regard to the assessment of Todd and his presenting problems:

- *Family structure*: the presence of extended family in the home in a caretaking role, lacking contact with male family members; no siblings; triangulation pattern with three family members in the home; and possible divorce or dissolution of marriage or partnership between Todd's mother and father.
- *Family process*: Todd presents with anxiety (particularly in relation to school functioning and need for structure), Todd's mother externalizes blame regarding Todd's presenting problems to school procedures, Todd's mother also has difficulty

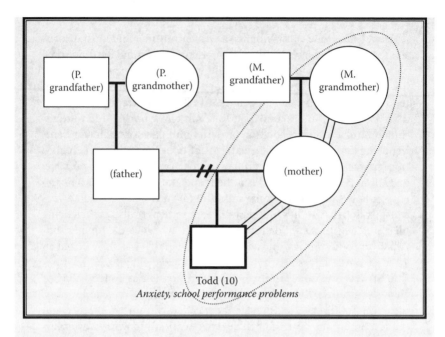

Figure 10.1 Genogram for Todd

> following school recommendations about limiting his home-
> work completion because of Todd's emotional reactions, and
> Todd's family seems more closed in its adaptability to external
> influences.

Additional assessment information would be beneficial to the family
systems therapist, including behaviors engaged in by Todd's mother
and grandmother surrounding his academic behavior and homework
completion more specifically. For instance, it will be important to
discern whether Todd is trying to reduce his mother's anxiety about
his ability to be successful in school. There may also be additional
pressures for Todd to represent his family as a high school or college
graduate. This may be exacerbated if Todd would be a first-generation
college student within his family. Much of this information would be
collected during treatment sessions, when Todd and his family can also
be observed by the therapist.

TREATMENT PROCESS

From a family systems perspective, Todd's mother (and possibly his
grandmother) would likely be viewed as the main change agents in

therapy. Although the primary referral reason is to identify sources of Todd's academic difficulties and related emotional distress, there would be a primary focus on family patterns that may be reflected in, and further exacerbated by, Todd's behavior. Both Todd's mother and grandmother would explore their own contribution to Todd's academic behavior and concerns and distress regarding his academic functioning. Specifically, the therapist would assist Todd's mother in reducing the use of externalized blame and recognize her role in effectively assisting Todd. Todd's mother and grandmother may also have to examine their relationship in the parenting role within the family to determine whether Todd is serving in a triangle by working to reduce their anxiety or distress as his caretakers. For example, if Todd's mother and grandmother both had spouses who proved unsuccessful occupationally, he may experience undue pressure during his early childhood years to make up for their errors.

The specific techniques utilized in family systems therapy would also be applicable to work with Todd and his family. First, *process questions* could be used to elicit self-exploration on the part of Todd's mother to examine her role in contributing to Todd's recent decline in his academics and behavior. In this, Todd's mother may be asked, "How do you respond when Todd's teacher suggests that you limit his homework time in the evening?" or "Describe your reaction right now to your mother's suggestions and advice in session." Second, *relationship experiments* may be used in the context of sessions to help Todd's grandmother better understand her daughter's tension as both a parent and a child within the household, and to reduce her tendency to undermine Todd's mother's discipline. Third, the detriangling technique may be helpful in examining the potential triangulation pattern among Todd's family members, including (a) who within the triangle serves as the "insider" and "outsider," and (b) the relative degree of tension stability in the triangle. For instance, it is possible that Todd's mother finds herself regularly shifting from taking sides with Todd to taking the side of her mother depending on the circumstances. This shift in alliance may be both confusing and anxiety provoking to Todd, who may be often forced into the "outsider" role. Fourth, Todd's mother and grandmother may particularly benefit from the therapist acting as a neutral *coach* or consultant, in order to help them reduce their own anxiety. Fifth, if the family system is not well differentiated, such that there is too much emotional interdependence, Todd's mother and grandmother may benefit from learning I-positions to promote development of their differentiated selves. The emphasis of autonomy among family members may serve to increase parenting efficacy for Todd's mother and a clearer, more stable family relational pattern that will provide Todd a greater sense of predictability and security in his home. Sixth, both Todd's mother and grandmother may share insights based on the experience of their own friends and coworkers (i.e., *displacement stories*) that inform strategies they would like to test in their own family.

As Todd's presenting problems involve school-related concerns, it may also be helpful to apply family systems theory to the societal emotional processes that may be present within the school setting. In this, the therapist may be able to identify unique (and possibly disparate) cultural influences on Todd's family system as compared to those that affect practices within the school system. For instance, within Todd's family system, male family members may be expected to adopt leadership roles and may be less supported in their experience of internalizing problems such as anxiety and worry. Alternatively, staff working with Todd in the school system may have received recent training on stigma associated with the mental health needs of students and, as a result, may be better prepared to adjust their expectations to match Todd's presenting needs.

Summary

Bowen's family system therapy offers a well-developed, theoretically derived approach to treatment of a range of presenting problems that is considered revolutionary in the field of family therapy. Its goals are focused on improving family members' understanding of their contribution to problematic family systems and increasing their likelihood to take responsibility for change. This is done in a therapeutic environment that promotes a reduction of anxiety and negative emotionality among family members.

Although not originally developed for use in the school setting, knowledge of the theoretical background and techniques of family systems therapy may be beneficial to school professionals as they work with students of all sorts. This approach encourages professionals to move away from child-focused blame for his or her presenting problems and to understand the context in which the behavior presents. School professionals may serve to assist with the assessment process (e.g., observation of child behavior), and can support parents who are trying to take a more active role in the intervention of their children's needs. Furthermore, as Bowen would advocate, all individuals can benefit from self-examination and exploration of family-of-origin issues that may play into their interactions with others and their functioning in both personal and professional realms.

References

Bowen, M. (1978). *Family therapy in clinical practice*. New York: Aronson.

Comella, J. D. (2003). Observations of reciprocal functioning in a challenging environment. *Family Systems, 6*, 101–116.

Fine, M. (1992). Family therapy training: Part II. Hypothesizing & story telling. *Journal of Family Psychotherapy, 3*, 61–79.

Fisher, S., & Mendell, D. (1958). The spread of psychotherapeutic effects from the patient to his family group. *Psychiatry, 21*, 133–140.

Gilbert, R. (2003b). Bridging cutoff in a divorced family. In P. Titelman (Ed.), *Emotional cutoff: Bowen family system theory perspectives*. Binghamton, NY: Haworth.

Harrison, V. (1997). Family emotional process, reactivity, and patterns of ovulation. *Family Systems, 4*, 49–61.

Jackson, D. (1959). Family interaction, family homeostasis and some implications for conjoint family therapy. In J. Masserman (Ed.), *Individual & Familial Dynamics* (pp. 122–141). New York: Grune & Stratton.

Kazdin, A. E., & Wassell, G. (1999). Barriers to treatment participation and therapeutic change among children referred for conduct disorder. *Journal of Clinical Child Psychology, 28*, 160–172.

Kerr, M. E. (1992). Physical illness and the family emotional system: Psoriasis as a model. *Behavioral Medicine, 18*, 101–113.

Krauss, M. W., & Jacobs, F. (1990). Family assessment: Purposes and techniques. In S. J. Meisels & J. P. Shonkoff (Eds.), *Handbook of early childhood intervention* (pp. 303–325). New York: Cambridge University Press.

Papero, D. V. (1990). *Bowen family systems theory*. Boston: Allyn & Bacon.

Rauseo, L. (2003). Migration and emotional cutoff. In P. Titelman (Ed.), *Emotional cutoff: Bowen family system theory perspectives*. Binghamton, NY: Haworth.

Stafford, L., & Bayer, C. L. (1993). *Interaction between parents and children*, Newbury Park, CA: Sage.

Taylor, L., & Adelman, H. S. (2000). Connecting schools, families, and communities. *Professional School Counseling, 3*(5), 298–307.

Walsb, F. (Eds.) (1982. *Normal family processes*, New York: Guilford.

11

Applying Adlerian Therapy in the Schools

Linda C. Caterino

Amanda L. Sullivan

Although Alfred Adler's first works were written more than 100 years ago, his theories are remarkably relevant to modern psychology. For example, Adler was one of the first practitioners to focus on the ecological nature of child development. Although we tend to look at the child's needs by considering family, school, and community systems, he even included the larger systems of human nature, the planet, and the cosmos. He emphasized the social nature of the individual and the connectedness between persons as the basis of mental health. Adler also recognized the value of prevention, particularly in the treatment of children. In 1919, during an educational reform movement, he established 22 child guidance clinics in his native city of Vienna, Austria, as well as 28 additional clinics that were in operation throughout Europe, where Adler and his followers provided therapy to children, adolescents, and their families, while simultaneously training physicians, teachers, and social workers. Adler's theories (e.g., 1963) laid the foundation for most modern therapeutic approaches. Like Carl Rogers (1951), Adler stressed the importance of developing a strong relationship with clients and advocated that the best way to understand the client is to enter into his or her subjective world. In essence, Adlerian therapy is more educational than medical in its orientation. Clients are viewed as basically healthy individuals who may need guidance and education to help them cope with their discouragement, low self-esteem, faulty thought patterns, and useless behaviors, so that they can develop a more appropriate lifestyle and a more meaningful social existence. Therapy is seen as a "corrective learning experience" where the therapist may assist the client in gaining insight into "mistakes" in his or her cognitive schema by challenging faulty assumptions and beliefs (i.e., cognitive distortions) and by adopting a process quite similar to that used in cognitive therapy (Beck, Rush, Shaw, & Emery, 1979; Burns, 1980) and rational emotive therapy (Ellis, 1957).

Overview of the Therapeutic Approach

Alfred Adler was born in Vienna in 1870, the second son in a family of six children. Inspired by his own childhood health problems, Adler decided to become a physician and received a medical degree from the University of Vienna in 1895. He began to practice psychiatry in 1907, and he was invited to join the Viennese Analytic Society, Sigmund Freud's discussion group. Adler began writing on the topic of organ inferiority, the idea that everyone has both weak and strong parts of their anatomy, and the aggression instinct, which he considered one's reaction to a blocked need. Adler criticized many of Freud's concepts, especially his concept of sex as a fundamental motivator of behavior, and in 1911, Adler and nine of his followers resigned from the group and went on to form the Society for Individual Psychology.

In developing his theory, Adler was influenced by the philosopher Hans Vaihinger (1911/1952). In his famous work, *Philosophie des Asl Ob* (*Philosophy of "As If"*), Vaihinger expressed the view that the ultimate truths in life were beyond human understanding, but that people create partial truths or "fictions" to guide them in daily life. Adler referred to this concept as *fictional finalism*, the idea that future-based fictions (e.g., the existence of heaven) influence people's behavior. These fictions form the basis for each person's individual lifestyle. Another influence on Adlerian psychology was Jan Smuts, the South African philosopher and statesman. He described the concept of wholism (1926), or the belief that people can truly be understood only as unified wholes within the context of their environments. Adler interpreted wholism to mean that people should be seen as integrated individuals, not as fragmented parts. Ironically, he then labeled his socially based theory *individual psychology*, as the word *individual* translates to "undivided."

Adler believed that a desire to fulfill one's potential and reach one's ideal motivated all human behavior. This approach, called *teleology*, emphasizes that people move toward personal competence and that their goals and ideals are dynamic, rather than the static, mechanistic conceptualizations of Freud. However, they may or may not be consciously aware of their goals, thoughts, and behaviors (Dumont & Corsini, 2000).

One of the guiding concepts in Adler's approach was *Gemeinschafts-gefuhl*, which is roughly translated as social interest or a feeling of a caring or concern for others. This concept of social interest was based on his belief that humans are social animals who exist in an inherently social environment and have a fundamental need for belonging. Social concern is inextricably tied to one's sense of purpose, which is based on being useful to others. Adler believed that mental illness and various social ills were the result of inadequate social interest, often because people become overwhelmed by a sense of inferiority in some aspect of their physical or psychological features, and may develop an "inferiority complex." In response to these feelings of inadequacy, some individuals may develop a "superiority complex," which may be manifested in inappropriate behavior such as bullying or prejudice. Adler distinguished between three basic psychological types caused by inadequate social interest. The ruling type tends to be aggressive and dominant. The leaning type is introverted and internalizing, and depends on others to carry him or her through life's problems. The avoiding type withdraws from all social contact and can become psychotic when faced with difficulties.

Adler (1963) eschewed the disease model of psychological disorder in all but a few cases and viewed behaviorally and emotionally disordered individuals as discouraged, rather than sick. He theorized that discouraged people perceive themselves as being unable to face the three challenges of life: work, love, and community. Adler postulated that the roots of discouragement came from overambition, a feeling that one must be better than others, a lack of courage, and a pessimistic attitude (Dinkmeyer, Pew, & Dinkmeyer, 1979). He believed that one's thoughts, feelings, and behavior can only be understood in the context of his or her lifestyle, which is the approach each individual takes to coping with life's problems and interpersonal relationships, and how one expresses oneself and behaves in an environment. Lifestyle is developed early, and usually by 5 years of age, children have already developed their own interpretations about life and have identified the best way to cope with their problems (Blamires, 2006). According to Adler, an unhealthy or maladaptive lifestyle can be shaped by organ inferiorities, pampering, and/or neglect. One's earliest childhood memories and childhood problems (e.g., eating habits, fears, and problem behaviors) were regarded as important to understanding the basis of one's lifestyle.

The family constellation is also believed to influence the child's behavior and the development of his or her unique lifestyle. Adlerian views on birth order have been incorporated into popular psychology. He supposed that only children are likely to be pampered and may not learn to take care of themselves. They may be egocentric and attention seeking and may not have the ability to collaborate, compromise, and cooperate with peers. They may have difficulties in transitioning from their homes to schools, where they may not experience the same level of support that they have received from their parents. On the positive side, they may have advanced intellectual and language development and skills in relating to adults.

In families with multiple children, the first child may bear the brunt of the parents' expectations and ambitions and may feel anxious and pressured to achieve. First children may try to please their parents and may be especially conforming, responsible, and highly motivated. However, these children may become very impressed with their power and position and may become overly competitive, controlling, and dominant. Once a second child is born, the first child may feel "dethroned." Although initially the first child may battle for the lost position, by becoming disobedient, or sullen and withdrawn, he or she may then lose confidence and become discouraged. Adler suggested that first children may be conservative, solitary, and successful, but may also be more likely than any other group to develop problems.

The second child may be extroverted, rambunctious, and oppositional. They may be very different from the first, especially if they are of the same gender and close in age. The second child may react with anger, resentment, and oppositional behavior after the birth of the third child. The youngest child, who is never dethroned, may be pampered and provided with few expectations for success. This child may develop feelings of entitlement and privilege, and may become manipulative or overly dependent on others. Some youngest children may become competitive with their older siblings. Adler saw this group as the second most likely to exhibit problem behaviors. With the current growth of single-family and alternative family structures, and the rise in the number of only children and adopted children, and the increase in the number of single-parent households, there are other factors to consider.

In addition to understanding the family constellation, Adler recommended that the therapist examine the family atmosphere. The family atmosphere is the accepted coping style of the family that will then become a model for the child. For example, the atmosphere may be authoritarian, where unquestioned obedience is demanded; rejecting, where children feel unloved and unaccepted; suppressive, where children are not permitted to express their thoughts and feelings; inharmonious, where family members may frequently argue; inconsistent, where there is a great deal of confusion and lack of routine; overprotective, where children may be taught to over rely on parents; happy; relaxed; warm; or optimistic. Adler hypothesized that children from authoritarian households will have very different coping styles than children from permissive or authoritative atmospheres. The discipline styles adopted by the parents, the consistency within the environment, and the message parents provide about the acceptance of the child as an individual will shape the child's developing lifestyle. If children do not receive the proper support from family and others, they may experience a feeling of inferiority, become discouraged, and anticipate failure.

Although Adler wrote that it was important to understand a child's history, he did not regard one's past as being completely deterministic; instead, he believed that the individual could create his or her own judgments and values. In this way, individuals are seen as responsible for their own lives and actions, and are not merely the consequence of their early histories.

Adlerians believe that all behavior is purposive. Dreikurs and Soltz (1964) identified four goals of misbehavior: attention seeking, power, revenge, and assumed disability. They noted that although all young children seek attention, this behavior typically diminishes in the primary grades. Attention seeking can be active constructive or passive constructive. In the active constructive form, the child may be successful only to receive external rewards or self-elevation and may not be cooperative with others. Although the passive constructive child is similar to the active constructive, he or she may not be as vigorous in achieving his or her goals. The active destructive child may seek attention through misbehavior or "acting-out" behaviors, whereas the passive destructive child may appear unmotivated and fearful. The attention-seeking pattern is thought to develop from receiving either too little or too much parental attention. Children who choose attention seeking as their goal may demonstrate such disorders as generalized anxiety disorder or social phobia. By displaying these symptoms, they receive attention from sympathetic adults who provide them with special accommodations, and with time, these children come to believe that attention and special accommodations are necessary and that a display of anxious symptoms is the only way to receive them.

The second goal, power, is most evident in children who resist control from authority figures. In pursuit of this goal, the child may respond in an outwardly aggressive (active destructive) or rebellious way or in a passive aggressive or stubborn (passive destructive) manner. Children who are motivated by this goal gain a sense of importance by letting adults know that they will not be constrained by rules or intimidated by punishment.

They may often engage in power struggles with adults to demonstrate the adults' impotence. This behavior may be a result of inappropriate modeling by adults who have used threats and control in discipline. These children may develop symptoms consistent with oppositional defiant disorder.

The third goal of revenge or retaliation may develop when children perceive that they have been hurt, mistreated, and made to feel devalued by the adults in their lives. The goal here is to hurt others in order to get even, if possible, by choosing the most sensitive triggers for the adults in their lives. This pattern can be actively or passively destructive.

The final goal is assumed disability or inadequacy, where the child has lost his or her sense of personal significance, as well as any motivation for academic or social concerns. The child who chooses this goal of misbehavior is frequently characterized as discouraged and depressed. They may seek to withdraw or self-isolate from others in a passive destructive manner.

Assessment and Case Conceptualization

There are four stages in the individual therapy process: (a) building a relationship, (b) understanding the client, (c) explaining the client's behavior to him or her, and (d) strengthening social interest (Dreikurs, 1957). These phases or processes are not always sequential and may overlap. In phase 1, the therapist and client establish a collaborative therapeutic relationship. Mutual expectations are developed and agreed upon. It is in the first phase that the therapist begins to subjectively experience the client's world subjectively (Ansbacher & Ansbacher, 1956). Mosak (1987) indicated that during this phase, the therapist must convey hopefulness, faith, and care. The therapist should not assume an authoritarian role, but must display a nonjudgmental manner, emphathy, and encouragement. It is particularly important to provide reassurance to children and adolescents in this phase, because the decision to enter into therapy may not have been their own. Understanding and support may be conveyed to the client by reflecting feelings, restating content, providing explanations, and answering client questions.

In the next phase, psychological investigation, the therapist seeks out information through observation and interview regarding both current difficulties and past history in order to gain insight into the client's underlying convictions, goals, values, relationships, and early family history. The therapist may question the client about his or her early recollections (including happy experiences, early dangers, misdeeds, punishment, successes, and failures), dreams, and other childhood factors such as birth order and family atmosphere. Although initially information may emerge slowly, eventually the therapist will be able to notice a pattern of behavior so that he or she can formulate hypotheses regarding the client's lifestyle and its effect on the client's functioning in the three life tasks of work, love, and community.

In the third phase, interpretation, the therapist attempts to raise the client's understanding of his or her thoughts and motives and their consequences through a series of questions or a Socratic dialogue. The client's mistaken beliefs or cognitive distortions and useless behavior patterns are explored and gently challenged so that the client can gain insight into his or her goals, beliefs, and actions. This insight may be demonstrated through a verbal or nonverbal acknowledgement termed a *recognition response*. In working with children, Lee (2001) suggested that the therapist develop a Life Style Matrix and present this to the child. This matrix displays the child's comments regarding himself or herself, others, and life in each of the three life tasks, work (school), family (love), and community (friends). The child is then asked to describe his or her behaviors in each of these domains and to evaluate whether his or her actions are leading to the consequences they desire.

In the fourth and final phase called reorientation or reeducation, the therapist and the client collaborate to develop alternative thoughts and behaviors. The client is encouraged to break old patterns and to discontinue socially inappropriate behaviors, so that a healthier lifestyle can be fostered, one that centers on meaningful social contributions (Blamires, 2006). During the session, the therapist and the client may role-play a new behavior and then identify two or three actual life challenges (or homework assignments) in which the client may have to adopt new and different behaviors.

Adlerians use assessment to understand current functioning and how people perceive and operate in their worlds (Carlson, Watts, & Maniacci, 2006). They may employ formal instruments such as intelligence and achievement tests; projective measures; information assessments, such as drawing and sentence completion tasks; as well as lifestyle interviews in order to gain information about a client (Carmichael, 2006). The key elements of the lifestyle interview are identifying information, background data, current functioning, the presenting problem, and treatment expectations (Carlson et al., 2006). During the interview, the therapist may use a formal lifestyle questionnaire such as those developed by Stiles and

Wilborn (1992) or Shulman and Mosak (1988). Lee (2001) provided an example of a more informal interview procedure where she probed for information regarding family members, family atmosphere, family values, and discipline among other factors.

A therapist may also develop his or her own interview format. Lifestyle interviews typically include a description of current symptoms, perhaps using a Likert scale to convey severity, the circumstances under which these symptoms developed, and the client's description of what he or she would do if he or she did not experience these symptoms. This question, also referred to as the "magic question," could be phrased as, "If you woke up tomorrow and your problems were gone, what would be different?" Next, the therapist will explore current and past functioning in terms of friendships, school, work, and family or love relationships. It is particularly important to gather information about the family environment, which includes relationships between family members (including extended family), birth order, discipline methods, family values, division of household chores, and the child's perceptions of family members. For instance, the child might be asked to describe each of his or her family members by rating them across various dimensions (e.g., intelligence, helpfulness, rebelliousness, ambitiousness, friendliness, conformity, and good humor) and to identify which family member is most like them and which is least like them in order to determine family allies and competitors.

The family atmosphere should also be assessed. Shulman and Mosak (1988) described the family atmosphere on three dimensions: mood, order, and relationships. The *mood* is the emotional style of the family, which is usually established by the parents (e.g., depressed, angry, worried, happy, warm, tense, or optimistic). *Order* refers to the stability and structure of relationships and activity patterns (e.g., predictable, unpredictable, confusing, clear, rigid, or chaotic). *Relationships* describe the patterns of interaction between family members (e.g., dominant, submissive, distant, close, accepting, or rejecting).

Many practitioners also find it helpful to gather information about the child's earliest recollections because these are considered to provide the basis for the child's lifestyle (Kottman & Warlick, 1989). They may use the Early Childhood Memories questionnaire (Mosak, 1958) to gather this information. The child might be asked to describe his or her first recollection or even their first 10, depending on the age. He or she may respond verbally or may even draw out their earliest memories. A standardized instrument, the Manaster-Perryman Manifest Content Early Recollection Scoring Manual (Manaster, Berra, & Mays, 2001), can be used to analyze the content of early memories by considering the characters, setting, themes, affect, and locus of control demonstrated in the recollections. Statton and Wilborn (1991) have advocated the use of this type of technique with children. Another assessment measure is the BASIS-A (Curlette, Wheeler, & Kern, 1997), which measures the four lifestyle themes of belonging/social interest, going along (willingness to adhere to social standards) taking charge, and wanting recognition. There are also five supporting scales: Harshness, Entitlement, Liked by All, Striving for Perfection, and Softness. The therapist may also ask for a description of a typical day in the family's life. Through the lifestyle interview, the therapist may gain information on the child's private logic or personal value system, and his or her level of social involvement, and will then begin to conceptualize the case using the four goals of misbehavior as a guide.

The therapist will then reflect these hypotheses to the client. Initially, children may not be able to incorporate these insights to prevent misbehavior, but they may develop some realization after the fact. Eventually they may be able to develop a better sense of awareness so that they can monitor their misbehavior while they are in the course of an action until finally they may learn to prevent impending behavioral problems. Throughout the therapeutic process, the therapist should be encouraging. Encouragement, however, is not praise or reinforcement; rather, it focuses on helping the child through the therapeutic process, by acknowledging that he or she has the ability to rectify mistaken beliefs, change inappropriate behaviors, and solve problems. The child is urged to seek intrinsic satisfaction and reinforcement, instead of looking for external rewards. Punishment is also discouraged because it can lead to feelings of revenge in children and a need for power. Instead, the use of natural and logical consequences is fostered. Natural consequences are a direct result of the child's behavior. For example, a child who leaves his or her bicycle outside unlocked may suffer the consequences of having it stolen. Logical consequences are developed through family policies. They should be consistent and fair. An example of a logical consequence might be that a parent does not allow a child to go out on a weekend evening if he or she came in after curfew the weekend before.

Common therapeutic techniques employed in individual therapy include reframing, in which the therapist interprets the client's behavior in a more positive way; guided imagery; role-playing; and homework assignments or daily life challenges. Adler also suggested the use of paradoxical intention, where the therapist may direct the client to exaggerate the misbehavior. Although he noted that none of his clients ever followed his paradoxical advice, he believed that paradoxical intention would be useful in gaining the client's attention and lessening any feelings of resistance (Ansbacher & Ansbacher, 1956).

Play therapy techniques have also been incorporated into Individual Therapy. Adler believed that children's play was reflective of their individual lifestyles. Patterns of behavior can be observed in play, art, and even sandtray techniques (Bainum, Schneider, & Stone, 2006; Sweeney, Minnix, & Homeyer, 2003). Carmichael (2006) suggested that the child therapist can utilize play therapy to help children explore alternative perceptions of events and to help them develop a sense of power over the effect these events have on their sense of belonging and motivation. Kottman (1997) has been a strong proponent of the use of Adlerian techniques in play therapy. Her approach emphasizes the development of the four C's: connectedness with others, the belief in oneself as capable and confident, counting oneself as valuable, and the development of courage or the willingness to risk and confront difficult challenges.

The mutual storytelling technique, although more typically associated with psychoanalytic therapy, has also been used in Adlerian therapy with children. This technique entails having the child create a story with a beginning, middle, and end. The therapist then analyzes the story for metaphors indicative of faulty perceptions and a maladaptive lifestyle. The practitioner then retells the story, substituting the child's ending with a healthier resolution. The goal of this approach is to help the child learn alternative ways of perceiving events that lead to correct beliefs, increased social connectedness, and behaviors that are more appropriate (Kottman & Stiles, 1990).

Other Adlerian techniques may be seen as adjuncts to individual child therapy. These may include family or group therapy, as well as parent training (*Systematic Training for Effective Parenting*; Dinkmeyer and Dinkmeyer, 1976,), teacher training (*Systematic Training for Effective Teaching*; Dinkmeyer, McKay, & Dinkmeyer, 1980), or even a combination of all of these techniques.

Applications to School Settings

Adler and his followers were very interested in education. One of his students, Rudolf Dreikurs, wrote a classic book on Adlerian psychology in schools called *Psychology in the Classroom* (1957). In this book, he emphasized the four goals of misbehavior, as well as the concepts of natural and logical consequences.

Raymond Corsini (1977), a student of Dreikurs, was instrumental in developing the individual education (IE) and IE4R programs (Pierce, 1987). The individual education (IE) program began in two private parochial schools in Oahu, Hawaii, and currently there are six additional schools in the continental United States, and two overseas (Pryor & Tollerud, 1999). The school curriculum emphasizes the four R's of responsibility, respect, resourcefulness, and responsiveness through classroom discussions, community service, cooperative learning experiences, peer tutoring, and group problem solving. Administrators, teachers, and staff all receive training in discipline, classroom management, and encouragement techniques, while parents participate in parent education programs. The academic program of an IE school includes the traditional subjects of language arts, math, science, and social science, but in addition, students can petition to study a particular topic of interest so that they can develop their skills in resourcefulness. Students can choose to learn in the classroom, by independent study, or via computer. There are weekly examinations, and students and their personal mentors or teaching assistants keep progress charts. The IE model is based on a system of mastery learning, and no letter or number grades are assigned. Extrinsic rewards and punishment are not encouraged, nor is competition between students because it interferes with a feeling of belongingness and may negatively impact student self-esteem. The curriculum also includes socialization training (responsiveness), where students take part in classroom meetings and social skills training in order to improve their communication and problem-solving skills. Discipline is based on previously agreed upon logical consequences.

Adlerian techniques have also been incorporated in traditional school settings. In 1982, Dinkmeyer and Dinkmeyer developed a structured program for use with elementary students from prekindergarten through fourth grade called developing understanding of self and others (DUSO). In this program, young children are encouraged to develop positive self-images, to become aware of social relationships, and to recognize their own needs and goals. Structured activities such as role-play, fantasy, interactive exercises, and the like are used in the development of 42 different life skills. In Dinkmeyer et al.'s (1980) teacher-training program, *Systematic Training for Effective Teaching (STET)*, teachers are presented with techniques to help them to identify the four goals of misbehavior, to avoid power struggles, to encourage students, and to implement logical consequences.

Albert's (1995) cooperative discipline program utilized a similar approach to help teachers create effective educational environments.

Campbell (2003) formulated an Adlerian-based student peer-coaching model. The model uses real-life situations as opportunities for students to learn and practice social skills. In each session, the therapist takes the students through a five-step process in which actual problems encountered by the students are analyzed. The student is asked to (a) select the situation; (b) identify who is involved, explain the actual events, and hypothesize the reason for the event and what each participant may have been feeling; (c) brainstorm possible solutions and consequences; (d) implement a new behavior; and (e) provide feedback. Other school-based programs include Clark's (1995) social interest program, which can be fully integrated into a regular school curriculum; and Brigman and Molina's (1999) program, which emphasizes the multicultural aspects of social development, in addition to fostering the more traditional objectives of understanding, empathy, communication, cooperation, and responsibility through the use of group discussions and projects.

Adlerian theory can also be incorporated into school observations and consultation. Hardy (1984) suggested that school observation procedures take into consideration the four goals of misbehavior, and Dinkmeyer (2006) suggested that Adlerian therapy should be a basis for school consultation because the approach emphasizes mutual collaboration and seeks to develop hypotheses to explain student behaviors.

Since individual therapy is focused on the development of improved social skills, it is well suited to the school structure because it can be taught in the classroom, in small groups, as well as in individual therapy sessions. Teacher and parent training sessions can also be conducted concurrently.

Evidence Base

The research evidence in support of Adlerian therapy is limited, and much of it is quite dated. Previous reviews of the literature (Watkins, 1992) merely looked at the quantity of Adlerian research studies. Watkins found that the number of research studies increased from 75 in the 11 years between 1970 and 1981 to 103 in the 9 years between 1980 and 1991. He did not discuss, however, the quality of research. Although researchers claim that Adlerian approaches have been shown to be somewhat useful in the treatment of some emotional, behavioral, and academic problems (e.g., Bettner, 2005; Gilbert & Morawski, 2005), much of the research is based on case studies. Typically, research studies have included very few participants and have employed simple pre- and posttherapy comparisons without the correction afforded by analysis of covariance procedures. When the latter procedure has been used, findings have not always been significant (Gordon-Rosen & Rosen, 1984).

Because parenting programs tend to attract larger sample sizes, there has been some research on the efficacy of Adlerian parenting programs. Burnett (1988) reviewed 21 studies on the effectiveness of Adlerian parent programs and noted positive changes in children's behavior, children's self-concept, parent behaviors, and parent attitudes post treatment. Two doctoral dissertations (Johnson, 1991; Urbin, 1991), as cited by Farooq, Jefferson, and Fleming (2005), found that parents who had participated in an Adlerian parenting program had higher ratings of their children's behavior on posttest measures as compared to controls. Mullis (1999) reported that after attending Adlerian-based parent education programs, parents viewed their children more favorably and noted that they behaved more responsibly. Snow, Kern, and Penick (1997) worked with parents of 119 adolescents who were attending a day hospital. Parents participated in either a traditional parenting program or the Adlerian-based STEP program (Dinkmeyer & McKay, 1976). Their results indicated that the children of the STEP-trained parents were less likely to withdraw prematurely from the therapeutic program than were children whose parents were in a traditional parenting program. Farooq et al. (2005) found that after attending a 6-week video-based Adlerian parenting program, inner-city African American parents reported more positive perceptions of their children's behavior and increased authoritative parenting as compared to controls. Nystul (1984) noted that after a group of 14 Australian mothers participated in a STEP program, they were found to be more democratic in their child-rearing attitudes. They also showed an increase in encouraging behaviors and a decrease in strictness as compared to wait-list controls. Gordon-Rosen and Rosen (1984) conducted a nine-session Adlerian based training program for African American inner-city parents using Dreikurs and Soltz' book, *Children: The Challenge* (1964), and charts and handouts from the STEP program (Dinkmeyer & McKay, 1976). Prior to the training, immediately post training, and 4 months later, all parents completed an assessment of their children's behavior. Although simple gain scores comparing experimental and control groups revealed greater improvement in the experimental group, an analysis of covariance controlling for the pretest score was not significant. This process then makes one question whether the results of the previous studies would hold up under more rigorous statistical procedures. In addition, most of the studies did not include long-term ratings to show whether any improvement was merely a temporary change. Moreover, the studies cited used parent ratings and rarely incorporated more objective measures of children's behavior.

Morse and Brokoeven (1987) and Richie and Burnett (1985) supported the use of Dinkmeyer and Dinkmeyer's (1982) DUSO program in improving children's self-concepts. Platt (1971) and Porter and Hoedt (1985) cited a number of studies that support the efficacy of Adlerian group counseling.

White, Flynt, and Jones (1999) described an Adlerian-based teacher-training program called *kinder therapy*. In this program, six school staff members, both teachers and school counselors, were trained in the principles of Adlerian-based play therapy and then paired with six kindergarten students for individual play therapy sessions in the school playroom. Staff comments were assessed pretraining, and 6 weeks post therapy. Observers recorded the number of comments that teachers made in the following categories: encouraging statements, limit-setting (punishment, ineffective verbal responses, effective verbal responses, and logical consequences), and goal disclosure. Results indicated that encouraging, goal disclosure, and logical consequence statements tripled, and ineffective verbal responses decreased by two thirds. The staff also rated the target students both before and after therapy using the Student Encouragement Assessment Scale, which measures the teacher's perception of the child's view of self and others, openness to experience, and sense of belonging. Results indicated that the teachers' views of their students' level of encouragement increased in the cases of three of the six students, remained constant for two students, and decreased for one student. The Social Skills Rating System (Gresham & Elliot, 1990) and the Behavior Assessment Scale for Children (Reynolds & Kamphaus, 1992) revealed increases in positive behaviors (e.g., adaptability and social skills) and decreases in negative behaviors (e.g., hyperactivity, aggression, anxiety, depression, somatization, and withdrawal). Although this is an interesting study that attempts to use standardized test scores, there may be some confounding because the school staff implemented the therapy and also served as raters on the standardized instruments; in addition, there were only six subjects in the group, and no statistical analyses were used beyond simple frequency counts and gain scores.

Research has also been conducted to determine the efficacy of IE schools. Poch (1985) reported increased attendance and academic growth at an IE junior high school program. Pratt and Mastroainni (1981) found that academic performance at IE schools was equivalent or superior to that at traditional schools. Krebs (1982) reported that when compared with a control school, students at the IE school showed significantly better achievement as measured by the Iowa Test of Basic Skills. In addition, there were very few incidents of serious misbehavior (vandalism, school property damage, theft, fighting with injuries, substance abuse, and cheating) and truancy at the IE schools.

To summarize, it appears that, in general, Adlerian therapy has not been subjected to intense research scrutiny and does not meet the criteria for evidence-based practice (EBP), as determined by Division 12 of the American Psychological Association (i.e., has a treatment manual, clearly specified client samples, good design, a comparison to another technique or a placebo treatment, adequate statistical power for group studies, or several well-designed single case studies). An examination of the published Well-Established and Probably Efficacious Treatments listed does not include any strictly Adlerian studies (Chambless, 1996). Nor do the studies meet the suggested criteria of the Task Force on Evidence-Based Interventions in School Psychology sponsored by APA's Division 16 and the Society for the Study of School Psychology (n.d.; http://www.sp-ebi. org/documents/_workingfiles/EBImanual1.pdf). Future studies designed to assess the efficacy of individual therapy should be carefully designed to meet these criteria.

The Case of Todd

Ethically, before any therapy with Todd begins, parental consent must be obtained, as well as child assent. The concepts of therapy, confidentiality, and any grounds for breaking confidentiality should be clearly explained to Todd and his mother. It would be preferable for the therapist to meet personally with Todd's mother and grandmother, both individually and together, in order to observe their interactions. Todd's attendance at this interview might also provide important information for the therapist. Ideally, although it is important to include Todd's caretakers throughout the therapeutic procedures, this may not be possible due to parental work responsibilities. If individual or family therapy is not possible, the therapist should at least provide Todd's mother and grandmother with readings (e.g., *Children: The Challenge*; Dreikurs & Soltz, 1964), activities (Dinkmeyer & Dinkmeyer, 1976), and even videos that explain the principles of Adlerian therapy. Some Adlerian therapists may wish to treat their clients in a more social setting, such as group counseling or a classroom-based social skills program, but again this may not be feasible given the restrictions of the school environment; thus, a description of an individual counseling program is presented.

First, we need to establish what we know about the situation, and the referral concern. We actually know very little about the case beyond the fact that Todd is a 10-year-old African American boy being raised by his single mother and grandmother. We do know that Todd is experiencing some academic difficulties, either not completing all of his assignments, taking an excessively long time to complete them, or not turning them in. One of the first tasks should be to determine which one of these behaviors is occurring. We also know that although Todd has been well behaved in the past (at least at school), currently he is displaying some tantrum behaviors.

An in-depth interview with Todd's current teacher and his previous teachers should be undertaken to determine their perceptions of Todd's behavior. After the referral question is clearly defined, the therapist should review the effects of any previous interventions. Prior to meeting with Todd, it would be helpful for the therapist to observe Todd's behavior in the classroom using the goals of misbehavior as a framework for interpretation during both the consultation and the observation processes.

In the individual interview with Todd, the first step would be to build rapport, so that he and the therapist can develop a cooperative and collaborative relationship. Given his apparent anxiety and his need for structure and organization, he would benefit from a discussion of the goals of therapy and the guidelines of the sessions. Specific details related to therapy, such as location, time, length, and frequency of sessions, should be considered. For an anxious child such as Todd, a regular meeting time and place would be very important. Given that a lack of homework completion is one of his critical symptoms, it would be important for the therapist, Todd's teacher, and Todd to explore how classroom activities missed due to session attendance would be handled in terms of logical consequences. In addition, Todd may need to be reassured that he is not being referred for counseling due to failure or displeasure on the part of his teacher and his mother, but rather that meeting with the therapist should help him to cope with his problems.

After rapport is established, the therapist may wish to begin the life-style interview to gain information regarding Todd's subjective thought patterns. The therapist should begin with some open-ended questions where Todd can describe himself, his family, and his friends, as well as his attitude toward school, schoolwork, and other activities. He may also be asked to draw a picture of himself and describe what he likes and dislikes about himself. Subsequent to this broad interview, the therapist should assess specific aspects of Todd's life. Most importantly, a family constellation should be undertaken. Although we know that Todd is being raised by his mother and grandmother, we do not have any information regarding Todd's father or his extended family, and this information could be critical. Hildebrand, Phenice, Gray, and Hines (1996) reported that extended family relationships are an important part of the African American community and noted that child care is frequently shared among mothers, grandmothers, and other female relatives.

We also know that Todd is an only child, and according to Adler, this may suggest that he has advanced language and intellectual skills and that he may relate well to adults. Indeed, Todd's psychoeducational evaluation did reveal above-average intellectual ability, and his third grade teacher's comment that he "was a perfect little gentleman" may be an indication of his social abilities with adults. Adler also suggested that only children may be pampered and overly dependent on adults; however, this hypothesis needs to be explored in more depth. In addition, because Todd's mother and grandmother live together, it may also be interesting to gain information regarding the family constellation of his mother's and grandmother's families of origin.

Next, a review of the family atmosphere should be undertaken. The information we have so far relates only to "order" and suggests that the home is organized because there are established times for dinner, homework, and bedtime. However, information still needs to be gathered regarding the mood of the home, the relationships among family members, and whether there have been any changes in the home environment in the last year.

Although we have a description of a typical day for Todd, we do not have any information regarding his early recollections. He may be asked to provide his first memory or even his first five memories. If Todd prefers, he can be given the option of drawing his memory and then describing it or using a sandtray to depict the memory. During this activity, the therapist should observe the contents of the memory, the characters involved, and the feelings Todd associates with the memory. Again, this memory is interpreted within the concept of the four goals of misbehavior.

Adler indicated that the three tasks an individual must master are work, love, and community. It appears that Todd's problems are centered on "work"—or, in his case, schoolwork. The extended amount of time he spends engaged in schoolwork appears to be very problematic and may interfere with his development in the other two areas. For example, it appears as if he has very little time to interact with his mother and grandmother or even with peers. Findings from the psychoeducational evaluation suggest that the excessive amount of time engaged in schoolwork does not appear to be due to an actual learning problem or learning disability because Todd's cognitive and academic skills, as well as his previous school grades, have all been good.

As Todd's beliefs and goals become more evident, the therapist may continue to refine his or her hypotheses regarding Todd's behavior. After a review of the four goals of misbehavior, it appears that Todd's behavior may be an attempt to meet his goal of attention. Initially, Todd seemed to assume the active constructive form of attention seeking, working for the external rewards of good grades and positive adult attention. During the past school year, however, Todd, although still working hard on his homework, may be showing signs of passive destructive behavior by not turning in his completed work. Passive destructive children display symptoms of anxiety, and Todd's rating scales do show internalizing behaviors, including symptoms of anxiety and worry. These children may solicit attention from sympathetic adults who may attempt to provide special accommodations for them. Indeed, Todd's teacher did try to lessen his homework assignments, although interestingly, Todd refused the accommodation, indicating that he has not totally made the transition from an active constructive pattern to a passive destructive one. Todd's behavior could also be construed as maladaptive perfectionist. Maladaptive perfectionists tend to score higher on levels of external locus of control, need for recognition, and striving for perfection. They tend to be less willing to adapt their behaviors to social cues than adaptive perfectionists (LoCicero, Ashby, & Kern, 2000).

Next, the therapist will attempt to explore Todd's thoughts and beliefs, to help identify and then gently confront any mistaken beliefs. The therapist may then share his or her hypotheses with Todd. The therapist might offer empathic statements that link events, thoughts, and feelings to behaviors. For example, he or she might say, "I understand that you might believe that you are not valuable when you do not finish your homework. However, is there another way that you could feel? Let's take a look at those thoughts which lead you to believe that you are 'nothing' if you do not get an A, and let's figure out if this is a realistic thought." Given his rating scale results, another hypothesis may be that Todd is overly concerned with others' acceptance. By using the Socratic process, Todd might be asked to give evidence for these thoughts, as well as evidence to the contrary. He should be encouraged to look at things differently and to consider advantages to the alternative points of view. For example, it may be suggested to Todd that although his anxiety serves to protect him from the life task of schoolwork, and affords him special attention, sympathy, and concern, it may not be helpful in meeting his life goal of successful attention. For example, his grades have now fallen to C's, and he has no free time at home to gain attention from his mother and grandmother. As these hypotheses are presented to Todd, the therapist may closely observe him to detect the presence of a recognition reflex.

In the final phase of therapy, reorientation, the therapist and Todd will collaborate on identifying alternative thought patterns and behaviors. He will be encouraged to act "as if" he can work more quickly or turn in his work just for a brief period to see what the consequences will be. During the actual session, Todd may role-play different behavior patterns, and then he should be given several short assignments where he can demonstrate new behaviors outside of the session. For example, Todd may be asked to be courageous by spending 10 minutes less on homework each night and monitoring his progress. He may also be encouraged to develop a social interest in others, such as tutoring younger children, performing community service, or working on cooperative learning projects.

Although the therapist is working directly with Todd on these skills, he or she should also consult with Todd's teacher and caretakers. Logical consequences need to be developed for not turning in homework. The adults should also be counseled not to use praise so as to minimize Todd's belief in external reinforcement as a means of gaining self-worth. LoCicero et al. (2000) suggested that teachers should not praise students, but validate their progress toward academic mastery, and that teachers and parents should make a point of telling the student that they can have the courage to be imperfect and to "downplay rightness" (p. 458). In addition, competitive techniques should be discouraged as they may serve to intensify Todd's low self-esteem.

Todd's progress during the course of the counseling intervention should be consistently evaluated. Todd and his therapist may use a chart to monitor his progress in turning in homework, lessening time spent on homework, and mastering new academic skills. In this way, Todd can see his own growth as he meets appropriate goals.

Summary

Adlerian therapy has a long and impressive history. Many of its concepts have been influential in the development of more modern therapies such as cognitive-behavioral therapy (Beck et al., 1979; Burns, 1980), rational emotive therapy (Ellis, 1957), self-psychology (Karrel & Gill, 2004), positive psychology (Leak & Leak, 2006; Seligman & Csikszentmihalyi, 2000), reality therapy and choice theory (Glasser, 1965, 1998; Peterson, 2005; Wubbolding, 2000), constructivism (Watts, 2003), narrative therapy (Daigneault, 1999; Hester, 2004; White & Epson, 1990), and brief solution focused therapy (Watts & Pietrzak, 2000).

Adler's emphasis on the role of social contributions and social equality foreshadowed the importance of diversity and multiculturalism in psychotherapy. Adlerian therapy has been seen as well suited for use with diverse groups. For example, Salzman (2002) and Hunter and Sawyer (2006) described how they successfully incorporated Individual Therapy into their work with Native Americans. Perkins-Dock (2005) has advocated for the use of Adlerian therapy with African American families. Adlerian therapy has also been recommended for use with Mexican American clients (Frevert & Miranda, 1998), Asian Americans (Carlson & Carlson, 2005), Muslims (Johanson, 2005), Jews (Manaster, 2004; Rietveld, 2004), fundamental Christians (Watts, 2000), youth (Potter & Hoedt, 1985), the elderly (Penick, 2004), and the gay, lesbian, bisexual, and transgendered (GLBT) community (Friend, 1987; Kottman, Lingg, & Tisdell, 1995).

Adlerian approaches have several practical applications to school counseling. Whether utilized in individual or group applications, Adlerian therapy can be used to address issues of self-esteem and belongingness in schools. The Adlerian therapist should be encouraging and consistent, guiding child clients as they confront their faulty perceptions, beliefs, and behavior patterns to come to a more adaptive and prosocial coping style. Interventions should focus on natural consequences, fostering cooperation, developing one's sense of community, and preventing misbehaviors. As such, Adlerian approaches are also particularly useful for conceptualizing classroom management and behavior interventions. The parent and teacher training components of Adlerian therapy can also be helpful in prevention and consultation models. Through the study of Alfred Adler's individual psychology, the child therapist can gain an understanding of an important and influential therapeutic technique that after almost 100 years is still appropriate to our modern society.

Recommended Readings

Ansbacher, H. L., & Ansbacher, R. R. (1956). *The individual psychology of Alfred Adler*. New York: Harper & Row.

Carlson, J., Watts, R.E., & Maniacci, M. (2006). *Adlerian therapy: Theory and practice*. Washington, DC: American Psychological Association.

Dinkmeyer, D., Dinkmeyer, D., Jr., & Sperry, L. (2000). *Adlerian counseling and psychotherapy*. Columbus, OH: Merrill.

Dinkmeyer, D., & McKay, G. (1982). *Raising a responsible child*. New York: Simon and Schuster.

References

Adler, A. (1963). *The practice and theory of individual psychology*. Patterson, NJ: Littlefield, Adams.

Albert, L. (1995). *Cooperative discipline revised*. Circle Pines, MN: American Guidance Service.

Ansbacher, H. L., & Ansbacher, R. R. (1956). *The individual psychology of Alfred Adler: A systematic presentation in selections from his writings*. New York: Harper & Row.

Bainum, C. R., Schneider, M. F., & Stone, M. H. (2006). An Adlerian model for sand tray therapy. *Journal of Individual Psychology, 62*, 36–46.

Beck, A., Rush, A. J., Shaw, B. F., & Emery, G. (1979). *Cognitive therapy of depression*. New York: Guilford.

Bettner, B. L. (2005). Using early recollections to understand and help a failing student. *Journal of Individual Psychology, 61*, 100–105.

Blamires, M. (2006). Is there a point to wearing dead men's spectacles? How the theoretical insights of Adler and colleagues relate to current practice with children experiencing EBD. *Support for Learning, 21*(4), 182–187.

Brigman, G., & Molina, B. (1999). Social interest and school success. *Journal of Individual Psychology, 55*, 342–354.

Burnett, P. C. (1988). Evaluation of Adlerian parenting programs. Individual Psychology: *The Journal of Adlerian Therapy, 44*, 63–77.

Burns, D. D. (1980). *Feeling good: The new mood therapy*. New York: William Morrow.

Campbell, C. (2003). Student success skills training: An Adlerian approach to peer coaching. *Journal of Individual Psychology, 59*, 327–333.

Carlson, J., Watts, R. E., & Maniacci, M. (2006). *Adlerian therapy: Theory and practice*. Washington, DC: American Psychological Association.

Carlson, J. M., & Carlson, J. D. (2000). The application of Adlerian psychotherapy with Asian-American clients. *Journal of Individual Psychology, 56*, 214–226.

Carlson, M., & Carlson, J. (2000). The application of Adlerian psychotherapy with Asian American clients. *Journal of Individual Psychology, 56*, 214–225.

Carmichael, K. D. (2006). *Play therapy: An introduction.* Upper Saddle Ridge, NJ: Pearson Education.

Chambless, D. L. (1996). An update on empirically validated therapies. *Clinical Psychologist, 49,* 5–18.

Clark, A. (1995). The organization and implementation of a social interest program in the schools. *Individual Psychology, 51,* 317–331.

Corsini, R. (1977). Individual education: A system based on individual psychology. *Journal of Individual Psychology, 33,* 295–349.

Curlette, W., Wheeler, M. S., & Kern, R. (1997). *BASIS-A Inventory.* Highlands, NC: TRT Associates.

Daigneault, S. D. (1999). Narrative means to an Adlerian end: An illustrated comparison of narrative therapy and Adlerian play therapy. *Journal of Individual Psychology, 55,* 298–315.

Dinkmeyer, D., Jr. (2006). School consultation using individual psychology. *Journal of Individual Psychology, 62,* 180–187.

Dinkmeyer, D., Jr., Carlson, J., & Dinkmeyer, D., Sr. (1994). *Consultation: School mental health professionals as consultants.* Muncie, IN: Accelerated Development.

Dinkmeyer, D., & Dinkmeyer, D. (1976). *Systematic training for effective parenting (STEP).* Circle Pines, MN: American Guidance Service.

Dinkmeyer, D., & Dinkmeyer, D., Jr. (1982). *Developing understanding of self and others, D-1 and D-2 (Rev.).* Circle Pines, MN: American Guidance Service.

Dinkmeyer, D., McKay, G., & Dinkmeyer, D. (1980). *Systematic training for effective teaching (STET).* Circle Pines, MN: American Guidance Service.

Dinkmeyer, D., Pew, W., & Dinkmeyer, D., Jr. (1979). *Adlerian counseling and psychotherapy.* Monterey, CA: Brooks/Cole.

Dreikurs, R. (1957). *Psychology in the classroom.* New York: Harper & Row.

Dreikurs, R., & Soltz, V. (1964). *Children: The challenge.* New York: Hawthorn.

Dumont, F., & Corsini, R. (2000). *Six therapists and one client* (2nd ed.). New York: Springer.

Ellis, A. (1957). Rational psychotherapy and individual psychology. *Journal of Individual Psychology, 13,* 38–44.

Farooq, D. M., Jefferson, J. L., & Fleming, J. (2005). The effect of an Adlerian video-based parent education program on parent's perception of children's behavior: A study of African American parents. *Journal of Professional Counseling: Practice, Theory & Research, 33,* 21–34.

Frevert, V. S., & Miranda, A. O. (1998). A conceptual formulation of the Latin culture and the treatment of Latinos from an Adlerian psychology perspective. *Journal of Individual Psychology, 54,* 291–310.

Friend, R. A. (1987). The individual and social psychology of aging: Clinical implications for lesbians and gay men. *Journal of Homosexuality, 14,* 207–331.

Gilbert, J. N., & Morawski, C. (2005). Stress coping for elementary school children: A case for including lifestyle. *Journal of Individual Psychology, 61,* 314–328.

Glasser, R. (1965). *Reality therapy: A new approach to psychiatry.* New York: Harper & Row.

Glasser, R. (1998). *Choice therapy: A new psychology of personal freedom.* New York: Harper Collins.

Gordon-Rosen, M., & Rosen, A. (1984). Adlerian parent study groups and inner-city children. *Individual Psychology: The Journal of Adlerian Theory, Research & Practice, 40,* 309–317.

Gresham, F. M., & Elliott, S. N. (1990). *Social skills rating system manual.* Circle Pines, MN: American Guidance Service.

Hardy, C. A. (1984). The four goals of mistaken behavior as a focus for classroom observation. *Journal of Adlerian Theory, Research & Practice, 40,* 232–235.

Hester, R. L. (2004). Early memory and narrative therapy. *Journal of Individual Psychology, 60,* 338–347.

Hildebrand, V., Phenice, L. A., Gray, M. M., & Hines, R. P. (1996). *Knowing and serving diverse families.* Englewood Cliffs, NJ: Prentice Hall.

Hunter, D., & Sawyer, C. (2006). Blending Native American spirituality with individual psychology in work with children. *Journal of Individual Psychology, 62,* 234–250.

Johansen, T. (2005). Applying individual psychology to work with clients of the Islamic faith. *Journal of Individual Psychology, 61,* 174–184.

Johnson, J. C. (1991). The effects of parent education and authoritarian attitudes on parenting skills. *Dissertation Abstract International, 51,* 2552.

Karrel, A., & Gill, J. (2002). A comparison of Alfred Adler's and Heinz Kohut's conceptions of psychopathology. *Journal of Individual Psychology, 58,* 160–169.

Kottman, T., Lingg, M. A., & Tisdell, T. (1995). Gay and lesbian adolescence: Implications for Adlerian therapists. *Individual Psychology: Journal of Adlerian Theory, Research and Practice, 51,* 114–128.

Kottman, T., & Stiles, K. (1990). The mutual storytelling technique: An Adlerian application in child therapy. *Individual Psychology, 4,* 148–157.

Kottman, T., & Warlick, J. (1989). Adlerian play therapy: Practical considerations. *Individual Psychology, 45,* 433–446.

Krebs, L. L. (1982). A summary of research on an individual education (IE) school. *Individual Psychology, 38,* 245–252.

LaFountain, R., Garner, N., & Miedma, P. (2003). Adler's contributions to learning styles and multiple intelligence theories. *Journal of Individual Psychology, 59,* 213–222.

Leak, G. K., & Leak, K. (2006). Adlerian social interest and positive psychology: A conceptual and empirical integration. *Journal of Individual Psychology, 62,* 207–223.

Lee, R. S. (2001). A Modified Life Style Assessment and its use in the school setting. *Journal of Individual Psychology, 57,* 298–310.

LoCicero, K. A., Ashby, J. S., & Kern, R. M. (2000). Multidimensional perfectionism and lifestyle approaches in middle school students. *Journal of Individual Psychology, 56,* 449–461.

Manaster, G. J. (2004). Individual psychology and Judaism: A comparative essay. *Journal of Individual Psychology, 60,* 420–427.

Manaster, G. J., Berra, S., & Mays, M. (2001). Manaster-Perryman Early Recollections Scoring Manual: Findings and summary. *Journal of Individual Psychology, 57*, 413–419.

Morse, C., & Brokoven, J. (1987). The Oregon DUSO-R research studies series: Integrating a children's social skills curriculum in a family education/counseling center. *Individual Psychology, 43*, 101–114.

Mosak, H. (1958). Early recollections as a projective technique. *Journal of Projective Techniques, 22*, 302–311.

Mosak, H. (1987). Adlerian psychotherapy. In R. J. Corsini (Ed.), *Current psychotherapies*. Itasca, IL: Peacock.

Mullis, F. (1999). Active parenting: An evaluation of two Adlerian parent education programs. *Journal of Individual Psychology, 55*, 225–233.

Nystul, M. (1984). Positive parenting leads to self-actualizing children. *Individual Psychology: Journal of Adlerian Theory, Research and Practice, 40*, 177–183.

Penick, J. M. (2004). Purposeful aging: Teleological perspectives on the development of social interest in late adulthood. *Journal of Individual Psychology, 60*, 219–233.

Perkins-Dock, R. E. (2005). The application of Adlerian family therapy with African American families. *Journal of Individual Psychology, 61*, 233–249.

Peterson, S. (2005). Reality therapy and individual or Adlerian psychology: A comparison. *International Journal of Reality Therapy, 24*, 11–15.

Pierce, K. A. (1987). Individual education/Corsini's 4R schools: Another look. *Individual Psychology: The Journal of Adlerian Theory, Research & Practice, 43*, 370–378.

Platt, J. M. (1971). Efficacy of the Adlerian model in elementary school counseling. *Elementary School Counseling and Guidance, 6*(2), 86–91.

Poch, J. (1985). The Hufford Junior High School: A school within a school. *Individual Psychology: The Journal of Adlerian Theory, Research & Practice, 41*, 74–77.

Porter, B. A., & Hoedt, K. C. (1985). Differential effects of an Adlerian approach with preadolescent children. *Individual Psychology, 41*, 372–385.

Pratt, A. B. (1985). Summary of research on Individual Education to 1984. *Individual Psychology: The Journal of Adlerian Theory, Research & Practice, 41*, 39–56.

Pratt, A. B., & Mastroainni, T. (1981). Summary of research on individual education. *Journal of Individual Psychology, 37*, 232–246.

Pryor, D., & Tollerud, T. R. (1999). Applications of Adlerian principles in school settings, *Professional School Counseling, 24*, 299–304.

Reynolds, C. R., & Kamphaus, R. W. (1992). *Behavior assessment system for children*. Circle Pines, MN: American Guidance Service.

Richie, M. H., & Burnett, P. C. (1985). Evaluating the effectiveness of an Adlerian-based self-enhancement program for children. *Individual Psychology, 4*, 363–372.

Rieveld, G. (2004). Similarities between Jewish philosophical thought and Adler's Individual Psychology. *Journal of Individual Psychology, 60,* 209–218.

Rogers, C. R. (1951). *Client-centered therapy.* Boston: Houghton Mifflin.

Salzman, M. (2002). A culturally congruent consultation at a Bureau of Indian Affairs boarding school. *Journal of Individual Psychology, 58,* 132–146.

Seligman, M., & Csikszentmihalyi, M. (2000). Positive psychology: An introduction. *American Psychologist, 55,* 236–240.

Shulman, B. H., & Mosak, H. H. (1988). *A manual for life style assessment.* Muncie, IN: Accelerated Development.

Smuts, J. C. (1926). *Holism and evolution.* New York: MacMillan Compass/ Viking Press.

Snow, J. N., & Kern, R. M. (1997). The effects of STEP on patient progress in an adolescent day hospital. *Journal of Adlerian Theory, Research & Practice, 53,* 388–396.

Society for the Study of School Psychology. (N.d.). [Home page]. Retrieved July 9, 2008, from http://www.sp-ebi.org/documents/_workingfiles/EBImanual1.pdf

Statton, J. E. & Wilborn, B. (1991). Adlerian Counseling and the early recollections of children. *Individual Psychology: The Journal of Adlerian Theory, Research & Practice, 47,* 338–348.

Stiles, B., & Wilborn, M. (1992). A lifestyle instrument for children. *Individual Psychology, 48,* 96–105.

Sweeney, D. S., Minnix, G. M. & Homeyer, L. E. (2003). Using sand tray therapy in lifestyle analysis. *Journal of Individual Psychology, 59,* 376–387.

Task Force on Evidence-Based Interventions in School Psychology. (N.d.). [Home page]. Retrieved July 9, 2008, from http://www.sp-ebi.org/documents/_ workingfiles/EBImanual1.pdf

Urbin, T. A. (1991). A case study of the effects of an Adlerian parent education program on parent attitudes and child rearing techniques. *Dissertation Abstracts International, 52,* 4218.

Vaihinger, H. (1952). *The philosophy of "as if"* (C. K. Ogden, Trans. 1924). London: Routledge. (Originally published in 1911).

Watkins, C. (1992). Research activity with Adler's theory. *Journal of Adlerian Theory, Research & Practice, 48,* 1107–109.

Watts, R. (2000). Biblically based Christian spirituality and Adlerian psychotherapy, psychology, therapy. *Journal of Individual Psychology, 56,* 316–328.

Watts, R. (2003). Adlerian therapy as a relational constructivist approach. *Family Journal, 11,* 139–147.

Watts, R., & Pietrzak, D. (2000). Adlerian encouragement and the therapeutic process of solution focused brief therapy. *Journal of Counseling Development, 78,* 442–227.

White, J., Flynt, & M., Jones, N. (1999). Kinder therapy: An Adlerian approach for training teachers to be therapeutic agents through play. *Journal of Individual Psychology, 55,* 365–383.

White, M., & Epson, D. (1990). *Narrative means to therapeutic ends.* New York: Norton.

Wubbolding, R. (2000). *Reality therapy for the 21st century.* Philadelphia: Brunner-Routledge.

Section IV

Nontraditional Interventions

12

Applying Play Therapy in Schools

Athena A. Drewes

The need for and use of psychological services within the school system go back to the child guidance movement in the early 1900s, when societal changes occurred in how children were viewed. There was a shift to the child being seen more as an emotional family investment (Fagan, 2000). By 1920, compulsory education of children was mandated in all states, increasing the number of average days of the school year from 135 to 173 and doubling primary school enrollment (Drewes, 2001). Secondary school student enrollment went from 203,000 to 4.4 million (Snyder, Hoffman, & Geddes, 1997).

Consequently, classroom size is as high as 68 students along with the emergence of many administrative concerns over attendance and children's health issues (notably speech and hearing, as well as social work and psychological services; Fagan, 2000). School districts were forced to find ways to deal with rapidly multiplying referrals from teachers for help in dealing with students' behavioral, physical, and academic problems (Drewes, 2001a).

The National Committee for Mental Hygiene was formed in the early 1900s to provide information to the public regarding deplorable state hospital conditions, as well as to improve mental health treatment and encourage research on the prevention and treatment of mental illness (Carmichael, 2006). Consequently, mental hygiene programs and services began in schools, and child guidance clinics were established (Morris & Kratochwill, 1983). Almost 100 years later, school clinicians are still dealing with the same problems of referrals for the behavioral, physical, academic, and emotional problems of students (Drewes, 2001a).

In the 1960s, school districts included school psychologists and school counselors in order to meet the demands of classifying students as well as offer counseling mandated by the student's individualized education plan

(IEP). Graduate guidance, counseling, and school psychology programs were formed at universities and colleges to meet the demands of services in elementary and secondary schools. Professional journals were created for school psychologists and school counselors to keep up-to-date with assessment and treatment issues unique to the school setting. Writings about play therapy began to appear (Landreth, Jacquot, & Allen, 1968) and still continue to appear in such journals. These early authors promoted the use of play therapy to meet the developmental needs of schoolchildren, and the need for preventative interventions. Since 1980, play therapy has gained prominence and awareness within the school setting and among the public at large.

Today, there has been a rapidly increasing number of schoolchildren throughout the United States being identified as having special needs or disabilities. School clinicians, which include counselors, school psychologists, social workers, and even paraprofessionals such as child associates or youth and family workers, may find their counseling caseload filled with a majority of students having learning disabilities. Learning disabilities make up 46.2% of the school-aged students classified with disabilities and 5.9% of the overall school population (U.S. Department of Education, 1999). The U.S. Department of Education (1999) reported that approximately 2.7 million students with learning disabilities were served in the 1997–1998 school year alone. The number of children classified within the autism spectrum has shown an increase recently. The Autism Society (2005) reported that there has been an astounding 172% increase in the incidence of autism since the 1990s. Schoolchildren with an autism diagnosis also account for 3–7% of schoolchildren who are diagnosed with attention deficit/hyperactivity disorders (AD/HD; Children and Adults With Attention-Deficit/Hyperactivity Disorder, 2005). Furthermore, more than 25% of schoolchildren experience moderate to severe school adjustment problems due to emotional difficulties. As a result of these disabilities and learning difficulties, children who do not experience early school success are at risk of school failure, dropping out, becoming drug addicted and delinquent, and developing serious emotional disorders, which result in costly burdens to society (Drewes, 2001a).

Better and earlier identification practices and screening programs have contributed to the rising numbers of classified students with special needs. Consequently, school clinicians are now required to provide services to children at younger ages and throughout all the grades. Because of these rising numbers, it has never been more important for school clinicians to have the necessary knowledge and skill base for working with children with disabilities. Therefore, it also behooves supervisors of school clinicians to become familiar with the common issues that arise for children with special needs and their families, the barriers that prevent school clinicians from best meeting the needs of these individuals, and the various treatment modalities (both evidence based and empirically supported) that exist.

Therapeutic Powers of Play

Because children, as well as adolescents, with disabilities often have difficulty verbally communicating their concerns, behaviors, and problems due to emotional, cognitive, developmental, and speech and language difficulties, a nonverbal, play-based approach to counseling is needed. Play is the child's natural medium of expression. It is a special form of communication, and being primarily nonverbal it is a form that is full of images and emotions (Schaefer, 1993). Play contains several therapeutic factors. It can (a) allow children a way to enact thoughts and feelings that they might or might not be aware of, but cannot use words to express; (b) be a means of communicating; (c) allow for overcoming resistance; (d) increase a sense of mastery; (e) encourage creative thinking and problem-solving skills; (f) allow for catharsis in discharging positive and negative feelings; (g) also allow for the reliving of past stressful events and concomitant associated emotions; (h) offer the opportunity for role-playing in trying out alternative behaviors and actions; (i) enhance a flexible use of imagination; (j) use metaphor via storytelling, fantasy play, and drawings by the school clinician to allow for direct communication to the child's unconscious; (k) foster secure attachments; (l) form a relationship through play, creating a bond that is positive, is nonjudgmental, and contributes to the child's sense of well-being; (m) be fundamentally fun and enjoyable; (n) reduce anxiety through systematic desensitization and the neutralization of fears; and (o) offer older children and adolescents opportunities for socialization and understanding rules through playing various board games (Schaefer, 1993). The healing powers of play utilized in play therapy can alleviate behavioral difficulties and foster cognitive, emotional, academic, and developmental growth. The school clinician is able to utilize play and play-based techniques to create a trusting working alliance, create understanding and self-expression, help to develop the child's self-esteem, and help the child release emotions and practice and acquire new behaviors and empathy. As the relationship with the clinician increases, the child or adolescent can move into self-actualization and relationship enhancement resulting in growth, and development of mastery over fears and concerns as he or she develops ego strength (Schaefer, 1993). So it is no wonder that play therapy is a natural and very useful method of working with children in the school setting.

Play as Therapy Versus Play in Therapy

Play by itself is not therapy or counseling. However, there is play *as* therapy and play *in* therapy, as seen in play therapy. Play therapy allows for the use of play and play-based techniques in creating the therapeutic relationship as well as in working through a variety of emotional, developmental, and cognitive disabilities and issues.

Play therapy is both a treatment modality and a term that encompasses a variety of verbal and nonverbal treatment methods. Play therapy and the use of play-based interventions are not new and date back to the 1930s. Hermione Hug-Hellmuth, Anna Freud, and Melanie Klein saw the benefit of using toys as a means of communication with and by children in therapy, as children were not able to use the verbal treatment methods used with adults. Since that time, several adult talk therapies have been adapted for use with children along various theoretical lines. Some of these include psychoanalytic and psychodynamic play therapy; child-centered play therapies (Axline, 1969; Landreth, 2002), including filial therapy (Guerney, 1969; VanFleet, 1994) and child–parent relationship therapy (Landreth & Bratton, 2006); gestalt play therapy; child developmental play therapy, such as theraplay (Jernberg, 1979); Jungian analytical play therapy, including sand tray and sandplay therapy (Kalff, 1980; Lowenfeld, 1979); cognitive-behavioral play therapy (Knell, 1993); and integrative and prescriptive play therapy. These represent play *as* therapy.

Play therapy has also become a larger descriptor of a variety of methods used within treatment for children, such as art therapy, expressive arts therapy, narrative, and drama, music, and dance therapies, among others. These represent play in therapy.

In 1982, Dr. Charles Schaefer was instrumental in forming the Association for Play Therapy for the purpose of promoting the healing powers of play, play therapy, and credentialed play therapists. Over the past 25 years, through Dr. Schaefer's efforts and those of the association, there are over 5,000 members, in 45 state branches, who utilize play therapy in some form in their treatment of children and adolescents. Play therapy as defined by the Association for Play Therapy (APT) is "the systematic use of a theoretical model to establish an interpersonal process wherein trained play therapists use the therapeutic powers of play to help clients prevent or resolve psychosocial difficulties and achieve optimal growth and development" (APT, 2007). Since 1990, national training and registration criteria were established by APT for earning the title of *registered play therapist* and *registered play therapist-supervisor*. It has been only over the past 25 years, largely through the efforts of APT and Charles Schaefer, that play therapy, play, and credentialed play therapists have been actively promoted and have gained clinical and public recognition.

The appeal of using play therapy and play-based techniques is that it allows children or adolescents the freedom to express themselves without words, in the natural language of play. Just as birds may fly, and fish swim, so too is it natural for children to play. Play is as natural as breathing. Play is found in all cultures, and it transcends language barriers (Drewes, 2005). Play is the universal, natural language of children. Left on their own to entertain themselves, children of all cultures will play.

Play can provide the sense of power and control that comes from mastering new experiences, solving problems and concerns, creating social contact, stimulating creative expression and exploration, and allowing the child to rehearse roles and skills needed for survival (Drewes, 2001a; Landreth, 2002). The therapy toys become the child's words, and their play the child's language (Landreth, 2002). It is then up to the trained clinician to decipher the symbolic play and communicate back in a way that acknowledges to the child that he or she was heard and understood. Children from preschool on up are able to communicate nonverbally, through metaphor, and in an action-oriented way. By having toys, play, and expressive arts materials within the school clinician's room, the child immediately understands that this is a space where talk is not always necessary or expected in order for them to be understood.

Clinicians are able to utilize play therapy to strategically help children to express themselves when their verbal language fails to communicate troubling thoughts and feelings (Gil, 1991). Through an emotionally supportive environment, special therapeutic toys, and specialized training, the school clinician is able to respond to the child's metaphor and symbolism or through use of play-based interventions help the child resolve inner conflicts, distortions in thinking, and dysfunctional behaviors in a way that is consistent with his or her development (Reddy, Files-Hall, & Schaefer, 2005). Play therapy and play-based interventions and techniques can be easily paired with short-term treatments, which include cognitive-behavioral and behavioral management techniques in a directive manner, as well as in long-term treatment using a nondirective, combination, or integrative approach (Reddy et al., 2005).

Theoretical Overview

The school clinician can choose from a variety of play therapy theoretical approaches and intervention means. In the nondirective realm, there is the child-centered treatment approach in which the clinician follows the child's lead in play. Nondirective approaches for children were developed by Virginia Axline and refined by Garry Landreth, along with the psychodynamic and psychoanalytic approaches developed by Anna Freud, and the Jungian analytic approach utilizing sandtray therapy developed by Margaret Lowenfeld and Dora Kalff. In the directive realm, there is the cognitive-behavioral play therapy approach, in which the goals and objectives in symptom reduction drive the selection of the intervention and techniques to use; and Gestalt therapy, which utilizes multiple techniques and materials from working with clay and the sandtray, to drawings and guided imagery. There is the combined or integrative approach such as Adlerian in which the clinician will utilize nondirective as well as directive approaches that utilize storytelling and use of metaphor, among others. And, there is prescriptive play therapy that allows the clinician to select the treatment approach that best meets the symptoms and situation of the child at the moment. It allows for best practices in choosing evidence-based and empirically validated treatment approaches as well as moving from a nondirective approach in building a trusting therapeutic relationship and then into a directive approach for specific symptoms or skill building.

Nondirective Theoretical Approaches

Psychoanalytic and Psychodynamic

Evolving out of Sigmund Freud's (1909) psychoanalytic theories, Anna Freud (Freud & Clark, 1928) and Melanie Klein (Klein & Riviere, 1983) utilized play therapy as a means of understanding and healing the child. They viewed play much like Freud viewed free association. The goal of this nondirective approach not only is to change a behavior or symptom, but also goes deeper into the child's manner of coping with life and its stresses to help the child integrate various aspects of his or her personality (Bromfield, 2003, p. 2). In the safe and accepting therapeutic atmosphere, the therapist empathically listens and responds to the child's play and metaphor. This is a relationship-based therapy, whereby the therapist's role is to help the child recognize and interpret his or her unconscious motivations into the conscious. Through the formation of the therapeutic alliance and the process of transference and countertransference, the analysis of the transference relationship becomes important (Carmichael, 2006). Throughout the session, the therapist verbally responds to the child's play and metaphor, follows the child's lead, and eventually brings in interpretations to help process the play and transference issues.

Psychoanalytic and psychodynamic play therapy is good at helping children with anxiety, depression, trauma recovery, phobia elimination, borderline and psychotic functioning, chronic illness, learning disabilities, attachment disorders, and anger management (Bromfield, 2003).

Child-Centered (Virginia Axline and Garry Landreth)

The early work of Carl Rogers was adapted by his student Virginia Axline (1969) into nondirective play therapy. The clinician offers a therapeutic environment along with empathic listening and responding, unconditional positive regard, and genuine concern and feedback (Axline, 1947; Carmichael, 2006). The session allowed the child to play out feelings and concerns, similar to the talk therapist. She theorized that each child had a power force within that was striving toward complete self-realization and actualization. Given the proper therapeutic environment, the child could flourish and develop a well-balanced personality (Axline, 1947; Carmichael, 2006). Thus, by playing out feelings, the child externalizes them into a form whereby they can deal with them, control them, or abandon them (Carmichael, 2006). Landreth (2002) has extended Axline's views into a philosophical stance and life orientation that extend beyond the playroom. He postulated that children have an innate capacity for growth and resiliency so that they can direct and pace their own emotional growth and belief in self (Landreth, 1991). Consequently, "child-centered play therapy is an attitude, a philosophy, and a way of being" (Landreth, 1991, p. 55).

Jungian Analytic Play Therapy

Carl Jung, a contemporary of Freud, developed a theory in which he viewed the ego as having the responsibility to mediate between the inner drives and present reality. Jung believed in the curative aspect of play. One's psyche has the potential to self-heal. Archetypes assist in organizing the child's behavior, and play and its creative process, assist in transforming the child and leading to healing (Carmichael, 2006).

Jungian theory holds that there are both conscious (ego) and unconscious elements in the personality. These fundamental personality components, and structures of the psyche, emerge naturally and spontaneously (Peery, 2003). The inner world of the psyche strives to reconcile experiences and meaning with external reality (Carmichael, 2006). The healing process is initiated by opening the dialogue with the ego-self through the symbolic language of the self. These are explored through play, drawings, poetry, music, dreams, stories, and sandtray work. Once the ego-self becomes open to the symbolic expression in the safe and supportive therapeutic environment, the child is able to regain trust of self, and the healing process intuitively begins (Carmichael, 2006). The school clinician has three primary functions in Jungian analytical play therapy. First is to provide a safe, welcoming, and trusting environment. Second, the clinician joins with the child in witnessing his or her play and drama of the therapeutic process. Finally, the clinician maintains ego consciousness that is used to make meaning about and understand the significance of the play activity and archetypal themes (Peery, 2003).

Sandplay or Sandtray Therapy

Margaret Lowenfeld. Margaret Lowenfeld (1979), a contemporary of Anna Freud and Melanie Klein, viewed play as a cognitive process. She focused less on the therapist–child relationship and more on the organizational abilities of the child to make sense of the world and his or her life experiences (Carmichael, 2006). She believed the child had the capacity to work through problems on his or her own. She utilized a sandtray filled with moist sand that the child could mold and into which the child could insert a variety of miniatures that represented all aspects of his or her world (objects, people, animals, etc.). The child was directed to build his or her world in the sand, whereas the therapist was a passive witness to the process.

Dora Kalff. Dora Kalff (1980) studied under Jung and created the sandtray to allow children as well as adults a means of healing their psyche through the use of miniature figures (like those of Lowenfeld) to create a picture in the sandtray while the therapist is a witness to the process who is trying to understand the symbols and archetypes used.

Jungian play therapy works predominantly with metaphor and symbolism (Carmichael, 2006). Jungian therapists are predominantly nondirective with the therapist providing materials, such as art, drama, writing, and use of sandtrays, along with permissiveness, safety, and a nonjudgmental environment where children can safely explore their inner self.

Directive and Integrative Approaches

Gestalt Play Therapy

Working from the writing of Perls (1951), Oaklander (1988) adapted Gestalt theories and applied them to play therapy. The child's symptoms are viewed as masking the child's authentic expressions. Consequently, the school clinician's role is to help the child attempt to cope with and survive the stress in his or her world and to regain balance or homeostasis (Carmichael, 2006). Oaklander suggested that the work with the child is a delicate balance between directing and guiding the session while determining whether to move with the child or follow the child's lead in a therapeutic "dance" (Carmichael, 2006). The goal of therapy is to assist the child in becoming aware of self and the child's existence in the world. Expressive arts materials, including clay and paints, storytelling, poetry, puppets, and therapeutic games, are included (Oaklander, 1988) in the therapeutic space.

Adlerian Play Therapy

The underlying theory is that people are indivisible, social, decision-making beings, whose actions and psychological movement have purpose (Dinkmeyer, Dinkmeyer, & Sperry, 1987). The child's play reflects inner characteristics and manners of behavior or lifestyle (Adler, 2004).

Therefore, an Adlerian play therapist would help children to explore alternative perceptions about their life and experience, and utilize their goal-directed and purposeful behavior to move toward their desired goal.

The playroom includes toys to assist the child to create rapport with the therapist, convey a variety of emotions, role-play situations and relationships that exist in the child's life, provide a safe environment to test out behavioral and emotional limits, empower the child's sense of self, advance self-understanding, and improve the child's self-control and responsibility for his or her behavior and feelings. Toys are included to represent five basic groups: family-nurturing toys, scary toys, aggressive toys, expressive toys, and pretend and fantasy toys, including dolls, puppets, and games (Kottman, 1995).

Cognitive-Behavioral Play Therapy

This theory is based on behavioral and cognitive (Beck, 1976) theories of emotional development and psychopathology. It incorporates cognitive and behavioral interventions within a play therapy paradigm, with verbal and nonverbal communication during play activities. Sessions include forming therapeutic goals, having both the child and therapist select materials and activities, using play to teach skills and alternative behaviors, having the therapist verbalize the conflicts and irrational logic to the child, and use of praise by the therapist. Toys include books, stories, structured workbooks, drawing and art materials, puppets, and doll play. The therapist is guided by measurable objectives and specific interventions, and is directive in those interventions. The therapist chooses and directs the play activities to achieve goals established through the initial assessment (Knell, 1998).

Prescriptive Play Therapy

This approach is based on the core premise of differential therapeutics (Frances, Clarkin, & Perry, 1984), and it holds that some play interventions are more effective than others, for certain types of disorders (Schaefer, 2003). Thus, a child who does poorly in one type of play therapy may do well with another (Beutler, 1979). There is no "one size fits all" approach (Schaefer, 2003, p. 307), whereby one theoretical school is strong enough to make changes across all the many different and complex identifiable disorders. The prescriptive approach seeks to find the most effective play intervention to a specific disorder, matching the approach to the unique needs of the individual case (Norcross, 1991; Schaefer, 2003). The prescriptive approach utilizes eclecticism, selecting from various theories and techniques to create a therapeutic strategy that is best for the particular child. Thus multiple theories are embraced (directive and nondirective), rejecting a strict allegiance to just one particular school of treatment (Schaefer, 2003). The therapist researches evidence-based and empirically supported treatments, as well as identifies the change mechanisms underlying the effective outcome (Schaefer, 2003). Treatment goals and objectives need to be clearly delineated, along with a comprehensive assessment, in order to select the best treatment method to use. The play therapist must be familiar with the major theories of play and play therapy and have a clear understanding of play and how it is integrated into play therapy, the ways that play changes with development, and the many play materials and techniques currently available, along with the diverse ways these materials and techniques can be modified for a specific client and problem (Schaefer, 2003).

For all the theoretical formats, the school clinician needs a designated play area, either a playroom or a portion of his or her office devoted to the play materials. Inclusion of expressive arts materials (e.g., paper, scissors, markers, crayons, glue, magazines for making collages, clay for molding and pounding, and paints and markers with a variety of skins tones), culturally sensitive dolls and play foods, puppets, small vehicles (e.g., police, firemen, ambulance, and construction), a dollhouse, small doll figures, small animals (domestic and wild), small people figures, a sandtray (or Tupperware or a litter box container with dust-free and particle-free sand), and therapeutic board games are among some of the materials to include (Drewes, 2001b). These items can span across the age span from preschool on up to adolescents.

Assessment and Case Conceptualization

A measured, comprehensive, and sensitive assessment can both inform and initiate treatment (Gil, 2006). Assessment can be used to problem-solve the presenting problem, and what intervention would be best to use for this child, at this time. It should provide a comprehensive image of the child that gives useful and accurate information, with the primary aim of identifying and highlighting the child's strengths and weaknesses.

Aside from the standard evaluation and assessment tools used to determine whether a child needs special assistance or is eligible for classification, assessment of the child should be as comprehensive as possible. This will allow for identification of the problem, consideration of which treatment method or modality best suits the situation, and measurement of how the criteria will be met. Play therapy itself is process oriented, and assessment within play therapy should be ongoing and developmentally appropriate.

An initial intake meeting with the parent or caretaker should occur, whereby historical data, baseline behavioral concerns, levels of functioning within the home, outside activities (e.g., spiritual places and/or church, boy scouts, girl scouts, gymnastics, after-school activities, and family gatherings), and family and cultural history can be obtained.

A combination of play observations in naturalistic settings (classroom and playground), along with full developmental and family histories, formal play diagnostic tools, and observation in the playroom, should be used before proceeding with treatment. *Play Diagnosis and Assessment* (Schaefer, Gitlin, & Sandgrund, 1991) is an exhaustive, comprehensive catalog of a variety of play diagnostics that can be used for its research base and objectivity. The book is divided into sections covering developmental play assessments, diagnostic play assessments, parent–child interaction play assessments, family play assessments, peer interaction play assessments, and projective play assessments. Formal assessment tools, such as the Child Behavior Checklist, filled out by the parent and teacher can offer additional information on the child's level of functioning in different settings. The school clinician should always be sensitive to cultural, ethnic, and religious factors within the family that may influence formal diagnostic evaluations as well as interventions.

Play observation and informal play assessment can provide a wealth of information from children who especially may not be able to be tested in a more formal way, such as children with cognitive delays, selective mutism, autistic spectrum disorders, conduct disorders, or sensory and language limitations. Play assessment also allows children to gain a safe distance from sensitive, threatening, distasteful, or taboo issues, reducing their anxiety and allowing freer expression and recall that would have been limited through verbal interviews.

Informal observation should focus on the quality of the child's play, age appropriateness, and developmental level of play and use of play materials or whether the play is focused around a theme or is random, impulsive, listless, or the like. The school clinician should always be looking for the child's and family's strengths that can be worked with and built on.

Additional factors to look for are the quality of the child's peer interactions, whether they are a follower or initiator, the expansiveness of the play and use of materials, the frustration level, as well as the level of dependency and independence. Cognitive skills, language skills, level of self-control, relationships, self-concept, and emotional awareness should also be assessed for.

The school clinician can use play materials in the course of conducting both informal and formal assessments. For example, the school clinician can use puppets in asking questions to a younger child who seems withdrawn or reluctant to participate, have the child draw him or herself in the child's favorite weather or in the rain, or create a sandtray of his or her world, all of which assist in creating rapport while obtaining needed information prior to starting treatment. For example, the use of the Gingerbread Person Feelings Map (Drewes, 2001c) offers a quick and visual representations of the child's emotional and affective life. The child is given assorted crayons and an 8½" × 11" sheet of white paper with a gingerbread person shape drawn on it, with *happy, sad, angry, worried, love,* and *afraid* listed on the side. The child is asked to pick a color for each of the feelings listed. He or she is encouraged to add a few additional feelings to the list, and to select a separate color for each of those feelings. The child is asked to fill in on the gingerbread person where he or she might feel each of the feelings listed. Children are encouraged to try to remember a time when they felt each of those feelings, and where in their body they felt them. This informal measure, used as an "ice breaker," allows children or adolescents to show how much feeling identification and integration they are experiencing. The school clinician can then process the picture and how much or little affective awareness the child has and begin to use it in helping the child to become more aware on a bodily level of his or her feelings, particularly anger prior to "exploding." Intervention strategies, such as deep breathing, use of guided imagery, problem solving, and role-playing, might follow to help children not lose control when frustrated or upset once they become aware of their initial feelings.

Interviews can also be used for gathering information. They can be structured, unstructured, qualitative, quantitative, written, oral, or observational. The child is encouraged to use the puppets to tell a story of a recent situation or concern. The therapist can join in the puppet play to help role-play possible solutions or coping strategies.

Applications to School Settings

The Limitations

Often the strongest comments against using play therapy within the schools are that therapy is outside the scope and expertise of the school clinician, who is to offer only counseling. Often this becomes a matter of semantics. School clinicians may find that calling their play therapy sessions or use of play therapy techniques by another name helps to get around any administrative objections. Alternative descriptive terms that can be used instead include *developmental play, play counseling* (or *play counselor*), *play development, play media programs, counseling with toys, emotional growth through play,* and *developmental growth through play* (Landreth, 1983). In addition, administration, teachers, parents, or colleagues may lack awareness of what play therapy is, and assume it is nonproductive time spent "fooling around" or just "playing around." Consequently, the school clinician needs to spend time educating others about play therapy and its usefulness. This can be done by having brochures about play therapy (available from the Association for Play Therapy), explaining why play therapy is important and the training needed to be a play therapist, sharing research studies, and offering in-service training to the Parent Teacher Association or teachers and staff on the reasoning behind the use of the toys and their benefits in order to help dispel misconceptions.

Another limitation often encountered is that of the perceived expense of play materials and lack of a budget. Play therapy materials need not cost a lot of money for the school clinician. There are creative ways to obtain the needed materials through garage sales, thrift stores, dollar stores, hand-me-downs from siblings or relatives, sending a letter home to parents asking for certain supplies, or going to the Parent Teacher Association and offering to give a training on play therapy to the parents in exchange for obtaining some of the supplies needed (Drewes, 2001a).

School clinicians need to be aware of their own level of comfort using various materials that may become messy within their office or play room. Materials such as paints and Playdoh may require extra time for cleanup for messes that may occur. The toys and materials that should be avoided, for safety reasons, include those that are sharp, pointed, containing glass, and breakable. In addition, highly personal items and expensive, complicated, or mechanical toys should be avoided. Broken toys should be removed after the session and discarded, then replaced, if possible, with another one.

School clinicians need to be able to justify and explain the rationale behind including various items, especially those that release aggression. This is particularly notable regarding the inclusion of toy guns, rope, handcuffs, rubber or plastic knives, suction darts, dart guns, swords, punching bags (aka bobo or bop bags), and masks. Those clinicians trained in nondirective play therapy from the training programs in the Southwest may have been trained to include such items and may wish to use them. However, with the "zero tolerance" toward verbal and physical threats and acts of violence in many schools, children are expelled or suspended, often with police contact, if they are found with such materials on them (whether real or pretend) or even verbalizing intent. Consequently, the school clinician's inclusion of such material to facilitate fantasy aggression may create difficulties for the clinician and conflict for the child. School administrators will need to know about your inclusion of these items, as they may need to be able to support your decision to parents and staff, if comments or complaints arise. You will need to be able to explain the benefits of using such material and techniques in reducing the acting-out behaviors of children in school. You will also need to consider the child's feelings. They may feel conflicted if they perceive that there are two different standards. One that is imposed by the school, and one followed during their counseling time with the school clinician. They may feel uncomfortable using such materials, knowing the real-life consequences outside of the therapy room. Thus, you will need to weigh the value of each position and develop a clear and sound rationale for whichever decision you make. Alternative materials such as clay for pounding or throwing onto plastic mats, or building up and crashing down wooden block towers, may be even more effective in releasing and directing angry feelings and aggression than the above-mentioned items (Drewes, 2001b).

Another limitation in trying to use play therapy is the downsizing of personnel that may result in the increased workload of more buildings to service and more children to see, with varying space available, sharing space with other colleagues, and/or the inability to leave play therapy materials in a shared space that may result in the need to carry materials from building to building. A portable play therapy kit, using a suitcase on wheels, will allow the clinician to have the necessary materials available as well as portability.

Space limitations may also lead to difficulties in assuring child privacy and confidentiality. School clinicians sometimes are relegated to using the stage of an auditorium or "cafetorium," which doubles as the cafeteria and auditorium, or an empty book room, hallway, or other public access space. It is important for the child to know at the onset of working together that there is limited confidentiality to what is shared in the session due to the lack of privacy. Also, they may be seen, and their voices, if loud, may be heard by others nearby. The amount of noise generated in a session by a child expressing intense feelings could become disruptive to teachers or administrators trying to work nearby, so consideration needs to be given as to where you set up and the types of activities and techniques being planned.

There may also be a lack of adequate supervision available of clinical work and difficulty obtaining training in play therapy. The school clinician needs to remain flexible in problem solving as well as creative and innovative in meeting the demands and difficulties in conducting play therapy. The use of peer supervision groups, and attendance at various play therapy institutes and conferences, helps in alleviating the lack of supervision and training available within the school setting.

Scheduling limitations may also occur in trying to get a child released from his or her classroom setting for sessions. Sessions are usually limited to 30 minutes on the IEP, with some younger or hyperactive children unable to be seen for more than 15 minutes at a time. Limiting the amount of play materials used in the session, as well as structuring the time, will be necessary.

The Strengths

There are many benefits to using play therapy and play therapy techniques within a school setting. Primary mental health prevention services and enhancement of development through use of play-based interventions allow for children who are not classifiable but still manifesting behavioral problems or at risk for academic problems due to parental divorce, traumas, the birth or death of a sibling, hospitalization, and so on to receive services. More children can be reached within a school setting than through outside services. Families that have financial difficulties or who lack the motivation or resources to pursue mental health services can be helped. Further, children attend school daily, thereby making scheduling and rescheduling more flexible. Children are also already familiar with their school and the school clinician, allowing for less time needed to create a therapeutic relationship and the building of a trusting relationship with the clinician. Another positive is that paraprofessionals and the classroom teacher can be trained to work in creating a therapeutic environment that will help lessen the children's emotional issues and behaviors, thereby increasing the number of children served, as well as having critical staff part of the team coordination around the child.

Play therapy techniques allow for engagement with the child not only in individual sessions but also in group work with children facilitating the teaching of social skills and issues of self-control and impulsivity. Play therapy techniques also work well in groups addressing anger management skill development, as well as in dealing with specific issues, such as parental divorce or the death of a loved one. Play-based techniques and materials allow for the child or even adolescent to communicate through nondirective means when there are difficult issues to deal with. Such materials and techniques allow for the building of rapport, as well as the diffusion of angry and heightened emotions.

The school system becomes the ideal setting to provide ongoing early prevention, intervention, and therapeutic service delivery for mental health issues. More children are able to be reached within the school setting than through outside services, more families can be reached, children's daily attendance allows for ease of scheduling, the school setting is a familiar and safe treatment milieu, there is familiarity with the school clinician, and there is the availability of a team approach utilizing the classroom teacher in the therapeutic milieu. Because of the ever increasing referrals—notably of acting-out, angry, and aggressive children—along with administrative concerns about violence and suicide in the schools, coupled with increasing natural and human-made disasters, school clinicians having been looking for more and more techniques and effective ways to work with the students they see. Play therapy gives them the tools to effectively and playfully work with students who are unable to use verbal interventions or who refuse to participate or speak during their assigned counseling time.

Problems That Can Be Addressed

Play therapy as nondirective or directive or as an integrated treatment modality can be utilized for most problems that children are being referred to the school clinician for. A review of outcome studies on play therapy reveals ample evidence that play therapy is an effective treatment for a variety of social-emotional stressors, such as loss, divorce, relocation, hospitalization, physical or sexual abuse, trauma, domestic violence, and natural disasters, along with physical and behavioral disorders such as anxiety; depression; attention deficit/hyperactivity disorder (ADHD); autism or pervasive developmental, academic, and social delays; physical and learning disabilities; and conduct disorders (Bratton, Ray, & Rhine, 2005; Ray, Armstrong, Warren, & Balkin, 2005).

Evidence-based Research

For over 6 decades, play therapy has been recognized as the oldest and most popular form of child therapy in clinical practice. Play-based assessment and intervention approaches are being routinely taught in graduate master's and doctoral-level training programs around the world (Reddy, Files-Hall, & Schaefer, 2005). The main criticism of play interventions and play therapy has been that the field lacks rigorous research designs and data-analytic methods (Philips, 1985).

Over the past several decades, well-designed controlled research in play therapy has emerged. Although empirical studies comparing play therapy approaches have not yet emerged in any systematic way, individual theoretical approaches have conducted research dealing with specific populations using a specific treatment approach.

The Association for Play Therapy has produced the *International Journal of Play Therapy* over the past 20 years. It has included research as well as case studies and theoretical papers dealing with play and play therapy. In addition, its Research Committee has encouraged and supported research in the academic and public sectors through grants and awards. Recently, it has collaborated with the American Counseling Association to conduct a joint research project that is currently underway.

Two meta-analytic studies have examined the effectiveness of play therapy with children (LeBlanc & Ritchie, 1999; Ray, Bratton, Rhine, & Jones, 2001). Le Blanc and Ritchie's meta-analysis found that play therapy yielded an overall positive effect size of .66, indicating that play therapy has a moderate treatment effect. The authors found that parental involvement in the child's therapy and the duration of therapy were related to outcome success. Ray et al. found that the humanistic nondirective category demonstrated a slightly larger effect size than the behavioral-directive category. However, the authors cautioned that the disproportionate number of studies in the categories could account for the difference (Reddy et al., 2005).

The moderate to large positive effects of the combined meta-analytic studies indicate that play interventions appear to be effective for children across treatment modalities (group, individual), age groups (3–16 years), gender, referred versus nonreferred populations, and treatment orientations (humanistic-nondirective, behavioral-directive) (Reddy et al., 2005).

Reddy et al. (2005) offered empirically based play-based programs and interventions that are useful in the treatment of children from preschool to adolescents. Drewes, Carey, and Schaefer (2001) offered a text filled with various play therapy and play-based interventions, many with their own positive research outcomes that can be utilized in schools with ages from preschool to adolescence, and in group settings.

Files-Hall and Reddy (2005) reported that through the review of the literature, play interventions have shown success in treating children with disruptive behavior disorders, including ADHD (Reddy, Spencer, Hall, & Rubel, 2001) and oppositional defiant disorder (McNeil, Capage, Bahl, & Blanc, 1999), with overall externalizing behavior and parental stress reduced, and an increase in child compliance and social skills. Play-based interventions with children on the autism spectrum have resulted in significant improvement in symbolic play, social-emotional functioning, perceptual–fine motor skills, and language (Kim, Lombardino, Rothman, & Vinson, 1989; Restall & Magill-Evans, 1994; Rogers & Lewis, 1989).

Play-based intervention programs have also increased children's social and emotional health with at-risk children (Nafpaktitis & Perlmutter, 1998), child witnesses of domestic violence (Tyndall-Lind, Landreth, & Giordano, 2001), and child victims of abuse and neglect (Fantuzzo et al., 1996).

Treatment areas that still need more research include bereavement, children affected by HIV/AIDS, and children of substance-dependent parents (Files-Hall & Reddy, 2005). Recommendations for improving future research made by Reddy et al. (2005) are that research studies and journal publications should include clear documentation of the participants' age, gender, ethnicity, presenting problems, level of training of the intervention agents, complete protocol and research procedures, and inclusion and exclusion criteria. Clearer reporting and documentation of all aspects of studies will assist in the interpretation of results, and the replication and transportability of interventions to other settings and populations.

The Case of Todd

Currently there is not enough information to know exactly the best type of treatment method to use. More information would be needed first in order to rule out the possibility of emotional issues or even attention deficit/hyperactivity disorder. My first step would be to meet with the parent to obtain some additional family and developmental history. What are Todd's strengths? Is he involved in any outside activities, and how is his functioning in those settings (e.g. at church, at play dates, and with relatives)? Have there been any significant changes over the past year (e.g., moves, the death of a pet or relative, a loss of friends, divorce, the birth of a sibling, siblings having problems, or illnesses)? How are his eating and sleeping (does he have any difficulties falling asleep or staying asleep)? Does he have friends outside of school? How does he get along with each of his parents and/or siblings? Has a full physical been taken by the pediatrician to rule out anything medical? Have there been any other changes noted in his behavior that might appear obsessive or compulsive? What is the mother observing while Todd is working on his homework? Does she sit with him? Is he ripping up his work because of a mistake? Have there been any changes within the classroom, such as a new teacher, or a loss or addition of classmates? Is there any trauma history?

Next, I would conduct an informal observation of Todd within his classroom setting, in the playground or during free play, and even during lunchtime. A sampling across several different points in time would help to gather how Todd is functioning with peers and his teacher, what the quality of his play looks like, and how he is functioning during academics. I would be particularly interested in peer interactions to see if there might be any bullying or emotionally charged situations that may be contributing. I would try to rule out attention-deficit/hyperactivity disorder, which could be contributing to difficulty concentrating, focusing. and completing homework. I would next talk with the teacher and get her impressions, and try to see if there are particular times in the day that Todd does better. I would ask her if she had any ideas as to what may be contributing to the change, and any strategies that she uses in class that might help.

I would then conduct a play assessment. Having Todd come to my office, I would have him fill out the Gingerbread Feelings Map, and create a few additional pictures (e.g., "Draw a picture of yourself in the rain" and the Kinetic Family Drawing). I would encourage Todd to use the play materials in the room and observe what he does with them. What is his affect like? How does he handle the toys, and can he engage in symbolic and creative play? Does he go quickly to each item and not stay long with them? Is he easily frustrated? How does he interact with me? Is there good eye contact? Affect modulation and expression? Is he talkative or withdrawn? I would also explore with Todd if he knew why he was seeing me, tell him what I knew of the situation, explore what he thought I might be able to help him with and what he wanted to change, what his mother's concerns were, and how our sessions would be structured and when I would see him.

For a period of time (3–5 sessions), I would see Todd individually once per week. I would use an integrative-prescriptive approach in order to rule out various hypotheses I would be formulating. During those first 3–5 sessions, I would be nondirective and child centered, allowing Todd to utilize the toys as he wanted, following his lead, and verbally tracking his play. This would allow for the building of a safe, therapeutic environment, along with a sense of trust and rapport. As Todd played, I would note any play themes he might be showing and whether they changed within and across sessions.

Through this initial stage, I would hope to see the world through Todd's eyes and through his feelings and experiences. If Todd had not used the sandtray, I would direct Todd to create his world in the sand, making a sand picture for me. This directive use of the sandtray would allow Todd to access his unconscious issues and help to bring them forth. I would regularly meet with Todd's mother or call her weekly, if possible, or biweekly, to assess how things are at home and outside of school.

Depending on what further information was obtained, especially through the play, I might then either continue working nondirectively or I might bring in some directive techniques with the nondirective approach. I would utilize the sandtray more to have Todd create scenes around specific issues or scenarios about his family and school in order to try and rule out other issues. If issues appeared to be more related to peers, I might have Todd and another peer together in a dyad or create a small group to develop peer interactions and social skill building. We would be able to utilize role-play in creating scenarios and practicing problem-solving strategies in dealing with the peers.

I might utilize cognitive-behavioral play therapy to deal with underlying anxiety and fears, especially if Todd was able to share his fear, along with his view of his world and himself. If he had a negative self-image or negative worldview, we could work on his feelings and thoughts that led to this view. We would use deep breathing and guided imagery to help lessen his anxiety. I would work with his mother to develop a behavior modification plan that would help to structure and limit the amount of time spent on homework, and reward Todd's ability to finish it quicker and not feel he had to be perfect or complete it all. We'd also set up a reward system to help Todd hand in his homework so he receives credit for what he has completed. I would bring in his mother during some of the sessions to spend time together with Todd in family therapy and offer parent counseling for ways to work on lessening Todd's fears and anxiety (e.g., enrolling him in some after-school, outdoor activities).

Summary

Play therapy and a treatment method have been around for decades, dating back to Anna Freud and Melanie Klein. However, it has received special attention over the past 25 years through the formation of the Association for Play Therapy by Charles Schaefer.

Play therapy has grown out of a need to provide interventions and strategies to children and adolescents with problem behaviors and disabilities. Traditional therapies have required children and adolescents to be verbal participants. The child's lack of verbal skills and the resistance of adolescents have required the use of nonverbal means of treatment. Play therapy has grown beyond the simple use of toys for communication in a playroom (play as therapy) to include play in therapy through expressive arts, sandplay therapy, poetry, movement, art, drama, music, and storytelling. Play therapy is an intervention based on theoretical premises and accepted as a recognized therapy. The therapeutic powers of play and the child's ability to utilize the play materials symbolically help lead to emotional and behavioral changes.

As school referrals increase and include more and more children with special needs and emotional difficulties, school clinicians will need useful tools to help engage resistant, angry, and nonverbal children. Play therapy is a useful treatment modality that includes a variety of theoretical approaches, as well as utilizes play-based interventions within therapy to help children and adolescents deal with a myriad of difficulties. The school clinician will need support in getting supervision and training in how to utilize play-based techniques and play therapy.

Play therapy has much empirically supported research into its efficacy. Much more focused research will be needed for it to reach the level of *evidence-based*. However, there are many treatment approaches and therapeutic play-based programs that have shown statistical significance and positive treatment changes. More research will be needed to help bring play therapy into the forefront of the literature. Those interested in using play therapy and play-based techniques and treatment methods will need to have clinical supervision to help guide them, as well as additional training through a play therapy university course or workshops.

Recommended Readings

Carmichael, K. D. *Play therapy: An introduction.* Upper Saddle River, NJ: Pearson Merrill Prentice Hall.

Drewes, A. A., Carey, L. J., & Schaefer, C. E. (2001). *School-based play therapy.* New York: Wiley.

Gil, E., & Drewes, A. A. (2005). *Cultural issues in play therapy.* New York: Guilford.

Gitlin-Weiner, K., Sandgrund, A., & Schaefer, C. (2000). *Play diagnosis and assessment.* New York: Wiley.

Landreth, G. (1991). *Play therapy: The art of the relationship.* Muncie, IN: Accelerated Development.

Reddy, L. A., Files-Hall, T. M., & Schaefer, C. E. (2005). *Empirically based play interventions for children.* Washington, DC: American Psychological Association.

Schaefer, C. E. (2003). *Foundations of play therapy.* New York: Wiley.

References

Alfred Adler Institute. (2004). *Alfred Adler Institutes of San Francisco and Northwestern Washington.* Retrieved August 20, 2005, from http://Ourworld.compuserve.com/homepages/hstein/homepage.htm

Association for Play Therapy. (N.d.). About play therapy. Retrieved May 25, 2007, from www.a4pt.org

Autism Society of America. (2005). Autism facts. Retrieved April 1, 2007, from http://www.autism.org

Axline, V. M. (1969). *Play therapy.* New York: Ballantine.

Axline, V. M., & Carmichael, L. (1947). *Play therapy: The inner dynamics of childhood.* Boston: Houghton Mifflin.

Beck, A. T. (1976). *Cognitive therapy and the emotional disorders.* New York: International Universities Press.

Beutler, L. E. (1979). Toward specific psychological therapies for specific conditions. *Journal of Consulting and Clinical Psychology, 47,* 882–897.

Bromfield, R. (2003). Psychoanalytic play therapy. In C. E. Schaefer (Ed.), *Foundations of play therapy* (pp. 1–13). New York: Wiley.

Carmichael, K. D. (2006). *Play therapy: An introduction.* Upper Saddle River, NJ: Pearson Prentice Hall.

Children and Adults With Attention-Deficit/Hyperactivity Disorder. (2005). The disorder named AD/HD-CHADD fact sheet #1. Retrieved April 1, 2007, from www.chadd.org

Dinkmeyer, D. C., Dinkmeyer, J. D., & Sperry, L. (1987). *Adlerian counseling and psychotherapy* (2nd ed.). Columbus, OH: Merrill.

Drewes, A. A. (2001a). The possibilities and challenges in using play therapy in schools. In A. A. Drewes, L. J. Carey, & C. E. Schaefer (Eds.), *School-based play therapy* (pp. 41–61). New York: Wiley.

Drewes, A. A. (2001b). Play objects and play spaces. In A. A. Drewes, L. J. Carey, & C. E. Schaefer (Eds.), *School-based play therapy* (pp. 62–80). New York: Wiley.

Drewes, A. A. (2001c). The gingerbread feelings map. In H. G. Kaduson & C. E. Schaefer (Eds.), *101 more favorite play therapy techniques* (pp. 92–97). New York: Aronson.

Drewes, A. A. (2005). Play in selected cultures. Diversity and universality. In E. Gil & A.A. Drewes (Eds.), *Cultural issues in play therapy* (pp. 26–71). New York: Guilford.

Drewes, A. A., Carey, L. J., & Schaefer, C. E. (2001). *School-based play therapy*. New York: Wiley.

Fagan, T. K. (2000). Practicing school psychology. *American Psychologist, 55*, 754–757.

Fantuzzo, J., Sutton-Smith, B., Atkins, M., Meyers, R., Stevenson, H., Coolahan, K., et al. (1996). Community-based resilient peer treatment of withdrawn maltreated preschool children. *Journal of Consulting and Clinical Psychology, 64*(6), 1377–1386.

Files-Hall, T. M., & Reddy, L. A. (2005). Present status and future directions for empirically based play interventions for children. In L. A. Reddy, T. M. Files-Hall, & C. E. Schaefer (Eds.), *Empirically based play interventions for children* (pp. 267–279). Washington, DC: American Psychological Association.

Frances, A., Clarkin, J., & Perry, S. (1984). *Differential therapeutics in psychiatry*. New York: Brunner/Mazel.

Freud, A. (1928). *Introduction to the technic of child analysis* (L. P. Clark, Trans.). New York: Nervous and Mental Disease Publishing. (Original work published 1895)

Freud, S. (1909). Analysis of a phobic in a five-year-old boy. In S. Freud, *Standard edition* (Vol. 9). London: Hogarth.

Gil, E. (1991). *The healing power of play: Work with abused children*. New York: Guilford.

Gil, E. (2006). *Helping abused and traumatized children: Integrating directive and nondirective approaches*. New York: Guilford.

Gitlin-Weiner, K., Sandgrund, A., & Schaefer, C. (2000). *Play diagnosis and assessment*. New York: Wiley.

Guerney, B. G., Jr. (1964). Filial therapy: Description and rationale. *Journal of Consulting Psychology, 28*(4), 303–310.

Jernberg, A. (1979). *Theraplay: A new treatment using structured play for problem children and their families.* San Francisco: Jossey-Bass.

Kalff, D. (1980). *Sandplay.* Boston: Sigo Press.

Kim, Y. T., Lombardino, L. J., Rothman, H., & Vinson, B. (1989). Effects of symbolic play intervention with children who have mental retardation. *Mental Retardation, 27*(3), 159–165.

Klein, M., & Riviere, J. (1983). *Developments in psychoanalysis.* New York: Da Capo.

Knell, S. M. (1993). *Cognitive-behavioral play therapy.* Northvale, NJ: Aronson.

Knell, S. M. (1998). Cognitive-behavioral play therapy. *Journal of Clinical Child Psychology, 27,* 28.

Kottman, T. (1995). *Partners in play: An Adlerian approach to play therapy.* Alexandria, VA: American Counseling Association.

Landreth, G. (1982). *Play therapy: Dynamics of the process of counseling with children.* Springfield, IL: Thomas.

Landreth, G. (1991). *Play therapy: The art of the relationship.* Muncie, IN: Accelerated Development.

Landreth, G. (2002). *Play therapy: The art of the relationship* (2nd ed.). New York: Brunner-Routledge.

Landreth, G. L., & Bratton, S. C. (2006). *Child parent relationship therapy (CPRT).* New York: Routledge.

Landreth, G., Jacquot, W., & Allen, L. (1969). A team approach to learning disabilities. *Journal of Learning Disabilities, 2,* 82–87.

LeBlanc, M., & Ritchie, M. (1999). Predictors of play therapy outcomes. *International Journal of Play Therapy, 8*(2), 19–34.

Lowenfeld, M. (1979). *The world technique.* London: Allen & Unwin.

McNeil, C. B., Cappage, L. C., Bahl, A., & Blanc, H. (1999). Importance of early intervention for disruptive behavior problems: Comparisons of treatment and wait-list control groups. *Early Education and Development, 10,* 445–454.

Morris, R., & Kratochwill, T. (1983). *The practice of child therapy.* New York: Pergamon.

Nafpaktitis, M., & Perlmutter, B. F. (1998). School-based early mental health intervention with at-risk students. *School Psychology Review, 27,* 420–432.

Norcross, J. C. (1991). Prescriptive matching in psychotherapy: An introduction. *Psychotherapy, 28,* 439–443.

Oaklander, V. (1988). *Windows to our children.* Highland, NY: Center for Gestalt Development.

Peery, J. C. (2003). Jungian analytical play therapy. In C. Schaefer (Ed.), *Foundations of play therapy* (pp. 14–54). New York: Wiley.

Perls, F. S. (1951). *Gestalt therapy: Excitement and growth in the human personality.* New York: Julian.

Ray, D., Bratton, S., Rhine, T., & Jones, L. (2001). The effectiveness of play therapy: Responding to the critics. *International Journal of Play Therapy, 10*(1), 85–108.

Reddy, L. A., Files-Hall, T. M., & Schaefer, C. E. (2005). *Empirically based play interventions for children*. Washington, DC: American Psychological Association.

Reddy, L. A., Spencer, P., Hall, T. M., & Rubel, E. (2001). Use of developmentally appropriate games in a child group training program for young children with attention-deficit/hyperactivity disorder. In A. A. Drewes, L. J. Carey & C. E. Schaefer (Eds.), *School-based play therapy* (pp. 256–274). New York: Wiley.

Restal, G., & Magill-Evans, J. (1994). Play and preschool children with autism. *American Journal of Occupational Therapy, 48*(2), 113–120.

Rogers, S., & Lewis, H. (1989). An effective day treatment model for young children with pervasive developmental disorders. *Journal of the American Academy of Child and Adolescent Psychiatry, 28*(2), 207–214.

Schaefer, C. E. (1993). What is play and why is it therapeutic? In C. E. Schaefer (Ed.), *The therapeutic powers of play* (pp. 1–15). New York: Aronson.

Schaefer, C. E. (2003). Prescriptive play therapy. In Charles E. Schaefer (Ed.), *Foundations of play therapy* (pp. 306–320). New York: Wiley.

Schaefer, C., Gitlin, K., & Sandgrund, A. (1991). *Play diagnosis and assessment*. New York: Wiley.

Snyder, T. D., Hoffman, C. M., & Geddes, C. M. (1997). *Digest of educational statistics*. Washington, DC: U.S. Department of Education, Office of Educational Research and Improvement.

Tyndall-Lind, A., Landreth, G. L., & Giordano, M. A. (2001). Intensive group play therapy with child witnesses of domestic violence. *International Journal of Play Therapy, 10*(1), 53–83.

U.S. Department of Education, National Center for Education Statistics. (1999). Children 0 to 21 served in federally supported programs for the disabled by type of disability: 1976–77 to 1997–98. In *Digest for Educational Statistics 1999*. Washington, DC: U.S. Government Printing Office.

Van Fleet, R. (1994). *Filial therapy: Strengthening parent-child relationships through play*. Saratoga, FL: Professional Resource Press.

13

Applying Art Therapy in Schools

Marjory J. Levitt

To begin this discussion of art therapy in the schools, let's provide a context painted with a very broad brush. In the history of the field of art therapy as we know it today, there are two parallel streams that provide orientation and describe the origins and philosophy of the theory and practice of the arts in psychotherapy. Likewise, in the history and development of art, education, and art education, there are powerful and often colliding philosophical and theoretical positions. The conjunctions and collisions between and among these disciplines comprise a source of tension, controversy, and confusion affecting the practice of art and art therapy in today's schools. We do not have the time, space, or mandate to explore these themes in exhaustive detail here—though they might deserve such attention.

In creating context, then, let's go back in time to the turn of the last century, to Vienna, and join the radical band of physicians, educators, artists, and politicians experimenting with the revolutionary theories of Sigmund Freud and his collaborators (Danto, 2005). It is in this experimental community that we will find the seeds of what will flower into one hardy branch of art therapy—though at the time, the boundaries between art, education, therapeutic treatment, and general physical health promotion were indistinct. In fact, the perspective at this point in time was entirely holistic. Weimar Germany embraced the ideal of environments including creative arts in school reforms immediately following World War I, and the belief that art and art making possessed curative powers was widespread. By 1919 Anna Freud, exploring art making in her work with children, also found much to admire and emulate in the theory and practice of Maria Montessori's child-centered methods (Gitter, 1975), as did Erik Erikson, himself an artist and neophyte practitioner of psychoanalytic psychotherapy (Danto). It was a time of almost febrile experimentation and discovery, and the arts held a prominent position in these experiments, as they did in all of life in Europe at that time—at least among middle- and upper-class, well-educated practitioners (Danto).

It might be difficult for us to imagine that psychoanalytic theory and practice were at one time such controversial and incredibly creative, diverse activities. They were also boldly and unabashedly political, and many free clinics, schools, and alternative communities flourished between the two great wars. In this broad embrace, Anna Freud and others conducted child analysis and trainings for parents, educators, therapists, and even patients, in clinics and public schools, and made free use of the creative arts in this endeavor. Including the arts as integral to treatment and healing was natural—as arts appreciation, practice, and participation were deeply integrated into daily life. There was no question! Art as therapeutic??? Obviously! (Danto, 2005). The seeds of art therapy had been planted, however, and took root, and flourished in the fertile soil of the United States.

The Diaspora following the rise of fascism in Europe shattered many of these bold therapeutic, political, and philosophical communities and practices (Danto, 2005). Many practitioners came to the United States. Many more were influenced by the exciting, radical ideas and practices of psychoanalytic psychotherapy, and some of these practitioners experimented, consolidated, and developed psychoanalytic theory into a discrete practice known as art therapy (Kramer, 1971, 1975a, 1979; Levick, 1983; Naumberg, 1973; Ulman, 1975). Within this psychoanalytically based group of pioneering practitioners, a further distinction evolved between "art-in-therapy" (Naumberg) and "art-as-therapy" (Kramer, 1971, 1979). The source of the discipline of art therapy is in arts education (Levick) and its creative extrapolation into therapeutic practice. In its infancy, pioneers in art therapy with children developed and tested the approach in school settings (Danto; Naumberg). This will be discussed in more detail in the following section.

Second- and third-generation practitioners, influenced by Freudian and neo-Freudian theory and practice, and increasingly rebelling against what was becoming a stifling orthodoxy, and others caught up in the burgeoning "third wave" of humanistic therapies following World War II also incorporated art and art making into the practice of newly devised methods for helping and healing. Using the creative arts in therapeutic activities with children, often in school settings, also characterized many of these approaches (Oaklander, 1988; Somers-Flanagan, 2007). Art and therapy went to school because that's where children are (Romer & McIntosh, 2005), and where the needs of suffering children could and can be met most readily (Kramer, 1971; Levick, 1983; Silver, 1978; Ulman, 1975).

Before delving further into the particulars of the theory and practice of art therapy as a distinct modality, a brief look at simultaneous trends in education—and education with specific reference to the arts—will help to establish a meaningful context for our understanding.

Since the 1960s, the arts have gradually disappeared from our public schools due to budget cuts, preoccupation with teaching to the test and the emphasis on the acquisition of basic skills (Kozol, 2005), and the unfortunate perspective that art is an extravagance (Landsman & Gorski, 2007). That art making can be therapeutic and even transformational for young people in or out of school seems unquestionable, as illustrated in such wildly successful after-school programs as the Philadelphia Mural Arts Program, Pittsburgh's Manchester Craftsmen's Guild, New York City's All-Stars Talent Show Network, and many, many others. School-based programs have an equally illustrious track record, and often extravagant claims have been made for the power of the arts in therapeutic applications, and in and of themselves, in improving cognitive and behavioral performance (Carp, 2005; Gardner, 1989; Natale, 1996; Winner, 2007), keeping adolescents in school, building community and teamwork (Landsman & Gorski), and enhancing self-esteem (Ansary, 2007). Art therapy programs have been shown to be effective in schools in both individual and group formats and are especially useful following environmental challenges such as the San Francisco earthquake in 1989 and the floods in Moravia in the Czech Republic in 1997 (Dowling, 1998); following the terrorist attacks in New York City on September 11, 2001 (Whitehead, 2007); and subsequent to gang violence in New York City and Los Angeles (Cedars-Sinai, 2007; Star, 2005). Other promising areas of successful application of art therapy programs include interventions designed to ameliorate the effects of post-traumatic stress disorder (PTSD), detect depression (Wallace et al., 2004), and assist in the integration and assimilation of immigrant and refugee children (Rousseau, Drapeau, Lacroix, Bagilishya, & Heusch, 2005). An interesting finding in Rousseau et al. suggests that teachers were positively influenced by the art intervention and, following the program, saw their immigrant, non-English-speaking students as more like other students. Oaklander (1988) also reported a positive impact on teachers in her group art therapy activities with students in a classroom-based assignment to draw your family as animals. Teachers comments included, "[M]y students were happier, and I was happier!" following the activity (Oaklander, p. 315).

Simultaneously, therapeutic and counseling services in the public schools are similarly beleaguered—school psychologists and counselors have seen their numbers diminish, and those who remain spend more and more time on paperwork and planning than on direct therapeutic services to children (Kahn, 1999). Art therapy as a specialty available in schools has suffered along with counseling and psychological services and is now a rare exception rather than the rule (Bush, 2003), despite evidence supporting its utility, value, and unique contribution to the school milieu (e.g., see Dasgupta, 2006; Dowling, 1998; Natale, 1996; Star, 2005).

The surgeon general's report on the mental health of children suggests that one in 10 children in our country struggle with mental health challenges that are severe enough to interfere with functioning and cause "significant impairment" (Romer & McIntosh, 2005, p. 598). Given that most children between 5 and 18 attend schools (90%, according to 2000 U.S. Census data), schools provide a unique opportunity to promote the mental health of youth (Romer & McIntosh). In fact, the failure to address the mental health needs of students has severe and lasting consequences.

> Adolescents with mental health disorders are at increased risk for poor academic achievement as well as continued mental disability. Many youth who suffer from mental disorders also end up in the juvenile justice system, an outcome that could be prevented if they were treated while still in school. (Romer & McIntosh, p. 599)

These young people are also at increased risk for substance abuse and failing to complete school.

Despite empirical evidence in support of the value of art and art therapy programs in schools (Carp, 2005; Essex, 1996; Hamblen, 1993; Holzman, 1997; Jarboe, 2002; Kahn, 1999; Mattes et al., 1986; Ray, Perkins, & Oden, 2004; Riley, 2001; Rogers & Zaragoza-Lao, 2003; Rousseau et al., 2005; Treffiletti, 2003), it is not likely that this trend toward diminished direct service will change at any time soon. Therefore, mental health service professionals who remain in schools might find the addition of art making, and an understanding of the value, principles, and methodology of art therapy, useful additions to their repertoire. Of necessity, my training and experience as an artist–educator–therapist in the humanistic tradition will influence the exploration that follows. In subsequent sections, we will explore aspects of the creative arts therapies in schools, including definitions, theory, methodology, assessment, applications to schools settings, and the evidence base for inclusion of art therapy in schools. A case example of Todd, a 10-year-old African American boy, will also be explored using art therapy techniques in his evaluation, assessment, and treatment.

Overview of the Therapeutic Approach

Art therapy is a varied and creative approach to providing psychological help to those in need. In developing an appreciation for the unique contribution of the discipline, keep in mind its imaginative, inspired origins. Current art therapy practice embraces many therapeutic orientations and modalities, including cognitive and behavioral approaches, Gestalt, psychodrama, client-centered therapy, Jungian, choice theory, and solution-focused therapies. It is commonly practiced in individual, family, and group settings, with people of all ages, cultures (Chapman & Appleton, 1999; Rousseau et. al., 2005), and abilities (Ulman, 1975). It is developed and practiced by individuals with diverse trainings and skills, and integrates artistic, educational, and therapeutic theory and method; a brief overview of definitions and history follows. As mentioned above, the roots of the discipline are in arts education and psychotherapy (Levick, 1983), strongly influenced by psychoanalytic and psychodynamic thought, and characterized by ongoing creative infusions and often surprising collaborations.

Definition of Art Therapy

There is some controversy and disagreement in defining art therapy in the field, and the definition has changed through time. It is a term that covers a wide and varied aggregation of practices in education, therapy, and rehabilitation (Ulman, 1975), and the passage of time has only served to add complexity and variety to any attempt at definition. Levick (1983) stated simply that art therapy is "that discipline which combines elements of psychotherapy with untapped sources of creativity and expression in the patient" (p. 3). Janet Bush (2003, p. 1) quoted the more inclusive, therapeutically focused, and comprehensive American Art Therapy Association (AATA) definition:

> Art therapy is a human service profession that utilizes art media, images, creative art processes and patient/client responses to the created products as reflections of an individual's development, abilities, personality, interests, concerns and conflicts. Art Therapy practice is based on knowledge of human developmental and psychological theories which are implemented in the full spectrum of models of assessment and treatment including educational, psychodynamic, cognitive, transpersonal and other therapeutic means of reconciling emotional conflicts, fostering self awareness, developing social skills, managing behavior,

solving problems reducing anxiety, aiding reality orientation and increasing self-esteem. (AATA, 2003)

Kahn (1999) defined art therapy with specific reference to its practice in school settings as a "psychoeducational therapeutic intervention that focuses on art media as primary expressive and communicative channels" (Shostak, 1985, quoted in Kahn, p. 292). Flexibility and responsiveness to the environment and to the population served are hallmarks in the development of the discipline of art therapy, and can inspire the embrace of general and comprehensive definitions. For the purpose of examining the practice of art therapy in the schools, including the psychoeducational component is useful and prudent.

Overview of History and Theory

Much of the early practice, development of theory, and research took place in schools and among children—especially schools for handicapped, behavior-disordered, or otherwise "special" and sequestered youth populations (Kramer 1971, 1979; Levick, 1983; Naumberg 1973; Rubin, 1978; Silver, 1978). In these environments, where the need for effective treatment was so great and access to reliably efficient treatment sadly lacking, pioneers in the field began to systematically explore and apply creative arts techniques. Formal art therapy as a distinct discipline can be said to have begun in 1947, when Naumberg implemented a pilot study making use of the spontaneous art made by problem children in a residential treatment setting exploring ego mechanisms of defense, interpretation, free association, and other hallmarks of the psychoanalytic approach (Levick). This approach came to be known as "art-in-therapy" and was extremely influential in the development and systemization of the field. In 1958, Edith Kramer formulated a second theory of art therapy, also rooted in psychoanalytic and psychodynamic theory and influenced by Naumberg's work, which emphasized sublimation and the process of art making itself as curative (Kramer, 1971; Levick). This has come to be known as the *art-as-therapy approach* and was considered to be more in alliance with art education than psychotherapy (Kramer, 1971). In these approaches, the counselor-therapist could serve as an interpreter of images, an object of countertransference, a witness to an absorbing process, a collaborator, or an expert offering training in the use of art media. Formal art therapy training and credentialing follow in the tradition established by

Naumberg, Kramer, Silver, Ulman, and Levick, who have also focused on conducting and inspiring empirical studies in support of the efficacy of art therapy among underserved, disabled, and mentally ill populations. Much research and practice have focused on the needs and treatments of these at-risk youth both in and out of school settings (e.g., Avraham, 2005; Bratton & Ferebee, 1999; Carp, 2005; Essex, 1996; Jarboe, 2002; Kaiser et al., 2005; Mattes et al., 1986; McConaughy, 2000; Natale, 1996; Riley, 2001; Rose, 1998; Rousseau et al., 2005; Rubin; Wallace et al., 2004; Whitehead, 2007; Winner, 2007).

Person-centered and other humanistic practitioners, not surprisingly, experimented in less systematic ways with the inclusion of art making in therapy in the 1950s and 1960s (Somers-Flanagan, 2007), carrying some of their experimental and experiential activities into the schools with them (Oaklander, 1988; Ray et al., 2004). Key theoretical components of these humanistic therapies that encourage the inclusion of expressive arts involve being open to new learning and experience, valuing authentic expression and pushing personal boundaries, as well as fostering flexibility and responsiveness to the unexpected—all considered to be hallmarks of optimal human functioning (Somers-Flanagan). Contemporary proponents of art therapy and art education in the schools emphasize some of these same attributes for all students—considering art-making experience to be an aid in developing problem-solving skills, including learning to solve problems with more than one result, and functioning well in ambiguity (Ansary, 2007; Friedman, 2006). Carl Rogers considered the therapeutic process to provide access to creative, life force energy; in his view, what is creative is frequently therapeutic, and simply put, makes people feel better and freer to express the uniqueness of who they are (Bratton & Ferebee, 1999).

Whether contemporary art therapy follows from and builds upon psychoanalytic, psychodynamic, ego psychology, neo-Freudian, psychoeducational, or broadly humanistic theoretical underpinnings will determine the specific approach to an individual or a group of students in the schools. Rubin (1978) has stated that art therapy "is a technique in search of a theory; and has already found useful many different psychological frames of reference" (p. 18). She predicted that a definitive "theory about art therapy will have to emerge from art therapy itself" (Rubin, p. 18). Assessment, evaluation, diagnosis, and practice are difficult to generalize, given the multiplicity of influences; thus, this overview will be as broad and general as the field itself. Humanistic approaches do not emphasize assessment, diagnosis, or evaluation in the practice of art therapy in schools or elsewhere; therefore, structures for these activities will be based on the formal art therapy tradition of Naumberg, Kramer, and others.

Levick (1983) has postulated that as with other aspects of human development, all children before the age of 5 demonstrate the same developmental sequences in drawing from the scribble to shapes within shapes; to triangles, circles, squares, and rectangles; to recognizable images; and to pictorial representations. This is observable across cultures, class, and ethnic groups. Jarboe (2002) identified different developmental stages in drawing skill than Levick that appear to be more closely aligned with Piaget's developmental sequences from the scribble (emerging at around 18 months) to preschematic (4 years), schematic (7 years), and dawning realism (10 years). These stages coincide roughly with Piaget's stages of intellectual development (Ginsberg & Opper, 1969). Cultural and class differences appear to have an impact on Jarboe's research, and she has found significant differences in the development of children's drawings across the cultural spectrum. When art therapy is used in a school setting in a diagnostic or assessment framework, understanding normal artistic development is crucial. Through comparison with the appearance and structure of normal art production, an individual can be seen to diverge, or not, from typical developmental milestones by viewing his or her art production. How the child produces art is a source of data for the therapist-evaluator. What is the relationship established with the art materials? In the language of formal art therapy evaluation, unconscious forces are expressing in every aspect of the activity—not just in the final product (Naumberg, 1973). In this domain, some caution is necessary for the practitioner. An assumption that children—especially young children in poor communities and schools—have familiarity with art materials is unwise. I have worked with children in public schools who have never opened a box of crayons, and never worked in marker or colored pencil. In some cases, much of our initial encounter involved introduction of the materials and time to explore and experiment with them. Jarboe encouraged art therapists who are using art as an assessment tool to have familiarity with the art and images children are exposed to in the cultural-racial and ethnic environment in which they have been raised. A more detailed consideration of assessment and case conceptualization follows in the next section.

Although a humanistic approach does not view the product of art production in an evaluative or diagnostic way, the process of art making with a school-aged child is a crucial source of information for the practitioner. Central to the practice of art therapy is the establishment of a relationship with the child, and of a strong, safe, and spacious relationship in which the individual may explore, expand, experiment, and grow. Creating a meaning-ful dialectic between the child, the therapist, and the materials is an activity particular to each child. Decisions need to be made constantly—what materials will suit which child? How much structure? How much inquiry?

Much in art therapy is viewed along a continuum and requires attention with each individual or group session. Art materials themselves are viewed along a continuum from most controlled—such as pencil and marker—to least controlled, such as paint and wet clay. Similarly, structure in art therapy sessions ranges from tightly controlled—one or two choices of controlled media, specific instructions, and clear and firm time boundaries—to few restrictions of media and/or subject, and so on. The art therapist makes decisions and provides direction to the child or group based on environmental limitations, time constraints, the purpose of the session, and information from teachers and other school mental health providers.

Whatever theoretical position an art therapist holds, whether working with an individual or a group, art therapy sessions and activities can be seen to have four components: motivation or rationale, the activity itself, discussion of process and product, and closure (Chapman & Appleton, 1999). Theoretical affiliation determines the content of these components, including the diagnosis, assessment, and interpretation of activity and product.

Assessment and Case Conceptualization

Art therapy in individual and group settings can be helpful in assessment practices and procedures in school settings from the perspective of both art-in-therapy and art-as-therapy (Jarboe, 2002; Levick, 1983). Diagnostic art activities, including scribbles, portraits, and collages, "can help to identify advanced creative and visual intelligence among students who are less verbally adept" (such as those with autistic spectrum disorders, or who are learning disabled; Jarboe, p. 2) as well as those who are developmentally delayed. For any student unable or unwilling to use words to express internal states, art activities provide a more neutral vehicle for alternate means of expression. In diagnostic clinical interviews, the inclusion of nonverbal techniques, such as drawing, is a key strategy especially effective for young children who may not yet have the capacity to express themselves in language. A request for a kinetic family drawing (KFD; Burns, 2000) can provide a great deal of crucial background information that may otherwise be unavailable from children who are reluctant or unable to disclose information. In this technique, the interviewer provides a pencil and paper and asks for "a picture of your family doing something together," and then requests that the child describe the drawing and the figures represented. Oaklander (1988) used a version of this technique in art intervention activities in classrooms, wherein she asks students to draw their families as animals. Other creative variations can be offered with similar outcomes—providing respondents with imaginary and fanciful scenarios to describe mundane and potentially troublesome realities. Who is and is not included in these drawings can be important information. In art therapy activities in groups for children of divorce, family drawings that depict painful changes can help to diffuse emotions brought on by divorce, and help children to process unwanted change (Rose, 1998). How these drawings are produced can also be significant in both diagnostic and process-based assessments typical of humanistic approaches, focused on the activities of relationship building. How the student talks about the product—in this case, the family drawing—and how the therapist responds help to establish the relationship balance between the practitioner and the participant. In these exchanges, conducted in an environment of warmth, acceptance, and openness, therapist and student begin to develop the unique language of their relationship (Oaklander; Somers-Flanagan, 2007), a language that has been described as "qualitative, relational, connotative and affective" (Hamblen, 1993, p. 192).

The process of art production has been conceptualized as a form of nonverbal language (Levick, 1983), as part of the overall developmental process of learning (Gardner, 1989), as a form of visual problem solving (Arnheim, 1969, as cited in Levick), as an acceptable language to express strong emotion (Rubin, 1978), and as a source of vital information about the dynamic aspects of cognitive and psychosocial development (Levick). Participating in art making "is a mind-builder to the extent that it provides access to ways of knowing that may not be tapped by other forms of communication" (Hamblen, 1993, p. 193). For very young children, some boys, and those with expressive language difficulties, drawing can be useful as a means to express significant experiences and a safe, socially acceptable way to express and discharge anger, confusion, and other negative emotions (Rose, 1998). In one classroom-based art therapy session that I conducted with an elementary school special education class, students were instructed to draw a picture of something they wanted to share with the group. Controlled art media—pencils and markers and plain, white paper—were provided, and they had 10 minutes to draw. A quiet, withdrawn boy of 9 produced a surprisingly detailed, sophisticated illustration of his recent visit to a clinic for diagnostic medical tests, with blood dripping from the arms and hands of the small figure that represented himself. In this way, school personnel were made aware of his fragile health status, and we were able to follow up with his parents. In addition, his drawings impressed his peers, other students told him of their medical exploits, and he was, for a time, a bit of a hero in the classroom. As noted in Oaklander (1988) and Somers-Flanagan (2007), these group-level art therapy interventions serve to improve individual functioning, build group cohesion, encourage empathy, and provide important information for teachers and other school personnel.

Choosing materials and instructions appropriate for the developmental level of the student is crucial in assessment and case conceptualization in art therapy as well as in other areas (Levick, 1983; McConaughy, 2000; Rose, 1998). It is also possible to support the child to perform "a head taller than himself" (Holzman, 1997) by directing him or her to experiment with unfamiliar or more advanced materials and techniques and thereby promote the development of key learning skills such as learning by doing and the ability to imagine and create that which does not already exist (Ansary, 2007). Gardner (1989) contended that what is central to the arts is that they represent certain ways of knowing not necessarily developed in other ways in schools, and that arts support cognitive development in general. This is an area that demands more investigation and research.

Practitioners are cautioned to be mindful of the possibility of allergies to art materials prior to giving them to a student as well as to student disabilities and other limitations that may prevent or hinder a student in the use of any particular materials. The use of nontoxic materials is strongly encouraged, and these materials are readily available. In initial assessment interviews, students benefit from an introduction to materials, the establishment of ground rules including how and when to stop creating, expectations for cleanup, and general behavioral guidelines in the art room, if there is one, or with the art materials and therapist. Clarity in instruction is important in the assessment phase and throughout. Informing students of all ages that any thoughts, feelings, or reflections are acceptable, but not all *behavior* is appropriate, is an important ground rule (Somers-Flanagan, 2007). Time spent establishing this parameter is helpful in the development of the therapeutic alliance, and in successful art therapy experiences.

Whether or not there is a dedicated art–art therapy room, a safe and comfortable space is important with adequate storage, surfaces for creating artwork, and accessibility to students of all abilities. It is helpful in establishing therapeutic rapport and safety if the art therapy space does not change from meeting to meeting. Practitioners need to be familiar with the art materials provided and instructions given, and have a realistic sense of the match between the student developmental level, time constraints, goals and objectives of the activity, and complexity of the assignment. It is helpful, in some instances, to have examples of completed works of art, especially when using unfamiliar media or offering new activities. For the purposes of initial assessment and case conceptualization, simple, straightforward art activities such as drawings with pencil and marker and collages provide the most information with the least amount of distraction. Tailoring the activity to the time frame is important, as unfinished artwork can create a sense of anxiety and failure in the student, just as completed artwork can serve to bind anxiety and release physical and emotional energy (Kahn, 1999).

Establishing goals following assessment in art therapy is similar to other forms of therapeutic intervention. Goals are broad in scope and are written from the perspective of student behavior in concrete terms. Goals should address cognitive growth, improved emotional regulation, social behavior, and physical development (AATA, 2003).

Applications to School Settings

Art therapy interventions and techniques are extremely flexible and can be adapted to many circumstances and environments within schools. They can be adjunctive to other student mental health services or to classroom activities, or the focus of treatment in and of themselves. They can be conducted with individuals or in groups of almost any size. Art therapists can and do provide services to all students who have need of assistance—not just special education students. Art therapy is cost-effective, may improve academic performance, and meets a variety of student needs not otherwise addressed in the school setting (Carp, 2005; Natale, 1996). In addition, Kahn contended that art therapy can achieve the same goals as other techniques of time-effective counseling and is easily adaptable to other brief therapy models (1999). Including art therapy in school-based services has been encouraged by research to

> meet the rising needs of students who require more clinical assistance than is typically provided. Children entering school today face more challenging problems that place them at risk for school failure. For many, school is the only place they are exposed to structure and safety. (Jarboe, 2002, p. 8)

Among adolescents, participation in art therapy may actually seem less threatening and engender less resistance than participation in talk therapies, which have been lampooned and distorted in the media (Riley, 2001).

The American Art Therapy Association (2003) suggested that art therapy be included in individual education programs (IEPs) or student services plans in cases of serious emotional or traumatic experiences in the community and environment outside of school. In such circumstances, group-level art therapy interventions can also be helpful, for example (as mentioned above) in New York City after September 11 (Whitehead, 2007), in San Francisco following the 1989 earthquake (Dowling, 1998), and in 11 elementary schools in Los Angeles responding to gang violence (Cedars-Sinai, 2007).

Art therapy can also be useful—individually or in groups—for adolescents exploring career and college choices at the high school level. Making use of such techniques as collage and treasure mapping, students can be directed to explore, in image and fantasy, possible directions and consequences (Bratton & Ferebee, 1999). These kinds of techniques can also help students clarify goals and explore aspects of identity development. Group art therapy can also be explored to advantage with preadolescents as an aid in developing aspects of identity in the peer group setting, a salient aspect of growth at that time of life (Bratton & Ferebee). In fact, some very early practitioners pioneering group therapy, and group art therapy in particular, have asserted that group work is the modality of choice for preadolescent and adolescents (Ginott, 1975, and Slavson, 1944, as cited in Bratton & Ferebee). In group and in individual work, "[E]xperiences with art offer both symbolic and practical occasions to deal with change, ambiguity, and even chaos" (Hamblen, 1993, p. 194). Students are rewarded for trying new and different approaches and for taking appropriate risks in the expression of ideas and the manipulation of art materials (Hamblen).

Evidence Base

As mentioned in previous sections, experiments in art therapy as envisioned by Naumburg and Kramer in the late 1940s and 1950s took place in schools for problem behavior (Naumburg, 1973) and handicapped children (Kramer, 1971, 1975a, 1975b, 1979), as did much of the later work of Rubin (1978), Levick (1983), and Silver (1978). It is difficult to follow the trail of this early work, given that what was being studied and how it was being conceptualized varied as the field developed. For example, although

Levick asserted that the images produced by a child provide important information on the dynamic aspects of both cognitive and psychosocial development, research has not specifically investigated or confirmed that the process works in reverse, that is, that drawing and art activities assist children in the resolution of developmental impasses. More research is needed in this area, especially in establishing and confirming the relationship between artistic activities, cognitive development, and academic achievement. Researchers urge caution in demanding instrumental outcomes from activities and processes such as art and other creative pursuits (Arnheim, 1969, in Levick; Carp, 2005, Winner, 2007). In several recent empirical studies, Winner has found only weak scientific evidence that arts education and training are directly related to better school performance in other school subjects. Hamblen (1993) contends that artistic exposure and training yield benefits that "consist of abilities of translation and transfer, which give qualitative nuances to language, speech and social relations" (p. 194). In a study designed to test the development of cognitive skills in handicapped children via art therapy interventions, Silver discovered a statistically significant relationship, indicating that art experience can be educational and therapeutic at the same time. Language- and hearing-impaired children improved significantly in their ability to represent concepts of space, order, and class following art therapy intervention.

Several studies show promising results in the areas of art therapy interventions with elementary school children in the detection and prevention of PTSD following natural disasters, such as Project COPE following the San Francisco earthquake in 1989, and replicated in the Czech Republic following devastating floods in 1997 (Dowling, 1998). Visual art therapy has been found helpful in reducing symptoms of PTSD nightmares, with reductions in frequency and intensity (Kaiser et al., 2005). It is suggested by this and other studies (Avraham, 2005; Wallace et al., 2004) that the use of visual symbols in art provides a mechanism to express the visual phenomena of nightmares (Kaiser et al.) and aids in integration and containment, as well as symptom reduction. Wallace et al. found art therapy assessment helpful in identifying symptoms of depression and PTSD in pediatric and young adult renal transplant recipients. This is a promising area of research as the need for effective detection and treatment of PTSD and depression in children and youth is of extreme importance given the pervasiveness of these disorders (an estimated 10% of school-aged children are vulnerable to trauma, depression, and other disabling mental health disorders; Chapman & Appleton, 1999). Additionally, Kaiser and colleagues pointed out that art therapy, as a nonverbal activity, may be especially helpful in processing nonverbal events and experiences such as trauma (Kaiser et al.). As Ray et al. (2004) pointed out, talk therapy is often not effective with young children. Children's feelings are often inaccessible at the verbal level, and the use of imagery and art gives them another language for expressing thoughts, ideas, and feelings. In addition, fantasy drawings allow the child to remain at an emotional distance from the realities of life—realities that might be too painful or confusing to approach directly (Ray et al.).

Group art therapy in school has been demonstrated to be effective in reducing truancy among Native American youth (Chapman & Appleton, 1999) and in improving understanding and reducing stigma and feelings of isolation in pediatric asthma patients (Chapman & Appleton). Treffiletti asserted that new styles of expression discovered through art therapy interventions may be especially useful for children who are observed to be more withdrawn, passive, or intimidated in groups (2003). A Canadian study found some evidence that creative workshops in classrooms "can have a beneficial effect on the self esteem and symptomatology of immigrant and refugee children from various cultures and backgrounds" (Rousseau et al., 2005, p. 184). As mentioned previously, a surprising result of this study was the positive impact the art activity had on the teachers, an outcome also reported by Oaklander (1988). This unintentional benefit deserves more attention from the research community. A statistically significant positive association was found between the availability of arts and entertainment opportunities in the community and children's health (Rogers & Zaragoza-Lao, 2003), indicating the need for more serious evaluation of the overall impact of arts and art making for the health and well-being of our communities.

The Case of Todd

Using the case example of Todd, an art therapy treatment plan will be described. This plan is based on the assumption that we meet weekly, for a 45-minute session, in an art therapy room dedicated to this purpose. We are able to have sessions uninterrupted by loudspeaker announcements, bells, buzzers, phones ringing, and other school personnel. The environment is comfortable, uncluttered, functional, and orderly, with art materials to be used in the session prepared and at hand on a large table where we both sit together at a 90° angle from each other. This description begins with our first session. My specific approach is humanistically oriented, so that we are not engaged in activities that require formal assessment or diagnostic techniques and procedures. My initial sessions are diagnostic in that I will be carefully monitoring media, monitoring client response, and adjusting activities to meet the demonstrated readiness for activity as we progress. I have read Todd's case materials, including any diagnostic or assessment test results and reports of interviews with his mother, grandmother, and his teachers; and have met with other school personnel familiar with his situation.

My goal for our first session is to introduce myself, explain how art therapy will work, and begin to build a supportive and nurturing environment, including a helpful and trusting relationship with Todd (Oaklander, 1988). In subsequent sessions, we will not spend as much time talking at the start of our meeting. The format for the session is as follows:

- Welcome, introductions, and brief conversation about the purpose of our time together. Inquiry: Why do you think you have been asked to come to see me? Questions?
- Orientation and introduction to the space and the materials, discussion of the kinds of things we will be doing together, and the time frame for artwork, discussion, questions, and cleanup. Questions?
- Brief discussion of the limits of confidentiality (in age-appropriate language), ground rules for our work, and reiteration of how we will work together. Questions?
- Establish broad goals for our work together. What are the changes he would like to see? What is his experience with art? Does he like it? Is there anything he would like me to know before we begin?
- Set up for today's art activity, drawing time, process time, and clean up.
- Homework for our next meeting: things to think about, and things to try at home or in the classroom.

At the start of our work together, I am especially interested in building a solid and helpful relationship with Todd and in laying the groundwork for an environment of controlled freedom, openness, and trust. With limitations related to his age and cognitive understanding, I want Todd to be a collaborator in his journey of exploration in art therapy, following basic principles of person-centered counseling by believing deeply in my young client's ability to know what hurts, what direction to go in, and what problems are crucial (Somers-Flanagan, 2007). Although I want Todd to trust me to explore his troubles, I want to trust him as well, and be open to learning from him how to be of most help. I'll be looking for opportunities to communicate to him that just as I have found creative artwork to be helpful in difficult times, I am hopeful that he will find similar benefits (Somers-Flanagan).

In practical terms, I want to determine how much structure Todd needs to be able to grow and develop and will begin with controlled media by providing six colored pencils, regular #2 pencils with erasers, markers in six colors, and plain, white 8½" × 11" paper with a matte finish. He will have his choice from among these limited materials. Our first activity will be a request to draw a picture of his family doing something together that he enjoys. If additional verbal prompts or dialogue is indicated, I will provide them. Based on Todd's profile and presenting problems, I will provide clear boundaries and concise, short-term goals and directives, with a 5-minute time reminder before the activity phase ends. At the very beginning, I want Todd to know that there is no one right way to make a work of art, that he can have fun with this and all of our activities, and that we can both be surprised by whatever he decides to create. In our therapy, I would like Todd to learn that he can enjoy a process without undue concern for the product.

Although I am not specifically observing for the purpose of diagnosis, I am very interested in watching for signs of Todd's reported perfectionism. I'm curious: Will Todd work on his family drawing the way he reportedly works on his homework by taking hours and hours, and will he be able to finish the assignment? Will this structured but open-ended task create frustration or anxiety? Will he display obsessive-compulsive features in his drawing? I will be attentive to appearances and his verbal reports of excessive worry and inhibition as he works, gently encouraging spontaneity without inducing chaos or feelings of the loss of control. If I observe and/or he reports that he is tense, worried, or anxious, I might interrupt the artwork to teach him some simple relaxation techniques such as deep breathing, muscle tension and relaxation, or visualization. I like the idea of going very slowly with him and having an agenda and objectives that are flexible enough to give us time to work thoughtfully. This focus will be a hallmark of my work with Todd. Can we help him to develop more confidence in his products/creations? Can we discover how to help him be more efficient and effective in doing what he has been asked to do? Can we use our time to help him to relax? Can we figure out how he can ask for help, and receive it without being ashamed or upset? Even humanistic and experientially based therapeutic endeavors encourage practical application and the transfer of experience into other domains. Todd and I will talk about this—though not, perhaps, at our first session.

After we process Todd's thoughts and feelings about our first session and the artwork he has produced, we will see if we can identify a concrete and specific goal for him to take with him through the week. For example: If Todd has found that the drawing was fun or relaxing, I might instruct him to take a moment to remember this feeling before he sits down to do his homework. If he is willing and interested, I might ask him to create a quick pencil drawing before his homework to concretely remind him of the fun he has drawing. I might also have him write down our homework ideas to take along with him, exercising caution that we do not add to his sense of being burdened by all the demands made upon him. At the end of this session and all of our sessions, we will place Todd's completed artwork in a special portfolio with his name on it, thereby beginning to create a sense of the value of his creative activity and development. With some youngsters, and likely with Todd, periodic review of the contents of this portfolio can be helpful in visually representing progress and change. As we review our work through time, the artwork can help us assess our ability to meet the goals we have established. In some cases, and with Todd's permission, I may share selected works of art with his mother, grandmother, teacher, or other adults concerned with his performance and progress. Regular contact with school mental health providers, teachers, the administrative team, and Todd's mother and grandmother is an important part of the art therapists' professional responsibility (AATA, 2003). Change and improvement in the target symptoms that brought him into treatment will be noted regularly. Discussions with his teacher will help to keep the therapeutic work oriented toward the accomplishment of his broader academic and behavioral performance goals, including goals Todd identifies as most important to him.

Subsequent sessions will include a brief check-in as we begin to find out how Todd's week went, whether or not he has found anything that we did or said helpful to him, and anything else he might like to tell me before we begin our work. We will check in about his homework as well. Over the course of our sessions, and as we develop a positive and supportive relationship, I will gradually experiment with art materials, introducing less controlled, "messy" media such as wet clay, watercolor, and finger paints. As we explore using these potentially threatening materials (Chapman & Appleton, 1999), we might have an opportunity for him to represent and discuss his feelings about being in control. Participating in such messy activities in a safe environment may help him to learn something about the possibility of creating order out of chaos. It is possible also that exposure to messy media might be of help in desensitizing him to any fears he may have of the perceived danger of losing control. Questions in the background at this point are as follows: Is he allowed to fail? Does he feel he needs to be perfect? Where did he get this idea? What pressures are on him at home in his matriarchal household? Does he have to perform as the "man of the house" for his mother and grandmother? What are his ideas about being a man? What, if any, relationship does he have with his father, and with other men? What are the "shoulds" that underlie his caution, worry, and anxiety? I have many questions and some tentative theories about these and other concerns. In my directives and in the projects I assign, Todd and I will hopefully explore these and other ideas through the medium of art, and possibly also in language.

In the back of my mind is an understanding that many children entering fourth grade find the work more challenging and may falter from early years of success. The work is more difficult than it has ever been; a higher level of problem solving is required to demonstrate proficiency and mastery. I'd like Todd to know this and have some reassurance that he does not necessarily struggle alone. Again, via art explorations, we might discover what it means to come to a boundary where all that you know is not quite enough to help you solve the new problems that are just ahead. In fact, this perspective is a well-respected interpretation of the challenges of all growth and development (Holzman, 1997). Could we solve some of these problems together? Can we figure out, via art making, how to create something that has never existed before? Could Todd take this success and understanding out of the art room and into the classroom and home with him? I think Todd could learn to persist through what he feels are "mistakes" and to learn to work with his "messed-up" drawings or paintings. Art making and our verbal reflections of the processes and feelings that emerge for him might give him resources within and without to tolerate and even appreciate imperfection. I would also like to provide Todd with a place to play, to have fun and experiment without harsh consequences or fear of failure. The relationship between the art therapist and the child has great potential for providing space for safe and intimate play: transformative, developmental play (Holzman) as we engage in our wordless, rhythmic dialogue of creation. I'd like Todd to emerge from some of his sessions extremely proud of himself and what he has created out of nothing.

I am interested too in the classroom environment. What is the racial and ethnic mixture in his class? Are there other African American children—boys in particular? Does he like his teacher? What are his peer relationships like? Is he popular with other children? Directives given to explore some of these topics in our sessions might be to draw or paint a picture of you in your classroom. Draw how it is and how you would like it to be. We might also explore, via collage making, ideas he has about himself in his role as student or as son and grandson: Where is he now, and where would he like to be? Choosing images, cutting them to shape and size, and arranging and pasting them are indirect lessons in problem solving, as are much of creative art activity. I've hypothesized that some of Todd's struggles have to do with organizational skills that have not quite kept up with the more advanced demands of the fourth grade.

Given that Todd has been described as a "perfect gentleman" and a boy who likes to please others, I am hopeful that we will develop a warm, close, and trusting relationship. I hypothesize that the uncritical and accepting nature of our interactions will be helpful to him and provide an oasis in a young life fraught with disappointments and difficulties. I am hopeful also that this bright, pleasant, and essentially cooperative child will develop skills to help him learn how to learn, to be open to being ignorant and "not knowing how," and to proceed with more confidence and enthusiasm. The therapeutic activity of creation embodied in the humanistic tradition of expressive art therapy is nonsystematic, nonempirical, experimental, experiential, and idiosyncratic—and perhaps fluid and playful enough to provide respite for this youngster.

Todd seems to be an excellent candidate for creative art therapy, and it is likely that his schoolwork will improve as he internalizes more positive and realistic expectations of his capacities as a charming, intelligent 10-year-old boy, the pride of his mother and grandmother.

Summary

From its origins in the heady days of the early years of psychoanalysis between the two great wars, through the gradual systemization and theory building of the 1940s and 1950s by such practitioners as Margaret

Naumberg and Edith Kramer, the creative arts therapies have provided innovative practices to assist in the diagnosis and treatment of the mentally ill, the handicapped, and the learning disabled. Much of the early research and practice took place in schools with children suffering from disabilities and mental health problems, and art therapy in schools continues to be researched and developed in schools to this day. In addition to its immediate ameliorative capacity, "the use of expressive arts facilitates a process of creative self-development that can continue long after termination of treatment" (Bratton & Ferebee, 1999, p. 193). Easily adapted to individual and group formats, art therapy has much to offer in the K–12 mental health service provision environment.

Therapists do not need to be experts in order to use creative arts techniques in treatment. The discipline is flexible enough to allow for incorporation into most modalities currently in evidence in our schools. Cognitive behavioral, choice theory, psychodynamic, Jungian, and person-centered approaches all lend themselves to infusions of creative arts activity. It is recommended that therapists who wish to include arts activities in school-based interventions experiment themselves with the media and techniques they wish to employ. Consultations with art therapists, art teachers, creative arts workshops and continuing education seminars all provide opportunities to gain exposure and experience.

As Chapman and Appleton (1999) stated, "The therapeutic potential of art lies in two areas: the opportunity art offers for integration and the creation of meaning, and the vehicle art provides for mastery through creation and exploration of images" (pp. 189–190). As an adjunctive treatment or as the central focus of intervention, creative art therapy can serve to provide much needed help for students who might not be helped in other ways: for example language impaired, developmentally delayed, and some autistic spectrum disordered students. The use of visual imagery as a therapeutic device taps into very early ways of knowing and responding to the world. We could see, and make sense of what we saw long before we could talk about it. Tapping into the power and utility of imagery is not foreign to the experience of learning, and can provide access to understanding and growth in learning environments (Riley, 2001). Although more research needs to be done in contemporary school environments to establish clear links between learning, the arts, and art therapy, sufficient success has been demonstrated to recommend it as a helpful modality to include among mental health services in our schools.

Recommended Readings

Bush, J. (1997). *The handbook of school art therapy: Introducing art therapy into a school system*. Springfield, IL: Charles C. Thomas.

Malchiodi, C. (2006). *Art therapy sourcebook*. New York: McGraw-Hill.

Moriya, D. (2000). *Art therapy in schools: Effective integration of art therapists in schools*. Jerusalem, Israel: Author.

Rodriguez, S. (1984). *The special artist's handbook: Art activities and adaptive aids for handicapped students*. Englewood Cliffs, NJ: Prentice Hall.

Ross, C. (1997). *Something to draw on: Activities and interventions using an art therapy approach*. London: Jessica Kingsley.

Stack, P. J. (2006). *Art therapy activities: A practical guide for teachers, therapists and parents*. Springfield, IL: Charles C. Thomas.

Sweeney, D. S., & Homeyer, L. E. (Eds.). (1999). *The handbook of play therapy*. San Francisco: Jossey-Bass.

Wadeson, H. (2000). *Art therapy practice: Innovative approaches with diverse populations*. New York: John Wiley.

References

American Art Therapy Association (AATA). (2003). *Art therapy in the schools: Resource packet for school art therapists*. Mundelein, IL: Author.

Ansary, T. (2007). More art, better schools. *Arts at Risk* (Pts. I–IV). Retrieved April 22, 2007, from http://encarta.msn.com/encnet/Features/Columns/?article+artsatrisk

Avraham, D. (2005). Visual art therapy's unique contribution in the treatment of post-traumatic stress disorder. *Journal of Trauma & Dissociation, 6*(4), 5–38.

Bratton, S. B., & Ferebee, K. W. (1999). The use of structured expressive art activities in group activity therapy with pre-adolescents. In D. S. Sweeny & L. E. Homeyer (Eds.), *The handbook of group play therapy*. San Francisco: Jossey-Bass.

Burns, R. (1982). *Self-growth in families: Kinetic Family Drawings (K-F-D) research and application*, New York: Brunner/Mazel.

Bush, J. (2003). About art school therapy. Retrieved March 7, 2007, from http://www.schoolarttherapy.com/school_art_therapy.htm

Carp, J. G. (2005, June 17). [Art therapy testimony]. Prepared for IDEA hearings at Vanderbilt University, Nashville, TN. Retrieved March 7, 2007, from www.arttherapy.org/documents

Cedars-Sinai. (2007). Works of art depict fear and hope of students reaching out from trauma of gang violence. *Cedars-Sinai Medical Center News*. Retrieved April 27, 2007, from www.cedars-sinai.edu/pdf/PSYCHGangViolenceArt-38160.pdfIV

Chapman, L., & Appleton, V. (1999). Art in group play therapy. In D. S. Sweeny & L. E. Homeyer (Eds.). *The handbook of group play therapy*. San Francisco: Jossey-Bass.

Danto, E. A. (2005). *Freud's free clinics: Psychoanalysis and social justice, 1918–1938*. New York: Columbia University Press.

Dasgupta, A. (2006, June 14–20). Three elementary schools try to patch over feud with patchwork mandalas. *Villager, 76*(4). Retrieved April 28, 2007, from www.thevillager.com

Dowling, P. J. (1998). *Art therapy in Czech Republic elementary schools following the 1997 Moravian floods*. Washington, DC: U.S. Crisis Corps.

Essex, M. (1996). In the service of children: Art and other expressive therapies in public schools. *Journal of the American Art Therapy Association, 13*(3), 181–190.

Friedman, T. L. (2006). *The world is flat: A brief history of the twenty-first century*. New York: Farrar, Strauss & Giroux.

Gardner, H. (1989). *To open minds*. New York: Harper-Collins.

Ginsberg, H., & Opper, S. (1969). *Piaget's theory of intellectual development: An introduction*. Englewood Cliffs, NJ: Prentice Hall.

Gitter, L. (1975). Montessori and the compulsive cleanliness of severely retarded children. In E. Ulman & P. Dachinger (Eds.), *Art therapy in theory and practice*. New York: Schocken.

Hamblen, K. (1993). Theories and research that support art instruction for instrumental outcomes. *Theory Into Practice, 32*(4), 191–198.

Holzman, L. (1997). *Schools for growth*. Mahwah, NJ: Lawrence Erlbaum.

Jarboe, E. C. (2002). Art therapy: A proposal for inclusion in school settings. Retrieved March 7, 2007, from www.newhorizons.org/strategies/arts/jarboe.htm

Kahn, B. (1999). Art therapy with adolescents: Making it work for school counselors. *Professional School Counseling, 2*(4), 291–299.

Kaiser, D., Dunne, M., Malchiodi, C., Feen, H., Howie, P., Cutcher, D., et al. (2005). *Call for art therapy research on the treatment of PTSD*. Mundelein, IL: American Art Therapy Association.

Kozol, J. (2005). *The shame of the nation: The restoration of apartheid schooling in America*. New York: Three Rivers Press.

Kramer, E. (1971). *Art as therapy with children*. New York: Schocken.

Kramer, E. (1975a). Art and emptiness: New problems in art education and art therapy. In E. Ulman & P. Dachinger (Eds.), *Art therapy in theory and practice* (pp. 33–42). New York: Schocken.

Kramer, E. (1975b.). The practice of art therapy with children. In E. Ulman & P. Dachinger (Eds.), *Art therapy in theory and practice* (pp. 159–180). New York: Schocken.

Kramer, E. (1979). *Childhood and art therapy: Notes on theory and application*. New York: Schocken.

Landsman, J., & Gorski, P. (2007). Countering standardization. *Educational Leadership, 64*(8), 40–44.

Levick, M. F. (1983). *They could not talk and so they drew.* Springfield, IL: Charles C. Thomas.

Mattes, J., Pitak-Davis, S., Waronker, J., Goldstein, M., Mays, D. T., & Fink, M. (1986). Predictors of benefit from art, movement and poetry treatment: A pilot study. *Psychiatric Hospital, 17*(2), 87–90.

McConaughy, S. H. (2000). Self report: Child clinical interviews. In E. S. Shapiro & T. R. Kratochwill (Eds.), *Conducting school based assessments of child and adolescent behavior.* New York: Guilford.

Natale, J. (1996). Art as healer. *Executive Educator,* National School Board Association. Retrieved March 3, 2007, from www.enchantedway.com/articles/arthealer/htm

Naumberg, M. (1973). *An introduction to art therapy: Studies of the "free" art expression of behavior problem children and adolescents as a means of diagnosis and therapy* (Rev. ed.). New York: Columbia University, Teacher's College Press.

Oaklander, V. (1988). *Windows to our children.* Highland, NY: Gestalt Journal Press.

Ray, D. C., Perkins, S. R., & Oden, K. (2004). Rosebush fantasy technique with elementary school students. *Professional School Counseling, 7*(4), 277–282.

Riley, S. (2001). Art therapy with adolescents. *Western Journal of Medicine, 175*(1), 54–57.

Rogers, M. A. M., & Zaragoza-Lao, E. (2003). Happiness and children's health: An investigation of art, entertainment, and recreation. *American Journal of Public Health, 93*(2), 288–289.

Romer, D., & McIntosh, M. (2005). The roles and perspectives of school mental health professionals in promoting adolescent mental health. In D. L. Evans, E. B. Foa, R. E. Gur, H. Hendin, C. P. O'Brien, M. E. P. Seligman et al. (Eds.), *Treating and preventing adolescent mental health disorders* (pp. 598–615). New York: Oxford University Press.

Rose, S. R. (1998). *Group work with children and adolescents: Prevention and intervention in school and community systems.* Thousand Oaks, CA: Sage.

Rousseau, C., Drapeau, A., Lacroix, L., Bagilishya, D., & Heusch, N. (2005). Evaluation of a children's program of creative expression workshops for refugee and immigrant children. *Journal of Child Psychology and Psychiatry, 46*(2), 180–185.

Rubin, J. A. (1978). *Child art therapy.* New York: Van Nostrand Reinhold.

Shostak, B. (1985). Art therapy in the schools: A position paper of the American Art Therapy Association. *Art Therapy, 1,* 19–21.

Silver, R. A. (1978). *Developing cognitive and creative skills through art: Programs for children with communication disorders and learning disabilities.* Baltimore: University Park Press.

Somers-Flanagan, J. (2007). The development and evolution of person-centered expressive art therapy: A conversation with Natalie Rogers. *Journal of Counseling and Development, 85*(1), 120–125.

Star, L. (2005, November 28). The fine art of helping at-risk kids. Retrieved May 5, 2007, from http://www.connectforkids.org/node/3729

Treffiletti, M. L. (2003). Art therapy: A child's tool for understanding and communicating. Retrieved April 22, 2007, from http://web.syr.edu/~mltreffi/Research%20Review%20Report.htm

Ulman, E. (1975). Art therapy: Problems of definition. In E. Ulman & P. Dachinger (Eds.), *Art therapy in theory and practice* (pp. 3–13). New York: Schocken.

U.S. Census Bureau. (2000). Statistical abstract of the United States, Washington, DC: U.S. Government Printing Office.

Wallace, J., Yorgin, P. D., Carolan, R., Moore, H., Sanchez, J., Belson, A., et al. (2004). The use of art therapy to detect depression and PTSD in pediatric & young adult renal transplant recipients. *Journal of Pediatric Transplants*, 8(1), 52–59.

Whitehead, M. (2007). S. A. R. I.: Telling the story. *International Journal of Group Psychotherapy*, 57(2), 267–268.

Winner, E. (2007). Visual thinking in arts education: Homage to Rudolf Arnheim. *Psychology of Aesthetics, Creativity and the Arts*, 1(1), 25–31.

14

Applying Dance/Movement Therapy in School Settings

Elise Billock Tropea

Dianne Dulicai

William C. Freeman

All human beings communicate through the universal language of movement. The premise that body movement plays an important role in the development of the child is one that is certainly not new. "As parents, as educators or as therapists we have observed new infants and have marveled at their continual challenges as they move from one developmental stage to another" (Tropea, 1990, p. 15). At birth movement is, in fact, the primary form of expression infants have at their disposal. The wonder of newborns most often brings forth in us spontaneity as we relate with them predominantly through nonverbal interactions. We may delight in observing and responding to the baby naturally, encouraging connection through touch, cuddling, and rocking, and through imitation of their sounds and movement. "We are creative in devising ways to reach infants; in fact, in countless ways each of us has successfully encouraged, humored, cheered, soothed, reassured, coached and taught the children in our world" (Tropea, 1990, p. 15).

If one were to take a video of an infant and his or her caretaker and play it in slow motion, one would both see and hear that the infant's movements and sound are in synchrony with him or her (Condon, 1968). Most often, a parent knows intuitively when the child is not attuning or paying attention, and just not connecting. This body sense, called *kinesthetic awareness* by dance/movement therapists (DMTs), is an awareness that goes far beyond words themselves. As children develop, they incorporate this early learning in their relationship to others. Think of a 5-year-old child at the dinner table with his parents. When he laughs a bit too loud with a mouthful of food, his mother turns toward him and reaches to touch him firmly but gently. The child without any words reads her look and the quality of the touch, and he knows clearly that his behavior is not accepted. In fact, before words appear, he has learned about rules of behavior, understands what to expect, and feels the emotional atmosphere by how he is handled. Gesture, body attitude, tone of voice, and nonverbal interaction precede language and actually affect a child's relationship to and mastery of the spoken word.

Nonverbal communication, movement observation, relational skills, and developmental movement knowledge are, then, skills we all possess and utilize intuitively to some degree as we endeavor to build and expand relationships with children. Dance/movement therapy (DMT) begins with these basic principles and is grounded in a sound body of knowledge in the above areas as well as those involving psychological, cognitive, social, and family systems theories.

Although DMT is a relatively new form of therapy, it is derived from a very old concept. For thousands of years, every culture has celebrated both life and the body through ritual and dance. Whether we choose to engage in the experience, or bear witness as others do, the dance itself can evoke powerful physical and emotional responses. Have you ever watched a dance performance or a sporting event and experienced certain exhilaration, a sensation in your body, almost as though you were part of the performance or game? New brain research is teaching us about the way we respond to what we see and hear (Gallese, Keysers, & Rizzolatti, 2004). If a child observes another child eating a banana, the brain area that highlights eating fires just as if he or she were eating the banana him or herself. Although the research is new, caretakers know that, in this situation, the next request from the child will most likely be to have his or her own banana.

DMT came of age in the 1940s; its pioneers were dancers. Who better to use movement as expressive behavior, feel the attunement of another body to learn new dance patterns, and understand that rhythm organizes the body?

In this chapter, we will provide an overview of the therapeutic approach, including how the pioneers began work with children. A case example will demonstrate how therapeutic movement intervention with a particular child might proceed, and examples of the broad diverse use of movement intervention in various populations will be identified. We will focus narrowly on the best practices in a school setting and describe how assessment tools inform our practice with a description of how evidence-based research assists us to provide a continual analysis of service outcome.

DMT: An Overview

Any preliminary understanding and examination of DMT must begin with a truth that has pervaded its history over the last 70 years—that of the rootedness it takes from the creative artistry of dance. In specific, the revolutionary movement known as modern dance, more abstract in content and philosophy than classical ballet, came about in the early 1920s largely because of artists such as Ruth St. Denis and Ted Shawn. The Denishawn Company blazed the trail for other well-known dance artists such as Martha Graham, who was one of the original members of the Denishawn Company. Shawn said of their work, "I believe that dance communicates man's deepest, highest, and most truly spiritual thoughts and emotions far better than words, spoken or written" (quoted in BrainyQuote.com, n.d.). Although Martha Graham, also considered one of the founders of modern dance in this country, would not have perceived herself as a healer, her words were prescient and have guided the notion that the medium lends itself to full expression of the human spirit:

> There is a vitality, a life force, an energy, a quickening that is translated through you into action and because there is only one of you in all of time, this expression is unique. And if you block it, it will never exist through any other medium and be lost. The body says what words cannot. The body is a sacred garment. (About.com, 2007)

Today, almost a century later, the body–mind connection has become more widely accepted. More and more, people are inclined to try alternative or holistic methods to alleviate somatic issues through "body work." There has been considerable growth in body-oriented therapies and techniques. Advertising even uses the "new catchphrase" to sell products, suggesting that by driving a particular car the owner can be assured of finding the perfect balance of mind, body, and spirit! What, then, distinguishes DMT from other forms of body-oriented therapies?

As early as the 1940s, a small cadre of dancers who embraced the disciplines of modern and creative dance had begun to explore the power of dance and its elements in facilitating healing with people diagnosed with severe mental illnesses—Marian Chace on the east coast of the United States, and Mary Starks Whitehouse and Trudi Shoop on the west coast, to name a few. Chace was most noted for her role in founding the American Dance Therapy Association (ADTA) in 1966. Her history illustrates the profession's beginnings.

Trained as a modern dancer, she, like Martha Graham, performed with the Denishawn Dance Company and began teaching in her early adulthood. Through her own personal life experiences and in observing her students' movement repertoire, Chace realized that there was more to dance than performance. That is, she witnessed varying movement styles among her students and the connection of their moving to their emotions. Her interests led her to St. Elizabeth's Hospital, where she worked with patients with severe mental illness. Her work drew respect from psychiatrists and staff alike, and began to spread. Informal gatherings led these pioneers to pursue studies in psychology, child development, and group process, and together they created the ADTA. Today there are over 1,500 practicing therapists representing 43 countries. More information about the association and its educational requirements, standards and ethics, and research foundation may be found on the ADTA Web site (http:// www.adta.org).

The association expanded the professional title from *dance therapy* to *dance/movement therapy* in the early 1990s to more clearly represent the breadth and scope of the work and to assist others in understanding the nature of the profession. Still, its definition and process remain unchanged. "Dance/Movement Therapy is the psychotherapeutic use of movement as a process which furthers the emotional, social, cognitive, and physical integration of the individual" (ADTA, 2007). Although our orientations may differ, that is, our theoretical leanings toward certain psychological systems and our areas of specialization regarding the populations we serve, DMTs share a common reverence for the creative process, and honor expressiveness of the dance in its many forms. The foundation of dance is the cornerstone of our work and, in fact, distinguishes our profession from other forms of body-oriented techniques.

Therapeutic Aspects of Dance/Movement Therapy with Children

As early as the 1940s, pioneers such as Polk (1974), Leventhal (1980), Canner (1968), Kalish (1974), and Espenak (1979) had begun to explore their work with children with challenges: those who were diagnosed with communication and physical disorders, and those whom we may today diagnose with pervasive developmental delays (PDD), attention deficit disorders (ADD) with or without hyperactivity, learning style differences, and emotional, physical, and sexual trauma. Although each has had her own unique history and journey into the field, what becomes palpably clear as one either reads about or watches through video the work of these women is the integrity upon which their relationship to the child is grounded. Mary Starks Whitehouse (1987) stated that "the body is the physical aspect of the personality, and movement is the personality made visible." Mary Wigman (1966), noted pioneer of modern dance in Europe, in *The Language of Dance* conveyed the depth and wholeness of the movement experience. "A foot that smiles, a hand that can weep—well, the dance is not only an art of time and space, it also is the art of the consciously lived and fulfilled moment" (p. 110).

These artists' and pioneers' early work informed other DMTs, such as Beardall (1992), Duggan (1995), Erfer (1995), Freeman (Freeman et al., 1994), Kornblum (2002), and Tortora (2006), to explore and build on the work of these predecessors. From wellness and prevention to severe conditions in childhood, DMTs have interfaced with educators, and have witnessed the power of collaboration as members of school-based teams. Task analysis of movement-based experiences from their clinical practice, along with the willingness to translate movement vocabulary into more user-friendly terms, has resulted in increased understanding of our practice's efficacy among educators and therapists alike. As DMTs, we, too, address the following:

- Perceptual motor development and fine and gross motor coordination
- Verbal and nonverbal communication
- Impulse control
- Body image
- Socialization skills
- Emotional expression
- Ability to maintain boundaries
- Attention span and on-task behavior
- Critical thinking skills, problem solving, and creativity

In the 1960s, dance/movement therapist Janet Adler's work with both normal and severely disturbed preschoolers was captured on film. *Looking for Me*, almost 40 years later, continues to be a hallmark of our work with children. Its brilliance lies not only in her body-centered way of reaching children but also in her elucidation of dance/movement therapy in clear and easily understood language. Her expressive movement sessions with normal 3–5 year olds illustrate developmental movement characteristics typically found in children of that age. In contrast, the film also records individual sessions over several months with two very young children, diagnosed with autism and psychosis. It is here that viewers can truly bear witness to Adler's remarkable ability to begin where these children are, using movement and gesture to gently invite connection. Her recorded work with adults in an in-service training session serves to remind us all that as adults we tend to lose our spontaneity, favoring words over playful movement.

> At a certain point in the child's development, the emphasis seems to shift from free exploration to the more structured business of language development. When this shift occurs, too many of our (special) children are left without the sensory stimulation so vital to their growth. (Tropea, 1990, p. 15)

"For many children, moving through the early years can be painful and chaotic" (Adler, 1970, p.). As educators and as therapists, we are cognizant of the fact that developmental stages are guidelines we expect to see within the normally developing child. Although variations and time differentials are based on the individual child, there are typically, however, sequential constants that inform next steps in a child's growth. For many children, those fluid stages of "normal development" may appear out of sequence. Those who are challenged with sensory, cognitive, and emotional difficulties most often present with splinter skills, and it behooves those of us who work with these children to both know normal milestones and make adaptations for those who grow differently.

DMTs who work with children combine skills in nonverbal movement observation and behavioral assessment with sound knowledge of the developmental processes of childhood, from cognitive, social, emotional, behavioral, and physiological perspectives. Therapists provide movement experiences that integrate these areas while utilizing gentle, noninvasive techniques that rely on the senses, in particular one that we call *kinesthetic sense*. Sound relational skills coupled with kinesthesia inform our work. Kinesthetic empathy, simply put, and which we all possess to some degree, is the ability to feel and understand another person simply by being in physical awareness with that human being. Something we see or feel in another—a smile, a gesture, a movement—evokes in us an in-relational response as we take in the other's movement repertoire and try it on in our bodies, cycling back and in response moving in ways that create what we might call a dance of relationship. This fluid cycle really is the underpinning of DMT. In relationship with another, we listen with our bodies, and listen as well to the words, while observing and sensing areas in the body that are held. We acknowledge without physically or behaviorally changing that body. Instead, we employ methods such as amplifying, modulating, or mirroring the movement behavior, suggesting ways of broadening the repertoire of the children, and in so doing introduce new coping skills.

Growing research in the areas of psychiatry and neurobiology (Levine, 1999; van der Kolk, 1994) have yielded major breakthroughs in understanding the effects of trauma and stress and the connection between mind, brain, and body. The discovery that the body holds trauma on a cellular level and actually alters brain functioning has both supported and informed the work of many dance/movement therapists who work clinically with children, adolescents, and adults struggling with anxiety, trauma, posttraumatic stress disorders (PTSD), dissociative disorders, depression, severe body image distortions, and eating disorders. Dance/movement therapists continue to conduct research in this arena.

DMT Blanche Evan (1982) stated, "The object is first not to change the body of the client but to let the client become freer and freer in exposing the body that she has" (p. 5). Whether we are working in direct clinical services or providing preservice education, our starting point remains constant. Breath, rhythm, body attitude, use of space, and attunement are all incorporated in both the assessment phase and direct treatment with children.

These basic tenets have proven useful for teachers and other members of the school-based intervention teams. In-service training in educational settings offers school personnel and parents an overview of the modality and provides experiences that further their own understanding of individual movement styles and how they affect interaction with individuals and groups. Creative movement experiences can and do surprise many educators and non–dance/movement therapists. The following example represents a session with teachers I facilitated many years ago:

> Michael, a special educator[,] and his colleagues represented teachers from a variety of settings from elementary (middle) and high school. When (he) realized that we would be spending much of our time involved in active participation, Michael quickly voiced his reticence to join in, making it clear to the rest of the group that he did not "dance." As we began a simple warm-up, stretching body parts in time to a popular piece of music, (he) began to relax. Using rhythm as an organizer, we tapped our knees and our toes, laughing at the difficulty some of us had in doing so. We took turns saying our names and creating gestures to accompany them as we went around the circle. The group moved cautiously to start, concerned that there might be a right or wrong way to play. Its members were to discover for themselves that creative movement was a natural process, and one did not require as prerequisites, "grace" or "agility." We played with movements, speeding them up and slowing them down.

> (In) pairs we experimented with mirror imaging, taking turns leading and then following, trying on new movement behavior, and allowing ourselves to join with another in the process.... Michael expressed both his joy at "acting like a kid," and his surprise at the enjoyment of it.... Our closing ritual brought the group back together, once again emphasizing the non-verbal affective methods of interacting. Moving in and out of the circle in unison, using varying tempos and varied movement dynamics the group flowed in synchrony to music. (Tropea, 1990, pp. 16–17)

Discovering our own movement ranges and styles and those of others helps us to hone nonverbal observational skills and allows us to take more informed next steps in devising strategies and environments that best address the needs of our students.

> The arts are an area where there is no "right or wrong" and children are encouraged to express their thoughts, feelings, and fears in an acceptable way. If adults can have an ego enhancing experience in a nonverbal, or at least nonacademic mode, it is easier for them to see how children are benefited. (Lyons & Tropea, 1987, p. 245)

Models for personnel preparation (Freeman et al., 1994) may also include demonstrations with students within the school setting, offering personnel a look at how theory informs practice. Often, initial in-service training models lead to a more expansive relationship between DMTs and school-based teams. The case study to follow represents an example of such collaboration in motion. DMT within family systems facilitates that the same kind of personal growth with parents and siblings as they learn to be sensitive to the styles and dynamics that enhance overall family functioning. Dulicai (1977) saw the family as a system with its own rules and regulations recognized through nonverbal behavior that is often below the level of awareness. The first task for the clinician is to understand the system within which he or she is working (Dulicai, 1977).

The Case of Todd

As we described previously, the nature of our work, both in the assessment phase and in treatment planning and implementation, relies predominantly on observable movement behavior; but preliminary and ongoing dialogues utilizing the skills and assessments of the treatment-based team are vital to our process in providing effective services to the children and youth whom we serve. Team meetings inform the assessment session by identifying and then including any specific items that need to be tended to, as well as the ongoing work with the student.

Our case analysis of Todd is initially framed around the Child Movement Assessment: A School Based Service (CMA), further elucidated in the evidence-based research section of this chapter (below). In brief, following initial team meetings the DMT facilitates the nonverbal assessment session, which is videotaped. The tape is sent to an external evaluator, a specialist in movement assessment, who generates a report based on observable data. Among numerous movement factors and profiles, the report identifies the primary areas of the child's strength and needs, along with recommendations that may include direct services, consultation, and/or training. Where DMT is suggested as a treatment mode, the report includes recommendations regarding proposed frequency and duration, as well as strategies for application for school, home, and community settings. A team discussion follows in which observations, behavior, and interactional themes, along with other factors, are addressed.

Often our first communications from teachers and other members of the school-based team resemble the case history in chapter one. What immediately strikes us in reviewing this case history is the dearth of descriptors regarding Todd's physical self: his appearance, size, facial expression, and eye contact. What we do have to work with, however, provides us with a general sense of Todd, a 10-year-old boy who, unlike many at his age, appears to spend the majority of his time focused narrowly on "homework," both during the week and over the weekend. Key words and phrases found in the written case, such as "worry," "anxiety," "structure," "perfect little gentleman," and *tantrums*, provide markers for us as we prepare for the assessment phase of our work. Based on the inordinate amount of time Todd spends working at home, we would want to know how Todd functions during his "free time." Team meetings with school staff and his mother help to gather a fuller picture of this young boy.

Observation

We would begin by observing Todd in his school environments: during a free period such as lunch or recess, and in the classroom setting. It is important that observations include the student working or playing independently as well as cooperatively in interaction with others. Methods for notating movement may include Laban Movement Analysis (see the evidence-based section, below, for more description), as well as other nonverbal observational instruments. Observations yield information impressions regarding how the child uses his body through locomotion and articulation to communicate, interact, and attend to tasks. Notations include such elements as the nonverbal communication styles used: interactional dynamics, posture, gestures, motor skills, and other nonverbal movement abilities in the areas of communication and physical, social, and emotional functioning.

Assessment

The assessment itself brings the DMT and student together in a space large enough to engage in gross motor activities without distractions. The therapist facilitates activities that measure competencies in both functional and expressive movement. Obstacle courses, props, and music may often find their way into the session. It is important to note that the same skills of kinesthetic empathy and relationship described earlier are very much a part of this initial phase. Based on the written case description of Todd, we will assume that he has integrated movement characteristics that allow him to use the torso as a stabilizer while the arms and legs expand their task-oriented behavior. Abilities needed to throw and catch a ball, ride a bicycle, and use the appropriate force for an activity would be present in his repertoire, but the ability to exert appropriate inhibition when frustrated and use words to express frustration may not be demonstrated. From a developmental perspective, at his age, we might expect Todd to have full modulation of both strength and flow characteristics, as they relate to his ability to cope with frustration; but, judging from the written evaluation, we are likely to see a problem in this area. The assessment would include an activity that challenges Todd's ability to attend to multiple stimuli, in order to observe his movement response. Sequencing tasks such as an obstacle course would help identify to what extent he is inclined to repeat or redo, signaling indicators of perfectionism and anxiety.

Because his father is not mentioned, we assume that his contact is limited or not present. Movement games that relate to sports help us see to what extent Todd shows signs of male movement characteristics and style. We would look to see if his phrasing has clear beginnings and endings, with appropriate preparation and recovery. Lastly, we would want to test his ability to modulate the flow factor, providing us with an understanding regarding to what extent he can freely use expressive movement qualities or is restraining emotional responsiveness.

Treatment

The assessment is particularly important so that the therapist can measure the success or failure of the interventions and provide the most cost-efficient services to the school system that can later be translated to real-life behavior and hopefully behavioral change.

Upon this information, a treatment plan can be built. DMTs combine team-based reports, observations, and movement assessment material and begin at the body level. Goals for Todd's treatment include the following:

- Increasing his ability to use strength and discharge energy in a safe and appropriate way
- Channeling tantrum behavior to the therapy session rather than the home or classroom
- Increasing his ability to modulate from quickness to sustainment, thereby increasing his ability to self-regulate and reduce anxiety
- Reducing stress and increasing relaxation through developing techniques for self-soothing behavior (including the use of fine touch) that can be employed in difficult or stressful situations
- Decreasing perfectionist behavior by introducing movement-based experiences that are structuring while allowing him to use both single-focused and multifocused attention and stimulate creative thinking

Todd's need for structure and his anxiety regarding performance influence the beginning stages of treatment. It is by starting where the child is that we are able to create the safety and containment so vital to helping him explore other modes of moving, both functionally and expressively. Activities that promote strength—that is to say, a sense of groundedness in his body—make way for exploration and release. We know he has an inability to modulate strength that results in tantrum behavior. Therefore, we build a structured movement exploration rather than a free-flow expression of strength. We want to introduce the idea that assertiveness is a more mature quality than tantrums in a controlled way.

Anxiety, by its very nature, is energy that is trapped in the body. It is the result of being able to neither fight nor flee. The DMT works with Todd in ways that allow him to build the skills necessary to modulate energy, by both giving voice to it and releasing it through his body. The therapist will begin to encourage Todd to make sounds and later words that accompany expressions of strength later to be able to substitute words for acting out. Also he will be encouraged to bring his tantrums to the therapy session rather than the schoolroom or home. Enlisting the assistance of the teacher and mother in this request is extremely important. Returning to the concepts discussed earlier in this chapter, breath, rhythm, body attitude, use of space, and attunement are all incorporated in both the assessment phase and direct treatment with children.

Todd also needs an outlet for exploring less than perfect behavioral options to situations. Obstacle courses are a particularly good medium for this intervention, because they are set up so that there are many ways to go through them. There is no right answer but, rather, many ways to accomplish success. Sometimes it is easier for a child to gain insight through a concrete and pleasurable experience than through words alone. Thinking of alternate ways, even funny solutions, allows new behavior to evolve. The goals for behavior changes and more mature responses to life experiences are common goals with all forms of therapeutic intervention. This chapter attempts to describe the process in a school-based setting.

Evidence-Based Research

The widely accepted definition of evidence-based practice (EBP) is one adapted from Sackett and colleagues (Sackett, Straus, Richardson, Rosenberg, & Haynes, 2002) and by the Institute of Medicine (2001, p. 147): Evidence-based practice is the integration of best research evidence with clinical expertise and patient values. The United States expends more per capita in medical costs than any other industrial nation, though 15% of our population is uninsured and 24% have no mental health coverage (World Health Organization, 2001). During the 1990s, these facts caused funding agencies to examine ways to measure effective practices by requiring caregiving agencies to change their means of evaluation. The public has been offered the proposal that the problem is an uninformed practice rather than practice informed by research (Norcross & Levant, 2005). EBP as developed must include best practice evaluation, include the knowledge and skill of experienced clinicians, and be consistent with patient values. Though conflict still is present within discussions at the American

Psychological Association and the American Medical Association, funding agencies are regularly using EBP in issuing approved status.

The arts therapies including art, dance/movement, music, drama, psychotherapy, and poetry have a recent history of professional identity and research development, each advancing in its own time. The scientific side of our development came later when we began the dialogue—combining arts and science, both a part of our identity. Arts therapies address the whole person as each modality incorporates various channels of communication and draws on creativity. Creativity broadly defined and inclusive of an art form and less restricted thinking is incorporated in the process of therapy and in how the client entertains the possibility of different options of behavior. Dance/movement therapist (DMT) Robyn Cruz stated that this form of research can be used to measure the quality of DMT programs and results of their work in order to support the use of DMT. One aspect of EBP is the ability to assess treatment effectiveness—if treatment was actually delivered as it was intended (Cruz & Berrol, 2004). Traditionally, the purpose of research was to test a hypothesis moving theory forward and increasing the body of programs and results of their work in order to support use of DMT. Dance/movement therapists generated hypotheses early in our development, such as the 1974 early work by Schmais (1974), who stated,

1. Movement reflects personality.
2. The relationship established between the therapist and patient through movement supports and enables behavioral change.
3. Significant changes occur on the movement level that can affect total functioning (p. 10).

Thirty years of research mostly within graduate programs have worked through these original hypotheses and generated increasingly more intricate research questions. In the early 1990s, we, with our colleague William Freeman, began to research our work with children in school-based settings. As schools were mandated to include children with disabilities in public schools or contracted school clinics to insure inclusion, budgets were severely strained. The immediacy of controlling costs for new demands on school systems made investigating best practices urgent. Accessible Arts, Inc., was awarded a contract from the Kansas Department of Education, and DMTs Freeman, Dulicai, and Tropea developed an instrument to measure outcome of DMT intervention as a part of the broader creative arts enquiry (Dulicai, Freeman, & Tropea, 2005).

The project included developing in-service training for teachers and administrators, but for the purpose of this chapter we will speak to the research question alone. Research questions included developing a movement profile that would measure the cognitive emotional and social skills of the child as a baseline for repeated testing to measure change. Coordinating interventions with teachers and other service providers, integrating the individual education program (IEP), and building provider teams insured more effective treatment.

Inspiration for the development of the instrument rested on the shoulders of prior research by several major authors and researchers such as Rudolph Laban (1950), Marion North (1972), Judith Kestenberg (1965), and Beth Kalish (1974), to name but a few. Laban's work provided the conceptual language for the quality of movement in terms of flow (the ease or restraint of movement), space (the single-focused or multifocused attention of movement), time (the urgency or lingering pace of movement), and weight (the strength or sensitive quality of movement). North, a protégé of Laban, tested his hypotheses that these qualities were outward manifestations of personality in several longitudinal studies of infants and children. Kestenberg, also a protégé of Laban and a psychoanalyst, focused her work on the developmental stages of movement and the interaction of child and parent (Kestenberg, 1974). It was Kalish and colleagues who built on her predecessors, translating the research to clinical practice and assisting in the development of the Behavior Rating Instrument for Autistic and Other Atypical Children (BRIAAC; Ruttenberg, Kalish, Wenar, & Wolf, 1978). Others too numerous to mention here have built on this work, and the reader may wish to explore the listings of recommended readings and resources that follow.

Returning our focus to the Developmental Movement Assessment developed by us, it relies on notation of movement in interaction with other children, individual characteristics, movement in task behavior, movement sequences, and balance activity. Scores included how an activity and what activity was performed. For example, the child was able to repeat a sequence as it had been displayed using "strong" and "direct" qualities but was not able to use these qualities in the classroom. Movement scores compared behavioral academic self-esteem (BASE; Coopersmith & Gilberts, 1982) and thinking creatively in action and movement (TCAM; Torrance, 1981), and showed changes in behavior and self-esteem from pretest to post test on all items (Freeman, 1991).

Child Movement Assessment: A School Based Service (CMA) is the new title for the instrument used, to date, in 43 original assessments of children referred by school staff and used over time to test success or failure of dance/movement therapy to meet or to adjust goals of treatment (Amighi, Loman, Lewis & Sossin, 1999). Over time, revisions have improved the ability to report a child's physical, cognitive, and emotional strengths and weaknesses through movement assessment. The dance/movement therapist's report translates the specific movement details into a more general language appropriate for school personnel. The report concludes with recommended goals for dance/movement therapy treatment goals to meet IEP goals (Dulicai, Freeman, & Tropea, 2005). See the case example section, above, for a description from this project. The methods and procedures of the CMA include separating responsibilities in this process. One DMT conducts the observation and facilitates the assessment session or evaluation, the latter of which is videotaped. The other independently reviews the session on videotape to rate nonverbal behavior in a data-based computer program, providing data that serve as the basis of the report. In our initial development of this model, our goal was to separate out tasks and reduce possible conflicts of interest. Such a model separates out the observation and facilitation of the session from the analysis, report, and recommendations resulting from an assessment or evaluation session.

A sampling of work contributing to the body of knowledge of our evidence-based work with children includes Kornblum (2002), who measured the outcome of DMT intervention to reduce bullying in schools, producing excellent results. Galing measured creativity scores for normal and disturbed children before and after DMT intervention (Galing, 1989). Dance/movement therapy applied to an experimental group of disturbed preschoolers showed higher scores on a developmental movement rating instrument than a control group given non-body-centered groups (Gellman, 1995).

Conclusion

The field of dance/movement therapy has, at its core, the inviolate belief that the body is the container for our earliest relationship experiences, experiences that are primarily nonverbal in nature. It is through touch and bodily experience with self and other that we learn about our world. When children are nourished though an environment that both respects and provides sensory experiences, their ability to move through developmental stages so vital to cognitive, affective, and physical growth increases greatly. Research continues to support the efficacy of DMT with children who are at risk, and opens the way to increased collaboration with verbal therapists, educators, allied professionals, those in the medical profession, and families.

In 2007, statistics reveal that up to 50% of youth are obese. Researchers report poor nutrition and lack of physical exercise as major contributors to this alarming epidemic. Television and technologies such as the computer and handheld games have replaced outdoor activities. And, stress and violence among American children and adolescents have spiraled to a rate never before seen in our history. Therapists continue to report increasingly high numbers of youth, both male and female, who are struggling with negative body images. We must strive to collaborate and to build effective teams of educators, mental health professionals, and families if we are to create the environments that allow children to grow and to meet their educational and therapeutic goals.

Appendix: A Glossary of Movement-Related Terms

body boundaries: Movement demonstrating one's ability to differentiate between self and others and objects, and to attribute properties to them.

body level: Movement that includes use of the torso and its shape, integration, and patterning of limbs and torso.

communicative elements: Movements that define and regulate human communication, such as eyebrow flash, eye contact, aversion, and length of contact; for example, dominance displays.

effort/shape: System for notating body movement, providing researchers with a common language—it defines how the movement is done, rather than what is done, and appears in developmental hierarchy.

expressive body: Movements carrying affect messages, such as pounding fist, hand on chest, and appeasing gestures.

flow: The degree of tension accompanying a movement on a continuum from *free* to *bound*; according to North (1972), this is associated with feeling.

kinesphere: Individual's personal space measured from the center out as far as the limbs can reach.

modulation: One's ability to control motoric behavior.

phrasing: Movement sequence from beginning to end.

space: The quality of attention to movement displays on a continuum from *direct* (single-focused) to *indirect* (multifocused); according to North (1972), this is associated with thinking and organizing.

time: The urgency or lingering pace of movement on a continuum from *quick* to *sustained*; according to North (1972), this is associated with decision (doing).

transitions: Flow of motor activity from one sequence to another.

weight: The quality of how weight is used in relation to gravity on a continuum from *strong* to *light*; according to North (1972), this is associated with differentiation of self and intention.

Recommended Readings and Resources

Readings

American Dance Therapy Association (ADTA). http:// www.adta.org

American Journal of Dance Therapy. American Dance Therapy Association. http:// www.springerlink.com (subscription required to view).

Freeman, W. (1998). *You're okay right where you are: Expressive movement in education.* Unpublished doctoral dissertation, Union Institute, Cincinnati, OH.

Levy, J. F., & Leventhal, F. (Eds.). (1995). *Dance and other expressive arts therapies: When words are not enough.* London: Routledge.

Tortora, S. (2006). *The dancing dialogue: Using the communicative power of movement with young children.* Baltimore: Paul H. Brooks.

Films

Adler, J. (Prod.). (1970). *Looking for me.* Berkeley, CA: Berkeley Media.

American Dance Therapy Association (ADTA). (1983). *Dance therapy: The power of movement* (N. Brock, Dir.). Columbia, MD: ADTA.

Brownell, I., & Wilcoxen, W. (Dirs.). (1998). *A time to dance: The life and work of Norma Canner.* Medford, MA: Bushy Theater.

References

About.com. (2007). Graham, Martha. Retrieved May 2, 2007, from womenshistory.about.com/cs/quotes/a/gu/graham

Adler, J. (Prod.). (1970). *Looking for me.* Berkeley, CA: Berkeley Media.

Amighi, J., Loman, S., Lewis, P., & Sossin, K. M. (1999). *The meaning of movement: Developmental and clinical perspectives on the use of the Kestenberg Movement Profile.* Amsterdam: Gordon and Breach.

Barlett, V., & Brock, N. (Producers), & Adler (Writer). (1970). *Looking for me* [Film]. (Available from University of California Extension Center for Media and Independent Learning, 2000 Center St., 4th Floor, Berkeley, CA, 94704).

Beardall, N. (Producer). (1992). *In our voices: Dancing for development and discovery* [Video]. (Available from Newton, MA Public Schools.).

BrainyQuote.com. (N.d.). Ted Shawn quotes. Retrieved July 10, 2008, from http://www.brainyquote.com/quotes/authors/t/ted_shawn.html

Canner, N., & Klebanoff, H. (1968). *And a time to dance.* [2nd ed.] Boston: Beacon.

Condon, W. S. (1968). Linguistic-kinesic research and dance therapy. *American Dance Therapy Monograph, 3,* 21–42.

Coopersmith, S., & Gilberts, R. (1982). *Manual for behavioral academic self-esteem: A rating scale.* Palo Alto, CA: Consulting Psychologists Press.

Cruz, R. F. (2004). *Dance/Movement therapists in action: A working guide to research options.* Springfield, IL: Charles C. Thomas.

Duggan, D. (1995). The "4's": A dance therapy program for learning disabled adolescents. In F. Levy, J. Fried, & F. Leventhal (Eds.), *Dance and other expressive arts therapies: When words are not enough* (pp. 225–240). London: Routledge.

Dulicai, D. (1977). Movement therapy with families. *The Art of Psychotherapy, 4,* 77–80.

Dulicai, D., Freeman, W., & Tropea, E. (2005). *Child movement assessment: School-based services.* Unpublished manuscript.

Erfer, T. (1995). Treating autistic children in a public school system. In F. Levy, J. Fried, & F. Leventhal (Eds.), *Dance and other expressive arts therapies: When words are not enough* (pp. 191–213). London: Routledge.

Espenak, L. (1979). The Adlerian approach to dance therapy. In P. Bernstein (Ed.), *Eight theoretical approaches in dance-movement therapy.* Dubuque, IA: Kendall/Hunt.

Freeman, W. (1991) *Development of pre-service modules for arts related services* (Grant to U.S. Department of Education, Office of Special Education Programs). Kansas City, KS: Accessible Arts.

Freeman, W. (1998). *You're okay right where you are: Expressive movement in education.* Unpublished doctoral dissertation, Union Institute, Cincinnati, OH.

Freeman, W., Hoernicke, P. A., Kelly, S. N., McCormick, J. L., Klocke, T., & Wright, T. (1994). *Access to the arts: Education curricula modules in art, drama, dance/movement for the integration of the arts in the inclusive classroom.* Kansas City, KS: Accessible Arts.

Galing, A. J. (1989). The correlation of expressive movement qualities and creative potential in ego disturbed/developmentally delayed and normal children. Unpublished research, Drexel University, Philadelphia.

Gallese, V., Keysers, C., & Rizzolatti, G. (2004). A unifying view of the basis of social cognition. *Trends in Cognitive Sciences, 8*(9), 8.

Gellman, L. (1995). *The influence of dance/movement intervention on the development of normal preschoolers.* Unpublished master's thesis, Drexel University, Philadelphia.

Kalish, B. (1974). Working with an autistic child. *Dance Therapy: Focus on Dance, 7,* 38–41.

Kestenberg, J. (1965). The role of movement patterns in development: I. *Psychoanalytic Quarterly, 34,* 1–36.

Kestenberg, J. A. B. (1974). *Children and parents: Psychoanalytic studies in development.* New York: Aronson.

Kornblum, R. (2002). *Disarming the playground.* Oklahoma City, OK: Wood & Barnes.

Laban, R. (1950). *The mastery of movement.* Boston: Plays.

Leventhal, M. (1980). *Movement and growth: Dance therapy for the special child.* New York: New York University Press.

Levine, P. (1999). *Healing trauma* [Audiotapes]. Boulder, CO: Sounds True.

Lyons, S., & Tropea, E. (1987). Creative arts therapists as consultants: Methods and approaches to in-service training in the special education forum. *Arts in Psychotherapy, 14*(3), 243–247.

Institute of Medicine. (2001). *Crossing the quality chasm: A new health system for the 21st century.* Washington, DC: National Academy Press.

Norcross, J. C. B., & Levant, R. F. (Eds.). (2005). *Evidence-based practices in mental health.* Washington, DC: American Psychological Association.

North, M. (1972). *Personality assessment through movement.* London: Macdonald and Evans.

Polk, E. (1974). Dance therapy with special children. In K.C. Mason (Ed.), *Dance therapy: Focus on dance VII.* Reston, VA: American Alliance for Health, Physical Education, Recreation, and Dance.

Rifkin-Gainer, I., & Evan, B. (1982). An interview with Blanche Evan. *American Journal of Dance Therapy, 5,* 5–17.

Ruttenberg, B. A., Kalish, B. I., Wenar, C., & Wolf, E. G. (1978). *The Behavior Rating Instrument for Autistic and other Atypical Children (BRIAAC).* Chicago: Stoelting.

Sackett, D. L., Straus, S. E., Richardson, W. S., Rosenberg, W., & Haynes, R. B. (2002). *Evidence based medicine: How to practice and teach EBM* (2nd ed.). London: Churchill Livingstone.

Schmais, C. (1974). Dance therapy in perspective. In K. C. Mason (Ed.), *Dance therapy: Focus on dance VII.* Reston, VA: American Alliance for Health, Physical Education, Recreation, and Dance.

Torrance, E. P. (1981). *Thinking creatively in action and movement.* Bensenville, IL: Scholastic Testing Service.

Tortora, S. (2006). *The dancing dialogue: Using the communicative power of movement with young children.* Baltimore: Paul H. Brooks.

Tropea, E. B. (1990). Creative dance/movement: Personal perspectives. In P. A. Hoernicke (Ed.), *Arts with special needs students: Value, place and promise.* (pp. 5–19) Kansas City, KS: Accessible Arts.

van der Kolk, B. (1994). The body keeps the score: Memory ad the evolving psychobiology of posttraumatic stress. *Harvard Review of Psychiatry, 1,* 253–26.

Whitehouse, M. S. (1987). Retrieved August 25, 2008 from authenticmovement_usa.com/index.htm

Wigman, M. (1966). *The language of dance.* Middletown, CT: Wesleyan University Press.

World Health Organization. (2001). *The world health report 2000: Health systems: Improving performance.* Geneva: Author.

15

Seeing Through Clearer Eyes
Mindfulness and Acceptance-Based Behavioral Interventions in the School

Jennifer Block-Lerner

Michael A. Holston

Maggee Messing

> Soon the child's clear eye is clouded over by ideas and opinions, preconceptions and abstractions. Simple free being becomes encrusted with the burdensome armor of the ego. Not until years later does an instinct come that a vital sense of mystery has been withdrawn. The sun glints through the pines, and the heart is pierced in a moment of beauty and strange pain, like a memory of paradise. After that day … we become seekers.

This quote, by novelist and short story/nonfiction writer Peter Matthiessen (1987, p. xii), both captures the essence of a mindful stance toward experience and raises important questions with regard to the capacity of children and adolescents to be in such a place. In a sense, it might seem paradoxical to "teach" mindfulness and related practices to children, who naturally embody being in the present moment. At the same time, all too soon that "clear eye" is clouded over, perhaps by both naturally developing intellectual capacities and expectations/encouragement from all of those in their environment. Once children can reflect on the past, worry about the future, and compare themselves with others (among other abilities), it becomes that much more difficult to maintain "simple free being." Perhaps if children were taught skills to more frequently inhabit a mindful state, it wouldn't take "until years later" to come back to this place. Furthermore, such regular inhabiting might lead to improvements in academic performance, social skill development, and overall psychological functioning. Although the empirical literature that addresses such questions (to be reviewed below) is currently sparse, the few studies that exist (e.g., Semple, Reid, & Miller, 2005; Singh et al., 2007) do suggest that mindfulness-based methods hold promise with children and adolescents.

Definitional Issues

Mindfulness has been variously referred to as a set of methods or techniques, a psychological process that can produce outcomes, and an outcome in and of itself (Hayes & Wilson, 2003). As may be clear from the above paragraph, we are most concerned with mindfulness as a process. From our perspective, various methods may be used to facilitate this process, and a range of outcomes may be derived from such regular practice. What does this process entail?

An often-cited definition is that offered by Kabat-Zinn (1994), a pioneer in the extraction of mindfulness-based techniques from their context in Buddhism and other Eastern spiritual traditions (and importation into the realm of today's medicine, health care, and society; see http://www.umassmed.edu/cfm/mbsr/). Kabat-Zinn referred to mindfulness as "paying attention in a particular way: on purpose, in the present moment, and nonjudgmentally" (1994, p. 4).

Baer and colleagues (e.g., Baer, Smith, & Allen, 2004; Baer, Smith, Hopkins, Krietemeyer, & Toney, 2006), heeding the call of Dimidjian and Linehan (2003), have conceptualized mindfulness as involving various sets of skills. These researchers (Baer et al., 2006), through the factor analysis of existing instruments that assess the construct, recently identified five facets of mindfulness. The resulting measure, the Five Facet Mindfulness Questionnaire (FFMQ), assesses individuals with regard to their capacities for observing, describing, accepting without judgment, acting with awareness, and nonreactivity. Although much research remains to be done to determine the utility of this measure in various settings (especially those that are clinical in nature), and with populations of varying developmental levels, the FFMQ offers us a useful framework for thinking about the abilities that different approaches might foster.

To experience a "glimpse" of such nonjudgmental, present-moment awareness, or Baer et al.'s (2006) mindfulness skills in action, one might envision a scenario that involves a fifth grade student who tends to get very nervous before exams. "Maria" might be instructed to take a few minutes before a particular exam and, during this time, to use her breath as an anchor to the present moment. As she tries to keep her attention on her inhalations and exhalations, and the spaces between breaths, she will likely notice a plethora of bodily sensations (e.g., her heart beating very fast, and perhaps some tightness in her chest or butterflies in her stomach), thoughts about the exam ("I haven't studied enough" and "I'm going to fail this test"), and other experiences (e.g., memories from recent exams she has taken, or perhaps thoughts about what she has to do later in the day or what just happened at lunch). Maria's task is simply, as each of these experiences arises, to note its presence as a thought, bodily sensation, memory, or the like, and to bring her awareness back to her breath. In the process, she might also notice judgments (i.e., other thoughts) about her experiences (e.g., "I wish I didn't get so nervous before tests" and "Can't I ever get my heart to slow down? This is stupid"); these too are to be noted as they arise and fall.

Overview of the Therapeutic Approach

Although many forms of psychotherapy address one or more of Baer et al.'s (2006) identified facets of mindfulness (e.g., see Block-Lerner & Wulfert, under review, for a discussion of acceptance as a common factor in various psychotherapeutic approaches), with regard to method, the focus of this chapter will be on those we are referring to as mindfulness and acceptance-based behavioral approaches. In addition to mindfulness-based stress reduction (MBSR; Kabat-Zinn, 1990) and other approaches that emphasize the practice of mindfulness, we will also review research that has been done on several interventions from within the "third wave" of cognitive-behavioral therapy (i.e., Hayes, Strosahl, Bunting, Twohig, & Wilson, 2004). These include acceptance and commitment therapy (ACT; Hayes, Strosahl, & Wilson, 1999), dialectical behavior therapy (DBT; Linehan, 1993a, 1993b), and mindfulness-based cognitive therapy (MBCT; Segal, Williams, & Teasdale, 2002); all share an emphasis on integrating traditional behavioral (and/or cognitive) treatment strategies (e.g., exposure or thought monitoring) with those consistent with mindfulness or an "experientially accepting stance" toward experience (e.g., Block-Lerner, Plumb, & Orsillo, 2003). More specifically, these treatment packages attempt to implement many of the empirically supported active ingredients in CBT interventions from within a mindfulness or acceptance framework. Such approaches may aim to make existing CBT packages more palatable (e.g., Hannan & Tolin's [2005] incorporation of mindfulness into exposure and response prevention for obsessive compulsive disorder) and/or more clearly linked with quality of life or what matters most to clients (i.e., Wilson & Murrell's [2004] focus on "values").

At this point, most of the development and evaluation of these interventions have occurred in adult populations. However, attention is also being given to the ways that such treatment packages might be tailored to fit the unique needs of children, adolescents, and their families. In our brief introductions to each treatment approach, we offer an overview of the main components of each intervention as well as examples of how each is being adapted to address the unique needs of these populations.

Mindfulness-Based Stress Reduction and Mindfulness-Based Cognitive Therapy

A course of mindfulness-based stress reduction (MBSR) has traditionally involved eight weekly sessions (2.5 hours in length) of psychoeducation and experiential opportunities. These sessions are conducted in relatively large groups of 25–30 participants. Mindfulness practices introduced include a body scan meditation, yoga-based stretches, a sitting meditation, and a walking meditation. Participants are also presented with the idea of "informal" mindfulness practice, which involves bringing one's full awareness to the present-moment activity, be that eating, showering, walking into school or a store, or sitting and listening to a family member share a story about his or her day. Each session of the MBSR protocol involves homework assignments for practice during the week; typically, 45 minutes of some type of formal practice 6 days per week (often with the assistance of recorded instructions, e.g., on audiotapes or compact discs), along with informal mindfulness of daily activities (as well as other forms of monitoring and/or reading assignments), are encouraged. The MBSR curriculum also includes a full-day (typically weekend) mindfulness meditation retreat that involves long stretches of silence. One often forgotten aim of MBSR is to highlight participants' sense of interconnectedness with the world around them by bringing awareness to their own experiences as well as to the experience of others (e.g., Kabat-Zinn, 2005).

Mindfulness-based cognitive therapy (MBCT; Segal et al., 2002) represents an integration of MBSR and cognitive therapy (techniques such as thought monitoring and pleasant events scheduling are utilized) and is based on a cognitive vulnerability model of depressive relapse. MBCT has traditionally entailed eight weekly group sessions conducted with up to 12 participants who have experienced recurrent episodes of depression but are not currently depressed. The intervention aims to increase partici-pants' awareness of their unwanted thoughts, feelings, and bodily sensa-tions and to change their relationship to these experiences such that they are responded to intentionally and skillfully versus simply reacted to in an "automatic pilot" manner (Ma & Teasdale, 2004).

Although MBSR has typically been implemented and evaluated with various adult populations (for reviews, see Baer, 2003; Grossman, Niemann, Schmidt, & Wallach, 2004), few studies have reported on the use of MBSR with children. There are several notable exceptions that speak to the ways that this protocol may need to be adapted for younger populations. Semple et al. (2005), drawing from both MBSR and MBCT, developed a school-based intervention program that incorporated instruction, in-session prac-tice opportunities, and weekly home practice exercises for children 7 to 8 years of age experiencing anxiety. Each of six sessions emphasized a single sensory modality (i.e., kinesthetic, taste, sight, sound, smell, or touch). Based on the authors' assumption that children's attentional capacities are shorter than adults, sitting breathing meditation exercises were limited to 3 minutes each (and each session began and ended with this brief form of practice). Because this protocol was geared toward children experienc-ing anxiety (associated with significant levels of distress and functional impairment), Semple and colleagues' intervention also involved each child recording his or her most pressing worry on a piece of paper and throwing this paper in a "Worry Warts Wastebasket" (as a side note, when using a technique such as this, it is important to emphasize to participants that the exercise is in the service of getting some distance between them and their worries, not throwing their worries away).

Wall (2005) also incorporated elements of MBSR (and tai chi) in a 5-week educational program for middle school students. Elements described in this protocol said to be drawn from MBSR include a lying-down breath-ing meditation (based on Benson's [1975, as cited in Wall, 2005] relaxation response), the use of Zen koans (i.e., short, nonlinear stories or questions), sitting meditation with a bell, and mindful eating. Wall's use of a mindful eating exercise, in this case of an apple, incorporated both sensory ele-ments (i.e., guiding the students in smelling the apple, hearing its crunch, and noticing its textures) and those that were designed to highlight a sense of interconnectedness. For the latter, participants were instructed to con-sider all of the "non-apple" elements that went into producing the apple (e.g., sunlight, rain, and workers' labor) and to hold these in their minds as they went about eating the apple; similarly, the instructor noted that his interactions with the students involve all those who taught him, from elementary school through college and beyond.

Several additional mindfulness-based treatment approaches deserve note. Although not necessarily comprehensive packages that attempt to facilitate a mindful stance toward all experience (as MBSR and MBCT do), several research groups have developed treatment approaches for specific populations of children and adolescents. Singh et al. (2007) utilized a single-component mindfulness intervention deemed *Meditation on the Soles of the Feet*. This approach encouraged adolescents with conduct disorder to bring full awareness to their experiences of anger. After doing so, participants were instructed to shift the focus of their attention from anger to sensations present in their feet and, in practice sessions, to maintain focus on the latter for 10–15 minutes. Similarly, Harrison, Manocha, and Rubia (2004) presented a meditation-based family treatment approach for children with attention deficit/hyperactivity disorder (ADHD) specifically based on Sahaja yoga meditation (SYM). The SYM-based program utilized twice-weekly sessions over a 6-week period as well as parent-led home practice. However, the extent to which the state of "thoughtless awareness" that SYM attempts to facilitate is consistent with mindfulness (versus more of a one-pointed focused attention, similar to Transcendental Meditation practices) is unclear.

Dialectical Behavior Therapy

Dialectical behavior therapy (DBT) is an empirically supported and theoretically grounded psychological treatment created by Linehan (1993a, 1993b) to treat individuals who meet diagnostic criteria for borderline personality disorder (Katz & Cox, 2002). The framework of DBT is based on Linehan's (1993a) biosocial theory and the idea that reality is "continuous, dynamic and holistic" (Miller, Rathus, & Linehan, 2007, p. 39). In short, Linehan's biosocial theory attributes the client's emotional, behavioral, and cognitive dysregulation to a transactional process between an "emotionally vulnerable" individual and an "invalidating environment" (Woodberry, Miller, Glinski, Indik, & Mitchell, 2002).

DBT typically consists of at least a one-year commitment and requires clients to participate in group and individual therapy in tandem (Linehan, 1993b). Group treatment consists of four psychosocial skills modules. These modules target the development of core mindfulness skills, interpersonal effectiveness skills, emotion regulation skills, and distress tolerance skills

(Linehan, 1993b). Mindfulness skills are taught in two or three sessions and then integrated into the beginning of each of the other three modules. (Linehan, 1993b). Each of the other three modules lasts for 8 weeks, and, in institutions that conduct DBT "by the book," each module is run twice during the course of the year. The client's individual therapist should be using the skills taught in group to help the client develop solutions to the problems he or she may be dealing with. Within the DBT model, it is the responsibility of the individual therapist to address suicidal crises and other life- and therapy-interfering behaviors (Linehan, 1993b).

Based on Linehan's (1993a, 1993b) biosocial theory and the adult version of DBT, several researchers have developed modified versions of DBT to use with adolescent populations. One modified version of DBT is DBT-A, which was created by Miller, Rathus, Linehan, Wetzler, and Leigh (1997) for use with adolescents.

DBT-A differs from DBT in a number of ways. For example, the first phase of DBT (typically a year in the adult version) has been shortened to 12 weeks (Miller & Glinski, 2000). The adolescent version also differs in that parent skills training groups have been added. Although the adult version uses a therapist-to-client consultation model, environmental interventions with younger populations have been recommended because of minors' limited power over their environments (Miller & Glinski, 2000; Miller, Glinski, Woodberry, Mitchell, & Indik, 2002). Other modifications include having family members in individual therapy sessions when family issues seem paramount, simplifying language on skills handouts, and offering 12- to 24-week follow-up to those clients who graduate from the initial 12-week program (Miller et al., 2000). Similar to that in DBT targeting adults, the skills training in DBT-A includes mindfulness skills to help in the identification of emotion dysregulation, distress tolerance skills to help stabilize a sense of self, interpersonal skills to remedy social deficits, and emotion regulation skills to help effectively regulate mood (Katz & Cox, 2002).

Not all clinicians working with suicidal adolescents use the DBT-A model. Indeed, other researchers have modified DBT in different ways. In their own version of DBT, Turner, Barnett, and Korslund (1998) made the skills training lessons more concrete, used more action-oriented than dialectical thinking strategies, conducted skills training with the individual clients and/or their families as opposed to in groups, added family treatment, and shortened the length of treatment. These researchers found that their version of DBT was a viable option for minority, inner-city adolescents (Turner et al., 1998).

Acceptance and Commitment Therapy

Acceptance and commitment therapy (ACT) is a psychological treatment that uses mindfulness-based methods along with behavior change strategies to improve clients' quality of life. Consistent with other "third-wave" cognitive-behavioral therapies (Hayes, 2004), ACT's focus is on changing individuals' relationship to their thoughts and feelings, versus attempting to change the content of these private experiences themselves, as more traditional (i.e., "second-wave") cognitive-behavioral approaches emphasize. Mindfulness practices such as those described in the sections on MBSR and MBCT are but one set of experiences that are used in ACT in the service of helping clients to relate differently with their ongoing private experiences. An overriding goal of this treatment approach is to help individuals clarify what matters most to them and to take action in accordance with these personal values. Key to being able to do so is the development of psychological flexibility. *Psychological flexibility* has been defined in the literature as "contacting the present moment as a conscious human being, and, based on what that situation affords, acting in accordance with one's chosen values" (Hayes et al., 2004, p. 5).

It is also important to note that ACT is grounded in a comprehensive behavioral account of human language and cognition, relational frame theory (RFT; Hayes, Barnes-Holmes, & Roche, 2001). RFT holds that although our capacity for language has been pivotal in allowing us to rise above challenges faced by many other species (e.g., keeping warm, and attaining food and other items necessary for survival), basic language processes (e.g., those that allow us to reflect on the past, imagine a future, and compare ourselves to others) are also at the core of human suffering. A research base is developing in support of the main tenets of this theory, and conversations are also ongoing about the application of RFT principles within and outside of psychotherapy (Hayes et al., 2001).

ACT protocols have been developed and tested with adults who comprise various clinical and nonclinical populations (for reviews, see Hayes, Luoma, Bond, Masuda, & Lillis, 2006; Hayes, Masuda, Bissett, Luoma, & Guerrero, 2004). Very recent attempts have also been made to integrate acceptance and mindfulness-based therapeutic techniques into already existing psychosocial treatments for child and adolescent problematic behavior. For example, Greco, Blackledge, Coyne, and Ehrenreich (2005) reviewed ACT-based strategies for children and adolescents who exhibit anxious behavior. Murrell, Coyne, and Wilson (2004) discussed the use of

ACT with children, adolescents, and their parents more generally. Because we will draw primarily from ACT in our assessment and case conceptualization section and in the case example at the end of the chapter, we save a more detailed discussion of this approach for these sections.

Assessment and Case Conceptualization

For several reasons, we will emphasize an ACT-based approach to assessment and case conceptualization. Because MBSR is not a therapeutic intervention per se, offers general skills (versus targeting a particular presenting problem, though the skills may certainly be used to do so), and is typically conducted in relatively large groups, little emphasis is placed on conceptualizing any particular "problem," and less so on what this looks like in any given individual. MBCT, although grounded in the psychological literature and incorporating elements of traditional cognitive therapy, is based on an understanding of the processes underlying depressive relapse and thus targets a specific population of individuals. In fact, the developers of MBCT (Teasdale, Segal, & Williams, 2003) suggested that advances in the field are much more likely to come about through the development of mindfulness-based interventions grounded in empirically supported, theory-driven models of given psychological disorders. Such disorder-specific case formulations may be helpful in providing a rationale for clients with the targeted diagnosis (e.g., depression) considering participation in MBCT; they may also be helpful in tailoring more general protocols to the needs of a given population. Although MBCT has more recently been applied to populations other than individuals with a history of depression (e.g., Baer, Fischer, & Huss, 2005; Semple et al., 2005), the bulk of evidence in support of this intervention has been gleaned for depression. Thus, the applicability of the underlying model is more limited. Furthermore, because MBCT is almost always conducted as a group intervention, less emphasis is placed on using this model to shed light on any one client's presenting problems.

Various researchers and clinicians in recent years have attempted to extend DBT's applicability into clinical populations beyond borderline personality disorder (BPD; e.g., Goldstein, Axelson, Birmaher, & Brent, 2007; Nelson-Gray et al., 2005). However, most of the development and refinement of this intervention approach (and the model of psychopathology underlying it) have taken place with those individuals meeting criteria for BPD (or, in the case of DBT-A, in adolescents exhibiting self-harm and other behaviors consistent with a BPD diagnosis), and thus this model remains less generally applicable as well.

ACT, on the other hand, has been applied more universally as an intervention to reduce "human suffering." The underlying model upon which ACT is based (i.e., RFT; Hayes et al., 2001) draws on the basic properties of human language and cognition, and thus is much more broadly applicable. Because ACT has often been applied in an individual psychotherapy context, and because it is grounded in basic behavioral theory (i.e., "first-wave" CBT; Hayes, 2004), which values functional analyses of behavior, more effort seems to have gone into describing how the general ACT model may be used to inform idiographic case conceptualizations. Thus, although in later sections we will discuss ways that tools from MBSR, MBCT, and DBT may be used to facilitate a mindful stance and/or the psychological flexibility that ACT generally espouses, we rely heavily on the ACT literature (e.g., Hayes, Strosahl, Luoma, Varra, & Wilson, 2004; Murrell et al., 2004) in discussing case conceptualization and assessment.

From an ACT perspective, it is critical to assess the functional impact of the behaviors that are bringing the child into psychotherapy or to the attention of the school psychologist. In particular, the main factors to pay attention to are the degree of experiential avoidance (i.e., unwillingness to experience particular thoughts, bodily sensations, memories, etc.; Hayes, Wilson, Gifford, Follette, & Strosahl, 1996) inherent in a given behavioral pattern as well as the ways that valued life outcomes are restricted as a function of such attempts at avoidance (Murrell et al., 2004).

Specifically, Murrell et al. (2004) indicated that case conceptualization with children from an ACT perspective focuses on seven key components. Although we discuss these in turn, for the most part, the order in which each of these areas is assessed is not critical, as long as all relevant information is gathered. First, one needs to assess the form, frequency, and intensity of the problematic behavior(s). This may be done, in part, through the use of standardized interviews (e.g., the Anxiety Disorders Interview Schedule for Children—Parent Version; Silverman & Eisen, 1992) and/or rating scales (e.g., the Children's Depression Inventory; Kovacs, 1980; the Kids' Eating Disorders Survey; Childress, Brewerton, Hodges, & Jarrell, 1993) for particular types of problems or disorders. However, it is generally advisable to utilize a "broad-band" (Barkley, 1997) rating scale that assesses the major dimensions of child psychopathology (e.g., depression, anxiety, aggression, and hyperactive-impulsive behavior) as a starting point. Examples of such rating scales include the Child Behavior Checklist (CBCL; Achenbach, 1991) and the Behavioral Assessment System for

Children (BASC; Reynolds & Kamphaus, 1994); both have parent and teacher versions (as well as a self-report version for youth 11 years and older in the case of the CBCL "family" of instruments) and satisfactory norms (Barkley, 1997).

Next, the situational triggers (both internal private experiences and external events) for problematic behaviors should be determined. Is Jesse's avoidance of social situations precipitated by critical comments made by his mother? By self-critical thoughts that he experiences when faced with challenging homework assignments? Especially with children, it is important to assess behavior across multiple situations and contexts (e.g., at home, in various classes at school, with extended family members, and during extracurricular activities) to get a clear and comprehensive picture of the problem behaviors and their triggers.

It is also critical to identify the particular distressing thoughts, feelings, memories, sensations, or events that the problematic behavior pattern is helping the child to avoid. For example, perhaps Tasha turns to alcohol each time that she recalls an instance of her uncle molesting her, or each time that she experiences sensations in particular regions of her body. Furthermore, she may have a particularly hard time "sitting with" thoughts that suggest that she may have played a role in her uncle's choosing to victimize both her and her younger cousin; each time such a thought arises, Tasha quickly tries to distract herself or otherwise avoid the cognitive activity.

The next step specified by Murrell et al. (2004) involves taking a closer look at the specific experiential avoidance strategies used to control or manage painful psychological events. Alcohol or other substance use, overeating, and suicidal or self-harming behavior are all examples of behaviorally focused emotional control strategies (Hayes et al., 2004); examples of internally based emotional control strategies offered by Hayes and colleagues include distraction, self-instruction, excessive self-monitoring, and dissociation.

Experiential avoidance strategies typically work—at least in the short term. Another step in the case conceptualization process discussed by Murrell et al. (2004) is identifying the short-term reinforcers for the control and avoidance strategies utilized. For example, smoking cigarettes might immediately allow an adolescent to feel less anxious; avoiding gym class might immediately bring relief to a young child who is teased about his weight and athletic abilities in that context.

From an ACT perspective, it is essential to assess the child's valued directions in domains such as school, recreation, family, and friendships.

Because not every child will understand the meaning of the word *values*, therapists might instead opt to inquire about what and who are most important to him or her. Similarly, Murrell and colleagues (2004) noted that introduction of the idea of "vitality" may be useful in this process. These authors present a transcript of a group session involving a discussion of valuing with children ages 7 to 10. After asking the children to draw pictures of or write down the important things that our hearts do, the therapist noted that our hearts are "vital"; they are very important, and they keep us alive by pumping our blood. The therapist then shows the children a heart-shaped box and says,

> But this kind of heart is different. It keeps you alive in a different way. This kind of heart is about the things that are really important to you. They are not important for keeping your body alive, but they are really important for having and keeping special stuff in your life. This stuff is the people, things, and ideas that you really want in your life because you care about them a lot. These are called your values ... the things that we do that bring us close to our values are vital. (Murrell et al., 2004, p. 255)

The Valued Living Questionnaire (VLQ: Wilson & Groom, 2002, as cited in Murrell et al., 2004) and its recent modifications for children, adolescents, and their parents (Greco, 2002) may also be helpful in determining what is most important to these individuals, as well as how consistently they are acting in accordance with these values. Murrell et al. (2004) highlighted the potential (especially with younger children) of using more concrete strategies. For example, a clinician might indicate that "living exactly as your values and your heart would tell you how to live" (p. 256) is at the center of a target and ask the child to place a Velcro-covered ball somewhere around this target to assess how closely the child feels he or she is living in accordance with what matters most.

Finally, after exploring children's valued directions, clinicians working from an ACT perspective will want to assess the extent to which problematic behaviors are interfering with any or all of these desired life outcomes. Essentially, although avoidance strategies may have short-term benefits, it is important to determine how, in the longer term, such efforts at avoidance only compound suffering by reducing the vitality in the lives of children and their families.

Assessment of ACT-relevant processes may also be aided by a recently developed measure, the Willingness and Action Measure for Children and Adolescents (WAM-C/A; Greco, Murrell, & Coyne, 2004, as cited in Greco et al., 2005). The WAM-C/A is a 50-item instrument that assesses willingness to experience private events, values-oriented action, and cognitive fusion (i.e., "the treatment of thoughts as though they are what our minds say they are"; Gardner & Moore, 2007, p. 90); the measure's psychometric properties are currently being assessed in community and clinic samples (Greco et al., 2005). It seems that increased attention should be paid to the development and validation of such standardized, developmentally appropriate assessment instruments for children and adolescents.

Treatment Implications

Pointing out the essential "unworkability" of control strategies (when considered from the perspective of what matters most and not just "feeling better" in the short term) may serve to heighten a sense of what ACT proponents call "creative hopelessness" (i.e., a felt sense of the unworkability of a control or change agenda) and a willingness to try to do things differently. In particular, children and their families may then be more open to the idea that "control is the problem" and willing to take steps toward both changing their relationship to their private experiences (being more accepting of these and experiencing them from a more defused stance) and taking action in line with their values with or without these thoughts, feelings, and so on "on board." Please see the case example below for further discussion of these and other components of ACT and ways to make such components more understandable and relevant for children, adolescents, and their families.

Application to School Settings

As beautifully articulated in Peter Matthiessen's piece that opened this chapter, the main goal of mindfulness and acceptance-based approaches is to either maintain or reinstate the "child's clear mind," allowing for more instances of "paying attention: on purpose, in the present moment, and nonjudgmentally" (Kabat-Zinn, 1994, p. 4). ACT takes this a step further and says that developing such "mindfulness" or "experientially accepting" skills is often in the service of increasing values-consistent action. However, ACT also recognizes the power (or perhaps value) of present-moment experiencing for its own sake, leading to the statement that "values are the process through which process becomes the outcome" (Hayes et al., 1999, p. 219).

In any case, in school settings, there are many ways that the development of such present-moment experiencing might be fostered. As suggested by the case conceptualization section, an ACT-based model might be utilized to guide a school psychologist's work with an individual student. Such an approach will be illustrated in the case example toward the end of this chapter. It is also possible that ACT-consistent skills might be developed in more of a group context, perhaps targeting a small group of students who are struggling with similar sets of problems (e.g., avoidance of social interaction because of [fusion with] fears of evaluation). Similarly, DBT might be employed, in both individual and skills training contexts, within a school setting, although careful attention would need to be paid to making clear who the appropriate contact person(s) is (or are), for example in the case of a need for phone consultation between sessions (most likely the school psychologist seeing the student individually, but this might vary from school to school).

In an earlier section, we briefly reviewed several examples of MBSR- or MBCT-based approaches that have been conducted in school settings. These were conducted in small groups with children identified by school personnel, either because of a specific presenting problem (in the case of Semple et al., 2005) or because of a lack of serious emotional problems (in Wall, 2005). These studies certainly provide preliminary support for the viability of carrying out such interventions on school grounds; Semple and colleagues also highlight the cost-effectiveness of conducting mindfulness-based interventions in this context (in groups in schools) as opposed to providing individual clinic-based services.

Mindfulness-based approaches might also be incorporated into school settings more generally. Although ACT- and DBT-based work incorporate mindfulness practice (ACT as one of several tools to build cognitive defusion skills, and DBT as the foundation for skills training in emotion regulation, distress tolerance, and interpersonal effectiveness), some of the protocols that emphasize mindfulness practice, especially MBSR, nicely lend themselves to implementation on a broader scale in school settings. In this way, MBSR and related protocols might be seen as examples of emotional education curricula, similar to the ways that REBT-based approaches (see Vernon, this volume, for a review) and work based on emotional intelligence (e.g., Brackett et al., in press) have recently been transported into the classroom and other parts of the school building. Such approaches might be seen as helping students address any existing psychological difficulties they have, building skills to assist them in coping with life's challenges to come, and allowing them to live more fully in the present moment and enjoy the process.

Mindfulness practices might be incorporated into school curricula in a number of ways. First, it is possible that health education classes might be utilized to implement an MBSR protocol. Although the shorter "session" time would have to be taken into account, it seems that this could easily be balanced out with a greater number (than eight; perhaps three times as many, based on a typical class session of 45 minutes) of class meetings. Rather than thinking about this option as cutting into the time that health teachers have to address other topics (e.g., substance use and the characteristics of healthy relationships), it seems that MBSR could easily incorporate discussion of all such "healthy lifestyle" issues. Alternatively, or perhaps related, covering the MBSR curriculum early on in an academic year (and perhaps then beginning each subsequent class session with a brief practice) would nicely "set the scene" for more detailed coverage of these other topics. Students could be encouraged to draw upon practices and skills learned in MBSR training (e.g., "Three-Minute Breathing Space") when considering and making challenging choices related to these other topics in their daily lives.

Incorporating MBSR into the health curriculum clearly requires that health teachers be trained in (and receptive toward) this approach. Furthermore, Wall (2005) recommended that teachers and facilitators of such approaches have a "working command" of the skills involved: "a working command means that the facilitator personally practices these skills daily with an intention to see and experience life directly" (p. 236).

If existing health education teachers are not willing to take on such a personal practice or are otherwise unable or unwilling to "embody" the skills taught in MBSR; if, for other reasons, the health curriculum does not allow for such training; or if, for some reason, MBSR cannot be offered to the entire student body, the MBSR protocol might be shared with interested students as an after-school offering or as part of a summer enrichment program.

In the event that the entire MBSR protocol cannot or will not be offered along any of the lines suggested above, mindfulness-based practices may still be incorporated into the school day. Perhaps after a longer training (e.g., a full- or half-day retreat that allows for a fuller introduction to the spirit and rationale behind mindfulness training, along with some longer practice sessions), the simplest way for this to happen is for classroom teachers or other school personnel to be equipped to lead the class in brief practices, potentially at the beginning of each day or class period. Teachers who themselves regularly practice taking a "mindful stance" toward experiences as they arise will also be in a position (in addition to potentially being more patient and otherwise wise in their interactions with students) to seize "teachable moments" (Vernon, chapter 6, this volume). For example, after a physical or verbal altercation between students, those involved might be encouraged to sit with the particular thoughts, bodily sensations, and other aspects of emotions that are arising, and also to notice that they can fully experience emotions (e.g., anger), while still choosing to take action in line with their values. As teachers learn to incorporate more of the approach into their classroom practices, they might benefit from the opportunity to talk through and/or walk through (in vivo) case examples with the school psychologist and/or child study team.

In whatever ways MBSR and/or related mindfulness practices are brought into the school setting, a few issues become important to consider; many of these are not unique to mindfulness-based practices but instead hold for the incorporation of any kind of "emotional education" or similar curriculum. First, it is imperative that everyone involved, directly or indirectly, is as "on board" as possible. Ideally, all levels of educational personnel (from the Board of Education to administrators to child study team members to teachers to teachers' aides) would have the opportunity to be exposed to mindfulness-based practices, to express any reservations they might have about the approach, and to have their questions addressed. Similarly, for any mindfulness-based training to have its full impact, parents of students need to be informed, and perhaps even themselves offered the opportunity to at least get a "taste" of mindfulness, maybe through an evening or weekend workshop. Potential concerns that might arise and would need to be addressed include the overlap and/or consistency between mindfulness-based interventions and various religious beliefs or practices (although mindfulness practice has its roots in Buddhism and other spiritual traditions, the ways in which it is being implemented and studied are not tied to any particular religion; this is clearly a complicated issue, however); the frustrations that many have in attempting to practice mindfulness, given how prone we are to acting "mindlessly" (student participants, school personnel, and parents alike should be reminded that it is challenging to develop such skills, even those that tend to come naturally in children earlier on, and of the importance of bringing compassion to these experiences); and the reactivity that comes anytime such a program is made mandatory (giving voice to this concern from the beginning might be valuable).

Evidence Base for Mindfulness and Acceptance-Based Behavioral Approaches with Children

As mentioned previously, the development and evaluation of mindfulness and acceptance-based behavioral interventions specifically for children and adolescents have barely begun. In our brief review of the evidence base here, we focus on presenting results from the few studies that have implemented such methods. In addition to describing study results, we also present more general conclusions offered by the researchers, where applicable. Finally, we briefly evaluate the status of this evidence base and indicate what we consider to be key directions for future research.

Mindfulness-Based Stress Reduction and Mindfulness-Based Cognitive Therapy

As reviewed above, Semple and colleagues (2005) developed an intervention based on MBSR and MBCT tailored for children (7 to 8 years of age) with clinically significant levels of anxiety. Interestingly, contradicting teachers' reports and the authors' clinical observations, participants themselves reported low levels of anxiety at baseline (the authors note that this may be related to the fact that anxiety measures were geared toward older children and may not have been developmentally appropriate for younger participants). In any case, by the end of the 6-week program, teachers of these children reported improvements in academic functioning or reductions in symptom scales for four of the five children. Furthermore, four of the five participants demonstrated enthusiasm for and interest in mindfulness practice and requested that the program continue. The question "How much did I like class today?" was given an overall average rating of 4.13 on a 5-point scale. Semple et al. also presented detailed clinical observations of all five participants' progress through the intervention that would likely prove useful for those interested in implementing similar approaches.

The intervention described by Wall (2005) that incorporated MBSR-based practices with those based in tai chi was less formally evaluated. Wall reported that subjective statements made by middle school student participants suggested that they experienced well-being, relaxation, improved sleep, less reactivity, increased self-care, self-awareness, and a sense of interconnection or interdependence with nature. Future research along these lines should clearly attempt to operationally define and measure such important changes in the context of controlled empirical studies.

Utilizing a multiple baseline design, Singh and colleagues (2007) evaluated an intervention based on *Meditation on the Soles of the Feet* in adolescents with conduct disorder. Decreases in aggression were exhibited by all three participants, and these gains were maintained through the end of the school year (i.e., middle school graduation), which was notable given participants' initial risk for expulsion from school. Interestingly, improvements were not demonstrated over the course of the intervention for other maladaptive behaviors (e.g., noncompliance, and cruelty to animals) that participants had chosen not to address.

As mentioned above, the extent to which Sahaja yoga meditation is consistent with fostering a mindful stance toward experience is unclear. However, given the relative paucity of empirical research in this area, and the ways in which studies of related approaches might shed light on mechanisms of action, we briefly review the findings of Harrison et al. (2004). This approach was implemented in children with a wide range of ages (4–12 years of age) with ADHD. Changes in parent-reported ADHD behaviors, self-esteem, and relationship quality, as well as child-reported benefits at home (e.g., less anxiety, and better sleep patterns) and at school (increased abilities to concentrate, and less conflict), were described from pretreatment to post treatment. Parents additionally reported feeling happier and less stressed themselves, along with an increased perceived ability to manage their children's behavior. Children on a waiting list for the treatment provided a quasi-control group. However, it is also important to note that there was a fairly high dropout rate in this study (25–30%), which was likely related to the high demand placed on parents with regard to involvement in treatment (i.e., the protocol involved parent-led meditation practices at home).

Dialectical Behavior Therapy

Several versions of DBT tailored to adolescents have been empirically examined in various types of studies. A case study of a 16-year-old female exhibiting suicidal behaviors in an inpatient setting found that DBT-A was effective in reducing her maladaptive behaviors (Katz & Cox, 2002). Based on this case study and other work in this area, Katz and Cox suggested that at the core of the effectiveness of DBT is the clinician's comprehensive understanding of Linehan's (1993a) biosocial theory and acknowledgment that patients' maladaptive behaviors are due to their emotional dysregulation.

Another study done in an outpatient setting, with adolescents displaying features of BPD, compared a 12-week application of DBT group skills training with those receiving treatment as usual. These researchers found that those adolescents receiving DBT exhibited a lower rate of treatment dropout and fewer days of psychiatric inpatient care as compared with those in the control condition (Robins & Chapman, 2004). Although the fact that participants were assigned to groups based on symptomatology (e.g., suicidal behavior) versus random assignment limits the conclusions that can be drawn, this study suggests that DBT is a viable approach for adolescents with features of BPD.

In a study of 32 nonsuicidal outpatient young adolescents with oppositional defiant disorder (ODD), Nelson-Gray et al. (2005) found that a 16-week group DBT skills training program resulted in a reduction in negative behaviors (externalizing behaviors and ODD symptoms, as well as internalizing symptoms, including depression) as well as an increase in positive behaviors (caregivers' rating of interpersonal strength). Notably, this study also included various incentives for participation (e.g., pizza at the beginning of each session, and up to $10 weekly for completing homework assignments and participating appropriately in sessions) as well as ways to maximize attendance (e.g., the provision of taxi rides for those without other transportation). Although the lack of a control group and the potentially limited generalizability of results (based on incentives that these researchers were able to provide that might not be possible in other contexts) limit the conclusions we may draw from this study, Nelson-Gray and colleagues' work adds to the growing body of literature suggesting that DBT may be an effective approach for adolescents outside of those who meet criteria for BPD. A study conducted by Goldstein et al. (2007) similarly provides preliminary support for the use of DBT in adolescents with bipolar disorder.

Acceptance and Commitment Therapy

Empirical evidence in support of ACT with children and adolescents is currently quite limited. Several case studies suggest promise with an adolescent female with anorexia nervosa (Heffner, Sperry, Eifert, & Detweiler, 2002) and an adolescent female with chronic pain (Wicksell, Dahl, Magnusson, & Olsson, 2005). Furthermore, Wicksell and colleagues

(Wicksell, Melin, & Olsson, 2007) presented the results of a pilot study examining the efficacy of an ACT-based approach for 14 adolescents experiencing chronic pain. At posttreatment and 3- and 6-month follow-up assessments, improvements were seen in functional ability, school attendance, catastrophizing, and pain. Controlled research should continue to examine the viability of such an approach with this population.

A randomized controlled trial of a behavioral intervention that incorporated ACT-based methods in an attempt to reduce risky sexual behavior was conducted by Metzler, Biglan, Noell, Ary, and Ochs (2000). Those participants who received the individualized five-session treatment approach reported gains, including fewer sexual partners, fewer sexual contacts with strangers in the previous 3 months, and less use of marijuana before or during sex as compared with those in a treatment-as-usual control condition. It is important to note that this intervention targeted several processes unrelated to ACT (i.e., decision-making and social skills), and the extent to which outcomes were dependent on the ACT components (metaphors and other strategies to facilitate acceptance of unwanted thoughts and feelings) is unclear. The authors acknowledged that "further research is needed to distill out the essential elements of the intervention and put them into a format that would be cost-effective in an STD clinic setting" (p. 50). However, the possibility certainly exists that the ACT-based framework in which the other treatment components were conducted facilitated their acceptability and/or overall potency.

Final Comment on the Evidence Base

Although the studies reviewed above do suggest that these interventions have potential with young people with a variety of presenting problems, empirical research on mindfulness and acceptance-based behavioral approaches with children and adolescents is clearly still in its infancy. In addition to better controlled, more rigorous outcome studies, it is imperative that researchers attempt to shed light on the active ingredients of multicomponent treatment packages (including such parameters as optimal amounts of practice time for individuals of varying developmental levels and/or the moderators of such effects), as well as the mechanisms by which such components exert their effects. It is only through such thoughtful, theory-driven research that science will be advanced (Hayes & Wilson, 2003) and that we stand in the best position to offer our services to the young people with whom we work.

The Case of Todd

Before jumping into conceptualization and treatment of the presenting problems described in the case example, we would want to be sure that we are aware of all potentially problematic behavior that is occurring for Todd. Although this largely seems limited to anxiety-related signs and symptoms (including worry), and these appear to be most closely related to performance-based concerns, we would still want to look closely at the data from general behavioral rating scales, as well as those more specifically targeting internalizing symptoms, including depression and various types of anxiety. We also want to keep in mind that assessment is an ongoing process; as we develop our conceptualization and begin to implement a treatment plan based on this, we are open to new pieces of information and new ways of thinking about Todd's experiences.

In accordance with the ACT model of case conceptualization presented above (Murrell et al., 2004), in order to gain a sense of the function that Todd's problematic behaviors serve, we need to first assess the situational triggers for these behaviors. We might learn, for example, that Todd's anxiety seems most intense on the nights when he has the most math homework, and that math has always been the subject with which he has struggled the most. Or perhaps we find out that Todd's mother started dating someone new approximately 3 months ago, and that his anxious behaviors (e.g., spending an especially long time on his schoolwork, and increased worry and irritability) appear to be heightened on the nights before and after his mother goes out with this man.

Related, because there is a high likelihood that Todd's problematic behaviors are forms of experiential avoidance, we need to get more detailed information about the specific distressing thoughts, feelings, memories, bodily sensations, or events that Todd's problematic behavior is helping him escape or avoid. We might find that thoughts such as "Having trouble with my math homework means that I am a failure," or "If I don't do well in school, then Mom and Grandma will be so ashamed," or "If Mom and this guy get really serious, then she'll never have enough time for me" are particularly unacceptable to Todd. He might be especially unwilling to experience the bodily sensations of an accelerated heart rate and butterflies in his stomach, along with memories of past exams when he did not know the answer to more than one or two questions. Greco and colleagues (2005) noted that distinctions between "internal" and "external" events and among thoughts, sensations, and memories (often useful in working from an ACT perspective) may be made through the use of visual aids or diagrams. For example, Todd might be asked to think about "everything you have been struggling with" and then given a full-size sketch of a person. He would then be helped to write painful thoughts near the person's head and painful emotions near his heart; unwanted sensations could be indicated near those parts of the body in which they are experienced. External events and/or overt behaviors with which Todd is struggling could be recorded outside of the boundaries of the sketched body (Greco et al., 2005).

With regard to specific experiential avoidance or control strategies, we already know that Todd is spending an inordinate amount of time on his homework assignments. It is essential to understand, however, other ways in which Todd might be attempting to avoid or control his private experiences (thoughts, feelings, sensations, etc.), during and outside of the time that he spends "working." For example, when Todd experiences the above-mentioned cognitions, does he attempt to engage in distraction or suppression of these thoughts? Does he repeatedly tell himself that he should not care as much about his schoolwork or feel the way he does about Mom's new boyfriend? Has he engaged in any other problematic behaviors in an attempt to control the way he feels, such as over- or undereating, substance use, or excessive television watching or video game playing? Although he likely doesn't have time for these activities during the week, we do not know what his weekends look like. Related, what does he do in his interactions with the school counselor that might serve an experientially avoidant function? For example, when the topic of Mom's beau comes up, does Todd change the subject or refuse to engage in the conversation? In addition to all of the information gathering inherent in the above questions, such in-session observations will likely be invaluable in further elucidating the function of such problematic behaviors.

We next want to focus our attention on the short-term reinforcers that likely maintain Todd's attempts at control and avoidance of his emotional experiences. If Todd is engaging in distraction when uncomfortable thoughts and sensations arise, he may experience a temporary reduction in anxiety, immediately negatively reinforcing such behavior. Todd's current method of completing his homework assignments has also elicited a lot of attention from his mother and grandmother, his teacher, and other school personnel. It is possible that this attention, even if at times tense or negatively charged (especially in a child who fears not being the center of attention of his immediate family members), is also serving to reinforce Todd's behavior.

Perhaps most important to our work with Todd is gaining an understanding of his values, or what matters the most to him. We might, in so doing, talk in terms of "vitality" (Murrell et al., 2004), as described in the session transcript in the case conceptualization section above. Todd might also be asked to think about the times when he has felt most alive and/or to share information about the people and things that he cares the most about. Our guess is that Todd values his relationships with his mother and grandmother a great deal. In this domain, we would want to learn more about the type of son or grandson that Todd would most like to be. In our values assessment, we might also learn that Todd values having several close friendships with other children who like to do the same things he does. He might value engaging in activities such as biking and playing Frisbee, those that allow him to both engage in physical movement and spend time in nature. Todd might also value participating in activities such as sculpting and cooking that allow him to express his creativity and take some risks as he tries new art media or new recipes.

In conducting a values assessment with Todd, it is important to keep a few things in mind. First, because it seems as if Todd spends so much of his time and energy trying to avoid or control parts of his experience, he may be out of contact with what he cares about and the things he enjoys doing (Murrell et al., 2004). He may need to be prompted to think back to the things he enjoyed in previous years; showing him a pleasant events schedule or similar listing of activities might also be helpful in reminding Todd of the kinds of things that he enjoys and/ or that matter the most to him. Todd might be asked to consider the aspects of various activities he seems interested in that are particularly appealing to him; this might also help to derive a sense of his valued directions. It is also extremely important to sidestep talk about whether a valued outcome is realistic or not (Murrell et al., 2004). It should be emphasized to Todd that although we are often not in complete control of outcomes, we do control the direction in which we move our feet; values are the directions in which we walk. Finally, especially given what we know about his desire to please, it is critical to be vigilant for signs that Todd is endorsing values that are not really his own, but instead that reflect what he thinks his mother, grandmother, teacher, or others want him to care about.

Finally, we need to get a clear picture of how Todd's problematic behaviors are interfering with his taking values-consistent action. Given how much time Todd is spending on his homework, at least during the school week, it is readily apparent that he is *not* engaging in values-consistent action much of the time. Although some time spent on schoolwork is probably essential (and may even be consistent with values related to learning new things or engaging in creative problem solving), based on feedback from Todd's teacher, it is clear that he could be using more of his after-school time to engage in activities that he enjoys. It sounds like Todd's teacher typically does not assign homework over the weekends; this is other time that needs to be further assessed. What happens on Saturday and Sunday when Todd could be riding his bike to the park with friends or trying a new recipe with his grandmother? Is he too busy worrying about how much work he will need to do in the upcoming week? Is he so focused on berating himself for not wanting his mother to spend time with her boyfriend (or actually trying to prevent that from happening) that he is missing valuable opportunities to interact with her?

Based on the results of this case conceptualization process, we will be in a position to develop treatment goals for Todd. Our primary ACT-based goals for work with Todd include helping him to recognize that the ways he has been trying to control his experiences are not working; to increase his willingness to experience the sometimes painful events from which he has been running; and to engage in values-directed behavior even with these thoughts, feelings, sensations, and so on "on board." Before beginning to work toward these goals, we will want to consider how best to orient Todd and others involved in his treatment to this perspective. As a side note, it is important to recognize that although parent and teacher consultations are part of the mental health services granted to Todd, it may, in practice, be difficult to have much face-to-face contact with Todd's family members. Although it may be challenging to work in person with Todd's mother and/or grandmother around the constraints of the school day (especially in light of all of the additional demands on school psychologists' or counselors' time), meaningful contact that reinforces the messages that Todd is getting through counseling may be made via phone calls and/or other forms of communication (e.g., e-mail).

Informed consent is an important part of ACT because it is an exposure-based treatment and, as should already be clear, is emotionally demanding, requiring a willingness to explore and experience painful thoughts, memories, and situations (Murrell et al., 2004). As such, it should be explained to Todd that the work that he will do in therapy is going to be hard and that he will almost surely "fall" and have to "get back up" again (Murrell et al., p. 264). It should also be explained to Todd's mother and grandmother that they will likely not see instant improvements in Todd's behavior; this is important in guarding against possible discouragement and subsequent early treatment dropout. Some mindfulness and related work might also be done with Todd's family members (and perhaps his teacher) so that they become more open to their own discomfort in seeing Todd struggle and do not inadvertently send inconsistent messages to him about the acceptability (or lack thereof) of particular private experiences.

The "Mud in the Glass" metaphor illustrates the often painful treatment process (Murrell et al., 2004). Todd might be given a glass of muddy water that has been allowed to settle. He could then be told that his life is similar to the glass and that this therapy is about getting the glass clean (i.e., getting the mud out of the glass). Todd will soon realize that this task cannot be achieved without getting the water dirty. The purpose of this metaphor is to help Todd recognize that making the water muddy might be worth it (especially when this is framed in terms of building a life consistent with his values, not necessarily one that is free of pain). This exercise should also help to validate that it is hard to experience the pain of "cleaning the glass" and emphasize that the counseling and his mother's, grandmother's, and teacher's involvement are all in the spirit of helping him to scoop the mud out.

As may already be apparent, much of ACT work with children involves finding ways to make metaphors more concrete in order to impart treatment messages. In order to help Todd to recognize that the ways he has been trying to control his experiences have not been working (i.e., developing a sense of creative hopelessness and highlighting that "control is the problem"), such paradoxes may be highlighted concretely through the use of Chinese handcuffs. The objective of bringing this toy into session is to illustrate that attempting to get out of the trap through doing the logical and obvious thing (i.e., pulling hard) only creates additional tension and perpetuates the struggle. In contrast, pushing the fingers in, rather than out, creates more space to move, perhaps allowing for something new to occur (Greco et al., 2005). In this way, Todd might be more open to letting go of some of his unworkable control strategies and might be more willing to at least look more closely at that with which he has been struggling.

Our next target is to attempt to increase Todd's willingness to experience the sometimes painful events from which he has been running. Part of this process will involve helping Todd to develop a sense of "self-as-context," as distinct from the content (i.e., thoughts, feelings, sensations, and memories) with which he has been struggling. This may be done through various forms of mindfulness practice (e.g., a sitting or lying down meditation or a walking meditation, perhaps taught in the context of his health education class or individually in his counseling sessions) that entail Todd focusing on a particular stimulus (e.g., the breath or awareness of sounds), noticing each time that his mind wanders (noting whatever thoughts and feelings are present at the time), and gently bringing his attention back to the particular chosen anchor over and over again. Over time, Todd will likely become increasingly aware of the transient nature of his thoughts and feelings. The Chessboard metaphor (e.g., Twohig, Masuda, Varra, & Hayes, 2005), in which Todd would be encouraged to look at his feelings and thoughts as "chess pieces" and not the board itself, might convey a similar message or experience. Hopefully, with time and practice, Todd will have developed more of a "safe place" from which he might choose to experience even previously feared or disliked private experiences.

It will also be important to highlight the distinction between willingness and wanting. We can very much not want to experience something and still be willing to have it. For example, Todd might be asked if he goes to the dentist regularly. If so, and if he readily admits that he does not love going to the dentist, we might point out that just because we do not want to go to the dentist, most people are typically willing to show up at the dentist's office once or twice per year in the service of taking care of their teeth or their health more generally. Todd might also be presented with the metaphor of *Joe, the Annoying Classmate* (based on *Joe the Bum* [Hayes et al., 1999] and *Joe the Annoying Neighbor* [Orsillo, Roemer, Block-Lerner, LeJeune, and Herbert, 2004]). Todd would be asked to imagine that he decided to invite all of his classmates to his 11th birthday party. Everyone is having a wonderful time at the party, until Joe, the last person you expected to come, shows up. You have always found Joe to be annoying; he only talks about himself and is always interrupting people. In this scenario, you have a choice: You can spend the entire party trying to get rid of Joe and making sure that he does not come back in, or you can welcome Joe to your house (even though you still hold a negative opinion of him) and go on with the business of enjoying the party.

Finally, Todd will be encouraged to make commitments to values-consistent behavior, even when such thoughts, feelings, or sensations arise. This can essentially be done through exposure exercises, for example, in which Todd is instructed to spend an hour on his homework and then to go out to play Frisbee with some other children before dinner (it seems that Todd's teacher would be supportive of this particular exercise, given her earlier attempts in a similar vein). As the hour comes to a close, Todd will likely experience all kinds of thoughts and feelings about how poorly his work will be received or about how his mother and grandmother will be so disappointed if he does not earn A's for this marking period. He will be encouraged to notice that he can experience these thoughts and feelings while still moving in the direction of getting his things together and going out to meet his friends. Similarly (assuming that he expresses developing open and honest relationships as a value), Todd might be encouraged to talk with his mother about his feelings related to her new boyfriend (versus just assuming that she knows how he feels) and to ask her to do something that they would both enjoy on a Saturday. Again, facing such a task would likely bring up uncomfortable thoughts and feelings that Todd could practice being willing to experience. Furthermore, Todd might practice his mindfulness skills while he and his mother work with clay together or bake a loaf of bread. Continually bringing his awareness back to the present-moment experience each time he notices that his mind has wandered (to judgments, evaluations, his to-do list, etc.) would likely heighten Todd's experience of the present moment and at least give him glimpses through those "clear eyes," with which he saw everything several years previously.

Conclusion

Mindfulness and acceptance-based behavioral approaches appear to offer a lot of promise in the alleviation of suffering faced by children and adolescents. Although these approaches have been developed and empirically examined in multiple adult populations in recent years, extant research with younger individuals, especially in school settings, is quite limited. We hope that our brief descriptions of several of these treatment packages, as well as their application in the case of Todd, will inspire some to learn more about these approaches, to implement them creatively, and perhaps even to be involved in research that will help us to best tailor these interventions for those with different presenting problems and at various developmental levels.

Recommended Readings

Both the Center for Mindfulness (http://www.umassmed.edu/cfm/mbsr/) and the Association for Contextual Science (http://www.contextualpsychology.org) offer valuable information about trainings and other resources in MBSR, ACT, and related approaches. The Web sites of Amy Saltzman, M.D. (http://www.foryourselfhealth.com/Dr__Amy.htm), and Wellness Works in Schools (http://www.wellnessworksinschools.com/) provide helpful information about incorporating mindfulness in school settings.

Those interested in learning more about any of the "third-wave" behavioral approaches more generally are referred to the three books by Hayes and colleagues. The first two are largely conceptual-empirical, whereas the third (Hayes & Smith, 2005) is a self-help version of ACT (although it also contains discussion of the rationale behind many of the approach's techniques). Finally, Kabat-Zinn (2005) is an excellent resource for those interested in learning more about mindfulness and its implications more generally.

Hayes, S. C., Follette, V., & Linehan, M. M. (2004). *Mindfulness and acceptance: Expanding the cognitive-behavioral tradition.* New York: Guilford.

Hayes, S. C., & Strosahl, K. D. (2004). *A practical guide to acceptance and commitment therapy.* New York: Springer.

Hayes, S. C., & Smith, S. (2005). *Get out of your mind and into your life: The new acceptance and commitment therapy.* Oakland, CA: New Harbinger.

Kabat-Zinn, J. (2005). *Coming to our senses: Healing ourselves and the world through mindfulness.* New York: Hyperion.

References

Achenbach, T. M. (1991). *Integrative guide for the 1991 CBCL/4-18, YSR, and TRF profiles.* Burlington: University of Vermont, Department of Psychiatry.

Baer, R. A. (2003). Mindfulness training as a clinical intervention: A conceptual and empirical review. *Clinical Psychology: Science & Practice, 10,* 125–143.

Baer, R. A., Fischer, S., & Huss, D. B. (2005). Mindfulness-based cognitive therapy applied to binge eating: A case study. *Cognitive and Behavioral Practice, 12,* 351–358.

Baer, R. A., Smith, G. T., & Allen, K. B. (2004). Assessment of mindfulness by self-report: The Kentucky Inventory of Mindfulness Skills. *Assessment, 11,* 191–206.

Baer, R. A., Smith, G. T., Hopkins, J., Krietemeyer, J., & Toney, L. (2006). Using self-report assessment methods to explore facets of mindfulness. *Assessment, 13*, 27–45.

Barkley, R. A. (1997). Attention-deficit/hyperactivity disorder. In E. J. Mash & L. G. Terdal (Eds.), *Assessment of childhood disorders* (pp. 71–129). New York: Guilford.

Block-Lerner, J., Plumb, J. C., & Orsillo, S. M. (2003, November). Facilitating an experientially accepting stance in the laboratory: Can we design manipulations to test mechanisms of change? Paper presented at the meeting of the Association for Advancement of Behavior Therapy, Boston.

Block-Lerner, J., & Wulfert, E. (Under review). (An) ACT in context: The history of acceptance and its potential value in treating social anxiety.

Childress, A. C., Brewerton, T. D., Hodges, E. L., & Jarrell, M. P. (1993). The Kids' Eating Disorders Survey (KEDS): A study of middle school students. *Journal of the American Academy of Child and Adolescent Psychiatry, 32*, 843–850.

Dimidjian, S., & Linehan, M. M. (2003). Defining an agenda for future research on the clinical application of mindfulness practice. *Clinical Psychology: Science & Practice, 10*, 166–171.

Gardner, F. L. & Moore, Z. E. (2007). *The psychology of enhancing human performance: The mindfulness-acceptance-commitment (MAC) approach.* New York: Springer.

Goldstein, T. R., Axelson, D. A., Birmaher, B., & Brent, D. A. (2007). Dialectical behavior therapy for adolescents with bipolar disorder: A 1-year open trial. *Journal of the American Academy of Child and Adolescent Psychiatry, 46*, 820–830.

Greco, L. A. (2002, November). Creating a context of acceptance in child clinical and pediatric settings. Paper presented at the annual meeting of the Association for the Advancement of Behavior Therapy, Reno, NV.

Greco, L. A., Blackledge, J. T., Coyne, L. W., & Ehrenreich, J. (2005). Integrating acceptance and mindfulness into treatments for child and adolescent anxiety disorders: Acceptance and commitment therapy as an example. In S. M. Orsillo & L. Roemer (Eds.), *Acceptance and mindfulness-based approaches to anxiety: Conceptualization and treatment* (pp. 301–322). New York: Plenum/Kluwer.

Grossman, P., Niemann, L., Schmidt, S., & Walach, H. (2004). Mindfulness-based stress reduction and health benefits: A meta-analysis. *Journal of Psychosomatic Research, 57*, 35–43.

Hannan, S. E., & Tolin, D. F. (2005). Acceptance and mindfulness-based behavior therapy for obsessive-compulsive disorder. In S. M. Orsillo & L. Roemer (Eds.), *Acceptance and mindfulness-based approaches to anxiety: Conceptualization and treatment.* (pp. 271–299). New York: Plenum/Kluwer.

Harrison, L. J., Manocha, R., & Rubia, K. (2004). Sahaja yoga meditation as a family treatment programme for children with attention deficit-hyperactivity disorder. *Clinical Child Psychology and Psychiatry, 9*, 479–497.

Hayes, S. C. (2004). Acceptance and commitment therapy and the new behavior therapies: Mindfulness, acceptance, and relationship. In S. C. Hayes, V. Follette, & M. M. Linehan (Eds.), *Mindfulness and acceptance: Expanding the cognitive-behavioral tradition* (pp. 1–29). New York: Guilford.

Hayes, S. C., Barnes-Holmes, D., & Roche, B. (Eds.). (2001). *Relational frame theory: A post-Skinnerian account of human language and cognition.* New York: Plenum.

Hayes, S. C., Luoma, J. B., Bond, F. W., Masuda, A., & Lillis, J. (2006). Acceptance and commitment therapy: Model, processes, and outcomes. *Behaviour Research and Therapy, 44,* 1–25.

Hayes, S. C., Masuda, A., Bissett, R., Luoma, J., & Guerrero, L. F. (2004). DBT, FAP, and ACT: How empirically oriented are the new behavior therapy technologies? *Behavior Therapy, 35,* 35–54.

Hayes, S. C., Strosahl, K. D., Bunting, K., Twohig, M., & Wilson, K. G. (2004). What is acceptance and commitment therapy? In S. C. Hayes & K. D. Strosahl (Eds.), *A practical guide to acceptance and commitment therapy.* (pp. 1–29). New York: Springer.

Hayes, S. C., Strosahl, K. D., Luoma, J., Varra, A. A., & Wilson, K. G. (2004). ACT case formulation. In S. C. Hayes & K. D. Strosahl (Eds.), *A practical guide to acceptance and commitment therapy* (pp. 59–73). New York: Springer.

Hayes, S. C., Strosahl, K. D., & Wilson, K. G. (1999). *Acceptance and commitment therapy: An experiential approach to behavior change.* New York: Guilford.

Hayes, S. C., & Wilson, K. G. (2003). Mindfulness: Method and process. *Clinical Psychology: Science & Practice, 10,* 161–165.

Hayes, S. C., Wilson, K. G., Gifford, E. V., Follette, V. M., & Strosahl, K. (1996). Experiential avoidance and behavioral disorders: A functional dimensional approach to diagnosis and treatment. *Journal of Consulting and Clinical Psychology, 64,* 1152–1168.

Heffner, M., Sperry, J., Eifert, G. H., & Detweiler, M. (2002). Acceptance and commitment therapy in the treatment of an adolescent female with anorexia nervosa: A case example. *Cognitive and Behavioral Practice, 9,* 232–236.

Kabat-Zinn, J. (1990). *Full catastrophe living: Using the wisdom of your body and mind to face stress, pain, and illness.* New York: Dell.

Kabat-Zinn, J. (1994). *Wherever you go there you are: Mindfulness meditation in everyday life.* New York: Hyperion.

Kabat-Zinn, J. (2005). *Coming to our senses: Healing ourselves and the world through mindfulness.* New York: Hyperion.

Katz, L. Y., & Cox, B. J. (2002). Dialectical behavior therapy for suicidal adolescent inpatients: A case study. *Clinical Case Studies, 1,* 81–92.

Kovacs, M. (1980). Rating scale to assess depression in school-aged children. *Acta Paediatrica, 46,* 305–315.

Linehan, M. M. (1993a). *Cognitive-behavioral treatment of borderline personality disorder.* New York: Guilford.

Linehan, M. M. (1993b). *Skills training manual for treating borderline personality disorder.* New York: Guilford.

Ma, S. H., & Teasdale, J. D. (2004). Mindfulness-based cognitive therapy for depression: Replication and exploration of differential relapse prevention effects. *Journal of Consulting and Clinical Psychology, 72*, 31–40.

Matthiessen, P. (1987). On becoming a seeker. In P. Matthiessen, *Nine-headed Dragon River: Zen journals 1969–1985* (p. xii). Boston: Shambhala.

Metzler, C. W., Biglan, A., Noell, J., Ary, D. V., & Ochs, L. (2000). A randomized controlled trial of a behavioral intervention to reduce high-risk sexual behavior among adolescents in STD clinics. *Behavior Therapy, 31*(1), 27–54.

Miller, A. L., & Glinski, J. (2000). Youth suicidal behavior: Assessment and intervention. *Journal of Clinical Psychology, 56*, 1131–1152.

Miller, A. L. Glinski, J., Woodberry, K. A., Mitchell, A. G., & Indik, J. (2002). Family therapy and dialectical behavior therapy with adolescents: Part I: Proposing a clinical synthesis. *American Journal of Psychotherapy, 56*, 568–584.

Miller, A. L., Rathus, J. H., & Linehan, M. M. (2007). *Dialectical behavior therapy with suicidal adolescents.* New York: Guilford.

Miller, A. L., Rathus, J. H., Linehan, M. M., Wetzler, S., & Leigh, E. (1997). Dialectical behavior therapy adapted for suicidal adolescents. *Journal of Practice Psychiatry and Behavioral Health, 3*, 78–86.

Murrell, A. R., Coyne, L. W., & Wilson, K. G. (2004). ACT with children, adolescents, and their parents. In S. C. Hayes & K. D. Strosahl (Eds.), *A practical guide to acceptance and commitment therapy* (pp. 249–273). New York: Springer.

Nelson-Gray, R. O., Keane, S. P., Hurst, R. M., Mitchell, J. T., Wartburn, J. B., Chok, J. T., et al. (2005). A modified DBT skills training program for oppositional defiant adolescents: Promising preliminary findings. *Behavior Research and Therapy, 44*, 1811–1820.

Orsillo, S. M., Roemer, L., Block-Lerner, J., LeJeune, C., & Herbert, J. D. (2004). ACT with anxiety disorders. In S. C. Hayes & K. Strosahl (Eds.), *A practical guide to acceptance and commitment therapy* (pp. 103–132). New York: Plenum/Kluwer.

Reynolds, C., & Kamphaus, R. (1994). *Behavioral assessment system for children.* Circle Pines, MN: American Guidance Service.

Robins, C. J., & Chapman, A. L. (2004). Dialectical behavior therapy: Current status, recent developments, and future directions. *Journal of Personality Disorders, 18*, 73–89.

Segal, Z. V., Williams, J. M., & Teasdale, J. D. (2002). *Mindfulness-based cognitive therapy for depression: A new approach to preventing relapse.* New York: Guilford Press.

Semple, R. J., Reid, E. F. G., & Miller, L. (2005). Treating anxiety with mindfulness: An open trial of mindfulness training for anxiety children. *Journal of Cognitive Psychotherapy, 19*, 379–392.

Silverman, W. K., & Eisen, A. R. (1992). Age differences in the reliability of parent and child reports of child anxious symptomatology using a structured interview. *Journal of American Academy of Child and Adolescent Psychiatry, 31*, 117–124.

Singh, N. N., Lancioni, G. E., Singh Joy, S. D., Winton, A. S. W., Sabaawi, M., Wahler, R. G., et al. (2007). Adolescents with conduct disorder can be mindful of their aggressive behavior. *Journal of Emotional and Behavioral Disorders, 15,* 56–63.

Teasdale, J. D., Segal, Z. V., & Williams, J. M. G. (2003). Mindfulness training and problem formulation. *Clinical Psychology: Science & Practice, 10,* 157–160.

Turner, R. M., Barnett, B. E., & Korslund, K. E. (1998). The application of dialectical behavior therapy to adolescent borderline clients. *In Session: Psychotherapy in Practice, 4,* 45–66.

Twohig, M. P., Masuda, A., Varra, A. A., & Hayes, S. C. (2005). Acceptance and commitment therapy as a treatment for anxiety disorders. In S. M. Orsillo & L. Roemer (Eds.), *Acceptance and mindfulness-based approaches to anxiety: Conceptualization and treatment* (pp. 101–129). New York: Plenum/Kluwer.

Wall, R. B. (2005). Tai chi and mindfulness-based stress reduction in a Boston public middle school. *Journal of Pediatric Health Care, 19,* 230–237.

Wicksell, R. K., Dahl, J., Magnusson, B., & Olsson, G. L. (2005). Using acceptance and commitment therapy in the rehabilitation of an adolescent female with chronic pain: A case example. *Cognitive and Behavioral Practice, 12,* 415–423.

Wicksell, R. K., Melin, L., & Olsson, G. L. (2007). Exposure and acceptance in the rehabilitation of adolescents with idiopathic chronic pain: A pilot study. *European Journal of Pain, 11,* 267–274.

Wilson, K. G., & Groom, J. M. (2002). *The Valued Living Questionnaire (version 11-13-02).* Unpublished manuscript.

Wilson, K. G., & Murrell, A. R. (2004). Values-centered interventions: Setting a course for behavioral treatment. In S. C. Hayes, V. Follette, & M. M. Linehan (Eds.), *Mindfulness and acceptance: Expanding the cognitive-behavioral tradition* (pp. 120–151). New York: Guilford.

Woodberry, K., Miller, A. L., Glinski, J., Indik, J., & Mitchell, A. (2002). Family therapy and dialectical behavior therapy with adolescents: Part 2. A theoretical review. *American Journal of Psychotherapy, 56,* 585–602.

Section V

Summary

16

Integrating Perspectives into Practice

Rosemary B. Mennuti

Ray W. Christner

Elana Weinstein

Throughout this book, we have exposed you to multiple levels of school-based mental health service, as well as to various theoretical orientations that were used in reaction to Todd's referring problems, each of which examined its position regarding psychological processes and provided a review of a number of prescribed interventions. What we have not done is provide you a specific comparison and contrast of each model. Rather we presented you the general process of each model, and in this chapter, we will offer you some guiding thoughts to help facilitate your personal theoretical style to direct your practice.

In the past, it was common for practitioners to adhere strictly to one theoretical orientation and a set of interventions that could be applied in various combinations to help children with emotional and behavioral problems. The therapist used this single orientation as a means of conceptualizing the case, interpreting and understanding the problems, complaints, and behaviors. Based on this conceptualization, the therapist selected strategies and techniques that fell within his or her theoretical approach, and aimed to heal, restore, and resolve concerns. Although we agree that using a solid case conceptualization to guide intervention selection and implementation is best practice in conducting therapy with children and adolescents, we recognize that many professionals may find it useful to incorporate the ideas and procedures from more than one orientation. Let us clarify, however, that we do not support the idea of being *theoretically eclectic*—that is, conceptualizing a case from multiple views. Nevertheless, we do support the usefulness of being *technically eclectic*, in that you conceptualize your cases from one theoretical perspective and use interventions from your approach with a supplement of strategies from other models to enhance treatment outcomes. It is important to determine what might work best for a specific child given his or her individual characteristics, the situation, and his or her needs. This allows for many varied interventions that are more appealing to children. By gaining an understanding of all theories, you will have broader insights and knowledge upon which you can establish your theoretical orientation and be integrative in your intervention selection.

The goal of this chapter is to provide you a summary of the key concepts in the mental health process as it relates to different theories and perspectives. Again, this is not to offer a step-by-step comparison of each theory, but to provide you "grist for mill" when thinking about each chapter presented in this book. The key is for you to ponder about how each of these chapters will enhance the service you provide to children and how the processes and techniques discussed can be combined to achieve effectiveness. For this chapter to accomplish its goal, it is necessary for you to think critically about this information in order to determine the approach that best fits your personal style and perspective, as well as to glean elements from other models that will complement and support your practice.

Similarities and Differences in Therapeutic Approaches

The theories presented are found to have more in common than they have differences, and each continues to evolve in terms of theory, research, and practice. Most of the approaches discussed in this book for use in schools have roots in earlier theories and principles, and they incorporate constructs at various levels. For example, each explains the importance of understanding development and earlier life experiences, though the focus of this key concept varies in degree. For some of the "classic" theories, early life experiences serve as the bases for their view of human nature in that behavior is formulated by the unconscious urges of psychosexual or psychosocial experience during the first several years of life. Others may find analyzing early life experiences as a way of understanding core beliefs and schemas to help frame current cognitions. The most extensive differences can be seen in the divergence on the basic view of human nature and what is seen as pathology, therefore leading to distinct ways for interpreting concerns, understanding the student, and developing goals for change. However, there are many similarities to what most therapists view as important. For instance, building the relationship between the practitioner and child is agreed to be at the heart of the majority of approaches.

All of the approaches discussed in this book can have a place within a school setting to help meet the needs of children and adolescents. Some approaches have a framework that can be added to the curriculum and integrated into daily school activities, whereas others are offered for a specific situation or individual. Some have a prominent role within schools because they are better suited to the entire student population, whereas other therapies serve to address individuals identified as at-risk or with diagnosed disorders.

Mechanisms of Change

What accounts for the changes that occur as a result of providing mental health service to children? The process of change in children can be accounted for by several factors. These include the therapeutic relationship; the consideration of developmental level; the use of knowledge related to risk, resiliency, and protective factors; the understanding of the home and school contexts; and the attention to motivation and attitude of the students as well as others within the system. All of the approaches attend to these factors, albeit they do so at varying degrees and their use is in a manner that matches the tenets of the specific theory.

Approaches to Assessment

Assessment for each approach is relatively similar, although some utilize formal assessments (standardized measures), some employ informal assessments (observations and interpretation), and some utilize a combination. Any type of prescribed treatment begins with a comprehensive assessment to identify the problem and set a treatment goal. All approaches use interviews, observations, and some form of formal assessment. Although assessments can range in types of procedures, all approaches typically combine these procedures to assist practitioners in determining clear treatment goals and objectives, establish a baseline of the identified problem, integrate information about the context and diversity of settings, and use some form of assessment to evaluate progress and the current level of client functioning. Keep in mind that it is necessary that all theoretical approaches used within schools, at a minimum, use assessment in these aforementioned ways. The data obtained provide the backdrop for a comprehensive and well-thought-out case conceptualization. What differs in the assessment process is who is being assessed—that is, it could be the individual child, a group of children, or the school or family system. The distinguishing feature is how the information is interpreted and used to formulate the concerns and guide the intervention approach, which varies depending on the specific theory's focus.

Case Conceptualization

Before conceptualizing a school case, it is important to consider whether approaches are prevention or intervention focused, are schoolwide or individually implemented, involve systemic or individual change, and are process oriented or goal oriented. Comparison across theoretical perspectives reveals important commonalities, namely, using conceptualization to identify the multitude of issues, understanding development, linking understanding to interventions, and reconceptualizing based on evaluation outcomes.

Another area to consider when conceptualizing an individual case is the problem's basis. The basis for most students' problems within the school setting is typically behavior, cognitive, or emotionally related. It is imperative to discover what causes and maintains the presenting issues in order to treat the child. For example, an inappropriate or nonfunctional behavior may help a student avoid schoolwork or an activity he or she does not enjoy. Behaviors are functions of their consequences, and therefore, behavior is learned and the environment typically contributes to inappropriate and nonfunctional behaviors. On the other hand, REBT, CBT, and Adlerian approaches hold that problems arise from irrational thoughts and false beliefs. Although some theories such as behavioral-based theories may overlap or share similar viewpoints in the understanding of a problem's basis, several theories have established unique opinions on a problem's origins.

For effective therapeutic intervention in schools, family and teachers play an important role in the case conceptualization of the students' problems in addition to the mental health practitioner. Because teachers and parents spend the most time with the student, these individuals can typically can provide valuable information not readily apparent to the practitioner and should be part of the intervention team. Family members and teachers are usually involved in the early stages of case conceptualization through interviews, questionnaires, and rating scales; however, these individuals can play a role in all types of interventions prescribed for the student. Yet, the intensity and frequency of involvement may vary significantly by approach or by the availability of those involved with the child. Across models, students need to take personal responsibility for the problems they face and their process and engagement in change; yet, improvements tend to be made with the collaborative help and support of parents, teachers, and other supportive figures in their lives.

Strategies and Interventions

Interventions can be applied in a multitude of settings, for many purposes, and for many different psychological disorders, problem behaviors, and skills. Yet, all therapies have the same overarching goal—namely, to help improve daily functioning and move a student toward a more successful future. How the goal is achieved varies upon the orientation, research outcomes, environmental context, and personal style of the mental health practitioner. The strategies and techniques in all models are monitored, evaluated, and modified on an ongoing basis, as suggested through progress monitoring. In general, areas to consider when reviewing for commonalities and differences among strategies and interventions are therapy focus, session content, techniques used, materials, goals, environments, and cultural applicability.

Conclusion

The chapters in this book offered a review of a number of therapeutic approaches to working with children and adolescents in schools. In this chapter, we did not provide you the same details offered in each chapter, but attempted to highlight commonalities and differences that you should consider when selecting an approach that fits your personal style and beliefs. Although a number of essential components exist across the various orientations, there are also a number of unique differences for you to consider. In addition to using this information to select a model consistent with your practice, the information provided can also be used to help you find components of other approaches that will augment your work with children. No matter your approach, the main commonality is that the goal of school-based mental health is to help increase the social and emotional well-being of children and adolescents, to facilitate their functioning within the world, and to enhance their learning.

Practitioners working with children and adolescents in schools not only bring the skills and knowledge they have learned but also bring part of themselves into their work. When a practitioner moves his or her knowledge from theory to practice, the idea of personal style begins to develop and take hold. This is not something that will "just happen." Instead, this is something that develops through self-reflection of your beliefs about behavior and working with children, paired with knowledge of approaches grounded in theory and an evidence base. To conclude this book, we leave you with the notion that the development of this personal style will enhance your work with children, schools, and families. We offer you some guiding questions to begin this reflection and to help move you into the application of the knowledge gained. Keep in mind that this process is one of evolution that will continue to unfold and help you merge the art and science of practice. These questions serve as the foundation of this process from which you will begin your thinking and will continue to reflect as you develop throughout your career.

Guiding Questions to Develop Your Personal Approach

1. Think about a time when you have made a specific change in your life.
   a. How did you go about making the change?
   b. What theoretical perspective is consistent with how you approached your own change?
   c. What about that perspective appeals to you?
   d. Are there aspects of other approaches that you may have incorporated in your own life or your view of yourself?
2. Which theoretical approach is consistent with your beliefs about behavior and human nature (e.g., the character of people)?
3. Which theoretical approach resonates with your thoughts and beliefs about development and working with children?
4. What is your relational style when interacting with others—directive, nondirective, passive, authoritative, or the like?
5. What is your comfort level when working with multiple tiers of service (e.g., systems versus individuals)?
6. What are your thoughts about identifying the needs or challenges of children (e.g., formal versus informal assessment)?
7. What is your belief about change or improvement in people and how change occurs?
8. What approaches do you feel match your personality and will enable you to be yourself when doing interventions?

Author Index

Subject Index